PRAISE FOR JAMES L. HALEY'S *WOLF: THE LIVES OF JACK LONDON*

"These days we have little sense of the literary glory that was Jack London. Thanks to James Haley's zeal, the author of [the fiercely imaginative *Before Adam*], not just the man of *The Call of the Wild*, is before us again."

—*Wall Street Journal*

"James Haley's fascinating biography is as much about London's socialist politics and domestic turmoil as his best sellers." —*USA Today*

"[A] wonderfully entertaining biography. . . . London told a friend, shortly before his departure to England, that he might conduct 'some survey of the London slums' while he was there, but then added: 'my main idea is to get a vacation.' That, as James L. Haley shows, was characteristic of a man plagued by contradictions. London was a committed socialist who was also a lifelong capitalist, an entrepreneur who built up a successful ranch and licensed his famous name to commercial products."

—*Literary Review (London)*

"[V]ividly drawn. . . . Haley has done a fine job. His book is a compelling story about a man who, after the death of Mark Twain in 1910, was America's most prominent author." —*Seattle Times*

"[London] was America's first great West Coast writer and his love for the Pacific Ocean marked him out from the East Coast authors of his day. But as James Haley recounts, London tempered the über-Western spirit of his work with a commitment to socialism. . . . Haley's account winds down like a clock." —*The Economist*

"Haley stakes a claim here as a rising voice of the West, with a biography that's perfectly suited to London's two-fisted, fortune-seeking life."
—*Outside Magazine*

"London, according to . . . Haley, is one of 'the most misunderstood figures in the American literary canon.' . . . London perhaps deserves to be misunderstood more than most because his personal circumstances draw attention to one of the big challenges faced by all writers. To write for money, or to write for oneself? To risk greatness? To sacrifice reward? . . . Haley retells London's adventures with great relish—and who wouldn't."
—*Guardian* (London)

"Highly readable. . . . This is an absorbing examination of a writer who we hope will continue to influence and seduce each generation of Americans."
—*Minneapolis-St. Paul Star Tribune*

"A splendid new biography." —*Washington Times*

"[A] solid and competent biography." —*Slate*

"A fast-moving narrative. . . . [*Wolf*] is consistently interesting, and it moves along through plentiful information. . . . [A] very useful and well-written introduction to London's exciting life." —*San Antonio Express-News*

"Haley has written a comprehensive biography, giving a complete picture of Jack London."
—*Oklahoman*

"[Haley] weaves together the often contradictory aspects of London's fierce personality and scarcely more bland public persona. . . . Haley escapes the trap of holding London's literary merit hostage to his political beliefs, making a convincing case for an economic crusader who also happened to be a great writer." —*Maclean's* (Toronto)

"Altogether an interesting tale of the man who associated himself with the wolf. . . . Recommended."
—*Choice*

"Haley has no ax to grind, nothing to prove, and, most importantly, no one to please; and it is perhaps this combination of freedoms that helps him provide the most complete biography of London, the man, to date."
—*Sacramento Book Review*

"Haley is a no-nonsense writer who gets down in the stacks of material written about Jack London, giving us a fine overview of the man born a 'working class, fatherless Californian in 1876' and sorts things out for us in his new biography." —*Buffalo News*

"The 'real' writer, as revealed in this riveting biography, isn't wholly admirable, but London was a passionately committed artist and a suffering soul." —*The Scotsman* (Edinburgh), Four Stars

"Dozens of Jack London biographies have been published since London's death in 1916. Is there room for one more? James L. Haley shows that there is, with *Wolf*. . . . Add in a life that included stints as an oyster pirate, fisheries official, hobo, sealer, Klondike sourdough, war correspondent, muckraker and adventurer—and you have the material for an epic story. Haley takes this material and puts it together in a focused and fascinating picture. He untangles the threads of London's early life and shows the path that led London to writing. . . . *Wolf* is a comprehensive, concise and readable biography. It is well worth reading." —*Galveston Daily News*

"[*Wolf*] reads smoothly, and for any who lack a knowledge about this iconoclastic and sensational writer of the early 20th century, it will make a pleasant bedside companion." —*Dallas Morning News*

"*Wolf* is a glorious achievement which will encourage readers to seek out more about and by Jack London." —*Irish Examiner* (Cork)

"Haley's work is the sympathetically told story of a man unlucky in his birth to foolish parents, unlucky enough in his health to die at 40, and unlucky with women until his second wife, Charmian. Recommended."
—*Library Journal*

"Although a great deal has been written about London, we have lacked a first-rate modern biography to give a complete picture of his achievement. James L. Haley has now provided one in *Wolf*. . . . In a well-organized, lucid exposition, Mr. Haley has produced a compelling account of his resistant subject."
—*New Criterion*

"In *Wolf*, James L. Haley gives us a terrific, compact biography that helps to restore London as a complex, prodigious writer of much (perhaps too much) more than tales of adventure."
—*Crosscut.com*

"A fascinating detailed account of the legendary author's life. Haley writes in a style that is engaging and gives insight into a complicated life. . . . For anyone who loves American literature as well as history."
—*Digital Journal*

"Careful research illuminates the creative process through which London forged such powerful works as *Call of the Wild, White Fang*, and *The Game*. . . . [A]ny reader who shares even a spark of London's incandescent curiosity will relish this vivid portrait."
—*Booklist*, starred review

WOLF

Also by James L. Haley

FICTION

Final Refuge

The Lions of Tsavo

The Kings of San Carlos

NONFICTION

Passionate Nation: The Epic History of Texas

Stephen F. Austin and the Founding of Texas

Sam Houston

Texas: From Spindletop Through World War II

Most Excellent Sir: Letters Received by Sam Houston, President of the Republic of Texas, at Columbia, 1836–1837

Texas: An Album of History

Apaches: A History and Culture Portrait

The Buffalo War: The History of the Red River Indian Uprising of 1874–1875

CO-AUTHOR

One Ranger Returns (with H. Joaquin Jackson)

WOLF

The Lives of Jack London

James L. Haley

BASIC BOOKS
New York

Hardcover first published in 2010 by Basic Books,
An imprint of Perseus Books, LLC, a subsidiary of Hachette Book Group, Inc.
Paperback first published in 2011 by Basic Books

Designed by Timm Bryson

The Library of Congress has cataloged the hardcover as follows:
Haley, James L.
Wolf : the lives of Jack London / James L. Haley.
p. cm.
Includes bibliographical references and index.
ISBN 978-0-465-00478-2 (alk. paper)
1. London, Jack, 1876–1916. 2. Authors, American—19th century—Biography. 3. Authors, American—20th century—Biography. I. Title. II. Title: Lives of Jack London.
PS3523.O46Z636 2010
813'.52—dc22
[B]

2010000536

Paperback ISBN: 978-0-465-02503-9
E-book ISBN: 978-0-465-02167-3

To Greg Walden, with love and thanks

He was youth, adventure, romance.
He was a poet and a thinker.
He had a genius for friendship.
He loved greatly and was greatly loved.

—ANNA STRUNSKY

He just jumped into life with both feet in that courageous way of his, and he got romance and mystery and beauty out of it where other men could see only labor. That's genius.

—JOHNNY HEINOLD

His eyes were those of a dreamer, and there was almost a feminine wistfulness about him. Yet at the same time he gave the feeling of a terrific and unconquerable physical force.

—ARNOLD GENTHE

Here was youth, exuberance, throbbing life.
Here was the good comrade, all concern and affection.

—EMMA GOLDMAN

CONTENTS

PREFACE

Nearly a decade before the death of Samuel Clemens, Mark Twain's place as America's favorite author was usurped by a California adventurer not yet thirty years old. In 1902, Jack London was regarded merely as an up-and-coming short story craftsman, but during the following year he took the American literary stage by storm with no fewer than three significant books: an introspective probe into the nature of affection and relationships in *The Kempton-Wace Letters*; a conscience-searing cri de coeur for social justice in *The People of the Abyss*; and then, the major sensation, a muscular Alaskan adventure novel titled *The Call of the Wild*. Following these in 1904 with the darkly hair-raising *The Sea-Wolf*, London fast became a full-fledged literary phenomenon, a front-page celebrity, and the highest-paid writer in America.

The mass of readers who lionized the gentle humor of Mark Twain were unaware that he had hidden his true feelings from them—his anguish at the human condition and his disgust with the moral failure of American capitalism and militarism. London shared these feelings, but in him the readership encountered a vastly different artist. He was an angry young man who could enthrall them with his adventure stories, but he also wrote flame-throwing jeremiads against the social injustices of his day. London's early circumstances—illegitimacy and poverty, years of brutish child labor and numerous personal and galling experiences with class prejudice—kindled a socialist fire in his belly that never abated. After he attained the national stage, his dismay was unassuageable that the public who adored his novels and stories did not care to hear his political opinions. After his death, memory of his politics was conveniently erased and he was refashioned as the quintessential author of boys' adventure stories. He thus became, and remains, perhaps the most misunderstood figure in the American literary canon. (He is not the only hero in our historical pantheon to have been given a bath before inclusion there—Charles Lindbergh comes to mind, from the right, and Helen Keller, from the left.)

London's books and stories were wildly popular during his lifetime, and just as quickly dismissed as a fad after his untimely death at age forty in 1916. During the "Red Scares" of the 1920s and 1950s his attacks on capitalism called his American loyalties so much into question that, though he was long dead, the FBI opened a dossier on him. Too popular to suppress, he was retained as a literary icon of juvenile adventure, and his keen sense of social justice was quietly forgotten, except by college professors and dedicated socialists.

Jack London was a socialist not because he was lazy or sought to live on the labor of others; few American writers have ever worked harder to educate and improve themselves, or have produced a more prolific stream of work. He was a socialist because of the manifest evil that he saw result from the abuses of unrestrained capitalism—the operative word being "unrestrained." London himself was a lifelong capitalist, an entrepreneur; he built up a successful ranch with innovative demonstration projects, he licensed his famous name to commercial products, he took risks and did not whine when gambles failed. But the United States of the late nineteenth and early twentieth centuries was the heyday of the ugliest excesses of unfettered, laissez-faire capitalism, the "Gilded Age" (Mark Twain's term) of corporate oligarchy, of worker abuse and oppression. The result was breathtaking social injustice as vividly displayed as it is in today's very comparable era. London witnessed the lower-class laborers slaving all their lives with no chance of getting an even break, and it represented to him a betrayal of the American dream that he unforgivingly set his face against. When London resigned from the American Socialist Party not long before his death, it was not because he had lost his zeal; he resigned because its members had lost theirs.

His political views, however, were not the only source of controversy about this immensely complex figure. He vigorously defended the rights of native peoples against exploitation by white, industrialized, Western society, but he was also a "racialist" who believed that those people were better off not mixing with whites. The difference between this and a racist was a distinction too subtle for many people in his own time as well as today, and he has proven vulnerable to a charge of racism. He was a robustly physical and highly sexualized man who struggled to find expression in a society still bound by the pruderies of the Victorian age. A spiritual man with a lifelong interest in the passion and teachings of Jesus, he was mortified at the role religion played in maintaining an unjust society, and claimed to embrace atheism to the end. Throughout his life he was tortured by the self-imposed imperative to do right by those whom fate had placed close to him, and despite the generous advances he received for his books, he often lived in poverty as he supported them. Yet he would have to be counted as a poor husband and a disastrous father. While in some ways he was never a child, in other ways he never grew up. When London met and ultimately married the woman who should have been ideally suited for him, maturity and even fidelity still eluded him.

❧ ❧ ❧

There have been many Jack London biographies, primarily of three types. The first and most numerous has been the biography for juvenile readers, meant to satisfy their curiosity about this fascinating man who fired their imaginations with *The Call of the Wild, White Fang,* and *The Sea-Wolf.* The second approach has been the general biography, fast and punchy, recounting his extraordinary life while avoiding interpretation that might get in the way of reading it as an adventure story. They are necessarily short and, excepting certain occasional flashes of insight, superficial. In addition to these books of Jack London "lite," there have been many volumes of limited scope: Jack London and Alaska, Jack London and the South Seas, Jack London and socialism, Jack London and women.

The third type of Jack London biographies have approached his life as literary criticism, principally emanating from a tight circle of scholars intent on vindicating London as a Great Writer. At this they have succeeded, even while admitting that there were two marked tiers of quality in London's prolific output. First there were the works of stunning originality and descriptive power, written in service either to his deeply studied craft of the novel wedded to his own high adventures, or to stinging the nation's conscience for its callous disregard of its most vulnerable members. Beneath that, though, was what even London called his hackwork, written in service to putting out a thousand words a day, every day, to make enough money to support his shrewish mother, and his demanding, unforgiving first wife and their two daughters; help his aged African-American wet nurse; provide handouts for an endless stream of wanderers down on their luck; and support his own expansive lifestyle. Nevertheless, the literary-critics-as-biographers have shown that London was a leader, not a follower, of the early twentieth-century "muckrakers," an admired correspondent of Upton Sinclair and others. He was also the first of the gritty American naturalistic writers, paving the way with his own rejection slips and controversy for Dos Passos, Steinbeck, and others whose standard fare was the humble and the disenfranchised. In general, however, these books have given London biography a "lit-crit" complexion that doesn't adequately plumb his deep and complicated psyche.

From the time I first began seriously reading Jack London, and reading about Jack London, this project has raised fundamental questions for me about the art of biography that were different from those I had to navigate with my own biography of Sam Houston. Both men have been written about not just extensively, but exhaustively. With Houston I had the advantage of working with hundreds of newly discovered papers, whereas London's entire known canon of letters has been meticulously catalogued and cross-referenced. Both men are the subject of regular conferences, symposia, and round tables, and yet for all the discussion and all the London books already on the shelf, I do not believe that his story has really been told.

I have noticed that much the same kinds of controversies swirl about Jack London as they do Sam Houston. Just as great pieces of art affect every individual uniquely, providing as many interpretations as there are persons to consider it, even so the important figures from our past reveal themselves differently to different students. Often it seems that we regard them, not for their own stories, but for what we ourselves need for them to represent to us, and scholars to date have given us irreconcilable portraits of this artist: Jack

London drank himself to death, or Jack London was never actually seen to be drunk. Jack London treated his first wife, Bessie, with kindness and consideration, or he was horrible to her. His second wife, Charmian, was a childish tomboy whom he had to humor and accommodate, or Charmian was a massively intelligent and dedicated helpmate who facilitated his success. Jack London never cheated on Charmian, or Jack London jumped anything in a dress. Jack London ended his life a suicide, or Jack London died of natural causes. And as with Sam Houston, much of the circular criticism delivered in conferences and printed reviews, which decry "errors" in the findings of others, is often merely strongly held interpretation, with the real Jack London dwelling somewhere within the staked and defended parameters of their collective theses.

Further mirroring the writing on Sam Houston, many of the previous works on Jack London were produced to deliver a certain spin. As a biographer, I do not feel that hiding the ball, telling only selective and sometimes misleading episodes of his life, as his widow, Charmian, did in her two-volume *The Book of Jack London* (1921), gives good or honest biography. Nor do I feel that for a writer to shamelessly ingratiate himself to heirs and executors, as Irving Stone is alleged to have done to obtain their cooperation for *Sailor on Horseback* (1938), gives good or honest biography. An interview conducted in 2000 with London's great-nephew Milo Shepard, who helped prepare Earle Labor's magnificent three-volume collection of London papers, contains horror stories of scholarly sycophancy and misprision, of documents purloined from collections of papers, of whole collections artfully gutted, or of collections withheld from view unless heirs felt confident that only a certain impression would result from using them.[1] From all this I have concluded that what London needs is a biographer's eye—not the eye of a vestal flametender, nor an acolyte, nor a revisionist, but a biographer's eye—from totally outside the existing circle. If this is seen therefore as a guerrilla piece, or unauthorized, or unblessed, that's because it is. My Jack London must necessarily be different from Labor's, or Kershaw's, or Sinclair's, or Stasz's, or Kingman's. That is the nature of biography. No one will understand Jack London by reading only one or two books, any more than any figure worthy of biography can be understood from reading only one or two books. Reading in depth, pro and con, light and heavy, is the only way to gain a nuanced understanding of the figures in our history who are worth knowing.

And often this is a question not of researching the subject, but of penumbral investigation, researching *around* the subject. One example that struck me in the present case: when London traveled to England in the summer of 1902 to write *The People of the Abyss*, he crossed the Atlantic on the R.M.S. *Majestic*. Only a couple of the previous biographers mention the name of the ship at all, and even then only in passing (so to speak), but the vessel would have been fraught with meaning for London and his experiences and his vehement socialist beliefs. London the lifelong sailor must have been breathless at the sight of her; but London the socialist must have been repelled. The great Atlantic liners—and the *Majestic* was the mightiest at the time—made their reputations by transporting the wealthy in elegance, but their operating expenses were paid with steerage warrens crammed with hopeful immigrants, most of whom were merely trading their English abyss for an American one. Indeed, London's first letter written from onboard the *Majestic* shows so clearly that the prevalent class injustice was foremost in his mind. Nothing could more clearly demonstrate his mental attitude at the time he commenced this important book, but previous treatments have overlooked this element for want of some related, but indirectly related, maritime history.

There are also times when biography must cast an eye forward. London's dispatches from the Mexican Revolution in 1914, which caused dismay and rage within the American socialist movement when they were printed, need to be seen in the context of Mexican history since then to understand that London's journalistic eye had cut straight to the heart of the issues as they were, not as they were imagined by armchair ideologues. The question was not whether he had betrayed his socialist ideals; the lasting importance of those pieces is that he was right. Biography requires context, and context requires research a bit broader than the subject himself. And that is perhaps the greatest missing element in the long shelf of Jack London books already published. People who were close to him and shaped him and were important to him have in the books about him been reduced to figures about whom little is illuminated, from Ina Coolbrith to Cloudesley Johns to George Brett to Mary Austin and many others; they need to be presented on his canvas with enough detail to give his own portrait depth and shading, and not be merely exponents of his massive correspondence.

It would be presumptuous indeed to claim that this volume is definitive; of course it is not. But I do believe that in portraying him in a more detailed setting I have made his story accessible to a larger audience that needs to know why he was important.

I was at a Christmas party the first time I related to a writer friend that I was beginning work on Jack London. A prominent magazine editor nearby suddenly stood in and began reciting—not talking about but *reciting*—"To Build a Fire." London's stories still thrill. But what I want readers to reflect on is why he was, and is, an important writer, what his experience meant and how our country has, and has not, changed since his time. The disparity of wealth and income in the United States is at the greatest extreme it has been since London's own time. And as class divisions again solidify, as increasing millions of Americans slip into poverty, and as the need to have even the most basic social safety net is called into question by establishment reactionaries, no writer in our national canon speaks with greater authority to the America of the twenty-first century than Jack London.

Talking about London with another writer friend, over lunch at the Texas Chili Parlor, a passing busboy noticed my copy of *The People of the Abyss* on the table. He was young and blond and poor, and I learned later that he was hopeless and drank too much, but he set down his plastic tub of dirty dishes, made free to leaf through the book, joined our conversation with gusto—and landed intelligent points. Nothing would have pleased Wolf more.

AUSTIN, TEXAS
NOVEMBER 2009

PROLOGUE

On July 14, 1897, the steamship *Excelsior* docked in San Francisco, California. It brought with it the first news that gold had been discovered in the Klondike region of the Canadian Yukon. Unremarkable men who once had only modest means now swaggered down the gangplank with gold dust and nuggets enough to set themselves up in business and live—some comfortably, a few fabulously. The news rocked the country to its foundations, not least because it gave hope to America's teeming ranks of the poor.

The United States was still wallowing in the malaise of the Panic of 1893 and its subsequent depression. The economic excesses of what Mark Twain had called the Gilded Age, the high-water mark of unrestrained capitalism and gaudy wealth for the tiny class of industrialist robber barons, now cruelly tormented the lower class. Jobs were scarce and miserably paid; the standard wage for backbreaking labor was ten cents an hour. Shirkers and troublemakers, and especially anyone who even looked like he might be a unionizer or a socialist, were fired in a heartbeat and replaced from the long line of the unemployed who were desperate to have that dime an hour.

Typical of them—in fact, archetypical of them—was a disaffected young intellectual of twenty-one who drifted about the dockside bars of Oakland, California. He was the illegitimate son of an unbalanced, free-loving spiritualist mother, who had been steadied somewhat by marriage to a kindly but partially disabled Civil War veteran. The boy was sensitive and unusually gifted, and he came to adore books, but in his existence there was little time to read.

From his earliest memory, life had been little more than a series of chores. As soon as he left primary school he had been set to work in a cannery, stuffing pickles into jars for the ubiquitous ten cents an hour. At fifteen he realized he could make vastly more money as a thief. He borrowed the funds to buy a small sloop, taught himself to sail, and became an oyster pirate, raiding San Francisco Bay's guarded tidal farms that were the monopoly of the Southern Pacific Railroad. He bought rounds of drinks for the waterfront toughs who became his friends, hiding from them his love of books and learning. Wary of prison or the violent death that other pirates met, he soon switched sides and made a small living for a while as a deputy for the California Fish Patrol.

Still poor, seventeen, and suffocating, he signed aboard a sealing schooner hoping that his share of the profits would rescue his family from their poverty. He was at sea for seven months, pulling his boat, slaughtering seals, and fending off the bullying and indecent advances of older sailors. Alone on his watch he had steered the ship through a roaring typhoon and returned home a man. But the little money he made was soon gone.

The economy had crashed during his absence, and he was lucky to find a job loading bobbins in a jute mill—for ten cents an hour. Knowing his love of books and gift of expression, his mother urged him to enter a literary contest sponsored by a local newspaper. Sacrificing precious hours of sleep, he wrote of the typhoon off the coast of Japan, and won the first prize of $25—a month's wages. It set him on a flurry of writing other articles, but no one would buy them.

He had read Horatio Alger stories as a boy, and still needed to believe that he could rise as a result of his honest labor. He took a job shoveling coal in the powerhouse of an electric railway company. The manager promised that he could advance in the business if he started at the bottom. The pay was $30 a month: ten hours a day, seven days a week—only they habitually gave him at least twelve hours' worth of coal to shovel. His actual pay was even less than a dime an hour. His whole body would seize up with cramps, and he sprained his wrists, forcing him to wear heavy leather splints to do the job. Advancement never came, and another employee eventually confessed that in shoveling coal he was the replacement of two men, who had been paid forty dollars a month—each.

He quit in a rage and became a hobo, riding the rails and experiencing the penniless subculture of vagrancy. To his surprise he met brilliantly read men among the tramps, men who introduced him to the egalitarian doctrines of socialism and gave him a cause to live for. Their disdain for capitalism and its minions who enforced order and conformity became brutally vivid in Buffalo, New York, where he was unjustly imprisoned for a month after being denied access to a lawyer.

He worked his way back home and returned to high school. He was years older than the other students. Some of his classmates mocked him for earning his keep as the school janitor, but others were mesmerized by the stories he wrote of his wide-roaming life, no fewer than eight of which were published in the school's literary journal. Looking ahead to college, he entered a prep school but was soon dismissed. The headmaster determined that he could not afford to have their wealthy students outshone by this working-class ruffian.

Stung but defiant, he studied on his own, and passed the three-day entrance exam to the University of California at Berkeley. He borrowed the tuition from a kindly barkeeper, but family poverty forced him to withdraw after a single semester. The institution was not sorry to see him go, for his effectiveness as an editorialist and street-corner socialist was raising consternation among students and faculty alike. He returned to his labors, for ten cents an hour, ironing shirts in the steam laundry—exquisite irony—of a prep school.

When the *Excelsior* docked with news of gold in the Yukon, the young malcontent knew he had to go. That there would be adventure was certain. There was also the possibility of wealth, perhaps great wealth. He approached his stepsister to lend him the money for a "grubstake." He was uncertain whether she would support him, until he discovered that her much older husband had also determined to go seek a fortune.

Only eleven days after the *Excelsior* had tied up, the pair boarded a coastal steamer dangerously overloaded with hundreds of other hopeful Klondikers, and headed north. They changed ships in Seattle and engaged an Indian canoe in Juneau to paddle them the last hundred miles to the prospectors' beachhead at Dyea.

He was greeted with chaos. Three thousand would-be prospectors, nearly all of them *cheechakoes,* the derisive local term for a tenderfoot, were all trying to get themselves organized to hike into the gold fields. It was nearly a three-week haul just to reach the first large resting camp, after which the elevation increased more and more steeply. London had brought a half-ton of supplies, all of which he had to carry in on his back, lugging seventy-five to one hundred pounds in each one-mile stage before trekking back for another load.

Many of his ill-prepared competitors had stupidly brought horses to do their hauling. This was a country with no forage. Overloaded and whipped, the horses soon dropped dead or fell into ravines. All his life he had adored horses, and now he saw to his horror how Dead Horse Gulch got its name.

The last obstacle was the worst. Chilkoot Pass presented him with a trek of three-quarters of a mile, upward at a 45-degree angle, after which the Canadian authorities at the border were satisfied that he could maintain himself and motioned him on. From there, he and his partners reached Lake Lindemann, the headwaters of the Yukon, where they built boats to float down to the gold region.

"Float," he discovered, did not begin to describe the terrors that followed. The lakes were connected by rivers fraught with gargantuan rapids. They saw others' boats dashed on rocks, or swallowed by gaping whirlpools. Men drowned before their eyes. Miraculously they made it through to Lake Bennett and Lake Tagish, and his sailing experience on San Francisco Bay got them through to Marsh Lake, which poured out into the gruesome rapids of 50-Mile River. As other outfits came to grief, and death, on chutes called the Ridge and the Horse's Mane, he got them through to Lake Laberge, and there winter overtook them.

Twice they were defeated by icy headwinds while trying to cross the lake before it froze. The third time they sailed by night, exiting the lake into 30-Mile River just in time to see the sheet of ice form behind them. Outfits less hardy would have to spend the winter where they were.

Almost at their destination, only eighty miles from the freezing boomtown of Dawson, they were met by discouraged would-be prospectors on their way back. The good claims had already been staked, they said, and there was barely enough food in town to get through the winter—a bad omen for them and the thousands of others who had come north to get rich. He and his partners appropriated an abandoned line shack and set up housekeeping, having decided they might as well hunker down for the advancing Arctic winter where they were, and conditions were deteriorating steadily.

Some days after, he set off alone up a nearby creek to do some exploratory panning, sheltering himself in a log dugout. The gold he found amounted to no more than a fingertip of flakes. Already he was showing the early signs of "Klondike Plague": scurvy. His gums bled, and his skin was slack and pallid. A passing doctor told him he would die without medical care. He could not go back the way he came; if he lived until the ice broke he would somehow have to sail down the entire length of the Yukon to civilization.

In this frozen crucible he reached a personal epiphany. He would never advance in life as a laborer. When he could no longer shovel coal he would be tossed aside like any other used-up, disabled worker. He had just turned twenty-two; if he lived through this winter, he vowed to himself, he would become a writer. If people were ignorant, he would educate them. If society was unjust, he would preach justice. He had shown a talent for writing; if he made it back home, he would train himself to write professionally, no matter what it took.

Cold, sick, lonely and miserable, the young man whose penmanship had never developed beyond what he could manage in grammar school scrawled some highly prophetic graffiti onto the log next to his bunk:

JACK LONDON MINER AUTHOR JAN 27, 1898

1 THE WORK BEAST

Readers of the San Francisco *Chronicle* snapped open the June 4, 1875, edition and were confronted by a lurid tale of domestic abuse and wifely desperation. The story was melodramatic, the writing turgid and breathless. A DISCARDED WIFE, shrilled the headline, WHY MRS. CHANEY TWICE ATTEMPTED SUICIDE.[1]

The husband-villain was "Professor" William Chaney, an astrologer, which was a respectable calling in the wide-open San Francisco of the 1870s. He was known in the Bay Area for his well-attended lectures and his forceful and nimble debating skills. The aggrieved spouse was Flora Wellman, not actually his wife although she called herself Flora Chaney. She was a spiritualist who supported herself by conducting séances and—being from a cultured family—piano lessons. Both principals were of a dubious social rank, belonging to a community of widely vilified nonconformists. "Husband and wife have been known for a year past as the center of a little band of extreme Spiritualists," clucked the reporter, "most of whom professed, if they did not practice, the offensive free-love doctrines.... It is hard to see what attracted her toward this man, to whom she was united after a short acquaintance. The union seems to have been the result of a mania like, and yet unlike, that which drew Desdemona toward the sooty Moor." She became pregnant and he, according to the newspaper, demanded that she obtain an abortion. Torn between devotion and degradation, Flora twice tried to take her own life.

William Chaney and Flora Wellman were both social rebels, but they had followed vastly different paths to this violent intersection of their lives. Chaney was fifty-four at the time their domestic strife became public scandal; Flora was thirty-one. Chaney was from Maine, born into harsh poverty in a log cabin on a farm near Chesterville, raw country twenty miles northwest of Augusta, in 1821. He was nine when his father was killed in an accident, and he was sent out to labor on nearby farms, seven of them in seven years; he loathed the work and was sometimes beaten for his sour attitude. In contrast, Flora was born into luxury in 1843 in Massillon, Ohio, a few miles west of Canton in the eastern part of the state. She had tutors and her family indulged her whims, but she was wild and willful; after her mother's death, from the age of four she terrorized her stepmother. Despite lessons in music and elocution and social graces, she remained spoiled and rebellious—traits that only worsened after she was ravaged by a fever thought to have been typhus. The disease arrested her growth at perhaps only four and a half feet tall, caused much of her hair to fall out, ruined her eyesight, and left her brittle, prone to hysterical rages that bordered on madness.

Before they met, both Chaney and Flora survived years in personal wilderness. Sick of farm labor, Chaney worked in a sawmill and tried to become a carpenter, always resentful of having to perform manual labor when he would have preferred a more learned life. At sixteen he determined to take his revenge on a cruel world by becoming a pirate, and spent two years on a fishing boat to learn seamanship. Late in 1839 he enlisted in the Navy, but after he found himself assigned to the dock-bound receiving ship *Columbus*, he deserted and as a wanted man began drifting toward New Orleans, once the haunt of the last great Gulf buccaneer, Jean Lafitte. When Chaney took sick and could not earn his passage on the flatboat he had signed aboard, the captain put him ashore, but Chaney at twenty was treated so kindly by local farmers that his faith in humanity was, briefly, restored.

Despite her family's repeated attempts to humor and pacify her, Flora became increasingly alienated. Like Chaney she was sixteen when she left home, living with one and then another of her three married sisters before deserting her family entirely. Where she roamed and how she supported herself for the next decade remained her own secret, but at some point she turned, as did so many turbulent spirits, to the West. By 1873, at age thirty, she was boarding in the Seattle home of Henry and Sarah Yesler. He was one of Seattle's most prominent citizens, entrepreneur of the first steam-powered sawmill on Puget

Sound; probably Flora's family had known him when he was a sawyer for a time in her hometown.

At some point in her wanderings, Flora had become enamored of spiritualism, an occult fad that swept America in the mid-nineteenth century and centered on the belief that the dead could be contacted through entranced mediums. First Lady Mary Todd Lincoln publicized the practice and even convinced her husband to attend séances in the White House.

Massillon itself had been rocked by a famous case when Flora was eight. Abby Warner, an eighteen-year-old illiterate who was believed to have been mildly retarded, was presented to the public as a medium capable of receiving messages from as many as three spirits at once. Naysayers were put to flight when Abby was taken to Christmas Eve services at St. Timothy's Episcopal Church, and the proceedings were reduced to confusion by loud knockings emanating from Abby's pew, although she herself was perfectly still. The authorities brought her to trial for disrupting a church service nevertheless, but she was acquitted for want of any witnesses able to swear that they had seen her causing the commotion. In Ohio more generally, the sisters Tennie and Victoria Claflin were drawing almost as much attention. To Flora, who already knew how to make herself the center of attention, the events were both spellbinding and instructive. Then, too, one of the most celebrated spiritualists of the day, Achsa Sprague, attributed her surviving a siege of rheumatic fever to the intercession of spirits, and Achsa's experience, so similar to Flora's own, may have given her the idea to become a practitioner. She found willing hosts in the Yeslers, who were devotees of spiritualism.

The Yeslers were unconventional in other ways as well. While they did not advocate free love, they certainly held liberal views; Henry Yesler acknowledged a daughter he had fathered with an Indian woman before his wife joined him from Ohio, and Sarah was known to have had at least one lesbian lover. Yesler also believed in astrology, and during the time that Flora was living with them he frequently welcomed into his home a man who had become a leader in this field, William Chaney.

After his riverbank rescue, Chaney had realized his dream of becoming better educated, but he remained a disagreeable rebel. As a teacher he alienated other teachers by spurning established science and philosophy. He read for the law in Wheeling, Virginia, but alienated other attorneys with his certainty that a legal system based on precedent was humbug. Eventually his contrariness cost him his law practice, and he was reduced to working in a match factory. Chaney's life took the cerebral turn that he craved in 1866, when by chance he fell in with Dr. Luke Broughton, a British astrologer who settled in the United States; he had practiced in Philadelphia until that town passed an ordinance against fortune-telling, then he removed to a studio at 814 Broadway in New York, where he made a convert, heart and soul, of Chaney.[2] Chaney became virtually one of the Broughton household, and their partnership proved lucrative, to the extent that they drew first an unfavorable press, then the determination of Broughton's landlord to evict them despite two years remaining on his lease. Months of harassment ended with Chaney being jailed, for want of bail, for twenty-eight weeks on unsubstantiated charges.

Once he was released, Chaney determined to search out a more open-minded community. He had married and was widowed, married again and was divorced, and despite the stars being aligned against the union he married a third time, to a woman he had met while incarcerated. Within a month of the completion of the Transcontinental Railroad he entrained for the West, telling his wife that the trip was purely exploratory and he would return soon.

Chaney worked and resided across much of the West. By turns, he was a lawyer and a surveyor—and always an evangelizing astrologer—in Nevada, Oregon, Washington, and California. He rewrote and published a British astrological tract as a kind of American manifesto of the art, and he lectured successfully in the San Francisco area before settling in Salem, Oregon, in 1871, frequently visiting Seattle. His third wife was left to languish and fume in New York as he took advantage of the West's more open-minded attitude toward astrology—open-mindedness, of course, that stopped short of public acknowledgment. "I enjoyed the friendship, 'in private,'" he recalled, "of U.S. Senators, Congressmen, Governors, Judges of the Supreme and lower courts, etc., but they were timid about recognizing me in public, except to salute me pleasantly." He believed to his core that his abilities had helped many of them to their high stations, "but they dare not reward me openly, although in private they were my best and truest friends."[3] It was surely in this connection that Chaney gained the friendship of Seattle's Henry Yesler, although had it been generally known that Yesler was consorting with and even consulting an astrologer, he likely would not have been elected mayor of Seattle, as he was in 1874.

In October 1873, Chaney was passing through San Francisco and encountered a turn of fortune that surely only an astrologer would have believed. First, a pickpocket stole his money even as he was intending to purchase a ticket home to New York; then an unidentified "gentleman" advanced him the money to hire Dashaway Hall and lecture, in exchange for half the proceeds. Chaney was a crack speaker and debater, and was soon set up again, spending the winter in San Jose. By May 1874 he had again saved money for a fare home, when he received a letter from his wife that she had divorced him, proclaiming her own freedom to remarry but threatening that if he dared to wed again she would expose him as a cad and bounder. Three weeks later Chaney defiantly opened his relationship with Flora Wellman. While in his memoir he claimed her as his fourth wife, there is no evidence that they married, and he later denied that they had.[4] They ensconced themselves in the San Francisco boardinghouse where the *Chronicle*'s reporter later found them, with all its color and nonconformity. She gave séances and piano lessons, and promoted his lectures and publications.

The times were lively. San Francisco had become a center of interest in spiritualism, and many of the best-known mediums visited and lectured there. Chaney and Flora came into the circle of William N. Slocum and his wife, Amanda. Slocum worked for the *Chronicle*'s competitor, the *San Francisco Bulletin*, and edited a brand-new reformist periodical called *Common Sense, A Journal of Live Ideas*, which advocated a hodgepodge of spiritualism, astrology, labor reform, women's rights, and free love, and to which Chaney began contributing articles.[5] When it went under in May 1875, Chaney undertook to edit and publish his own pamphlet-size periodical, the *Philomathean* ("lover of learning"), but that effort was disrupted with Flora's announcement of her pregnancy and her admission (according to Chaney) of an affair with a man named Lee Smith, because of which, he said, "the lodgers were leaving on account of her being known as 'Miss Wellman,' 'Mrs. Smith' & 'Mrs. Chaney' all at the same time."[6]

Soon after came her suicide attempts. She ventured to kill herself once with laudanum and once with a handgun that partially misfired, if it fired at all, as related in the sensational article in the San Francisco *Chronicle*. The piece was reprinted as far away as New England, where two of Chaney's sisters saw it, believed it, and cut off all contact with him. Amid the recriminations that followed, a small mob threatened to hang Chaney from a lamppost. Eventually he fled the city in December 1875 for Oregon, St. Louis, and eventually Chicago—acquiring and shedding two more wives along the way.

Abandoned and destitute, Flora was cast onto the mercy of friends and moved in with the Slocums at 615 Third Street. It was in their house, on January 12, 1876, that Flora was delivered of a baby boy.

❧ ❧ ❧

Whether for legal reasons or to insist upon recognition of her principal relationship, she named the infant John Griffith (the name of a favorite nephew) Chaney. Always waiflike in size and appearance, Flora now appeared wan and listless to a degree that was judged dangerous. Weighing just ninety pounds, she had given birth to a boy who weighed nine. The doctor recommended that she engage a wet nurse and suggested Virginia Prentiss, an African-American woman who had suffered a stillbirth on the same day Flora's son was born. At first people judged Flora's indifference to her baby as a result of her exhaustion, but over time, and with repeated reference to him as her "Badge of Shame," it became clear that she was barren of maternal instinct and felt no affection for him whatsoever. His illegitimacy was no secret, for Flora had used her increasingly obvious condition to decry the wrong done her and to win the sympathy of understanding clients.

Virginia Prentiss took the infant to her house near Nob Hill, where she lived with her carpenter husband, Alonzo, who was sometimes described as being white but who was actually a light-skinned quadroon—three-quarters white but still legally black.[7] So recently bereaved herself, "Jennie" Prentiss poured affection on "Johnny." She called him her "white pickaninny," and after a fever caused his black hair to fall and regrow for a time as white, he was her "cottonball." She became the first mother figure in Jack London's life. She herself had had a shattered childhood; born a slave and torn from her mother at the auction block, she took the name Virginia for the state where she had been born. Relocated to Tennessee and the Nashville-area plantation of a family named Parker, she at least had the fortune to be a house servant and not a field hand, serving as companion to the family's youngest daughter. After the plantation was sacked by Union troops, she endured all the horrors of the refugee, not being spared even the humiliation of roadside begging for herself and her former mistress.[8] They reached St. Louis, where relatives took in Mrs. Parker but turned Virginia away. She supported herself with domestic work until she could return to Nashville, where she kept house for the family of Alonzo and Ruth Prentiss. He had been an officer with the 49th Ohio during the war, but his career was cut short when it was discovered that his mother was a mulatto and he was discharged—albeit honorably, in deference to his creditable service to that point. After the Prentiss's marriage ended, Alonzo married Virginia and they had two children of their own, Will and Annie. They relocated to Chicago and then in 1873 to San Francisco, where they believed his carpentry skills would still be in demand despite the financial panic that seized the nation that year.

From all she had observed of white people and the black experience, Jennie Prentiss formed the opinion, which she was never shy about expressing, that black people were superior to whites. She carried herself with pride, dressed with taste, and regarded her own exceptionally dark pigmentation as a badge of distinction, but the affection she gave to her cottonball, Johnny Chaney, was no less than she gave her own children. In partial payment for Virginia Prentiss's taking Johnny off her hands, Flora, a gifted seamstress, stitched several fine shirts for Alonzo. In his carpentry, he had done some work for one John London, a forty-eight-year-old widower from Iowa with a fine, prominent brow and vast beard, with two small daughters then living in the Protestant

Orphanage for want of a household. The possibility of a match seemed to be there, and the Prentisses introduced him to Flora.

London had grown up hale, a Pennsylvania farmer and then a crew boss laying railroad track, but his Civil War service in the Illinois Volunteers cost him several sieges of pneumonia and the use of one lung. He had moved his family to Iowa to build a railroad bridge and then settled them on a farm near Moscow, where his pleasant fairness and generosity won him the friendship of local Pawnee Indians. His wife died soon after giving birth to their eleventh child (and the ninth to survive). London had come to California when doctors had recommended the climate for his son, who had suffered a chest injury playing baseball. In spite of the change, the boy died soon after the move, leaving London with his two youngest daughters who had come with them, compelling him to place the girls in the orphanage until he could make a home for them. Though partially disabled, John London was yet a man of steady habits, high morals, and a kind and sympathetic nature, and he was willing to work as hard as his health would permit. The recent deaths in his family had shaken his once solid Methodist faith to the point that he was dabbling in spiritualism, making Flora a natural confidante. In John London, Flora found a second chance at respectability, and she was willing to raise Eliza, then eight, and Ida, who was five.

They exchanged wedding vows on September 7, 1876. Her name on the marriage certificate read "Flora Chaney," although the record is silent on her having ever undertaken the formality of a divorce. London's girls were redeemed from the orphanage, leaving young Johnny the only child left out of the equation; Flora was in no hurry to reclaim him, so he remained with his wet nurse. Exactly when he joined the London family is uncertain, but even after nominal custody was restored, he often stayed with the Prentiss family when Flora needed to be free of him. He grew up adoring his "Mammy Jennie," a name that, considering her antebellum history, she thoroughly disliked, but could never break him of calling her, even after he grew up.

Home life was unstable. At home, the greater part of caring for the baby fell on his stepsister, Eliza London, and the resulting bond lasted throughout Johnny's life. London was eking out a living as a carpenter and door-to-door salesman for the Victor Sewing Machine Company, and within a couple of years the family had moved four times. They were living in a rented six-room flat on Folsom Street when Eliza was ten and Johnny was two and both contracted diphtheria, at one point lying so near death that Flora made an inquiry as to whether they might save some money by burying them together in one coffin. After their recovery, on the doctor's advice, John London fled San Francisco and its rampant diphtheria, not to mention its cost of living, and moved his family across the bay to Oakland. There he acquired enough land to resume his former farming life, and his small market garden prospered, to the degree that he acquired a certain fame for the quality of his produce. It was a lower-middle-class living, honest and rewarding and adequate, but it was never good enough for Flora, who remembered her childhood of luxury in a seventeen-room mansion.

London was able to open his own store at the corner of Campbell Street and Seventh, and at Flora's urging he took on a partner named Sowell to expand the operation more rapidly. They even moved in with the Sowell family, but within a short time, somehow, London lost his half of the business to his unsavory partner and in 1881 the family packed up and moved down the bay to work a small farm near Alameda. As an adult Jack London recalled being left alone briefly in a room full of packed boxes, seized with the terror of abandonment, hearing only the sound of the woman next door beating out her carpet in the yard.

The following year, Johnny at age six started primary education at the West End School. Unlike most boys of his class and era, he took to formal schooling willingly, thanks in part to his mother's early efforts. There were some ways in which the later Jack London, and through London his biographers, have painted the bitter and frustrated Flora in too dark colors. She did teach him to read at a very early age—Eliza recalled that he could already read when he started school—and once he attended regularly, Flora visited with his teachers to check on his progress.

Johnny's education in life also assimilated an important lesson at this time. One of his daily chores was to take his stepfather a pail of beer for afternoon refreshment from plowing. One day he grew curious about the brew, and one sip led to another. "First I sipped the foam," he wrote of it later. "The preciousness evaded me. Evidently it did not reside in the foam. Besides, the taste was not good." Remembering that grown-ups often blew the foam from the top of the brew, he got down to the beer and liked it even less, but with the experiment begun, it had to go forward. "I was gulping it down like medicine, in nauseous haste to get the ordeal over." Worried at having drunk so much, he remembered something else he had seen grown-ups do, and he took a stick and whipped up a new head of foam. "My father never noticed. He emptied the pail with the wide thirst of the sweating ploughman." Johnny attempted to walk beside the horses but fell almost before the moving plow, narrowly escaping a terrible injury. Seeing that the boy was roundly drunk, John London carried him to some trees at the side of the field and laid him in the shade; by the time they returned to the house Johnny had become violently ill. In a later life of great familiarity with alcohol, beer was never his preference.[9]

Life in Alameda proved transitory. Ever busy and ever carping, Flora prevailed on John London to move again, on the day Johnny turned seven, to a larger farm in San Mateo County, south of San Francisco, six miles from the city of Colma. It was a more commercial venture to produce potatoes, and again London's hard work started to make a success of it. He would take Johnny along with him on the great rumbling potato wagon as he made his deliveries, often stopping at the saloon in Colma for company and a beer. Here Johnny got his first taste of the warm and easy company of men, reveled in their solicitation and small gifts of a soda cracker or—an unforgettable occasion—a soft drink. This was a principal diversion, for life on the ranch was lonely, the school was inferior, and he had no playmates. Such neighbors as they had, some nearby Italians, thought it hilarious to get Johnny loaded on red wine, which also made him ill.

London's success led to greater expansion, and before long the family moved again, back to the east side of the bay and twenty miles inland in Alameda County, to an eighty-seven-acre ranch near Livermore. Here London diversified: poultry, grapes, and fruit and olive trees, in addition to vegetables, and again London's hard labor was rewarded. His "J.L." brand of corn especially was sought out, and the family enjoyed the best conditions they had yet known. Johnny had a hard regimen of chores on the farm, but the school was better, and he remembered trying on his first pair of store-bought underwear. He also noted his father's custom of selling only the most attractive produce; the Prentisses, who had moved across the bay so Mammy Jennie could be near her white child, got their pick of the culls, and the rest he gave to the poor.

Sensitive and reflective by nature, Johnny during these years fell in love with books. Always a precocious reader, he later recalled his enjoyment of John Townsend Trowbridge's books for boys at the age of six. The following year he discovered the works of French author Paul du Chaillu, some of whose romantic adventures were cast in editions for young children, and just one of whose titles could set an excitable boy's heart racing: *Explorations & Adventures in Equatorial Africa; with Accounts of the Manners and Customs of the People, and of the Chace of the Gorilla, Crocodile, Leopard, Elephant, Hippopotamus, and Other Animals.* Johnny was so taken with Washington Irving's *The Alhambra: A Series of Tales and Sketches of the Moors and Spaniards* that he built his own miniature Moorish palace with bricks that had fallen from the chimney, augmented with bits of wood and plaster. He had borrowed the book from a teacher, and after he had returned it, he wept the entire long distance home because he was not offered another one to borrow. Among the first nonfiction he remembered reading was a life of President James Garfield, who was assassinated in 1881. The book was titled *From Canal Boy to President,* and its author was Horatio Alger, with whose fictional works of optimism, hard work, and success Johnny also became familiar. He read the voyages of Captain Cook, which opened his lifelong love affair with works of the sea. He was also able to borrow dime novels and several titles of the popular Seaside Library of cheap reprints.[10]

By eight, he had read Ouida's *Signa,* and throughout his life London averred that this was a transforming experience, a literary epiphany that set his feet down the road to becoming a writer. All this, even though he had found his copy of the work discarded on the roadside and missing its final forty pages. It was many years before he even learned the outcome of the story. This was a weighty testimonial for London to have made throughout his maturity; he wrote about it, among other places, in his autobiographical *John Barleycorn* and near the close of his life in a letter to a leader of the California Writer's Club. Yet London's biographers have shown a singular lack of curiosity about Ouida, and *Signa* itself.

"Ouida" was the nom de plume of Maria Louise Ramé, an English novelist with a French father, born in 1839, and best known today for her novels *Under Two Flags* (1867) and *A Dog of Flanders* (1872). She was prolific, and imagined herself the center of an influential salon that she sometimes hosted languidly from her bed, and she was wounded at being lampooned in *Punch*.[11] Published the year before Jack London was born and the year after Ouida moved to Italy, *Signa* was the story of a simple Italian peasant boy, an illegitimate, who grows up to become a famous opera composer. Its opening lines demonstrate clearly the qualities that riveted the attention of a lonely boy who craved adventure, but they also show that London was not exaggerating when he described the book's consciousness-altering effect on him, for the taproot of his own style is just as clearly seen there:

> He was only a little lad coming singing through the summer weather; singing as the birds do in the thickets, as the crickets do in the wheat at night, as the acacia bees do all the day long in the high tree tops in the sunshine.
>
> Only a little lad with brown eyes and bare feet, and a wistful heart driving his sheep and his goats, and carrying his sheaves of cane or millet, and working among the ripe grapes when the time came. . . .
>
> Passengers come and go from the sea to the city, from the city to the sea, along the great iron highway, and perhaps they glance at the stern, ruined walls, at the white houses on the cliffs, at the broad river with its shining sands, at the blue hills with the poplars at their base, and the pines at the summits, and they say to one another that this is Signa.
>
> But it is all that they ever do; it is only a glance.[12]

The prose is evocative but simple, employing repetitive similes using words not difficult, with a rich use of color and texture, leading to a breakneck change of focus. *Signa* indeed is Jack London in the literary womb, and for him to have assimilated the rough marble of his later chiseled style, in a lump, at the age of eight, testifies to a frighteningly precocious little mind. He once confided to Eliza that he would not marry before he was forty, and he intended to have a huge house, one great room of which would be chock-full of books. This was, however, to be one of the last childhood confidences that he shared with the stepsister who was his rock and his comfort.

To Flora, the hard life of a farm wife was merely a waystation on the road back to luxury; only the hope of a future of ease sustained her through her labors. She bossed the family mercilessly, feigning heart attacks if she encountered resistance. Eliza and Johnny puzzled between themselves where the household money went. The truth was that Flora was sinking it in one and then another get-rich-quick scheme, or buying tickets in the Chinese lottery, always certain that her luck was about to change and she would recapture the life she had known as a child. She still held séances, and determined that the family could use the extra income of taking in a boarder. To that end she spoke with one James Shepard. Like her husband, he was a widowed Civil War veteran, a sea captain with three children. Where in Captain Shepard Flora saw rent money, sixteen-year-old Eliza saw a ticket to freedom, and she struck rapidly. Their marriage in 1884 left Flora with no boarders and no nanny to look after Johnny. Her appraising eye fell upon her younger stepdaughter, thirteen-year-old Ida, who however was more rebellious than Eliza and would have run away if imposed upon with her sister's full load. Losing Eliza was only the first shock of rapidly progressing calamity. Almost as suddenly the London poultry flock was wiped out by disease. Between this, Flora's gambling, and the costs of the rapid improvement of the farm, when the mortgage came due there was no money to pay it, and the London farm that once looked so promising was foreclosed on.

Starting anew, London loaded up his remaining family once more in the potato wagon and moved back into Oakland. He had done remarkably well for a farmer with one functioning lung, but undoubtedly the prospect of success had lent him strength; losing the farm in Livermore broke him in more ways than merely financially. Back in the city he took a succession of urban jobs—constable, night watchman—lesser and lesser jobs as his health entered a long and gradual decline. Oakland, however, held some rewards for Johnny.

The house the Londons took on East Seventeenth Street in March 1886, modest but with twin bay windows flanking the front door, was only a short walk from the Shepards, where Eliza had settled in to raising three stepchildren. Even more to his joy, Alonzo and Jennie Prentiss had moved to Oakland from San Francisco, so he once again basked in the warmth of his Mammy Jennie. Disappointed yet again with the failure of the Livermore farm, Flora quickly seized on the opportunities presented by once more living in the city: piano lessons, séances, a kindergarten—her fortunes might be recouped yet. This time the big scheme was to operate a boardinghouse for Scottish girls who had immigrated to work in the textile mills. Again they sank money into a project in which, when the riches proved ephemeral, Flora lost interest, and it failed.

Johnny was now ten and attended the Garfield School across the street from their house, but he was now put to work to supplement the family income, and work he did, to a degree exhausting even to read about. In later years Jack London never found joy in recalling those joyless years: his paper route—up as early as three to throw morning papers, then to school, and after school he threw evening papers. Saturdays he worked on an ice wagon, and on Sundays he set pins in a bowling alley "for a drunken Dutchman."

Nearly all his earnings were surrendered to his mother, and in hindsight he referred to himself as the "Work Beast." Indeed, London remembered these years with such bitterness that he later exaggerated the hardships, claiming to have once stolen a piece of meat from a girl's lunch box at school. This he may well have done, but the circumstances of the London household were not that desperate. Between John London's small earnings, Flora's piano lessons and séances, Ida's work as a laundress, and Johnny's multiple jobs, they ate steak and potatoes almost nightly. This was not for luxury's sake—it was what Flora cooked best and it was said to have been wonderful. On those rare occasions when they had company for dinner she deflected compliments, saying that the quality came from searing and dry-frying the beef in a big cast-iron skillet that she husbanded and continued to use even after a great chunk broke out of its side.

Loss of the boardinghouse engendered a succession of moves, occasionally an improvement but generally and inexorably downward in mobility, toward the poorest neighborhoods of West Oakland, ending in an austere cottage at 944 Thirty-Sixth Street, with the principal rooms on the second floor, entered by a tiny high stoop. The gradual drift toward poverty finally robbed Flora of her dogged optimism, and her bitterness made her almost impossible to live with. She took refuge in her white heritage, warning Johnny of the inferiority of the darker races now surrounding them in the ethnic mixture of West Oakland—a stance directly opposite that of Mammy Jennie, which caused him to question racism in a way that most ten-year-olds in the 1880s never had to. Home life was made more bearable by Johnny's affectionate alliance with his stepfather. Partly to establish their own bond and partly to escape Flora's rages, they spent a great deal of time together, duck hunting in the expansive marshes and fishing in the bay in rented rowboats. Jack London later wrote that his stepfather was the best man he ever knew.

The move to West Oakland led to Johnny's enrollment in the Cole Grammar School, a two-story Victorian maze that was the largest school he had yet attended, presided over by a principal with the unfortunate name of Mr. Garlick. By now accustomed to being the new boy in school and slow to make friends, Johnny retreated increasingly into the world of books, often at the cost of having to fight schoolyard bullies who would strike them from his hands. The leader of the Cole School's toughs was a budding young thug named Mike Pinella, who called Johnny a sissy, threw the book he was reading across the schoolyard, and was surprised to discover that the "sissy" could hold his own. Both boys wound up in Mr. Garlick's office, who ruled that they would not be punished if they would embrace and make up. Mike Pinella was willing, but Johnny, his keen and growing sense of justice offended, refused.

"I'll take the licking, Mr. Garlick," he said. "I know I was in the right, and I'll do it again if I have to."[13] (Principal Garlick acquired a measure of respect for the independent boy; once when Johnny was sent to the office for refusing to sing in music class, he explained to the principal that it was impossible to sing properly when the music teacher herself could not carry a tune. Johnny returned to class bearing a note that during music class he was to be allowed to write compositions instead.)[14]

Resorting to violence to preserve his right to read in peace became less frequent as word spread that he was a boy to be left alone. His love of books even gained a powerful ally, for the move to Oakland had brought him into contact with a new mentor, who soon took an unparalleled place in his development. At ten he entered for the first time the Oakland Free Library, a remarkable institution presided over by an even more remarkable woman. Oakland's library was only the second in the state (after the one in Eureka) and it was the product of preparation that extended back to the founding of a library association in 1868. The residential-looking, Italianate frame structure was built in 1872, then moved to City Hall Park and had a second story added in 1878. "It stood a little back from the street," as a frequent early patron remembered, "and one climbed a few steps to enter a hallway about ten feet wide; there in front of you loomed two large, swinging doors, covered with a dark green material like oil cloth of slightly rough texture." The ground floor was devoted to newspapers and periodicals, and a winder staircase before the swinging doors led up to the book room. "This main room, about thirty-five feet square, seemed rather dark on afternoons as you entered. . . . On the west side where there were no windows, the shelves reached nearly to the ceiling and a narrow balcony, half-way up the wall, made possible the use of these high shelves."[15]

Of frail construction, one contemporary described the Oakland Free Library as "leaning" against the city hall. To young Johnny London, however, it was a temple of wonders. He first visited it while throwing his paper route, a sheaf of newspapers squeezed beneath his arm. He asked the librarian for something good to read. Over the weeks she kept him supplied and encouraged his reading, but she was unable to coax him into talking about himself or his family. She perceived that there was some family secret or shame in play, but being herself a divorcée and an estranged granddaughter of the Mormon patriarch Joseph Smith, she knew that some family matters are best not pried into. When he presented a history of Pizarro's conquest of Peru to take home, the librarian complimented him on his choice. It was the first time anyone had taken an interest in what he read, and in exchange he finally took some cognizance of her.

Across the counter from him he beheld a matronly, handsome woman of forty-five. Born Josephine ("Ina") Donna Smith, she took her mother's maiden name to publish her own poems under the nom de plume of Ina Coolbrith. She had come to California as a child, over the Sierra Nevada in a wagon train; she was only thirteen when her first poems were published, and after moving to San Francisco her writing for and helping to edit *Overland Monthly* gained her the fast friendship of Bret Harte and even Mark Twain. After that magazine folded she was hired as Oakland's librarian when it was still a private subscription library in 1873, and continued when it was opened to the public. In 1886 this immensely read and capable woman became Johnny London's literary coach, and she gave his reading an organization and purpose that stayed with him throughout his life. Beginning at age ten, he undertook to check two books per week out of the library, and did so faithfully, on a vast range of subjects far above his grade level.[16]

London later memorialized the Oakland Free Library in both *John Barleycorn* and *The Valley of the Moon*. He acknowledged that those scenes represented his actual experiences and were not fictional elements of the stories. He admitted that, had it not been for such institutions, he likely could not have fashioned himself into a writer.[17]

Into his early teens, he began discarding the name "Johnny" for the tougher-sounding "Jack," even as he developed voracious loves of books and hard candy.

The books were free and the candy cost dearly, but identification with either commodity was enough to brand him a weakling and a sissy, a target for Oakland's budding dockside bullies just old enough to begin throwing their weight around. For his own defense, Johnny began cultivating his alter ego, the incorrigible delinquent, and transforming himself into a walleyed brawler. "I guess Jack was a pretty good boy when you come to figure it all out," his mother later told journalist Joseph Noel, "but he fell in with bad company. He used to have terrible fights with the boys of the neighborhood. He got to going down to the water front. He became awfully bossy in the house. We couldn't stand him sometimes."[18] When he was on the losing end of a fight, he at least learned that he gained respect in that world by taking a licking without complaint.

One of the worst times—exactly when is not known—was when he learned the definition of the word "bastard," and that he was one. According to Flora, he threw himself on the floor in a tantrum and ran away from home for two days. He returned, the injured child having retreated deep into his psyche, where he abided until the day the whole being died. But throughout his life, the injured child would surface in sudden, puerile outbursts that were usually quickly mastered. London was always ashamed of his illegitimacy, and in summary accounts of his life sketched down for correspondents, John London appears as his father without elaboration.

While at the Cole Grammar School, Johnny made the one close friend of his childhood, Frank Atherton. Johnny was the quiet, unpopular boy who preferred reading over roughhousing; Frank was the new boy in school, slow to make friends. Their relationship began over trading cards, which could be acquired by redeeming tobacco coupons; there were different sets to complete, the most popular being celebrated racehorses, boxers, or actors. No longer doomed to solitude, Johnny sometimes brought Frank home to dinner. Flora made him welcome, but there were times when her savage temper flashed, as when she once heard Johnny explaining to Frank (in a joke perhaps instigated by John London) that the table was spread with newspapers because they were too poor for linens. Flora stormed to a closet and returned with a full set of white tablecloth and napkins, not quickly mollified by the protests that they had merely been teasing. One stint was noted and admitted, however: dessert was unknown in the London household. Flora economized there to be able to afford higher-grade cuts of meat—reason enough, if not the principal reason, for Johnny's lifelong affliction with an incorrigible sweet tooth.

Frank was also aware of Flora's more exotic vocation as a spiritualist. In the mid to late 1880s interest in spiritualism generally was declining, but she was able to maintain an active practice. Their West Coast location was a help, for the Bay Area clung to its nonconformist heritage; her poor eyesight and dwarfish size—even as an adult she wore a girl's size twelve shoe—made her seem like a more authentic candidate as a medium. And she discovered an effective "hook" for a show, channeling communications from a long-deceased Indian warrior named Plume, and her séances were punctuated with unexpected war whoops. Oakland-area children called the London home the spook house, and Johnny became accustomed to sitting on the front stoop in mortification, sometimes with Frank, while Flora held a session with clients.

Like most boys, Johnny and Frank made great plans together, usually having to do with making their fortunes. Their greatest caper began with their crafting slingshots more powerful than the hip-pocket variety all the neighborhood boys carried. Armed with scrap-lead "bullets" that they shaped themselves, they practiced assiduously to improve their aim and determined to go duck hunting on the bay. Repeated expeditions netted only frustration, until one day they managed to kill two inedible mud hens and one hapless duck that the tide carried away as the two boys wrangled over which one had actually struck it. On their way home a Chinese laundryman offered them twenty cents apiece for the mud hens, and suddenly their avenue to fortune seemed paved for them. Quickly the hunting of ducks graduated to a scheme to hunt wildcats in the hills behind the city. Members of the Chinese *tongs* (organized gangs) prized the body parts of wildcats, believing they would assimilate their ferocity. This then led to a scheme to engender trouble between rival tongs to spike the demand for wildcat parts, and Jack and Frank made elaborate preparations, including a list of all they would need to commence business. Sadly for their enterprise, their first expedition found no sign of a wildcat.

Undeterred, the boys gathered and sold enough scrap to buy a couple of used handguns and returned to the duck hunting iteration of the plan. Their marksmanship, however, was not much improved over the slingshots, and moreover Jack's weapon proved to be so defective that its bullets splashed into the water only yards away. Furious, he slammed the pistol onto the gunwale so hard that it flew from his hand and disappeared into the bay. Frank could swim but Jack could not, and they nearly came to blows over Frank's refusal to dive in and try to retrieve the weapon. Angrier than ever, Jack ripped the oars from their locks and cast them as far away as he could, challenging Frank to swim after them. At this Frank offered Jack his own pistol, Jack realized his stupidity, and the remainder of the day was occupied in sculling the boat by hand until they were in range of snagging the oars with fishing line and rowing home. With their friendship sealed by a violent quarrel and making up, it lasted for life.[19]

This friendship also afforded Jack the beginnings of a cultural life. He knew the rudiments of music from his mother's piano lessons, and found it pleasant, but would not have dared betray such sissified notions to most other boys. Frank proved to be of the same bent, however, and together they spent precious small change haunting the upper balconies of concerts and operas.

In 1891 the newly minted "Jack" London graduated from the Cole Grammar School, having completed eight grades of primary education. His "easy" life now over, it was time to find a real job. The chronic financial needs of the family made it impossible for him to pursue any higher education, and even to farm him out as a trade apprentice would have deprived them of his earning power during any period of training. As the London family's luck had continued its decline, they moved farther out into West Oakland, a poorer area, ethnically mixed, home to most of the area's Chinese and increasingly the locus of Portuguese immigrants. One of the houses that the Londons rented, at 807 Pine Street, lay directly next to the railyards that serviced West Oakland's increasing industrialization. Near the residence was a former stable that now housed the R. Hickmott Canning Company, a business that, amid a cacophony of whirling, exposed machine belts, put up a variety of produce, including asparagus, tomatoes, and peaches. Jack London, fresh from grammar school, obtained employment in Hickmott's dingy, smelly, steamy cannery stuffing pickles into jars for ten cents an hour.

Mercifully, he enjoyed a brief respite in the few months between leaving Cole Grammar School and entering the Dickensian gloom of Hickmott's cannery. Frank Atherton's parents moved to Auburn, in the historic gold mining country northeast of Sacramento, and they invited Jack to spend the summer with them. For those few months Jack and Frank lived a boy's idyll of romping and mischief making, an adventure that an examination of London's later days makes one wonder whether he didn't spend the rest of his life trying to some extent to recapture. The summer also afforded him an opportunity to bond with Northern California nature in ways not provided by doing chores on the farms near Colma and Livermore. The land, and his love of the land, opened a theme for him that was ultimately realized in his closing years on the Beauty Ranch.

After this summer, however, his life revolved around Hickmott's Cannery. Even as Mark Twain and Edith Wharton were writing of America's "Gilded Age" of white gloves and liveried servants and Newport mansions, with Twain questioning its economic justice and Wharton lamenting its social consequences for wealthy women trapped in gilded cages, Jack London and other child laborers experienced its ugly, all-too-real underbelly. Theirs was a world of brutish and dangerous labor to the point of physical collapse, where workers were discarded without help if they fell ill or injured in factories where the loss of digits and even limbs was commonplace. His resentment of it never abated, and even as he exaggerated his family's poverty in his later telling of this period of time, his claim to have sometimes earned $50 a month at a dime an hour, if not an exaggeration, surely described labor at the outer limit of human endurance, especially for a fourteen-year-old. That arithmetic required sixteen hours per day, seven days each week, for an entire month. However, London always insisted that there were times he worked shifts for twenty-four hours straight and even longer, so five hundred hours—$50—in a month was possible.

2 ❧ THE OYSTER PIRATE

Jack London's consoling joy through these years, apart from his books, was hunting ducks at the edge of the marshes with his stepfather. Occasionally John London would find the money to rent a rowboat, and they would pull out onto the bay and fish for rock cod. It was the beginning of Jack London's courtship of the sea.

By saving small change over several months, he managed to hoard $5, more than half the purchase price of his own small skiff. But his mother soon learned that he had been holding out on her. One day during his shift at the cannery, Flora stormed into the place, upbraided him, and held out her hand for the money. Crestfallen and humiliated, he handed it over, but at the cost of his remaining affection for her. He always respected her for her hard labor and made allowances for her innumerable disappointments in life, but in his mental ledger he compounded this incident with another, in which she had punished him summarily and wrongly.

Young as he was, he was already turning into his own man. There were times, before he moved out of the London house, he still deferred to his mother's judgment, but his several months of hard labor in Hickmott's finished the job begun with the paper route, of forging him into a bleakly independent spirit, his own judge of what was right and wrong and reasonable. Raised but little loved, taught toughness by dockside brawling, taught that tenderness would be detected and attacked as weakness, assimilating that an intellectual curiosity only led to frustration in one fated to be a Work Beast, Jack London by age fifteen already looked out on the world through the eyes of the Wolf.

More cunning in his second attempt, London finally saved up enough money to acquire a small boat. John London's declining health, and his subsequent injury in a railyard accident, ended their fishing trips together, but of his own accord, Jack began teaching himself to sail. This was no easy endeavor on San Francisco Bay, which isn't a single body of water at all, but an intricate complex of a great bay fed by smaller estuaries that are themselves linked by swift-current narrows. The entire watery expanse stretches forty miles from southeast to northwest with the Golden Gate opening to the Pacific Ocean about halfway up, and at the northern end doglegs east through the Carquinez Straits to the complex of inland bays that receives runoff from the whole central valley. There are treacherous shallows, nearly irresistible currents, and the constant imperative to dodge commercial traffic and fishermen—all in all it was a tough school in which to train himself in the art of boat handling.

Sailing naturally brought him into closer contact with the waterfront and its denizens, and his favorite haunt became the J. M. Heinold Saloon. It was a tiny cracker box of a bar, built on pilings over the water at the end of Webster Street, constructed of timbers salvaged from a scrapped whaler. Originally erected in 1880 as a bunkhouse for oyster tenders, it was purchased three years later by "Johnny" Heinold, a slightly built but tough Pennsylvania German, a seaman who had ploughed into San Francisco Bay on a windjammer the year London was born. The affable, rubber-faced, stogie-mouthing Heinold reconfigured the bunkhouse into a saloon, which he managed for the next five decades, its congeniality underwritten by the sign over the bar:

ALL NATIONS WELCOME . . . EXCEPT CARRIE

In the off-season he dispensed drinks to the crews of the few dozen whaling and sealing ships that laid up in port for the winter, and when the men were at sea he held their mail for them. In season and out Heinold's became the favored saloon of the Oakland waterfront, as well as a regular stopping place for draymen hauling their loads across the estuary bridge. Only one rule was perennially enforced: fights had to be taken outside.

From this establishment, Heinold often observed young London working his skiff, a decked-over fourteen-footer with a centerboard, in chop that often threatened to swamp him. Heinold also marked London's endless enterprise, how the boy would take a load of onions and potatoes out to anchored vessels, whose cooks would hand over empty kerosene cans that London could sell for scrap at a dime apiece—each tin the equivalent of an hour's wage slavery at Hickmott's cannery. During these months, at age fifteen, he met real deep-water sailors—and these acquaintances came to have signal importance to the developing youth. Anchored across the estuary was a sloop, the *Idler*, arrived from Hawaii, where she was rumored to have been an opium smuggler. He had seen her tended by an impressive-looking young man, but felt himself unworthy to sail over, hail him, and make an acquaintance.

One day a youth who identified himself as Scotty, a British deserter who had jumped ship in Australia and made his way to California, asked London to sail him over to the *Idler*; her caretaker was a harpooner who intended to go out with the whaler *Bonanza* when she next sailed, and Scotty wanted to go, too. Tingling with anticipation, London sailed him over; they were invited aboard and below, and suddenly he was breathing the air of a new world, a man's world that electrified him.

> It was the first sea-interior I had ever seen. The clothing . . . smelled musty. But what of that? Was it not the sea-gear of men?—leather jackets lined with corduroy, blue coats of pilot cloth, sou'westers, sea boots, oilskins. And everywhere was in evidence the economy of space—the narrow bunks, the swinging tables, the incredible lockers. There were the tell-tale compass, the sea-lamps in their gimbals, the blue-backed charts carelessly rolled and tucked away, the signal-flags in alphabetical order, and a mariner's dividers jammed into the woodwork to hold a calendar. At last I was living.

Inevitably, the two older teens—Scotty was sixteen and the harpooner nineteen—began pouring drinks, offering London to join in. Jawing and singing, the older boys eventually passed out, leaving London not only their equal, but their superior for having drunk them under the table. To emphasize this point, when he might easily have sought an empty bunk and slept it off, he untied his skiff, and in the vicious chop of a heavy wind and an equally heavy tide opposing each other, he sailed the skiff back to Oakland. There the slack tide had left the water's edge a hundred yards from the wharf; only when he jumped down to haul it across the ooze and fell face-first into the mud did he realize he was still drunk. He cut his arms on a piling, from which he acquired painful barnacle poisoning, but that night below deck on the *Idler* cemented Jack London's betrothal to the sea.

The adolescent sailor bidding for acceptance was one identity he accommodated; still, he had to do something with the other, the reader and dreamer that he felt compelled to stow away. Within the gaslight of Heinold's bar, in addition to the hale company and the warmth from the wood-burning stove, London was also drawn to an enormous dictionary kept on a table by the window. It was at this table that Jack London would occasionally revert to his open, inquisitive nature. When he wanted to learn new words, recalled Heinold, "never a bit of attention would he pay to the men drinkin' and smokin' and jokin' up here at the bar—just fell to on that old book and read it like he'd like to learn everything in it." Ever alert to the accusation of being a sissy, London sometimes had to vindicate his manliness. "He was gentler than a woman," said Heinold, "yet he wasn't to be walked over—I don't care how big the guy was. He never fought much, but he'd set his jaw a certain way, and look with them flashing deep eyes of his, and that was all he needed to do. You see, he never bluffed."[1]

Heinold's shrewd appraisal of him at fifteen gave ample hints that London's life had now reached a critical dissonance. On the one hand, Ina Coolbrith and her library books were filling his head with history and adventure, mighty deeds, and a sense of life's possibilities. Yet against this was set his reality, canning pickles for a dime an hour at least ten hours a day, unable to get even $5 ahead without it being impounded by his imbalanced mother. Such an existence held no charms for a youth bursting at the seams of his life. By London's own later admission, he now was drinking beer when he would rather have been eating candy; and indeed it was his alter ego, the novice ne'er-do-well of the waterfront, swearing and drinking and brawling, who came up with a plan to shatter the cycle.

Oakland was born to serve San Francisco. When Horace Carpentier started the town in 1852, it was to operate a ferry from the eastern shore of the bay across three miles of open water to San Francisco, saving travelers a trek of eighty miles around the southern portion of the bay and up the mountainous peninsula to the settlement on the Golden Gate. His business acumen was later confirmed when Sacramento became the state capital, and traffic increased— it increased again in 1869 when Oakland became the terminus of the new Transcontinental Railroad. Carpentier had chosen a site of great geographical importance, but Oakland was merely the last way station; San Francisco, with its Nob Hill and its wharves of sleek, mighty clipper ships remained the destination that beckoned. Oakland's own tatty waterfront serviced far less romantic vessels—the ferry, the blood-greased whaling ships and sealing schooners, and the tired, shallow-draft fishing sloops. Thus when John London packed up Flora, Jack, and his daughters and relocated from San Francisco to Oakland, the move had about it some sense of water finding its own level.

San Francisco first gained prominence after 1849, as the gateway to the goldfields near Sacramento, but within a few years the bay was devastated by polluted runoff from the mining camps in the Sierra Nevada. Native species of fish and shellfish were all but wiped out; exotic species had to be imported to take their place. By 1890, after the gold played out, the tidal flats had recovered enough that they were once again an important source of pot hunting and fishing for the laboring class, especially in Oakland.

At the instance of investors, the Southern Pacific Railroad began to lease out large tracts of its coastal acreage, which had formerly been considered a public resource, so that oyster farmers could raise imported Atlantic oysters, superior in flavor to the native Pacific species. Some of the very first trains to arrive in California from the East on the new Transcontinental Railroad hauled cars containing barrels of "spat," juvenile oysters attached to chips of shell, ready to transplant. Wide stretches of the adjoining shallow water were dredged up into artificial reefs, and the Atlantic oysters they produced commanded a hefty premium in swanky restaurants.

Being a monopoly, the beds of Atlantic oysters were guarded, and the legislature, pliant to corporate lobbying, made stealing from them a felony. Many of the working-class people in Oakland who had lost their usual foraging grounds regarded this as an insult, even a provocation, so much so that local police sometimes looked the other way when hard-hauling Oakland fishermen raided the oyster beds for a quick supplement to their income. Such "oyster pirates" represented a kind of local folk hero—which may have been one reason the California Fish Commission yanked jurisdiction away from local authorities and created its own enforcement service in 1883.[2]

Looking at the danger to be braved and the money to be made, Jack London decided he would become an oyster pirate. He had learned of a small sloop, the *Razzle Dazzle*, that was for sale. She belonged to a regular at the Heinold Saloon who went by the moniker of "French Frank"; he was Gallic, debonair, about fifty, and an acknowledged leader of that shady waterfront community. To London, the $300 price might as well have been $3 million, but there was one person from whom he might confidentially borrow that kind of money, and he went to visit Mammy Jennie.

The Prentiss family had been living and prospering in Alameda, a racially mixed community in which families of color could achieve economic parity, or even live in better circumstances than white families who were down on their luck. Virginia had been steadily working as a nurse and had sizable savings, even as her husband's health had declined and he took on less work as a carpenter. The families had remained close; with the exception of Frank Atherton, Jack had never fit in well with the Cole School crowd and had spent at least as much time playing with Will Prentiss and his black chums, oblivious to the racial implications of the day. (Once during their roughhousing, Jack accidentally socked Will in the nose and exclaimed apologetically that he had mashed it "as flat as a nigger's," utterly unaware of any insult.)

Virginia Prentiss tried mightily to talk her white child out of becoming an outlaw, but Jack's arguments were unanswerable: he had become as tough as any of the other oyster pirates and could handle a boat better. So what if he got caught? Prison would be preferable to his present existence—the convicts worked shorter hours in better conditions, anyway. In the end, she counted out fifteen $20 gold pieces. "They fixed up the deal in here," recalled Heinold many years later. "Jack hands French Frank the money, and then they have drinks all around to celebrate."[3]

He took possession of the *Razzle Dazzle,* retaining her crew: a "wharf rat" who went by "Spider" Healey, twenty years old and sporting black whiskers, and Healey's niece, a girl London named "Mamie" for purposes of retelling, but whose real name he always held in confidence. London's biographers generally rely on his later written adventures to cite events from his months as an oyster pirate—London's fondness for artful devices to heighten the dramatic potential of his stories make this a dicey route to reconstructing his escapades. According to one of his own accounts, London's transition from being a Work Beast in the cannery to feeling the cold sting of salt spray on his face aboard the *Razzle Dazzle* happened in the space of one day, simply disappearing from the cannery and reappearing at the helm of his raiding sloop, which may or may not have been true. In the same rendition, the purchase was celebrated aboard the boat that night by London, Healey, Mamie, her sister, and others as a demijohn of red wine was liberally passed. During this revelry Mamie supposedly led London up onto the deck and "made love" to him. London and Mamie did become lovers, but whether it happened as described is doubtful.[4]

What London was not aware of was that French Frank was in love with Mamie, actually had proposed to her, and was sorely jealous of her preference for a fifteen-year-old. Even worse was the ripple of laughter through the saloons at French Frank's expense (Heinold was still chuckling about it forty years later), which allegedly prompted the older man to attempt to run down the *Razzle Dazzle* in another vessel during a rainstorm. London was alert to the danger and steered with his feet while brandishing a shotgun to keep French Frank at bay.

The ongoing drama, especially in light of the fact that virtually none of the other oyster pirates kept a woman on board, led Mamie to be dubbed Queen of the Oyster Pirates. By extension, Jack London became Prince of the Oyster Pirates, a sobriquet equally earned by his own quick success and acknowledged daring. In Mamie London discovered a quality in a woman that was new to him: a tomboyish relish of adventure that mirrored his own. "I could not help admiring a certain pluck that she had about her," he said later, "good fellow all through, unafraid of God or man or devil." Even so, she knew the terms of their relationship going into it, and abided by them, never asking for more, materially or emotionally, than he had signed on for, never intruding when he needed to be, as he often cast it, a man among men. It would be many years before he encountered this same combination of qualities in a woman, and when he finally did, he married her.[5]

The day-to-day labor of oyster pirating was a challenging and dangerous game of cat-and-mouse. Oyster beds were spaced up and down the coast within the bay. Oysters that were taken from abandoned beds were legal, and without an eyewitness to the theft it was impossible to prove which beds a given cargo of oysters came from. The better-protected beds were watched over by armed guards who kept vigil on platforms set on pilings. Successful pirating required cunning built on an intimate knowledge of the water's depth and the vessel's draft, allowing one to go where pursuing boats could not follow; a keen awareness of lunar phases, to blend in with the darkness of the night; and an ability to operate in absolute silence over still waters where even tiny knocks and bumps could travel with shocking clarity.

At moonless low tides the thieves would drop from their boats and fan out across the dank mud flats, the goal always to be first at the Oakland docks in the morning with a haul of fat fresh oysters commanding the highest price of the day from buyers who could not have cared less that they were enabling an ongoing felony. Twenty-five dollars for a night's labor was common, with London keeping two-thirds of the money and paying Spider the other third.

The satisfaction was not lost on him, as he later chuckled to his daughter, that now he had turned the tables on the system, that he was now the employer, with a hireling to pay, although for his share of the risks, Spider's one-third was much more generous than the going rate of ten cents an hour for common labor.[6] With daring that approached a death wish, London earned the deference of the entire fleet of oyster pirates. And this London parlayed into acceptance as that man among men, buying rounds of drinks for everybody at the Heinold Saloon, fighting rarely but fighting to win, and honing the art—significantly for his later career—of holding an audience rapt while he spun a yarn.

❧ ❧ ❧

As much as he relished the adventure and the chase, the times that London most enjoyed on the *Razzle Dazzle* were the nights when he knew that Spider and Mamie would be ashore. In advance of such occasions he would sortie to the Oakland Public Library to change out his books, and now being a young man of means, he would stoke up on a quarter's worth of candy. Late into the night, locked in his cabin and safe from discovery, he would debauch on Melville and Kipling and Flaubert, and taffy, and hard cannonballs—"big lumps of the most delicious lastingness," he later called them, proud of his ability to make one last an hour. It was heaven, but in the morning he knew he would have to resume his identity as Prince of the Oyster Pirates. "All the time I was striving to be a man amongst men," he wrote, "and all the time I nursed secret and shameful desires for candy. But I would have died before I'd let anybody guess it."[7]

He made good money stealing oysters from the Southern Pacific's leased reefs, later acknowledging that he made more in one week with the *Razzle Dazzle* than he could in a year at the pickle cannery. He repaid Mammy Jennie's $300 and made far bigger contributions to his family than even Flora could have dared demand from a boy making ten cents an hour. It was a signal experience for him psychologically as well. As one who grew up experiencing the ugly underbelly of the social and economic hierarchy that Mark Twain dubbed the "Gilded Age," for the first time he was able to get a little of his own back on the system.

But he also knew that he was pushing his luck. He was fortunate to have eluded capture thus far, but beyond that lay another worry: the competition was increasing, and he hardly needed to be told that there was, indeed, no honor among thieves. The oyster beds, rich as they were, were a finite resource, and one night a rival set the *Razzle Dazzle* afire. Arsonists also struck the *Reindeer,* owned by London's friend "Young Scratch" Nelson. London had long indulged a distant fascination with Nelson's father, "Old Scratch," a big, burly Scandinavian nicknamed for his brawling technique, in which the elder Nelson ended an altercation quickly by simply clawing off a piece of his opponent's face. Great was London's thrill the time he bid to increase his social standing by offering to buy Old Scratch a drink, and was accepted; he gained the friendship with Young Scratch in the bargain.[8] Nelson *fils* was an illiterate, but perhaps the strongest man on the waterfront, a Viking he seemed to London, and a daredevil who put the rest of them, even London, to shame.

Nelson's *Reindeer* was less damaged than London's *Razzle Dazzle,* so the two became partners, provisioning the *Reindeer* with a quick loan from Heinold. A few months more of successful oyster pirating with Nelson followed, months London always said he never regretted, except on the score that Nelson was tone-deaf, and London claimed his own ear for music was permanently warped by his partner's artless bawling of naughty sea chanties. Nevertheless, London's growing awareness of the gamble, and the growing odds that he would wind up dead or in prison, continued to nag him. Eventually he told Nelson that he wanted out, and the two parted as friends.

London confided his dilemma to Johnny Heinold, one of the few who understood that his whole persona was an act, a bid to belong, and that there was more to this boy than his buying rounds of drinks for the house and trying overeagerly to fit in with such rough company. Returning to a dime an hour wage was unthinkable for a youth who had been hailed as Prince of the Oyster Pirates, and who had once blown $180 buying drinks for his buddies in a single night. And that night below deck on the *Idler* continued to haunt and lure him.

At some point, exactly when can't be determined, he revealed to Heinold that he wanted to go to sea—to leave San Francisco Bay behind and head through the majestic Golden Gate, pitting himself against the vast Pacific itself. Heinold dissuaded him by suggesting that he join the California Fish Patrol. It made sense. Having mastered all the artful dodges of the law during his life as an oyster pirate, why should he not simply market himself to the other side of the law? North of Oakland, on the jut of land between San Pablo and Suisun bays, was the town of Benicia, where was located one of the first two offices of the Bureau of Patrol and Law Enforcement of the California Fish Commission, known in short as the California Fish Patrol. On one occasion London and Young Scratch had been in Benicia on the *Reindeer* to market a cargo of oysters, which was a rather cheeky thing to do right under the Fish Patrol's nose, and the station's boss, Charley LeGrant, offered them a job. London and, briefly, Nelson entered the service in the grade of deputy patrolmen, the equivalent of game wardens. They would receive no salary, but they would get to keep half the fines levied against lawbreakers they apprehended.

These new environs were not without interest for the inquisitive young sailor. Benicia boasted the *Solano*, the largest steam ferry in the world, her main deck laid with railroad tracks for transporting locomotives and cars across the estuary. To reach Benicia London sailed past Vallejo and the vast Navy yard at Mare Island, not really an island but a spindly peninsula that separated the Napa River from the east shore of San Pablo Bay. The yard's cavernous new dry dock was an architectural and engineering wonder, and nearby, her identity cruelly obscured by a shingle roof pocked with dormers and skylights, with windows where her gun ports used to be, was one of the most storied ships in American history. Laid down during the War of 1812 as the first U.S. ship of the line, a ninety-gun behemoth built to take on the best of the British fleet, she had cowed Barbary pirates and fought in the war with Mexico. For more than a generation she had been designated a receiving ship, a floating office warren, and only her three truncated masts that had once soared to topgallants poked defiantly above her crudely hipped roof to proclaim the last station of the U.S.S. *Independence*.

Benicia itself had a colorful history—the first city in California to be founded by Anglo Americans, it served as the state capital for a year before the government moved to Sacramento. The Pacific Mail Steamship Company's refueling and repair yard was the state's first large industrial facility, but London's own world centered on a more human and frowsy section of the waterfront, the community of fishermen and patrolmen, many of whom lived on their boats.

Living and sailing on Young Scratch's *Reindeer*, which the state had chartered, London employed his considerable cunning now on the side of the law. The oyster pirates of the lower bay came within his purview, but the primary targets of California's early conservation law were Chinese shrimpers who used illegal nets. Neither London nor the law took issue with them when small junks began dredging the bay for shrimp. But, as London wrote in *Tales of the Fish Patrol*, "This in itself would not be bad, were it not for the small mesh of the nets, so small that the tiniest fishes, little new-hatched things not a quarter of an inch long, cannot pass through. The beautiful beaches of Points Pedro and Pablo, where are the shrimp-catchers' villages, are made fearful by the stench from myriads of decaying fish."[9] Brought to the United States by the thousands for railroad construction, then resented for being there and entering into commerce, the Chinese immigrants withdrew into a society largely closed to Anglos and felt little loyalty to such western concepts as game conservation. Their defiance of the shrimping regulations was sullen and persistent.

Most of what is known of London's activities as a lawman comes from *Tales of the Fish Patrol*, his own somewhat heroically ginned-up memoir in the form of adventure stories for juvenile readers. Beginning in 1905, at the height of his fame and sandwiched between *The Sea-Wolf* and *White Fang*, its seven stories were published separately before being collected into book form. Melodramatic and vaguely Eurocentric in its action sequences, London nevertheless displays a keen ear for pidgin dialect, and the stories accurately reflect conditions on the bay in 1892.

In one of the less believable segments of the memoir, London and Charley LeGrant infiltrate the Oakland oyster pirates by posing as thieves themselves. During a dark-of-night raid, the two tow the pirates' boats away at low tide while the pirates are working the mud flats, leaving them easy and indeed grateful to be arrested as the tide comes back in. This was not a credible charade for London to have pulled off, when less than a year before he had been loudly buying rounds of drinks for the house, and word must have spread like wildfire when he went over to the Fish Patrol. And indeed, this was one case where London did actually tease apart fact from fiction in a letter to the story's publisher: there had in fact been such a raid, except it was the company watchmen who were stranded on the mud flats as the tide washed in, and "the raid was successful and . . . not one of the pirates was captured."

As with all of London's writing drawn from his own life—and that means most of his output—separating creative warp from factual, contextual weft is the more difficult because that was precisely what created such a tight fabric of story.[10] Interestingly, this is the only one of the *Tales of the Fish Patrol* that concerns the oyster piracy with which he was intimately familiar. In addition to the illegal shrimp netting by the Chinese, other stories describe the apprehension of Greek sailors who set illegal salmon lines. Throughout the stories, London's nautical narration clips along under full sail, but whether because it was early in his career or because he was writing for a youthful audience, the characters are simplistic, and they spout slang-laden dialogue that does more to advance plot and reinforce non-American stereotypes than it does enrich character or even depict realistic exchanges.

London's pro rata share of fines that were levied on poachers he had apprehended was paltry compared to his take as an oyster pirate, and his contributions to his parents fell off. John London and Flora moved into a tiny, tatty cottage built of lumber salvaged from dismantled recreational buildings from Badger Park—where, ironically, Johnny London as a boy had set up bowling pins. Jack's failure to make up for his stepfather's inability to provide for the family surely lent an element of despair to his drinking, although to outward appearances he still bent the elbow in hearty male bonding with his new mates in the Fish Patrol—and he quickly discovered that they drank every bit as hard as the oyster pirates.

An important turning point in his life occurred one night after a Herculean toot. Weaving his way down the wharf, he boarded a handy boat out near the channel to sleep it off, but then lost his footing and plunged overboard, where the sloughing tide carried him rapidly away. London was suddenly enveloped in disgust at the turns of his life thus far—unloved and forced to menial labor, shown through books a great sense of life and its possibilities, and then denied that life for his own squalid existence. And this was what he had come to: a stumbling teenage drunk who didn't even like to drink, but that was the price of admission to the camaraderie of men who would have howled and scoffed had they but known of his love of poetry and literature. A surreal sort of calm swept over him as the current took him down the Carquinez Straits, making it seem almost poetically appropriate that his wastrel's tale should come to such an end, and he oddly did not mind the shore lights slipping farther into the distance; he floated, weeping, waiting for the waters to close over him.

Four hours in the cold bay sobered him up, and with sobriety came a resurgence of his will not just to live, but to have great adventures and triumph. And with this unstoppable animal instinct to fight for survival came the reality that he very likely was going to die. The swirl of currents in the lower straits was lethal; he was aware of the vicious riptide off Mare Island with its pathetic hulk of the *Independence*, and before it could suck him under he shucked his clothes and, though exhausted, began stroking for the middle of the channel. Fighting, ardently convinced that he wanted to live, becoming acutely aware of the coldness of the water and of the numberless slaps of salt water in the growing chop he had already swallowed, a rapidly failing Jack London was plucked from the tide at dawn by a Greek salmon fisherman who happened by on his way into nearby Vallejo.

London quit the Fish Patrol, adding that experience to his growing résumé of adventurous employment, and left the San Francisco oyster industry to choke in the sewage and industrial pollution that was increasingly fouling the bay.[11] Restless over what to do with himself now, he returned to Oakland, his visible life resuming its slide into delinquency of drinking and slumming as his deeper self pondered the next move.

He was around the shabby London cottage irregularly, angering his mother, who needed his income, and troubling his increasingly disabled stepfather, who worried over the boy's future. Jack London loved sailing; the thrill of man against water had been the best thing about both oyster pirating and working for the law. He had been telling Heinold that he wanted to put to sea, but when it came time to act, he moved in the opposite direction: for $10 he and a friend agreed to sail a stolen and recovered boat from Oakland deep into the inland delta to Port Costa. When the boat's rightful owner stiffed them for the reward, they made off with the boat instead, eluding capture by sailing up the Sacramento River. They came across a gang of youthful hoboes skinny-dipping in the river near Sacramento. Suddenly fascinated by such a freewheeling lifestyle, London sent his friend on his way in the stolen boat and briefly took up life on the road as a tramp.

The other boys dubbed him "Sailor Kid," and for a brief lark he traveled with them so far inland as to cross the Sierra Nevada—a new sight indeed for such a coastal youth—and, it was said, he learned the essentials of rolling hapless immigrants for clothing or petty cash. The thrill of running with a gang soon wore off, for in its reduction it promised the same pointless end, prison or a violent death, as had oyster pirating. He gained skills that served him in future tramping adventures, but for the present he returned to the Oakland waterfront and the comfort of its familiar, if not uplifting, circumstances. He dallied with one and then another of West Oakland's collections of thugs, the Boo Gang and the Sporting Life Gang, but finding himself ill at ease with them, regularly returned to Young Scratch Nelson and the wharf rats clustered about Heinold's saloon, now renamed Heinold's First and Last Chance for its position at the departure point on the wharf, where travelers could have their first drink upon arriving from across the bay or their last drink before departing.

During the 1892 election season, London endured another tussle with alcohol that was in its way as grave a warning as when he had fallen overboard into the Carquinez Straits. He was loafing, penniless, about the Overland House, when an oyster pirate he knew called Joe Goose entered on a mission to round up men to fill out a torchlight parade at the Hancock Fire Brigade. The whiskey, as much as they could drink, was free to all who would come. In company with Young Scratch and others, they were herded onto a train for Hayward, a city a few miles in from the eastern shore of the Bay, fifteen miles southeast of Oakland. Once there, they cooperatively donned red shirts and fire helmets, and paraded with lighted torches for the local politicians who were supplying the booze. And they got drunk beyond description.

The parade's sponsors were not about to risk a horde of drunken wharf rats rampaging through Hayward, and quickly herded the crowd back onto the train. Dizzy and hyperventilating, London was beginning to show the symptoms of acute alcohol poisoning, and in a panic he tried to flee, falling down with each attempt to run, to a chorus of guffaws from the rest. Young Scratch finally carried him onto the train. Short of breath in his seat, London began clawing at a window and failing to open it—it was screwed shut—he seized someone's torch and broke the glass in a desperate bid for fresh air. Young Scratch thought he was trying to throw himself from the train and attempted to restrain him, but London resisted with all the violence his drunkenness could summon. A general brawl ensued, and London was knocked out cold.

If London's 1913 roman à clef of his struggle against alcohol, *John Barleycorn*, tells the truth without varnish, and there is a general agreement among his biographers that in this case it does, the incident shook him badly. "I often think that was the nearest to death I have ever been," he wrote. "I was scorching up, burning alive internally, in an agony of fire and suffocation, and I wanted air—I madly wanted air." And then all was blackness until he awoke again, seventeen hours later. With time and sobriety to reflect, he concluded that this could not go on.

3 THE SEAL HUNTER

Just a short time in the California Fish Patrol convinced Jack London that greater adventures must await him beyond the horizon. The day before his seventeenth birthday he announced to Johnny Heinold that he intended to go to sea—"before the mast," an expression that spiced his plan with a touch of Herman Melville and Richard Henry Dana and romance.

Heinold tried to persuade him to go back to school, but upon finding his arguments wasted he assayed the possibilities in the fleet laid up nearby. "The *Sophia Sutherland* was in port then, just bein' fixed up for a whalin' and sealin' voyage to Japan and the Bering Sea. I knew the skipper pretty well. He was a big hard-faced 'blue-noser' from Nova Scotia. . . . I think he was Irish-Scotch." The name of the vessel's captain was also Sutherland, so presumably she was named for wife or daughter.[1] He was the owner as well, nearly eighty, but his son managed the ship's day-to-day operation.

Heinold recommended London to Sutherland but was turned down flat when it came out that London was just turning seventeen. Over the course of an hour Heinold wore the captain down, detailing London's skill at handling his skiff, insisting that he was cut from a different cloth than others hanging around the bar, and hinting that he might turn out badly if he shipped out under a lesser captain. Heinold did not recall it in his short memoir, but he likely also told him of London's local fame as Prince of the Oyster Pirates turned lawman. The sale that Heinold began, London completed, impressing Sutherland with his maturity and determination.[2]

On January 20, 1893, barely a week after his seventeenth birthday, Jack London took leave of his parents. He was pricked only by the look of wistfulness in the eyes of his long-suffering stepfather, whom he loved and whose failing health did not guarantee that he would live to see a reunion. London signed aboard the *Sophia Sutherland*, a three-masted sealing schooner, topsail rigged, bound for the Bonin Islands, Japan, and then seal hunting in the Bering Sea. Gently swaybacked and of only modest displacement (conflicting accounts of her size average a hundred tons), her raked prow nevertheless had cut through a disreputable past. Apparently she had sailed under three other names, or more, smuggling and even "blackbirding"—kidnapping south sea island natives as slave labor for copra plantations.[3]

Three days later the *Sophia Sutherland* passed through the Golden Gate into the open Pacific. The precocious youth who watched the strait pass by and then drop astern could not have been more acutely conscious that he was entering a new life.

Like many boys who grow into their adult features precociously, he had been a homely child. Now at seventeen the ugly duckling of a boy had blossomed into a youth of head-turning beauty: light brown curly hair, large blue eyes with long lashes, and delicate features, but with a physique honed by constant labor and a constitution to match.

Banking on his experience at handling the sloops *Razzle Dazzle* and *Reindeer*, London signed aboard the much larger sealer as an able seaman, a rank that normally required three years' experience and an age of nineteen. This presumptuousness was sure to cause him trouble with the seasoned and unforgiving older sailors who would pounce on any excuse, any shirked task or poorly tied knot, to make this pretty boy's life a misery. Yet from the first day at sea, London determined to give no man cause to fault him; he quickly assimilated the names of ropes and knots that were new to him; he raced aloft without the least complaint whenever ordered; he was the first on deck for his watch and the last to go below after making certain that nothing assigned to him was left undone.

Still, the custom of the sea was that boys serve older sailors, and some of the crew of twenty-two were determined that London should pay his dues. His chief tormentor was a looming, ham-fisted Swede who went by Big Red John. Their altercation came when it was Big Red John's turn at "peggy-day," washing dishes and setting the fo'c'sle back in order after meals. Resenting doing chores while London was occupied only in weaving a rope mat, the older man ordered him to refill the molasses. London refused once, twice, and then three times, telling him to do it himself.

Every man in the cabin saw the fight coming. In a rage, Big Red John dropped a stack of dishes and moved to backhand him, but London lashed out with a punch that landed squarely between the Swede's eyes. Not for nothing had London observed the technique of Old Scratch Nelson back in Oakland: go for vital damage and end the fight quickly. Dodging one powerful but clumsy punch, London leapt on the Swede's back and began choking him. Big Red John did everything he could to dislodge London from his back, running him into bulkheads, cracking his head onto the beams that supported the deck above them, which dislodged the slush lamp and sent it crashing down. The seventeen-year-old took a terrible beating but Big Red John couldn't see it, and London's only way out was to squeeze harder and harder, bloodied but conscious of the sweet prize at the end if he could hang on: respect. As the Swede began to weaken, London cried out a curiously, almost comically boylike demand: "Will you promise to let me alone? Eh—will you promise?"

Big Red John, as London later said in an interview, "purple in the face, gurgled an assent, and when that viselike grip on his throat lessened, reeled and stumbled to his knees like a felled bullock." At the instant of victory the other ten men of the fo'c'sle crowded around him solicitously, their admiration palpable—a man among men, at last.[4]

Not all the establishment of dominance in the fo'c'sle revolved around menial labor, and it was aboard the *Sophia Sutherland* that Jack began to form his understanding of sexuality as a force of nature that would find expression without regard to social convention or taboo. The forward cabin of the *Sophia Sutherland* housed a dozen men, ten of them hardened seamen, and two, including Jack, inexperienced youths whom the older sailors sought to victimize. London hinted at it, apparently with chilling clarity, many years later in Manhattan, while walking with Michael Monahan, editor of an impoverished belles-lettres periodical called *Papyrus*, and journalist Joseph Noel, to whom he had licensed dramatic rights to one of his novels.

After an evening of drinking whiskey and listening to Chopin and Rachmaninoff at Victor Herbert's studio, London led Monahan and Noel on a drinking tour from one pub to another. At one point they passed a clot of rouged homosexuals loitering about the Flatiron Building at Fifth Avenue and Broadway, their principal gathering location, and Monahan lamented the perversion of Rimbaud, who, he said, had been led astray by troops in Paris during the Franco-Prussian War.

London asked particularly whether it was soldiers who had lured Rimbaud into same-sex activity, Monahan confirmed that it was, and London volunteered, "Sailors are that way, too. Prisoners in cells are also that way. Whenever you herd men together and deny them women their latent sex perversions come to the surface. It's a perfectly natural result of a natural cause." He did not say whether he ever participated aboard the sealing schooner or, in later years, in jail in Buffalo or snowbound with his fellows in Alaska, but he did nonplus Noel with a description of homosexual acts that Noel characterized as "brutal, frank, disgusting."

In passing the fey men in mascara—the third sex, as Noel called them in a reference to the eunuchs in India—Monahan declared, "I'd hang them all." London's rejoinder was more even-tempered. "A man should love women, and plenty of them," to keep from falling into such a state. In his view of the world, a view that later gave him the naturalistic, nonjudgmental voice of *Call of the Wild*, men denied one usage of sex would simply turn to an alternative.[5] That the alternative was practiced in dark corners of the *Sophia Sutherland* there can be little doubt, but whether London accepted this as a requisite of being a man among men in this womanless environment—his frank exposition of it to Michael Monahan suggests that he may have, but his full-bore heterosexuality in the company of women may suggest otherwise—we don't know.

London's cheek in posing as an able seaman was finally forgiven in his eagerness and assiduity in accomplishing every task given him. Another crewman who had also signed aboard for an able seaman's wage, a Midwesterner of about forty whom the other men called the Bricklayer, was less fortunate. As it became apparent that he had no idea what to do or how to do it, it was just as well for him that he took to his bunk and, the worse for him, entered the final stages of consumption. He was also regarded as an exceptionally vile human being, and the crew's contempt for him was not softened by any hint of compassion for a dying man. The sooner he expired, the better for them, and when the Bricklayer did die, he was sewn into his own blankets and weighted with coal.

Captain Sutherland lost his place in reading the burial service, at which his son seized the book and recited it, rapidly and without feeling, and the body was dumped overboard. London at seventeen watched the shroud disappear astern, and understood what a lonely place the sea could be. Even so, he did not waste a moment in claiming as his own, against all sailing superstition, the Bricklayer's drier bunk with better light for reading. He had brought books—*Moby Dick*, obviously, and *Anna Karenina*, a useful treatise on codes of behavior, and consequences.

The *Sophia Sutherland* proceeded west along the southern sea lanes without stopping in Hawaii, but London could make out the islands' peaks on the horizon. Then the ship steered west-northwest to her first destination, the Bonin Islands. For several hundred miles due south of Tokyo, a thin string of volcanic islands marks the western edge of the Izu Trench. At the southern end, two-thirds of the way to the Marianas, lie the Volcano Islands, including Iwo Jima. North of them, five hundred miles south of Tokyo, is the group called the Bonins, a dozen small, mountainous islands totaling only forty square miles, cloaked in subtropical jungle. The islands were uninhabited when they were discovered first by the Spanish in 1543 and separately by the Japanese fifty years later; in fact the name "Bonin" was a corruption of the Japanese word for "uninhabited."

During nineteenth-century imperial expansion, England and the United States quarreled over claims to the islands. The British based theirs on a visit by H.M.S. *Blossom* in 1827 and the Americans based their own on first settlement, as their descendants were still resident on the islands, although now outnumbered by Japanese immigrants who began arriving in 1861. Based on this plurality, and the islands' proximity to their homeland, the Japanese government managed to negotiate recognition of sovereignty with the western powers in 1876. The group's main island, Chichi Jima, became an important provisioning stop for Western vessels.

The *Sophia Sutherland*'s elderly owner-captain was a teetotaler (perhaps one reason that Johnny Heinold had sought him out) and the voyage was a dry one. Fifty-one days at sea, seven weeks plus two days, and Jack London was, apart from the captain, likely the only man on board who was not famished for alcohol. By the time they dropped anchor in the small, mountain-girdled harbor at Chichi Jima, dotted with some twenty other sealers and whalers lying at anchor, Oakland's dockside poison had been thoroughly cleansed from London's system. His every cell quivered with the excitement of adventure, of a dream realized, as though he were finally escaping into the pages of one of Ina Coolbrith's library books.

Since brawling his way to the respect of the other men in the fo'c'sle by besting Big Red John, London had become best friends with two in particular, a Swede named Victor and a Norwegian named Axel. When they moved about together, the rest of the crew called them the Three Sports, and they determined to explore the island. Taking one of the schooner's boats they set out for the sugar-white beach that fronted the settlement of Futami. From the water Victor pointed out a path that, after mounting a bare volcanic hillside, they could trace into the distance, rising higher and higher flanked by palms and flowers. Following this path to wherever it might lead was their first goal. The breeze was offshore, and London filled his lungs with the scents of cedar and sandalwood, glorying in the moment he would set foot on his first foreign sand.

They pulled their boat ashore but, walking into the beachfront town, discovered it in near pandemonium. "Several hundred riotous seamen from all the world, drinking prodigiously, singing prodigiously, dancing prodigiously—and all on the main street to the scandal of a helpless handful of Japanese police." London's Scandinavian companions decided to have a drink before locating that verdant path into the mountains, and since alcohol was still the ticket to acceptance, he joined them. He had no idea what local distillate they were drinking, but "it was hot as fire, pale as water, and quick as death with its kick."[6]

The binge quickly became the focus of the day. Victor and Axel met one acquaintance after another, and every reunion, every story of old times had to be recounted over an additional shot. By mid-afternoon Victor was ragingly, violently drunk, and London and Axel barely managed to get him back out to the ship, which he nearly tore apart before his mates managed to get him undressed and into his bunk.

Still determined to sample island culture, London and Axel returned to Futami and looked up a Japanese house of entertainment with its sliding doors and paper walls, and engaged some local musicians. No sooner had they arranged themselves in this more quiet activity than Victor found them again, crashing through a wall and scattering the group.

From this point London gave himself over to the inevitable, and the day dissolved into a staggering binge from which he could recall only an inchoate sequence of impressions. "I remember, somewhere, sitting in a circle of Japanese fishermen, kanaka boat-steerers from our own vessels, and a young Danish sailor fresh from cowboying in the Argentine with a penchant for native customs and ceremonials." In the swirl of memory he could recall politely drinking *sake* from tiny porcelain cups, and English runaways of his own age weeping from homesickness. When he awoke he was lying in the door of the harbor pilot's house, his money and his watch gone, along with his shoes, belt, and coat, with the pilot's wife bending over him in concern that he might not wake at all. After ten days in the Bonins the *Sophia Sutherland* weighed anchor and cleaved out of the harbor, with London still wistful that he had never explored that palm- and flower-fringed path into the mountains.

For the next three months the schooner plied her deadly trade. In following a herd of seals she would deploy six small boats, in one of which London was the oarsman; rifles and shotguns would bang throughout the day, and on gathering again at the mother ship the sailors would skin the carcasses and salt and store the skins, then wash the boats of blood before the next day's hunt. Steadily they worked their way north.

As the sun rose on April 10, 1893, the *Sophia Sutherland* was within sight of Cape Erimo, the prominent, triangular southern tip of Hokkaido. She hove to and launched all six boats, each with a crew of three. They had ventured far from the main seal herd, but there were enough seals nearby to make for a good hunt. London, pulling at his oars, heard one mate remark on the beauty of the morning; his steersman recited a famous dark aphorism: "Red sun in the morning, sailor take warning."[7] By mid-afternoon a dozen seals lay lifeless in the bottom of London's boat, but the weather had been deteriorating, a constant wind increasing from the west-northwest.

The schooner had worked her way to the lee of the boats to give them a swift run home, and at three o'clock they saw the return flag fluttering aloft. The sea turned from green to leaden as dark storm clouds rolled in, and the steersmen were challenged to keep their sterns to the growing swell or be swamped. Back aboard the schooner the falling barometer told all they needed to know about the coming night. Haste was made to skin the kill and secure the boats.

With darkness came the roaring terror of the typhoon. Mountainous waves, driving spray, all hands on deck securing gear that had broken loose, shouting at the top of their lungs without being heard, alert not to wash overboard in the crashing seas as rescue would have been impossible. There was no choice but to run before the storm; twice they shortened sail, the ship so hard to control that each man's turn, or "trick," at the wheel lasted only an hour before he stumbled below, exhausted. It was seven in the morning when London was called from the fo'c'sle to take his trick at the wheel. If ever he faced a moment of truth, this was it. Throughout the voyage he had done his job, done more than his share, and earned acceptance as an able seaman two years before it would even be legal to call himself one. But now all his greenness, all his inexperience, was on full display with the lives of the crew in his hands. The sailing master watched him grip the wheel, watched him for twenty minutes before feeling reassured that London could handle the job and not get them all killed. Then he went below, leaving London alone and responsible.

"Not a stitch of canvas was set," he wrote of it later. "We were running before [the storm] under bare poles, yet the schooner fairly tore along. The seas were all of an eighth of a mile apart, and the wind snatched the whitecaps from their summits, filling the air so thick with driving spray it was impossible to see more than two waves at a time. [She] was almost unmanageable, rolling her rail under to starboard and to port, veering and yawing anywhere from south-east to south-west, and threatening, when the huge seas lifted under her quarter, to broach to. Had she broached to, she would ultimately have been reported lost with all hands and no tidings." He fought to keep her stern to the swell, but even then, "once we were pooped. I saw it coming, and, half-drowned, with tons of water crushing me, I checked the schooner's rush to broach to. At the end of the hour, sweating and played out, I was relieved. But I had done it!"[8] The typhoon roared over them quickly, and by morning, conditions had lightened dramatically. London's turn at the wheel was, and remained, the proudest hour of his life.

As spring wore on, the *Sophia Sutherland* headed into the Bering Sea for more seals, an orgy of gore, sunup to sundown. The ship was little more than a floating charnel house in which a man of any sensitivity had no place. London later memorialized it in *The Sea-Wolf*, the decks "slippery with fat and blood, the scuppers running red, masts, ropes, and rails splattered . . . and the men, like butchers plying their trade, naked and red of arm and hand, hard at work with ripping and flensing knives, removing the skins from the pretty creatures they had killed." The meat was never eaten, the blubber never boiled for oil; the seal carcasses were thrown overboard. All, apparently, save one.

During the course of the voyage, the other crewmen in the fo'c'sle wearied sufficiently of Big Red John's bullying that they determined to exact a measure of revenge. Of all the men in the cabin, the Swede was the only one who habitually slept nude, notwithstanding season or weather. During the height of the seal hunt, one of the men distracted Big Red John long enough for others to conceal a big, cold-skinned carcass in his bunk. That night after his watch he stripped in the dark and dove under the covers—there followed a heart-stopping shriek and a good-faith effort at whipping every other man in the cabin.

Only when the hold was gorged with preserved sealskins did Captain Sutherland call a halt and head back south, putting into Yokohama for two weeks.[9] Perhaps thinking it funny, Sutherland entrusted all the men's pay to the seal shooters, sending them ashore to ensconce themselves in a public house before releasing the rest of the crew to try to find them. Having prepared himself for a foreign world, London was shocked and disappointed to discover that Yokohama was largely a Western city, very much in the vanguard of Japan's concerted effort to join and be recognized by the industrialized nations. It was not at all what he was led to expect from Ina Coolbrith's library books. Still, he took his first ride in a rickshaw, had his photograph taken, tanned and tough and confident, and experienced one incident that made his list of red-letter memories.

The story of London's adventure in Yokohama arose in his writing no fewer than four times, twice in fiction, and twice in nonfiction, but the details changed so much from one telling to another that the truth of what happened has been hopelessly lost. During one of his forays ashore, either he lost his money and could not afford the sampan fare back out to the ship, or he ran afoul of the police. After some wall-ripping escapades of his own through hapless tea houses, he plunged into the harbor, either of his own accord, or on a dare. Whatever the circumstance, he drunkenly swam the mile from the wharf out to the *Sophia Sutherland*, where the next day the harbor police, believing him drowned, brought out his clothes to have them identified, only to discover him safely sleeping it off. The story raced through the moored ships, and London found himself a harbor celebrity.[10]

At some point during the cruise of the *Sophia Sutherland*, London came down with a severe, indeed nearly fatal, siege of shingles. It dissipated by the end of the voyage, but it was the first indication he had that his physical constitution was not as impregnable as he posed, and needed to believe. Having departed San Francisco on January 23, the sealing schooner cleaved her way back through the Golden Gate on August 26, 1893, thirty-seven days out of Yokohama. The crew shared final rounds of drinks, and London went shopping: "A second-hand hat," he recalled, "some forty cent shirts, two fifty-cent suits of underclothes, and a second-hand coat and vest." Crossing the bay to Oakland, he spent another seventy cents on drinks for his old buddies, and looked up his family, whom he found hanging on in near ruin.[11] In a soul-suffocating moment his old life pattern asserted itself, and he handed over the balance of his seven months' wages to his mother to get the family back on their feet, and moved back into the London household.

* * *

Seven months at sea had sated the most urgent of Jack London's youthful wanderlust. Finding his family in trouble, he braced himself to begin looking for work, but his timing could not have been worse. The financial Panic of 1893 had sunk the country into one of the worst depressions it had ever known, and professional positions of any kind were unheard of. Even laboring jobs were scarce, and for them the near-universal wage was—how it must have deflated him—ten cents an hour, exactly the same as he had made stuffing pickle jars after primary school. Surely he could do better.

Returning to the oyster beds might have seemed lucrative, but he learned now how dangerous it actually had been. After London returned to Oakland he discovered that his former partner, Young Scratch Nelson, had been shot to death by police—a somber warning of what his own fate might have been had he not ended their partnership. French Frank was in hiding, and others of the old oyster pirates who had not evaded capture were doing hard time in San Quentin prison. There was no alternative for it; London must, for the present, become once more the Work Beast.

He learned of a job opening in a jute mill, keeping bobbins wound with fibers that were woven into burlap bags. For a young man who had lived such adventures as he, the jute mill, at a dollar a day for ten hours, loomed like the specter of failure itself. The only bright spot was that they promised him, if he stuck it out for a few months, that he would be raised to a dollar and a quarter per day. Late in August 1893, he bowed his head and put himself back under the yoke.

It was not the worst job he ever had. At a steady ten hours per day, there was even time left over for the beginnings of a social life, and he used the opportunity to embark on a program of self-improvement. He began attending the YMCA for physical conditioning, but he quickly realized this was a mistake. The youths there were wholesome, but callow and inexperienced in the world. Although many were of his own age, London realized that he had become a man in ways that they had not yet dreamed of in their complacent, circumscribed lives. Worse, their sheer innocence and lack of cares made him realize, with something of a shock, that (apart from that one summer spent with Frank Atherton's family) he had never really had a boyhood to enjoy. These pale boys at the YMCA could see him only as a bad influence, and their society was itself an unending reproach of his own social disability. It was a bad fit.

Fortunately for London, he chanced upon the very friend he needed, one who played the same role as once had Frank Atherton, during his time at the Cole Grammar School. His name was Louis Shattuck, "without one vicious trait . . . a real innocently devilish young fellow who was quite convinced that he was a sophisticated town-boy. . . . Louis was handsome, and graceful, and filled with love for the girls."[12] He was a blacksmith's apprentice, and therefore shared London's social class and understanding of the limitations of poverty. Even better, he understood the allure of candy, and best of all, Shattuck didn't drink. At last London had a chum with whom he could be himself, whose friendship was not bound up in men's obligation to down alcohol whether they wanted to or not. Neither one had a great deal of free time, but what they had they utilized in hanging out on street corners, smoking, their caps at angles they thought girls must find jaunty. London studied Shattuck's technique at accosting and picking up girls, and occasionally they would double-date, squandering a whole week's spare change to treat girls to street-vended hot tamales and ice cream.

Given the chance to follow Shattuck's suave template in meeting nice girls on his own, however, London foundered—with one exception. It happened at a Salvation Army meeting, in which he found himself seated next to the most adorable girl he believed he had ever seen. In his memoir he called her

"Haydee," but as with Mamie, the queen of the *Razzle Dazzle*, her real name was for his memory alone. She and her aunt came to the meeting out of curiosity, Haydee taking a seat next to London, who ever afterward claimed to have learned at that moment the truth of love at first sight. She was about fifteen, with brown hair and eyes under a tam o'shanter. They spent a half hour stealing glances and embarrassed blushes at each other. But London never said a word. He who had romanced the Queen of the Oyster Pirates and had called at sailors' pleasuring grounds on the other side of the Pacific, was never more at sea than at this moment, choking over how to open a conversation with a girl—a nice girl, an inhabitant of that innocent world of youth he had never known.[13] Haydee and her aunt soon left the hall, but when London tried to shadow them he was accosted by someone from his past, Young Scratch's girl, who knew they had been friends, and wanted—needed—to tell him how he died.

It turned out that he did get to see Haydee again; Louis Shattuck knew that she had a friend named Ruth, who was friends with Nita, who worked at the candy store they patronized. London entrusted a shy boyish note to Nita, which made its way to Haydee, who responded with encouragement. They met perhaps a dozen times, innocently, enjoyably, even if only to share a nickel sack of red hots. London always cherished her memory, as a memorial to the innocent adolescence that might have been his, had he not been a Work Beast from the time he was old enough to throw newspapers.

During the autumn of 1893 it was Flora London who noticed an announcement in the *San Francisco Morning Call*, a contest with first, second, and third prizes of $25, $15, and $10, for the best descriptive article by local writers no older than twenty-two. Jack should enter, she said, and write up his experience with that typhoon off Japan. London, exhausted every night from earning his dollar for ten hours at the jute mill, was initially unimpressed, but Flora, who had had to hear about the storm over and over again, kept after him. Finally he gave in and worked through two consecutive nights, almost hallucinating from lack of sleep. He produced a piece of 4,000 words, which he then cut in half to meet the contest rules.

> It was on the deck that the force of the wind could be fully appreciated. . . . It seemed to stand up against you like a wall, making it almost impossible to move on the heaving decks or to breathe as the fierce gusts came dashing by. . . . A soft light emanated from the movement of the ocean. Each mighty sea, all phosphorescent and glowing with the tiny lights of myriads of animalculae, threatened to overwhelm us with a deluge of fire. Higher and higher, thinner and thinner, the crest grew as it began to curve and overtop preparatory to breaking, until with a roar it fell over the bulwarks, a mass of soft glowing light and tons of water which sent the sailors sprawling in all directions. . . .
>
> The wild antics of the schooner were sickening as she forged along. She would almost stop, as though climbing a mountain, then rapidly rolling to right and left as she gained the summit of a huge sea, she steadied herself and paused for a moment. . . . Like an avalanche, she shot forward and down as the sea astern struck her . . . burying her bow to the catheads in the milky foam at the bottom.

He won first prize, beating out students from Stanford and Berkeley with his eighth-grade education from Cole Grammar School, his long hours of reading Johnny Heinold's dictionary on the corner table, and his fierce fondness for reading the great masters. "The Story of a Typhoon Off the Coast of Japan" was published on November 12, and Jack London, author, was born. So, too, was Flora London, author's mother. She had played longer odds than him in the Chinese lotteries for years, and now he had just made $25 for the family, nearly a month's laboring wages, with a very promising piece written in three days.

As most young writers discover, there is a vast difference between being acknowledged as having talent and making more than casual spending money at it. Immediately he spun out a couple of quick stories that he also submitted to the *Call*, but they were turned down. Newspapers, he discovered, did not publish fiction—a beginner's mistake.

❧ ❧ ❧

As time passed London inquired after the raise he had been promised if he stuck with the job at the jute mill, and when he found it was not forthcoming, he walked away. His family circumstances dictated that he must continue to generate an income, but he realized that it was time to start thinking more strategically about his future. He was still only seventeen; surely that was young enough to start afresh. Turning his mind to what sort of professional career might interest him, he concluded that he was sufficiently intrigued by the modern marvel of electricity to investigate becoming an electrician.

He obtained an interview with the superintendent of the Oakland, San Leandro, and Haywards Electric Railway. He desired, he said, to work his way up through the company and eventually become an electrician. The superintendent heard him out sympathetically. Yes, his was a laudable and workable plan, certainly he could rise in the company in time, but of course he must start at the bottom. Just then they needed a man to shovel coal in their power plant. It was as though he had walked into one of the Horatio Alger novels that had been a staple of his youthful reading. "I believed in the old myths," London wrote. "A canal boy could become president. Any boy . . . could, by thrift, energy, and sobriety, learn the business and rise."[14] Whatever was left in him of little Johnny London needed to believe that hard work, perseverance, and virtue could lead one to success in life. He had already shown on board the *Sophia Sutherland* that he could earn respect with determination, frankness, and a sincere effort to do a good job.

However, the coal passer's job at the electric railway was not as described. At $30 per month for working every day, including Sundays, with one day off per month, he was paid not by the hour but by the amount of coal he was given to shovel and barrow. As a result, every day he was saddled with far more labor than he could do in ten hours.

The power station was three miles from home, and London obtained a streetcar pass with the stipulation that he could sit down only when no other passenger needed the seat. His first day on the job, having arrived at seven in the morning, he finished at eight-thirty that night, weary and praying on the car home that it would not fill up so that he could take a seat. When it did, he was shocked to find that his body seized up, and he could not even stand. Through the course of days and weeks, he sprained both wrists and had to wear heavy leather splints to keep them from swelling. "But I was resolved," he wrote, "to show them what a husky young fellow determined to rise could do." There were no girls, no more library books; never had he been more the Work Beast.

Eventually one of the plant firemen took pity on the handsome teenager and confessed that in the job he was doing for $30 a month, he was replacing not one but two men who had made $40 a month—each. The fireman apologized: he would have spoken sooner, but he did not think London would actually stay and continue to labor under such ridiculous terms of employment. Even worse, one of the men he had replaced, according to an article in the newspaper, had just committed suicide in despair of finding another job and being able to support his wife and three children.

There was only so much lying, sly dealing, and ill usage that one young man could take. Had someone attempted to use him in this way on the waterfront, London would have beaten him to a pulp. Galled, scalded, betrayed, London quit the electric railway power station in a fury.

It was not hard work that he objected to—indeed he had already proved his love of physical exertion—it was the pointlessness and the drudgery of it, the idea of slaving at a pittance of a wage for a class of owners and investors who lived like lords and took their sense of entitlement for granted. It was being lied to and doubtless laughed at by owners who never questioned that a dollar a day was the best that people like him should expect for killing themselves.

In a very real sense, the coal he had been shoveling to stoke the boilers of the Oakland, San Leandro, and Haywards Electric Railway kindled another fire instead—hotter, angrier, more cynical. It was the fire lit in the deepest part of his soul to take up arms against this kind of evil.

4 THE TRAMP

Storming out of the power plant may have salved Jack London's bruised pride, but it was a terrible time to quit a job, no matter how demeaning. The economic downturn engendered by the Panic of 1893 had ossified into a depression that crippled agriculture nationwide, from Midwestern corn farmers to Southern sharecroppers, stagnated industry, and suffocated commerce. Ultimately 15,000 businesses went bankrupt.

Finding a new job, at even the most insulting wage, was almost unheard of at the time. Unemployment doubled from mid-1893 to early 1894, to 2 million workers; by June 1894 there were 3 million. By some estimates, the unemployment rate approached 20 percent, creating labor unrest on a scale unprecedented in American history. The national discourse began including words and concepts only recently thought too extreme for polite conversation: reform, socialism, even revolution. Not surprisingly, the San Francisco area was in the van of fearless thinking on the subject of social justice and institutional change.

Jack London was eighteen when he walked out of the power plant with the leather splints on his sprained wrists. He needed rest, and before he devoted himself to finding new employment he could at least renew his relationship with the Oakland Public Library. His reading took a more serious and more focused turn, as he was seized by a compulsion to understand, in effect, everything: how things came to be the way they were, why people believed what they did and behaved the way they did. He indulged a fascination for Darwin and the *Origin of Species*, which was given practical application in Herbert Spencer's *Synthetic Philosophy*. In the ongoing financial meltdown, Marx, as well as Nietzsche, made sense to him.

Even with his quick intelligence, however, London lacked coherent instruction while assimilating such raw source materials, and he occasionally misunderstood them. He became enamored of Nietzsche's expression "blond beast," equating the term with the super-race. The author actually meant that blond beasts were the segment of the population to be dominated. Understandably, given the white supremacy that was part of Flora London's daily conversation, it would not have naturally occurred to him that any race that was a candidate for domination could be white.

As the country seemed divided between the few very wealthy and millions of destitute, only one man in the tiny class of "haves" came to the fore in giving a damn about the plight of the poor. Jacob S. Coxey was a successful Ohio businessman—he was from Flora London's hometown—who began publicizing a plan for the federal government to print currency and use it to hire the unemployed on road construction, and to allow cities to trade their bonds into the U.S. Treasury in exchange for money to fund local projects. He accomplished his first step, getting his "Good Roads" bill introduced into the Congress, calling for an appropriation of the astronomical sum of half a billion dollars.

To the robber barons of the Gilded Age, the prospect of the federal government undertaking a jobs program for the poor was anathema. Such a scheme could dry up the labor market and force wages up from the widespread dime an hour. They were equally fearful of placing more money in circulation by backing it with silver. For many years after the Civil War, American currency had continued to be backed by gold, when the amount of paper money needed to service the growing economy far outstripped the new supplies of gold to guarantee the value of the greenbacks. Government monetary policy was to withdraw cash from circulation to maintain the value on what remained, which caused serious deflation. Home values, for instance, dropped below what was still owed on the mortgages. When silver, at the time being mined in much greater quantities, was finally allowed to help back the currency, American lenders, like European investors in the American economy, continued to want payment on demand in gold. As the pro-silver forces grew stronger, lenders preferred to seize assets rather than take payment in currency that they viewed as devalued. Loans were called in, forcing business failures by the thousands, mortgages were foreclosed, and the crisis deepened. The banks discovered that the foreclosed properties and seized assets were worth little in the sinking economy, and realized just how overextended they themselves had become; five hundred of them failed during the course of the depression.

In Oakland, the most public face of the corporate oligarchy was the railroad, which had been despised by most locals for years—as evidenced by popular sympathy for oyster pirates such as London—and their hatred only intensified when Southern Pacific attempted to press an ownership claim to the entire waterfront. Nationally their reputation was even worse. In this era before regulation, railroads were under no obligation to charge the same rates to all comers or on all lines. The rail barons gave active chase to obtain monopolies on routes by which they could bankrupt competitors' subsidiary companies by charging ruinous freight rates. The whole spectacle displayed laissez-faire capitalism at its ugliest, and like most depressions, that of the 1890s was brought on by overarching greed.

Coxey's "Good Roads" bill floundered in the Congress, so to demonstrate his popular support, he organized a march from his base in Ohio to Washington. Numbering only about a hundred when it left Ohio, his force grew until Coxey's marchers, officially named the Commonweal of Christ but widely termed the Industrial Army of the Unemployed, numbered over five hundred. Like streams flowing to a river, more groups of marchers began collecting in the West, intending to reinforce Coxey. One started from Denver, another from Los Angeles; one of the largest groups began forming about a young Oakland printer named Charles Kelly. "Kelly's Army" got a large boost when the mayor of San Francisco paid the fares to ship some six hundred recruits across the bay to Oakland to get them out of his city. The citizenry of Oakland gamely agreed to provision them, but then also intended to speed them on their way—an initial example of the opposing polarities that kept the Commonweal of Christ moving: widespread sympathy for their cause, combined with fear of being eaten out of house and home if they lingered too long in one place. Free transport was to be provided by Southern Pacific, motivated not by altruism, but by the civic quiet that would result from Kelly's malcontents, now numbering several hundred, moving out of the area. Temporarily bivouacked at Mills Tabernacle until they could be entrained, the fate of the mob was the subject of daily news and speculation during the brief period they were in Oakland.

Joined by a friend named Frank Davis, London decided to join the march. He had seen a big swatch of the world in crossing the Pacific, but apart from earning his credibility as a "road kid" by briefly crossing the Sierra Nevada, he had seen nothing of the United States. It was true that Kelly's and Coxey's armies were headed to Washington, D.C., and after his galling work experiences at the jute mill and power station, he might get to actually see whether that great American democracy that everyone seemed to revere so much could actually be spurred to effect some positive change for the benefit of someone other than rich plutocrats.

But politics aside, London hit the road in obedience to wanderlust. Without a job he was a burden to the family. He would be moving as one of a body of as many as 2,000 men, so it was unlikely he would starve, although he knew from previous experience that he could survive living hand to mouth if it came to that. More than anything else, it was adventure. He went to say goodbye to his stepsister Eliza Shepard, with whom he had continued a close relationship; when she learned that he was setting off with almost no money, she extracted from beneath the handkerchiefs in a bureau drawer a $10 gold piece that she had been hoarding to buy a new Easter bonnet and pressed it into his hand.

Kelly's Army was scheduled to leave Oakland for Sacramento on the morning of April 6, 1894, but a snag developed when Southern Pacific, which had agreed to transport them, suddenly clarified that it didn't mean to transport them in coaches, like paying passengers. Instead it provided a string of boxcars into which Kelly's "soldiers" could be loaded like cattle. On behalf of his army, Kelly declined. Realizing that it was the city of Oakland that was now being held hostage by the mob, a large force of policemen, firemen, and deputized citizens answered a fire alarm and converged on the Mills Tabernacle at two a.m. April 6, demanding that the army get onto the cars at once. Again Kelly refused, and he was taken to jail until the men agreed to decamp once he was released.

Kelly's Army departed Oakland in the boxcars at five in the morning, two hours before London and Davis reached the station at the announced departure time. Utilizing some of Eliza's gift, the two bought fares to Sacramento; arriving there at eight p.m. they discovered that Kelly and his army had already been hustled on to Ogden, Utah. Not surprisingly for an adolescent road trip with only minimal planning, London and Davis became separated, missed each other at the rendezvous they earlier had agreed upon, and wound up chasing each other through isolated whistle-stops across the Great Basin. To London it was a great lark, but to Davis it was a nightmare. By the time they finally reunited in Winnemucca, Nevada, Davis had had quite enough of the confusion and decided to return home. They shook hands and parted, but London committed to the diary he determined to keep of the experience that "though he has dicided [sic] to turn West again I am sure the expearience [sic] has done him good, broadened his thoughts, given a better understanding of the low strata of society & surely will have made him more charitable to the tramps he will meet hereafter when he is in better circumstances."[1]

In four days on the rails, London had come across many who, like himself, were trying to catch up to Kelly's Army or in the alternative link up with a separate eastbound contingent from Reno, Nevada. The quest led London on a wide circuit through the Great Basin, riding the rails, often in short hops until he was detected and thrown off the train by brakemen. His diary entries show an agile mind fascinated by his surroundings and soaking up every moment, from his surprise at how the high, clear, cold air made distant objects seem closer, to his first experience with what (he assumed) remained of the Wild West. "I went up to a Saloon," he wrote of Rock Springs, Wyoming, "got a glass of beer & had a fine wash in warm water. I am writing this in the saloon. It seems to be the wild & wooly west with a vengeance. . . . At the present moment a couple of cowboys or cattle punchers are raising cain generally. One is about 6 foot 4, while the other is a little shorty."[2]

Riding the rails on his own required London to outwit brakemen and conductors constantly. When caught, he was forced to negotiate their graft down to a level he could afford. Just after he crossed from Nevada into Utah, "I got one of the west bound tourists to lock me in a car bound east. Just before the train started the door was thrown open & a brakeman asked me how much I could 'shake up.' 'Fifteen cents' was my response. I had two dollars & fifteen cents on me & as the dollars were unbroken I did not propose to give them to him. He said he could carry me down the road a ways, but did not take the money. When we had traveled about 50 miles . . . the door was again thrown open, & the conductor & brakeman both appeared. After a long consultation they took my gold ring & left me the fifteen cents. The ring was good gold with a fine cameo setting."[3] Another common place for tramps to hide was on the "rods," stout struts that connected the trucks beneath the cars. It was a dangerous place to ride, only inches above the rails and ties blurring beneath, and London knew of hoboes who had lost their balance and come to an end in bloody pieces beneath the train's wheels. Indeed his own literary career almost came to a premature end when, once while he was riding down on the rods, a spark from the wheels caught his coat on fire, and he had to improvise the gymnastics to get out of it without falling onto the tracks.

Unknown to London, Kelly's progress eastward was interrupted by Southern Pacific's decision to strand him and his army in Ogden. The railroads had grown weary of the various contingents of the Industrial Army's penchant for "capturing" trains—essentially hijacking them, overwhelming them by sheer force of numbers and then forcing the crew to take them to their next destination. The railroads, with the warm editorial approval of the business class, devised an answer for these "captures." The first line of defense was to engage deputies to prevent marchers from boarding, which was what happened to one group in Denver. When that failed and a train was seized, compelling a railroad line to negotiate, they would agree to transport marchers of the Commonweal of Christ to their next stop. They would begin the trip, then the railroad would uncouple their cars and maroon the marchers in the middle of nowhere. Southern Pacific carried the Los Angeles contingent but then abandoned them at a desert switch eighty miles east of El Paso with no food or water. When Kelly's own army was similarly stranded in Ogden by the same line, they managed to get on a Union Pacific train to continue.

The depiction of Coxey's and Kelly's armies and the other marchers as bums and slackers gave artful cover to the railroads for such behavior, and served to discredit the marchers. Across America's heartland, however, where the depression was hitting the hardest, there was no shortage of sympathy for men marching for work. As Kelly's Army made its way through Colorado and into Nebraska, newspapers in their path took a supportive view. The "good people of Nebraska . . . need fear no violence or disturbance," according to the Omaha *Bee*. "These men are nearly all bona-fide workingmen." Nebraska of course was the home of William Jennings Bryan, the populist political champion of the movement who had staked his career on the unlimited coinage of silver, so Kelly's Army might well have expected their march to turn into a triumphal procession on that soil.

Moved, again, by the dual incentives of sympathy and a desire to keep the marchers moving on and not exhaust local resources, the communities through which they passed provisioned Kelly's Army. There were parades—a large crowd welcomed them at North Platte, seventy miles east of the Colorado line, to where the showman Buffalo Bill Cody had dispatched three beeves to feed them. More than 1,000 greeted them at Lexington, sixty miles farther on, the tracks following the Platte River. Often there were speeches, populist in tone and attacking the economic and social conditions of the day.

Some 3,000 people cheered Kelly's Army at Kearney, thirty miles east of Lexington, where the town *Journal* agreed that the march focused attention on "the desperation to which honest labor is being driven."[4] The twenty-seven boxcars, hung with American flags and banners proclaiming WEALTH PRODUCED ONLY BY LABOR and GOVERNMENT EMPLOYMENT FOR THE UNEMPLOYED were nowhere near sufficient to carry the 1,200 men, who rode in, on, under, and between them.

Jack London finally joined Kelly's Army at Grand Island, fifty miles downstream from Kearney, and his own recollection confirmed the carnival atmosphere. During the last several days of their approach to Des Moines, Iowa, townspeople would trek out to visit Kelly's Army where they camped. "The camp was thronged with citizens all day," he wrote on April 25. " . . . A game of baseball was also in progress between the Army & Town boys." The latter won, 16–12. "Every body expresses a good opinion of the army, & a great many were surprised at the gentlemanly bearing & honest appearance of the boys."[5] For these visits the more talented of London's fellow tramps sang or danced or vended little craft pieces for small change. Not to be outdone, London would seat himself alone by a fire, writing, looking as forlorn as he could. Upon making eye contact with a sympathetic-looking individual, he would volunteer, "If I had a postage stamp I would write a letter to my mother." He more than held his own, occasionally pocketing a dollar and a half for a day of wistfully bumming money for stamps.[6] It was as much as he made in fifteen hours of shoveling coal in Oakland.

On at least one occasion, May 16, he did use a stamp to write home. He must have told his mother that he was intending to leave Kelly's Army soon, because she knew to address her reply to general delivery in Chicago. It had been six months since, with Flora's encouragement, he had debuted in publication, and while her letter of May 22 has a tone of motherly care ("When we did not get a letter for three weeks I worried so that I could neither eat nor sleep") it was also apparent that she had an investment to protect. "Remember that you are all that I have and both papa and I are growing old and you are all that we have to look to in our old age." Almost prophetically she continued, "John under no circumstances place yourself in a position to be imprisoned, you have gone to see the country and not to spend your time behind the bars." She indicated that she had sent eight or ten letters to him in care of Chicago general delivery, each letter with stationery and stamps, and two with cash, a total of $5, "which you must stand very much in need of. John just as soon as we know whether you have got what we have already sent, we will try and send you some more." It is a wonder that, amid all the chase and confusion of riding the rails and dodging capture, London managed to save her letter.[7]

Crossing the Missouri River to Council Bluffs, Iowa, London had actually been with Kelly's Army less than 150 miles before he began to sour on the experience. To London's perception, Kelly was putting on airs, riding a handsome black horse, giving orders, and enforcing discipline that seemed excessive, even cruel. All his life, nothing crossed London like hypocrisy, and his retribution was not long in finding expression. London's own shoes had given out, and departing now from the railroad, he found himself marching, barefoot, and also having to help a sick man along the road. He was finally able to cadge a pair of boots by the time, at Des Moines, the army was provided flatboats to float them down the Des Moines River to Keokuk and the Mississippi. London made sure to station himself on the first one, knowing that being the first to dock in the evenings, they would receive the choice handouts from the locals, even though all such fare was required to be passed on to the army's commissary. At one point he noted in his diary, "We were overtaken by a round bottomed boat manned by two Commissary bucks. . . . They had orders to take possession of us but it was no go so they ordered us to wait for the main bunch while they proceeded to Harvey. I guess we will have to run past the town to night."[8] Some stretches along the river were so lined by well-wishers that they couldn't land on the bank in privacy to relieve themselves, but the army had also begun to be followed and harassed by Pinkerton detectives intent on disrupting their progress, and there had been violent clashes. "If any Pinkertons are captured," wrote London in his diary, "woe unto them."

By the time they reached Hannibal, Missouri, hard pulls on the river, thinning charity, skulking Pinkertons, and cheating the commissary had taken their toll. "Am going to pull out in the morning," he wrote. "I can't stand starvation." Striking out on his own to rendezvous with his mail in Chicago, London rode the rails alone again, braving the cat-and-mouse game with conductors and brakemen ever on the alert to throw tramps unceremoniously from the train. The chase was constant; one experience of jumping on a train with two fellow tramps he had fallen in with was not atypical:

> We waited till the train had almost run by when two of us jumped the palace cars & decked them [scaled up to the roofs] while the third went underneath on the rods. I climbed forward two cars to the other fellow

> & told him to come along the decks to the blind [an out-of-sight space between two cars whose doors were only on the sides] but he said it was too risky. I went forward about five cars & as the brakeman was on that platform I could proceed no further. . . . I waited & when the train stopped I climbed down & ran ahead to the blind. The brakeman . . . jumped off to catch me [but] I ran ahead & took the platform he had vacated. The fellow on the roof with me got ditched but I made her into Wells. . . . The brakeman was after us like a bloodhound so I climbed on the engine.

At the engine London persuaded the engineer to allow him to shovel coal into the boiler—one thing he knew how to do—and earn his fare to the end of the division. All in all, it was a harrowing way to travel.[9]

London later wrote enough of the tramping life to present a certain raffish but worldly wise self-image, positioning himself as polite society's correspondent in a seamy world they themselves would never dare enter. But life as a hobo had a darker side, a tangle of the secrets of lusty men with few options. He knew the public would never accept such a netherworld of sex and sexual servitude (not much different from what he had witnessed a year earlier aboard the *Sophia Sutherland*) and his knowledge of it would remain unwritten. Yet his knowledge of it is undeniable: he dedicated his later tramping memoir, *The Road*, to Josiah Flynt, a fellow hobo he had met on the rails, who was less reticent.

Flynt contributed an essay, "Homosexuality Among Tramps," to *Studies in the Psychology of Sex* by Havelock Ellis, the pathbreaking sex researcher whose books London later knew well and owned. Flynt offered the very modern estimate that 10 percent of tramps were homosexual.[10] In the tramps' well-established sexual hierarchy, a young novice who was vulnerable for being unfamiliar with hobo life, known as a "gay-cat," might well attach himself to an older and more accomplished tramp, a "profesh," exchanging security for sexual favors, after which the young ward became known as a "prushun." The phenomenon was well known enough that in *The Road* London was emphatic in his assertion that he had never been a prushun, but had graduated directly from road kid to profesh.

In Chicago London collected all of Flora's letters, using the money to outfit himself in used clothes ("after a great deal of wrangling . . . amongest [sic] the Jews of South Clark st."). After a shave and dinner he went sightseeing, attended the theater, and found lodging for fifteen cents—the first proper bed he had slept in since leaving home. He spent the next day, May 30, at the World's Fair, and the day after that boarded a lake steamer for the sixty-mile run to St. Joseph, Michigan, home of his mother's sister, Mary Everhard.

The sojourn with his aunt's family was restful—he liked his cousin so well that in later years he named the hero of his novel *The Iron Heel* after him, Ernest Everhard—and then he took to the rails again. He had always wanted to see Niagara Falls, and eluding the inevitable cons and shacks, hopped a convenient boxcar to Buffalo, New York. The sight did not disappoint, and he gazed at the falls transfixed until after eleven at night. His instincts warned him that Niagara Falls was not a community to welcome hoboes, and he walked all the way out of town before jumping a fence and bedding down in a field. He had slept only briefly when he awoke at very first light; he wanted one more look at the falls. He couldn't begin to beg for breakfast until eight, giving him plenty of time to appreciate the thundering waterfall. Walking down a quiet street, he saw three men walking toward him, whom he at first took for fellow tramps but then realized to his horror that it was two tramps in the custody of the constable who had arrested them. "I should have turned and run like the very devil," he wrote of it later. "He'd never have run after me, for two hoboes in the hand are worth more than one on the get-away. But like a dummy I stood still when he halted me."[11]

Unable to provide the name of a hotel where he was staying, London was arrested with the others and given the proverbial bum's rush to night court. He later excoriated the flatfoot who arrested him for working on commission (perhaps choosing to forget that he himself had worked on precisely the same terms for the California Fish Patrol). As it transpired, his arraignment was the only trial he would have. It consisted of the bailiff intoning for each case, "Vagrancy, your honor," to which the judge, Police Justice Charles Piper, would reply, "Thirty days." The accused were not allowed to speak. The one man before London who did speak was permitted to say he was homeless, but only because he had lost his job and had nowhere else to go. "Why did you quit your job?" demanded the judge. The man explained that he had not quit but had been let go; he was given thirty additional days for quitting his job. When London's turn came, he attempted to plead not guilty, to which the judge said, "Shut up," and he was taken away and shackled. His demand to see a lawyer was met by gusts of laughter.

If vagrancy was a crime, London had been committing it with abandon for weeks—the irony was that he had not committed it in Niagara Falls. Indeed he had taken trouble to walk on sore feet out of Niagara Falls before sleeping. Throughout London's written recollections of his life, he often changed the facts of various experiences to suit the dramatic needs of its telling. This was not one of them. Every time he wrote of it his vocabulary could barely contain his bitterness. Police Justice Piper, who heard these cases, could not possibly have known the effect he had on one of the most fertile young minds in America. To London, it was bad enough that the economy was engineered to benefit the wealthiest few, who held the means in such a powerful grip as to strangle any chance that lesser people might have for advancement. Now it was clear to him that the law, which in the United States was commonly trumpeted as the great leveler, was equally rigged. In his mind, what had been an ardent sympathy for economic reform began to harden into a case for revolution. For these thirty days, he thought, he would do his time and await his release, and when he was free he would write such a tract, file such a lawsuit, as would shake the American judiciary to its foundations.[12]

His home for the next month was the Erie County Penitentiary, and for the journey he was handcuffed to a large, affable young black man, whose only reaction was to laugh, shake his head, and repeat, "Oh, Lawdy." It was the new convict in the train seat behind them who most engaged London's attention. He described him as squat and powerful, but with a certain kindness and humor in his eyes. "As for the rest of him," he wrote, "he was a brute-beast, wholly unmoral," but as they talked London realized that he must attach himself to this man, that he could help him in prison. The man had an empty pipe, which London filled with his own tobacco, and divided the remainder with him. He became London's "meat," he referred to him as his pal, and he proved invaluable.

On June 29, 1894, the Erie County Penitentiary logged the entry of "John London, 18, single, father & mother living, occupation sailor, religion atheist . . . term of 30 days, charge of Tramp."[13] As they were being processed, his pal showed him how to toss a packet of his few personal effects to a trusty (an employed inmate) on an upper gallery so they would not be confiscated; when they were inoculated for smallpox, his pal advised him sternly to suck out the wound. London did so, escaping the gruesome, egg-sized boils that erupted on the arms of those who didn't know better.

At last London was placed in a cell and heard the lock snap behind him. Its other resident was young and seemed companionable enough, although he was a veteran of two years in an Ohio prison. As they talked, London's horror grew as he discerned that the walls and ceiling were alive with bedbugs, issuing from and disappearing into chinks in the masonry. Dinner was brought at noon, two chunks of bread and a quart of thin soup. Having already set to killing as many bedbugs as they could, the two drank the soup but chewed the bread to putty and used it to seal the vermin within the cracks in the mortar—effort that proved fruitless, as they were transferred to a new cell two galleries higher that evening.

In prison London discovered that there were two classes of men, the abusers and the abused. Although not vicious by nature, given the choice he would rather be one of the former than the latter, especially after watching an inoffensive black youth be bludgeoned and pushed down five flights of stairs, at last crumpling in a screaming heap at London's feet. The prison officials expected the trusties and hall-men to keep the pen running smoothly, and had no interest to inquire how that was done.

London had chosen well with whom to share his tobacco that first day. It turned out that the pal he made (he later wrote that they called each other "Jack," the only name by which we know him) was in a position to take care of him. The five hundred inmates were controlled by thirteen hall-men; his pal became one on the first day, and he let London know that he would get another one fired and arrange for London to replace him. The footsore teenager who had still been wearing leather splints on his wrists from shoveling coal had to work in the yard for only two days before his pal made good on his word. Thus London became part of the graft that was the prison commerce, and the terrible similarity between himself on the inside and the corporate barons on the outside was not lost on him:

> And at times, while all these men lay hungry in their cells, I have seen a hundred or so extra rations of bread hidden away in the cells of the hall-men. It would seem absurd, our retaining this bread. But it was one of our grafts. We were economic masters inside our hall, turning the trick in ways quite similar to the economic masters of civilization. We controlled the food-supply of the population, and, just like our brother bandits outside, we made the people pay through the nose for it.

Bread, while necessary, was not the coin of the realm; that was tobacco, and by extorting two or three rations of bread for a plug of tobacco, the trusties became wealthy, in prison terms, even to the point of accumulating cash. One with whom London shared a cell for a time counted out his $16 in savings every night, threatening London with a terrible fate if anything happened to it.[14]

Bread was only one graft, but in fact every aspect of the inmates' daily life was governed by some form of corruption, with order maintained by the most savage corporal discipline. If a man so much as looked like he was going to protest, even as London had tried to protest at his so-called trial, "Our own rule was to hit a man as soon as he opened his mouth—hit him hard, hit him with anything. A broom-handle, end-on, in the face, had a very sobering effect. . . . We could not permit the slightest insolence. If we did, we were lost."

Rarely in later years London alluded also to the prison's sexual brutality, but only in generalities. He hardly needed to spell it out that as a trusty, he was in a position to avoid abuse. Whether that meant that, as an element of keeping his place in the hierarchy, he was compelled to join in abusing others, he never said.[15]

Prison was not without some friendly cooperation, if not kindness. One inmate over whom he was the trusty was serving sixty days for being caught eating out of the dinner garbage of the Barnum & Bailey Circus. (It was good bread, he said, and the meat was "out of this world.") For him London procured a length of thin, stiff wire, which the man crafted into very serviceable safety pins; London began paying him for them in extra bread rations, while himself setting up a profitable trade in that otherwise unknown commodity. The commerce had a certain familiarity, not unlike his shrewdness with trading cards when he was a child, or sailing his skiff out to ships in the Oakland estuary to collect kerosene tins. Business was business.

London's pal Jack kept the expectation that when they got out, the two of them would become partners in something—if not crime, then perhaps life on the road. Indeed they were released together on the same day, July 29, and they started on foot for Buffalo, the pal thinking of a saloon, London planning his escape. As soon as they reached the city and entered a bar, London found a distracting moment to dart out the back door, jump the fence, and hop a southbound freight train. He rued the necessity of it. "I'd have liked to say good-bye. He had been good to me. But I did not dare."

Having had a month in the penitentiary to see how every pathetic attempt at redress, every feeble grasp for justice had resulted, somehow in some way, only in calling down punishment, he gave no further thought toward a lawsuit for violating his civil rights. All he wanted between himself and Buffalo was distance.

He continued south to Baltimore, then east to New York and, ironically, Boston, the cradle of American liberty. That irony, however, turned into an epiphany, for on this leg of the journey he met some truly learned hoboes who catalyzed his own intellectual quest. In Baltimore's Druid Hill Park he chanced upon a luxuriantly bearded tramp named Frank Strawn-Hamilton, a vivid socialist who all but bowled him over with his command of political and economic theory.

His mind suddenly alight with all the things he wanted to learn, London braced himself to ride the rails home as fast as he could. Looking to give commission-hunting American constables a wide berth, he finished his trek west through Canada, much of it in biting cold, ending in Vancouver, where he intended to earn his passage home on a ship. Discouraged at first that none would take him on, London was cheered by the discovery that Canadians were more forthcoming in their sympathy for the homeless unemployed. He wrote a few years later that he spent several weeks there. "I was never given a handout there in all the time I slammed back gates—always was 'set down' to tables. I was only refused twice, and both times because I came out of meal hours. And, further, at each of said places I was given a quarter of a dollar to make up for the refusal."[16] Canadian generosity left a deep impression.

Persistence finally paid off in employment as a stoker on the immigrant steamer S.S. *Umatilla* of the Pacific Steamship Company, a smallish vessel that for years plied the waters of the Northwest, ferrying human cargo who had to swear their age, nationality, race, health, wealth (including an amount if less than $500), and whether or not they were an anarchist or a polygamist. If there was one thing London could do, it was shovel coal, and the passage home went swiftly. He entered the Golden Gate once more, and now it was time for his life to begin.

5 THE STUDENT

Returning from his months on the road as 1894 waned, Jack London found himself stimulated by his discovery, especially in the East, that many tramps while monetarily down-and-out owned a deep wisdom about the world. The American economy and its society might claim that penury was the just lot of the masses who funneled the wealth they generated up to the drawing-room set. Among the hoboes, however, he found men who were able to compensate for their banishment from the economy with a vivid life of the mind. They lived on handouts, but they understood life in a way he did not. The experience presented him with a profound and alluring mystery.

Home again, he looked to the Oakland Public Library with renewed expectation for answers, and once again that institution proved a godsend. His treasured Ina Coolbrith had retired, but her nephew had been hired as reference librarian. His name was Frederick Irons Bamford, Canadian by birth and a Christian Scientist, lately an English professor at Hesperian College. A more bookish-looking librarian could not have been cast for a play—his desk in the library was never without a vase of fresh flowers—but by the greatest of good fortune he was the very man London needed to know: brilliantly well-read, an ardent socialist, eagerly introducing him to a stream of philosophy, economics, and political argument.

To London's previous acquaintance with Darwin was added Adam Smith and *The Wealth of Nations,* Benjamin Kidd and *Social Evolution,* and Kant and *The Critique of Pure Reason.* London's previous pass at Herbert Spencer's work had dazzled him with its brilliance but he never felt that he understood it. Now he could perceive in *First Principles* a kind of grand unifying theory, how Darwin's natural selection had also allowed dominant and subservient social classes to emerge, and how the very idea of natural selection, the survival of the fittest, necessarily meant that man was perfectible. And for man to be perfectible gave effect to Nietzsche in *Man and Superman*. The lit fuse of his mind sparked through master after master; this was life, and it began to make sense. At some level it snagged in his mind that Darwin's survival of the fittest and London's growing dedication to social justice conflicted, for unfairness and cruelty enforced the survival of the fittest. But he could set that aside to think through later; for now, the broad strokes had to be assimilated.

His time on the rails had been crucial in defining his cast of mind at this time. The country's wealthy might salve their consciences by clucking that hoboes were lazy and shiftless, and certainly he had met those who would rather wander than work, but they were not a majority. The whole reason for Coxey's Army was to demonstrate how badly most of them did want to work. Many of them had been as employed as he had been, as tied to pittance wages, until illness or injury cost them their jobs. Unless they had family to support them, they were cast out of the economic house to wander the country like pariahs until they starved, froze to death, or were imprisoned. What worried London most were the older ones; it was not a long leap to imagine what his own stepfather's fate would have been without him, Flora, and Eliza and Captain Shepard. London was young and strong, but he would not always be, and deep down he had to admit he was not as strong as he posed. His chest and back were brawny, but his extremities were delicate. He had sprained his wrists shoveling coal and had to wear splints for nearly a year; his small, flat feet had broken down after only several miles of walking with Kelly's Army. What he saw in the older tramps, toothless and hollow-chested, was his own inevitable end if he did not escape the clutches of physical dime-an-hour wage slavery.

London's months on the rails, followed by Bamford's tutelage, at last gave him clarity on what to do with his own life. To pull out of this lethal whirlpool was imperative, and he determined, within the fire of his avid, urgent new curiosity about everything, to find a way to make a living with his mind instead of his muscles. He would learn, and then he would write.

❧ ❧ ❧

Back in Oakland he found his family, for once, holding their own late in 1894. Home was a cottage at 1639 Twenty-Second Avenue, not the worst they had lived in, with a bay window and a lattice arch over the stoop at the head of a long flight of steps. His mother had returned to giving piano lessons, and his stepfather was able to hold modest employment as a "special policeman." His beloved stepsister Eliza, her much older husband, Captain Shepard, and their family lived around the corner from them and were also reasonably secure, supporting themselves as pension lawyers.

If ever there was a time when London could return to school and finish his education, this was it, and when he announced his intention, resuming his schooling became almost a family project: Flora furnished a room at the rear of the house for him, to serve as his dual study and bedroom. His earnings, when he was home, had helped anchor the family since he was about eight, and the more she could do to keep him there and out of saloons and off the waterfront, the better. Eliza gave him a table at which to study, and there was a wardrobe, a bed, and a nightstand with a lamp—an austere cell in which to undergo his metamorphosis, but also safe, dry, and dependable. (Flora was a stickler for comfortable beds. "I always have good beds in my house, if I haven't anything else.")[1]

All his life, London had known of his mother's penchant for playing financial long shots. As children he and Eliza wondered why it was the family never had any money when everyone was working at something, and usually more than one thing. John London also gambled, but only in a quietly amused, small-stakes way; with Flora it was an obsession. Putting herself in the hands of Plume, her Indian spirit guide, she played the Chinese lotteries, hectored her husband into insupportable business expansions, invested hard-earned money in financial jags like her failed boardinghouse for Scottish immigrant girls—all in a quest to recapture the life of ease that had spoiled her as a girl and that she had scorned as a disturbed young woman. By the mid 1890s she had virtually resigned herself to poverty. With no expectations, there could be no more disappointment. However, her first bet on her son's literary ability, encouraging him to enter the *Call*'s contest, paid off when he won. His chance of eventual success was certainly greater than her declining husband's, so preparing to pamper him during his coming academic rigors seemed less a long shot than an investment.

Assisting him further, Eliza gave him a bicycle on which to traverse the forty blocks to Oakland High School, although he took to it slowly and had numerous mishaps until she also provided a training wheel. Often he would ride around the corner in the mornings to breakfast with Eliza and show up "bruised, dripping wet and red in the face, his curls all tousled, fighting mad"[2] at having taken a fall in just that short distance. More important, Eliza gave him an improved chance at a social life by financing a regimen of dental work. Sailing and tramping had long since given him the habit of tobacco—chain smoking, and then chewing to ease the pain of his rapidly decaying teeth. He had never in his life owned a toothbrush, until now. With a new upper plate, he could once again smile without embarrassment, but Eliza extracted a promise to stop chewing tobacco.

On January 12, 1895, Jack London turned nineteen. Only recently had he enrolled in high school with students significantly younger than him. As he had discovered during his first attempt at gentrification in the YMCA, he had little in common with them. Not only were they younger, they were callow, even innocent, reminding him of the childhood he'd never had. He was also separated from them by poverty; he took a part-time job as the school's janitor. After school, the other students went home to their families; London stayed late to sweep up.

Yet for all that, his younger peers regarded him with something like awe. His physical beauty and maturity worked to his advantage, to be sure, but his worldly experience held many of them in a kind of rapture. He was a force of nature, set down before an impressionable audience. Certainly he acted the exotic part, never quite sure when he should put forward the dockside bully and when he could be himself, open and inquiring. Some were put off by him. Georgia Loring, in his French class, attributed his vacillating behavior to an inferiority complex arising from shame over his background. And then there was his profession of socialism. Fred Bamford at the Oakland Public Library, who had become a close friend, guided London's reading through the angriest seekers of social justice. London, with all the certitude of a nineteen-year-old, repeated their slogans with equal temper. The students at Oakland High, mostly very conventional children of very conventional parents, were alternately impressed by him and frightened of him.

London's main interest was writing, and a foreign-language teacher, Mollie Connors, once came across London moping over a composition that the English teacher had marked up beyond recognition. She asked what was wrong, and he answered, "It's no use, Miss Mollie. I'm going to quit. I came here to study English because I thought I could write—but I can't. Look at this." Miss Connors read through the paper and its corrections. "Never mind, Jack," she said calmly. "I'm going to tell you a secret: The only trouble is that you can write, and she can't. You keep right on."[3] Mollie Connors may have saved London's intellectual life that day.

The most popular extracurricular activity at the school was membership on the *Aegis*, the school publication. London lacked the underclass credits to join the staff, but he did submit stories and essays almost from the time he walked through the door. The work was far superior to that of students who had seen little and lived less, and although everyone knew he was the janitor, he made respectful friends and no fewer than eight of his pieces were published in the journal during the year.

In the *Aegis* pieces one sees the melding, the alloying of growing craft with life experiences, incorporating elements from the previous week and as far back as the first books he read. London's boyhood friend Frank Atherton was living in San Jose at the time, and he came up to accompany London to a concert and then explore the Barbary Coast. In one frowsy nightclub they found the crowd being entertained by a genuinely gifted violinist, which brought back memories of Ouida's *Signa*. London forged these pieces into a story, "One More Unfortunate," published in the *Aegis*, about a poor young violinist who dreams of a great concert career but drowns himself when the only engagements he can get are in tawdry dives. Another piece described the Bonin Islands, a personal travelogue that none of the other students could hope to match, and quite persuasive considering that he personally, contrary to his own regretful preference, never saw much of the islands beyond the waterfront stews. Under a thin veil of fiction, two other stories recounted life as a hobo riding the rails, but the ring of authenticity was so strong that the doubtful propriety of the stories for young readers was outweighed by their merit. Virtually alone among the high school students in knowing what he believed and why, he saw his socialist manifesto, the first he had attempted, published in March 1895 ("Arise, ye Americans, patriots and optimists! Awake! Seize the reins of a corrupted government and educate your masses!") to considerable consternation at his argument that social and moral degradation was the inevitable result of unregulated wage slavery.

London was also able to vent these opinions at the high school's Henry Clay Club, a debating society where his passion for oral argument could be given free rein. He made friends there, best among them Ted Applegarth, a young man with an English accent who came from a home of books and music and intellectual discourse. He visited the Oakland library one day just to strike up a conversation with London, an act that made a large impression. London's visits to the Applegarth home—he was amazed to see real oil paintings on the walls—set before him the banquet of the mind he had always hungered for; even better, Ted had an older sister, Mabel, who was a student at the University of California at Berkeley. London fell hard for her. She was a beauty, she was a muse; for her the Sailor Kid shed his crust and willingly became a pining schoolboy. She was enchanted, and just as willingly she undertook to sand his rough edges, teaching him propriety in both subject-verb agreement and which fork to pick up at dinner. Mabel's mother was her indefatigable chaperone, and London grew fond of her, "charming, witty and tactful as well as sympathetic with his strivings."[4] It was at least in part to impress Mabel that he spent some of his precious money on a dictionary, with the determination to learn twenty new words every day. Ted taught London to play chess, a game in which Mabel was not interested, but she was alert to express her shock when London followed a stupid move with an unstoppable expletive. Mabel was frail—in fact she had consumption—and to help her recover from the dangerous illness, the Applegarths took London with them on vacation to Yosemite. London later wrote his paeans to her as Ruth Morse in *Martin Eden*. He earned his keep with the Applegarths with his gift for storytelling, being careful to watch his language, and seeing the world through his eyes they came to appreciate him.

Along with the Applegarths, London grew close to Fred Jacobs. Small and slim and blond, he wore glasses, an assistant in the reference department at the Oakland library. Although he wrote at home, London read as much as he could in the library, just for the atmosphere of being surrounded by books, and Jacobs frequently helped him with homework. Chemistry was Jacobs's own interest, tending toward photography, a skill at which London later excelled. London also developed a fondness for Jacobs's girlfriend, Bess Maddern, who was a whiz in math class, and, unusually for girls, athletically inclined and a bicycle enthusiast. She was a great contrast to Mabel Applegarth; Bessie was raven-haired and independent, confident in areas of her knowledge but painfully insecure when discussions got out of her depth.

London had succeeded in making friends above his social station, but every time he might have allowed himself to think he had escaped his background, his past, the ball and chain of Twenty-Second Avenue would materialize at Oakland High to drag him back down, either in the need to visit Johnny Heinold and borrow some money, or in the person of John London, who would show up at school to visit and usually borrow money. There is no doubt that Jack London loved his stepfather, and the older man's decline had been hard to watch. He'd had to give up the job as special policeman for the less strenuous post of night watchman on the waterfront. In his pride to continue to try to do for himself, John even undertook to sell photographs door to door, but drawing on their old alliance of mutual support in the face of Flora's demands and rages, he would ask to borrow small amounts to avoid going home empty-handed. Often Jack had no money to lend him, and in turn had to borrow it from his friends on the *Aegis*. It would be difficult to imagine anything more humiliating.

In addition to Fred Bamford's guidance in reading, and classes at Oakland High School, London found a third source of edification, the "Speaker's Corner" on the courthouse square. Often on the way home from school he would pause to listen to the rhetoric, often socialist in nature, and one day heard a familiar eloquent voice. It was Frank Strawn-Hamilton, the tramp who had set London's mind on fire in Baltimore. In fact it was Strawn-Hamilton who, in company with the Socialist Labor Party's local financial secretary, had gotten the Speaker's Corner going. At first, the busy townsfolk were not interested in listening to lectures, but the speakers hit on the tactic of first arguing loudly, then hotly, with each other, and as a crowd gathered hoping to witness a fight, they would join forces for a public lecture, which, owing largely to Strawn-Hamilton's brilliance as a speaker, became a watched-for event.[5]

At the Speaker's Corner London also met the British Herman "Jim" Whitaker, who became a close friend and mentor. Like many of the men London selected for his inner orbit, Whitaker was several years older, a miller's son who became a career soldier before buying his freedom and immigrating to Canada. Relocating to Oakland with his wife and six children, he endured two months of grinding want before being hired by the local socialists to manage a grocery cooperative. Whitaker had been an instructor in the British army, and during after-hours at the co-op, he taught London the main points of boxing (where London on the waterfront had been merely brawling) and fencing, both of which sports London practiced enthusiastically for the rest of his life.

Before long, London was confident enough in his socialist grounding to begin taking the soapbox himself at Speaker's Corner. His debate practice in the Henry Clay Society had sharpened his speaking skills to such a degree that his energetic defense of socialism won him local fame; the San Francisco *Chronicle* presented an article about him in early 1896:

> Jack London, who is known as the boy socialist in Oakland, is holding forth nightly to the crowds that throng City Hall Park. There are other speakers in plenty, but London always gets the biggest crowd and the most respectful attention.
>
> London is young, scarcely 20, but he has seen many sides of the world and has travelled extensively. . . . He is a high school boy, and supports himself as a janitor in the institution. At present he is fitting himself for a

> course at the University of California, where he will make a specialty of social questions.
>
> The young man is a pleasant speaker, more earnest than eloquent, and while he is a broad socialist in every way, he is not an Anarchist. . . . Any man, in the opinion of London, is a socialist who strives for a better form of government than the one he is living under.[6]

Those students who were born of money, those who had never been Work Beasts, had no idea why he was so vituperative in his attacks on the capitalist system, and not everyone was enchanted after hearing the "boy socialist" hold forth. One of these naysayers was Georgia Loring from French class, who had been a student at the Hopkins Art School. "Beneath all his literary ambition," she recalled, "he was at heart, mind, and body, a Socialist. His blood was full of it. Boiling with it. His street speaking proved this, and the violence of his remarks that I have heard was terrifying in the extreme. When giving one of these talks he seemed to lose himself and to be clutching at the throats of his enemies in 'The class struggle.' His vigor and earnestness showed Ambition, but in the background there loomed the hideous red devil of Revenge—revenge for some fancied wrong."[7] Ironically, Georgia Loring would have to hear a lot more of socialism before all was said, for she became engaged to marry Fred Bamford, the reference librarian who had become London's coach in zeal to uplift the masses.

Indeed he was not an anarchist, but among those who heard the boy socialist hold forth was one very well-known anarchist, Emma Goldman, who marked him for future greatness, and future acquaintance. Throughout these months as student and janitor, London never lost sight of his ultimate ambition, and poured his energies into molding himself into a writer. He studied and copied antique forms of poetry, and in a later rapid exchange of letters with Ted Applegarth showed that he knew the compositional rules for "the ballade, the rondel, the rondeau, the roundel, the rondelay, the triolet, the sestina, or the villanelle. . . . They are all pretty structures, and so severe as to give the best of training in versification."[8] He scoured dictionary and thesaurus to increase his vocabulary beyond all need; once he criticized a phrase in one of Applegarth's poems as "pleonastic," when he might have simply written "redundant." He even found a use for "supererogatory," quite a word for a student whose handwriting still looked like a fourth grader's. Like many young writers, he was working his dictionary a little too hard.

The awkward chemistry of a twenty-year-old taking lessons with children four years younger began to make itself felt, both in his own frustration and in pressure from the other students' parents, through the PTA, that something be done about this young man who argued for socialism and told brutish stories to their children about skinning seals and stealing rides on railroads. When London dropped out there was probably some relief on both sides, but the question of college still presented itself. The entrance exams at Berkeley, where Mabel was a student, were exacting, but a diploma from an accredited preparatory school was just as acceptable as one from Oakland High. Both Ted Applegarth and Fred Jacobs enrolled in courses at a prep school called the University Academy, housed in a four-story Italianate villa in Alameda. It was a two-year curriculum, and expensive beyond his abilities, but the superintendent, a man named Anderson, recognized London's accomplishments to date and agreed that he need register only for the final term of courses, and an appeal to Eliza got the fees paid.

For once, London was able to steep himself in learning; under the tutelage of excellent teachers he threw himself into the courses, fully engaged and intellectually thriving. It was the experience of a lifetime, right up to the time, after five weeks, that Mr. Anderson called him into his office, told him his tuition would be refunded, and expelled him. The line handed him was that his classwork had been brilliant, but the academy's accreditation was in jeopardy by letting a student burn through the course work in one term that took other students two years. "He was very sorry," London wrote later of Anderson, "but . . . tongues were wagging about my case. In four months accomplish two years' work! It would be a scandal, and the universities were becoming severer in their treatment of accredited prep schools. He could n't [sic] afford such a scandal, therefore I must gracefully depart."[9] London was certain, however, that it was the students of the privileged who simply didn't want him there, were sick of being shown up by this raffish, unconventional delinquent, and brought the pressure to bear to get rid of him.

London's own vast vocabulary would have been paupered to describe what this abrupt dismissal did to him: he was outraged, heartbroken, humiliated. His disaffection with some highly touted but never quite defined American way, begun by the economic trap into which he was born, brought to a boil by his treatment as a Work Beast, perfected by Mr. Justice Piper in Buffalo's night court, was now given the only restatement London needed. He was not wanted. To excel in learning was the last chance for reconciliation between Jack London and the society that produced him; henceforward, it would be war.

He had begun learning as an autodidact; he could finish that way. He retreated to his back room in his parents' cottage, hunched with his cigarettes over the table Eliza had given him, and went to work. His close friends from Oakland High School were equally appalled over his treatment, and committed to help him. Jacobs and Bess Maddern were now engaged; Bessie tutored him in mathematics, and Fred tutored him in physics and chemistry. It would have been easier with access to a laboratory, but he would manage. Mabel Applegarth, with all her grace and social polish, and with whom he found himself increasingly in what he took to be love, helped him make up his shortcomings in English, and the vagaries of spelling that pocked his tramping diary disappeared from his letters. With sample exams from Berkeley in hand as his guide, for three months, nineteen hours a day, London labored in white heat to show up Mr. Anderson and the bluenoses at the University Academy, to prove to them that they could not get rid of him quite so easily.

London had no idea there was yet one more broadside he had to absorb, when he bicycled to Berkeley to begin the three-day regimen of entrance exams on August 10, 1896. The university had been inundated with applications and the school had recently raised its entrance standards. When he sat down to the first test he was horrified to discover it was far more difficult than what he had prepared for. For three days, for paper after paper, the certainty crept over him that he was in over his head. How could he explain such a failure? How could he accept life as a Work Beast?

Back home, he rolled some food and blankets into a knapsack, borrowed a small Whitehall, and sailed out onto the bay in a stiff wind, breathing in the salt air as though it were life itself. He turned north, entering San Pablo Bay, and then east through the Carquinez Straits, where he had so nearly drowned. He had intended to sail on to Suisun Bay, but with wind and tide behind him he put the tiller over to port and nosed into the tule flats of Benicia, and sought out the old Fish Patrol crowd. "For the first time in my life I consciously, deliberately desired to get drunk." Since entering Oakland High School, making friends with whom to study and play chess and write articles for the *Aegis,* he had not drunk and had not wanted to drink. He had visited Johnny Heinold at the First and Last Chance and occasionally borrowed money from him, but since leaving the waterfront and his need to hide his intellect and his curiosity, alcohol had held no appeal for him. Now, however, he intended to tie one on.

Charley LeGrant, his old boss at the California Fish Patrol, and his wife, Lizzie, greeted him with full hugs. "All the survivors of the old guard got around me and their arms around me." They invaded the local saloon, Jorgenson's, where "more old friends of the old free and easy times dropped in, fishermen, Greeks, and Russians, and French. They took turns in treating, and treated all around in turn again." Word spread that Jack was back; old-timers came and went, but London drank with them all. One who went by "Clam," who had been Young Scratch Nelson's partner before London, showed up, and Nelson's memory was hailed and toasted. Eventually LeGrant had London fetch his grip and shifted the party to a large Columbia River salmon boat, which he supplied with charcoal, a grill, and a fresh-caught black bass—but no more liquor. He let London, drunk or not, sail her defiantly out onto a wind-whipped Suisun Bay; they ripped through the chop, bawling out the old sea chanties—"Black Lulu," "I Wisht I Was a Little Bird," "The Boston Burglar"—as increasing bilge sloshed around their ankles.

They were out for a week, as far as Antioch; there they tied up to a potato sloop where old pals provided fishermen's stew redolent of garlic, and Italian bread and claret. In warm dry bunks, "we lay and smoked and yarned of old days, while overhead the wind screamed through the rigging and taut halyard drummed against the mast." If this was what life intended for him, it wasn't so bad.

But there were ends to tie up, and London returned to Oakland to await the result of his exams. When the verdict came it probably shocked him: he had passed, and was accepted to the University of California. Having been approved, there was still the matter of money, but Heinold had been counseling him for years to finish his education. He willingly lent London the $40 in tuition, allowing him to enter Berkeley for the fall term of 1896, a freshman in the Class of 1900, or as they referred to themselves, the "Naughty-Naughts."

* * *

At sixteen London had accomplished his need to be a man among men; now, at twenty, he was a student among students, and at Berkeley one he chanced across was Jimmy Hopper, whom he had known somewhat at Cole Grammar School. "He was going to take all the courses in English," wrote Hopper. "All of them, nothing less. Also, of course, he meant to take most of the courses in the natural sciences, many in history, and bite a respectable chunk out of the philosophies."

For once in his life, London looked about him and thought he must be happy. "Sunshine," Hopper characterized him, "a strange combination of Scandinavian sailor and Greek god." He rolled on sea legs when he walked, dressed with no thought to fashion, his brown hair sun-bleached to gold and seldom trimmed, but with a friendly openness "that was like a flood of sunshine."[10]

At Berkeley London worked off his stress with boxing gloves in the gymnasium, employing the rudiments of the sport that Jim Whitaker had taught him, augmented with a youth spent fighting without rules, and it was in the gym that he learned an important lesson. After one particular round, one of the upper-class young men that London had come to sneer at criticized him for whaling on an over-matched opponent. London's insolent challenge in response was at first ignored, but accepted after he backed it up with a quick swing that was dodged. "As you wish," said the upper-class snot. A crowd gathered as London attacked him with everything he had, but nothing landed, and after he winded himself, the bluenose laid him out with two punches, one in the nose and the second in the throat. London hated it when people judged him because of his background; now he had done the same thing, and paid for it.

Even as he gratified his hunger for knowledge and culture, London became increasingly curious about his own beginnings. If he had ever snooped through his mother's papers he would have found, dated September 7, 1876, her marriage certificate to John London, under the name Flora Chaney. From his own birth date of January 12 of that year he knew he was eight months old when they married. Mammy Jennie must have told him many times the story of how she had introduced Flora to John London, who, therefore, could not have been his father. Searching back through the morgue of the San Francisco *Chronicle*, he discovered the June 1875 article with its lurid description of the trouble between Flora and William Chaney, of his alleged demand that she undergo an abortion, and of her attempted suicides.

Knowing that to ask his mother the details of that period would have spun her into a rage, London consulted a local astrologer to learn more about Chaney. He learned that Chaney had once been quite famous, that in 1890, long after leaving San Francisco, he had authored a *Primer of Astrology and Urania*, which contained a great deal of memoir as well, and now in advanced years he was working in the Chicago area at the so-called College of Astrology. Fearing the consequences if Flora learned that he had opened a correspondence with Chaney, London persuaded Ted to allow him to use the Applegarth home as his return address, and penned a letter on May 28, 1897.

Chaney answered promptly on June 4 and seemed forthcoming with the facts of his relationship with Jack's mother. "There was a time when I had a very tender affection for Flora; but there came a time when I hated her with all the intensity of my intense nature, & even thought of killing her & myself.... Time, however, has healed the wounds & I feel no unkindness towards her, while for you I feel a warm sympathy, for I can imagine what my emotions would be were I in your place." However, probably fearing that the young man wanted something, perhaps money, he denied paternity. "I was never married to Flora Wellman . . . but she lived with me from June 11th, 1874 till June 3rd 1875. I was impotent at that time, the result of hardship, privation & too much brain-work." A young man who, like Flora, was from Ohio, was also living with them, and he might have been Jack's father. "The neighbors gossiped & talked scandal," wrote Chaney, "but I know nothing of my own knowledge." There was another candidate, as Flora had also "lived with Lee Smith of Seattle, as his wife, for a month," in the boardinghouse where Chaney took up residence, Smith's wife having deserted him to live with another man. Or still another possibility was a stockbroker who had paid Chaney $20 to cast a nativity for him. When it was finished, "Flora asked the privilege of taking it to him, to which I assented. A rumor reached me later that she frequently met him afterwards. His wife & daughter . . . were then in Europe." Chaney heard later that Flora had attempted to blackmail him. Beset by business reverses, the stockbroker moved to Oregon and a couple of months later killed himself. "I do not know as either was your father, nor do I know who is." Perhaps thinking to forestall any request for help, Chaney concluded, "I am past 76 & quite poor. But on the 15th inst. I am going to Michigan for a vacation, my first in 13 years. One of my students has offered me a home during summer in return for teaching her."[11]

Unsatisfied, London wrote him again, asking for more specifics. Chaney answered again with what seemed like dutiful patience, this time detailing his reason for ending the relationship:

> The cause of our separation began because Flora one day said to me:
>
> "You know that motherhood is the great great desire of my life, & as you are too old—now some time when I find a good, nice man are you not willing for me to have a child by him?"
>
> I said yes, only he must support her. No, she must always live with me & be the wife of "Prof. Chaney." A month or so later she said she was pregnant by me. I thought she was only trying me & did not think she was pregnant.

The fight that followed, according to Chaney, lasted a day and a night, after which he broke off their relationship. When he refused her hysterical pleas to continue as they had been, she rushed to the house of an acquaintance named Ruttley and there attempted her "suicides." According to Chaney it was a sham, and he cited witnesses whom London might still find in the San Francisco area to affirm that she never intended serious harm to herself.

Certainly Chaney would have been placing himself in the most favorable light possible in his relation of events, but London knew all too well that what Chaney described was well within Flora's established parameters. Besides, it did not take great calculation to realize that Flora was already three months along when she first broached the subject to Chaney, and she must have been testing the safety of revealing to him that she was expecting. A majority of London's biographers have concluded that Chaney was the likeliest possibility to be his real father; however, if that had indeed been the case, there would have been no need for Flora to frame the issue in terms of finding "a good, nice man" by whom she could get a baby. If Chaney had been the father, she would have simply announced her condition and importuned him to do the right thing. She must have already found a good, nice man, or else Chaney by 1897 had pondered his deception in sufficient detail to stand up to more than casual scrutiny.

Chaney had given London quite a shocking account of life among the San Francisco free lovers. "A very loose condition of society was fashionable . . . at the time & it was not thought disgraceful for two to live together without marriage. I mean the Spiritualists and those who claimed to be reformers." Within that context, he wrote, he had believed Flora's character honorable, but it was her rages that had driven him away—a point on which young London had plenty of history of his own. "Her temper was a great trial, & I had often thought before that time that I must leave her on account of it, & not for loose morals, for I did not ever suspect her up to that time."

Chaney may not have thought her conduct scandalous, but Flora's tempestuous libido succeeded in breaking up the boardinghouse where most of the involved parties had resided. "One day when I came home," Chaney wrote to

London, "I found all the lodgers moving away & great excitement throughout the house. As soon as I entered the room, Flora locked the door, fell on her knees before me & between sobs begged me to forgive her." It was then that he learned of her affairs, and his life, he wrote, would have been much happier had he abandoned her at that moment. After her pregnancy became known, and her "suicide" attempts, and the slanderous article appeared in the *Chronicle*, his own life became hell for the next decade, including a sister who blamed him in the matter and broke off contact. He had hired a detective to investigate Flora's would-be suicide, but the *Chronicle* refused to publish his findings and a retraction. "Then I gave up defending myself & for years life was a burden." Only recently, in his old age, had he cobbled a life together again, "and now I have a few friends who think me respectable."

If Jack London had known of the eerie parallels between his early life and Chaney's—his hatred of manual labor, his attempts to escape to sea, even embracing a flirtation with piracy, his obstinacy against accepting conventional wisdom, his wrongful imprisonment, his desire to grow a life of the mind through books, to say nothing of his serial philandering—he would have been amazed at the detail in which Chaney had pre-lived his own life, and might well have taken their similar paths for at least the possibility of Chaney's paternity. He might perhaps have tried to pursue a relationship with him, but all the evidence is that he dropped the matter after these two letters. Chaney lived for six more years, dying in Chicago in 1903 at age eighty-two.

London's semester at Berkeley had gone adequately, but he began to feel annoyed at spending so much time studying subjects that did not seem to bear on what he considered to be the large issues of life or that he could teach himself. And when the London family found their finances once again in peril, it became necessary for the gifted son, the one who had become used to being pampered at home with his cigarettes and fruit arranged just so on his studying table, to find a job.

He withdrew from the University of California, although he claimed he did so with minimal regret. He had, indeed, found other venues both of learning and of expressing himself. His brother-in-law, Captain Shepard, allowed him use of his newly acquired typewriting machine when it wasn't needed for his own business, although as with bicycles, it took some epic battles and a few injuries to train himself in its use. The brand name was Blickensdorfer, which London could have named the demon that lived within it. "The keys of that machine had to be hit so hard that to one outside the house it sounded like distant thunder or someone breaking up furniture. I had to hit the keys so hard that I strained my first fingers up to the elbows, while the ends of my fingers were blisters burst and blistered again. Had it been my machine I'd have operated it with a carpenter's hammer."[12]

Although he later acquired a fondness for bicycle trips, London's disgust with typewriters and his later disdain for automobiles evidenced a lifetime suspicion of technology. Shepard's typewriter, however, did yeoman service in turning out a stream of literature, London's first great burst, including letters expounding on socialism to local newspaper editors. They were closely reasoned, and for the most part quite good. "The labor of the United States is not the debtor class," he alleged in one. "They owe nothing for the simple reason that no one will trust them. Who composes this debtor class? The men of small capital—the men, who, when a debtless laborer produces ten dollars' worth of wealth, pockets eight of it and gives him two as a wage."[13]

The Applegarths had moved to San Jose, but in continuing to crave encouragement from Mabel, the depths of London's desire to make it as a writer became more apparent. At the upper end of the scale, published articles paid at a rate of two cents per word. To write only five publishable words was therefore the equivalent of an hour's laboring wage; he had to find a way to make it work. Deep down he knew that he was still learning, that what he was offering for sale now was rightly rejected. "I made ambitious efforts once," he later wrote of this period to Mabel Applegarth. "I was the greenest of tyros, dipping my brush into whitewash and coal tar . . . without a soul to say 'you are all wrong, herein you err; there is your mistake.' . . . My elephantine diction was superb—I out-Johnsoned Johnson. I was a fool—and no one to tell me."[14]

He joined the Socialist Labor Party, which brought him more contact with Whitaker and Strawn-Hamilton, but the crowds he attracted to his impromptu speeches on the courthouse square began to make the city take note of an ordinance against public gatherings held without the mayor's written permission. After a number of socialist speakers had been run out of the square, the party determined to challenge the law, and London volunteered to be the one taken. On February 10, 1897, he had just started a lecture on the Speaker's Corner when he was arrested and taken to jail. At his arraignment he demanded a jury trial, and unlike in Buffalo, this time he got one. Appealing to the Constitution's guarantee of free speech, and to the memory of Abraham Lincoln, whose birthday had just been celebrated, his impassioned argument managed to hang the jury, eleven to one voting to acquit, after which the city declined to refile the charges. Although the Applegarths stuck by him, the arrest marked him as an incendiary and cooled the ardor with which Oakland's polite element had begun to take an interest in him.

Nevertheless, the publicity won for the socialist cause was such that the Socialist Workers Party entered the twenty-one-year-old Berkeley dropout as a candidate for the Oakland School Board. It was becoming apparent, however, that his flight into political activism and writing was an indulgence that was hurting his family. The final straw landed when John London, feeble as he was becoming, offered to try to keep working to support Jack in his writing. That was unbearable.

In the previous couple of years he had reached high. He had left high school, but prepared for and been accepted into a leading university, and had his writing win contests and be published. That quickly became cold comfort now that he was staring again into the pit of menial labor, but for the summer of 1897 he agreed to accompany Herbert Shepard, Eliza's stepson, to work in the newly automated steam laundry of another preparatory academy, in Belmont on the peninsula southeast of San Francisco. The wage must have seemed like Fate's cruelest joke on him: $30 per month, the same as he had made shoveling coal at the electric train power station. Remembering daily the gall of being expelled from a prep school for daring to be smarter than the rich kids made the arrogance and superiority of the Belmont Academy students who dropped off and picked up their laundry that much harder to bear. They idled about, gossiping over iced drinks while London and Shepard sweat their pores out over the steam presses. ("So help me God," he told his second wife some years later, "no circumstance could make me touch an iron again if I died for it.")[15] Now a credentialed socialist, London made an attempt to organize the laundry workers but got nowhere;[16] he and Shepard had to content themselves with exacting an unmentionable form of revenge—over-starching the girls' underwear, knowing that the victims could never bring themselves to complain that they were being chafed raw. Dissimilarly from shoveling coal, here his $30 a month was in addition to bed and board, so he endured to the end of the term before retreating back to Oakland, desolate that having worked so hard to improve his mind, he was still a Work Beast. No matter what he did, it seemed he could not break the chains.

6 ❧ THE PROSPECTOR

By adulthood Jack London had come to understand desperation, and having nothing to lose. His memory was crowded with his mother's playing the Chinese lotteries and ruining his stepfather with one overreaching venture after another. Perhaps he should have recognized something of his mother in himself, when the grimy little steamship *Excelsior* docked in San Francisco on July 14, 1897, bringing news of the discovery of gold in the Klondike.

If gold is a fever, the gangplank of the *Excelsior* injected the disease into the United States. An owlish little one-time secretary of the YMCA and his wife trundled off the ship with $85,000 in gold; others rolled off even more. So too did the *Portland* when she tied up in Seattle two days later, and some of the first Klondikers had to hire porters to lug their sacks of nuggets and gold dust to the banks. The newspapers were not modest in their coverage:

> GOLD! GOLD! GOLD! SIXTY-EIGHT RICH MEN ON
> THE *PORTLAND*. STACKS OF THE YELLOW METAL!

Word of the Klondike had already reached Seattle when she docked and she was met by a crowd of 5,000 who watched more than a million dollars in gold come off the ship.

The news held immediate appeal for Jack London, Work Beast. Financial independence won with Alaskan gold would free him to pursue his writing while supporting his family. It would also give him license to marry Mabel Applegarth and maintain her in the state that her family would require.

At least minimally circumspect, London went to seek the advice of Joaquin Miller, California's most famous poet and an intimate of Ina Coolbrith—only to discover that he had already bolted for Alaska. London wanted to consult

Eliza, but he was already so much in her debt that he didn't dare—but then he received a shock: James Shepard, his aging and ailing brother-in-law, had also caught the fever and determined to go. Shepard declared that he and Eliza would bankroll the venture; Shepard would go with him, but London must do the hauling for them both. It seemed like a fair exchange. The Shepard house was in Eliza's name, and hopelessly she put a thousand-dollar mortgage on it. "They're both as crazy as loons," she said, "one no better than the other."

She might well have extended her remark to the whole stampede, which was, in essence, madness. Although the prospectors sailed to Alaska, the gold was not in Alaska. Thousands left the United States with no clue that the Klondike River emptied into the Yukon at the town of Dawson, in the heart of the Canadian Yukon Territory. That was a good five hundred miles of packing, climbing, boat-building, sailing, and rafting from where they came ashore. It should have been obvious that the locals had long since staked the best claims. It should have been obvious that by leaving the lower forty-eight in mid-summer, the survivors of that terrifying overland trek would arrive in the gold mining region just in time to confront the greatest terror of all, the Arctic winter, which they would have to survive before even thinking of prospecting for gold in the spring.

The Canadian government did its best to discourage this massive migration, barring entry to any who did not bring a year's supplies and $500 in cash. But the news stories of gold being disgorged by ships like the *Portland* and the *Excelsior* set in motion a horde that would not be denied, which said as much about the lingering depression that began in 1893 as it did about the lure of riches needing only to be plucked from streambeds. "Klondicitis," the newspapers called it.

Ironically for Northern California, which had endured its own gold rush a half century before, the history was conveniently forgotten that for every miner who struck a fortune, a vast number ended their venture penniless, and more than a few lay in unmarked graves. The odds were not good.

Some immediately saw the folly for what it was. Ambrose Bierce, the cynical Hearst columnist for the San Francisco *Examiner* and later a grudging familiar of London's, wrote of the Klondiker, "Will he clear the way for even a dog-sled civilization? . . . Nothing will come of him. He is a word in the wind, a brother to the fog. At the scene of his activity no memory of him will remain. The gravel that he thawed and sifted will freeze again. In the shanty that he builded, the she-wolf will raise her poddy litter. . . . The snows will cover his trail and all be as before."

Sharing Bierce's gloom was Mabel Applegarth's mother, the omnipresent chaperone who liked London in spite of himself. She wrote him three days before he was to sail: "We have just received the letter with the awful news that you are about to start for Alaska. Oh, dear John, do be persuaded to give up the idea for we feel certain that you are going to meet your death and we shall never see you again. . . . John, do give up the thought for you will never come back again, never. Your Father and Mother must be nearly crazed over it. Now, even at the eleventh hour, dear John, do change your mind and stay."[1]

Mrs. Applegarth's sentiment was understandable, but she was wrong on at least one count: his parents were not opposed. John London was now nearly seventy and confined to bed, his one functioning lung helping him cling to life. But his eyes lit up when he learned of his stepson's pending adventure; if only he could go, he said, he was sure the clean, cold climate would restore him. Jack was reduced almost to tears at the leave-taking, certain that it was a final goodbye. "Watch his smoke," John London said to comfort Eliza during the ensuing weeks when she sat up at night, keeping vigil over him. "He'll come out all right, and come out big, mark my words." Flora shared his confidence. If a typhoon in the open Pacific couldn't kill him, a little ice and some wolves would only make enough of an impression to write about later. Jack London did not go to the Klondike to gain material for the dozens of books, stories, and essays he produced in the following years; he went with the dream of returning a wealthy man. Mining the Yukon for literary wealth probably occurred to his mother first of all.

❧ ❧ ❧

The speed of it all was staggering. The *Excelsior* had docked on July 14; just ten days later, London and Shepard went to the outfitters and spent a large portion of Eliza's mortgage money within a few hours: "fur-lined coats, fur caps, heavy high boots, thick mittens; and red-flannel shirts and underdrawers of the warmest quality . . . a year's supply of grub, mining implements, tents, blankets, Klondike stoves, everything requisite to maintain life, build boats and cabins."[2] (The day before, when Shepard and Eliza were on a streetcar bound to meet London and finalize their plans, Shepard's excitement worked him into a small heart attack. The conductor stopped the car, and he and Eliza laid him gently on a lawn until a doctor could be sent for, who ordered Shepard to bed for two weeks, but the rendezvous was kept and Shepard insisted on persevering.) London's own drayage included items not common to the others: first and most important, a copy of Miner Bruce's *Alaska: Its History and Resources*, with its instructions detailed right down to which side of a river contained the main channel. He would have his own uses for Darwin and Spencer and Marx—and appropriately enough, Milton's *Paradise Lost* and Dante's *Inferno*.

The day after buying supplies, London and his wan brother-in-law boarded the S.S. *Umatilla*, the same vessel on which London had stoked coal on his way home from tramping. She was licensed to carry 290 passengers; this day she sailed with 471, most of them Klondikers with all their gear. She docked again at Port Townsend, Washington, just at the entrance to Puget Sound, where most of the would-be miners transferred to the S.S. *City of Topeka* and continued to Juneau, to arrive on August 2. Most of the men were traveling individually or in pairs, but by the time they got there, many of them had coalesced into larger partnerships to better bear the expense and the rigors of the coming test. London and Shepard fell in with three others: Fred C. Thompson, Jim Goodman, and Ira Merritt Sloper, who had been lately traveling in South America.

Their three days in Juneau were a fitting introduction to Alaska weather—it rained. Local natives were able to capitalize on the influx of northbound white men by charging them hefty fares to continue transport to the jumping-off point on the march for gold. On the 5th, London and Shepard engaged Indians to haul them and their gear in seventy-foot canoes up a sheltered arm of the inside passage called the Lynn Canal, past Haines to Skagway, finally beaching at Dyea. The hundred-mile paddle took three days, with London enjoying the presence of the Indians' "squaws, papooses & dogs." The previous summer London had vacationed with the Applegarths in the Yosemite Valley, which he recalled to Mabel in a letter written on their arrival. Their whole journey on the water "lay between mountains which formed a Yosemite Valley the whole length, & in many places the heights were stupendous. Glaciers & waterfalls on every side."

At Dyea he learned something else about the Alaskan summer. "I am laying on the grass within a score of glaciers, yet the slight exertion of writing causes me to sweat prodigiously." London had calculated carefully how to haul his and Shepard's outfit and avoid having to pay native porters. On a good trail he could carry a hundred pounds on his back, seventy-five on a bad trail. If he divided their half-ton of supplies into an average of fifteen loads, he could advance a mile, cache the pack, and return for another load. To move the whole outfit one mile up the trail would require him to walk twenty-nine miles, fifteen of it under burden. Such a thought did not faze him. "Am certain we will reach the lake in 30 days."[3]

London would certainly not be alone in plodding the trail. He estimated that there were about 3,000 novice Klondikers ready to start overland at this same time, but most of them were mired in confusion. Two-thirds of them landed at his location at the very head of the waterway, the rest five miles back down the coast at the slightly less raw town of Skagway. The head of the Lynn Canal was twice daily inundated with thirty-foot tides, so Dyea had no wharf. From where the ships dropped anchor, arrivals had to negotiate fees to load their gear onto lighters to ferry it to shore, which was nothing compared to the pandemonium on shore. Packs from different outfits were piled together, quarreling was hot, and fights were frequent. More local Indians were available to hire out as packers, but their rate had quintupled to forty cents per pound. London's party of five found it more economical to buy an old boat and pull their outfit the first six miles, up the Dyea River to where the boat grounded, then continue up its canyon, repeatedly fording the ice-cold stream. Following this narrow defile steadily, gradually upward, for eight miles he marched, carrying a pack, returning for another, carrying the second pack, returning for another, fifteen times for each mile. Thompson, a redhead of slender frame, lacked London's ability to haul his own gear and hired Indians at twenty-two cents per pound. The labor was backbreaking, and London, having worn his red flannels to Alaska, found himself sweating so profusely that he stripped off his outer layers to the red undershirt. He did begin to take some pride, though, that he was out-hauling nearly all the other white men, and a fair number of the hired Indian porters. Even with London doing the hauling, it took only a couple of days for Captain Shepard to come to his senses and realize that he would never survive to see the Yukon. After he turned back to catch a ship home, his place in the partnership was assumed by a man named Tarwater, later recalled by name and character in one of London's very last Alaska stories, "Like Argus of the Ancient Times," written the year he died and published posthumously.[4]

It took almost three weeks for them to reach the first resting place, a flat known as Sheep Camp. Four days more they continued through the rain, higher, crossing the tree line, until they reached a second campground near a large, block-shaped boulder called the Stone House. Of the Klondikers who eventually realized that they had sunk perhaps all their means into a project they could not consummate, some went mad, some killed themselves. Those who lasted a few more days saw their hope of accomplishment dashed as they looked up at the cruelest obstacle yet, the summit of Chilkoot Pass, a final ascent of three-quarters of a mile at a 45-degree angle, taken single file. London's party craned their necks upward to see it on August 27. There was an easier route to the interior, via White Pass a few miles to the south, but it required a trek of forty-five easier miles, as opposed to the twenty they had come. To save time, London's group, like most of the others, chose the shorter, harder trail.

All his life as a boy and young man, London had harbored a soft spot for animals, especially dogs and horses. What he beheld along the path up to the Chilkoot Pass made his heart ache. Many of the Klondikers had—stupidly—brought horses to do their hauling for them, despite the terrain, the season, and the lack of forage. As the trail became worse, they whipped the overloaded animals mercilessly. Some were beaten to death; some tumbled from the trail into gulches, where they lay flailing with broken legs or broken backs, with no one willing to spend a bullet on them to end their misery. Later, it was probably only a small exaggeration when it was said that one could walk the length of the trail to the Chilkoot Pass and never set foot on anything but dead horses. To London it was a soggy hell.[5]

London, Goodman, Thompson, Sloper, and Tarwater took their place in the long, thin line hiking slowly, painfully to the summit of the pass; London and the others who hauled their own gear one load at a time did so many times. The summit was also the Canadian border, and there Northwest Mounted Police weighed freight and determined who would be allowed to continue into the interior. From there to the Klondike would be downhill, but downhill, they soon learned, would be even worse than the climb. They would follow the watercourses for the five hundred miles through the upper tributaries of the Yukon to reach Dawson, but that five hundred miles contained some of the wildest water on the planet. Dawson was only fifty miles from the eastern boundary of Alaska, but from where they now stood it was north halfway to the Arctic Circle.

London and his partners followed the trail northeast, around the margins of small bodies of water, Long Lake and Deep Lake, continuing their grueling regimen. Eventually they hauled over an enormous rise to see the southern finger of narrow, glacial Lake Lindemann; one of the last stops on this leg was at a place called Pleasant Valley, whose name, they discovered, was something of a sick joke. Pleasant Valley was little more than a frigid marsh, and in places the weight of the packs drove London almost up to his knees in cold ooze.

Perhaps because London had studied Miner Bruce's book in such detail, they arrived on September 8, exactly one month after starting the trek, as he had predicted to Mabel Applegarth. Snow was already dusting the spikes of the tall spruces; the threat of winter, with the imperative to reach the gold region before the waterways froze up, was already in the air.

London's preparation, his strong back, and his dogged determination on the trail had been advantages over the less provident Klondikers; at Lake Lindemann he was to enjoy another, for if anyone knew how to build a small boat, he did, and Merritt Sloper was also knowledgeable. The advantage of having formed a partnership also became apparent, as Goodman, Thompson, and Tarwater took over packing their gear, while London, accompanied by Sloper, selected a campsite near a good stand of spruce and began felling trees to build their boat. Indeed, they found it helpful to pool their labor with another group of three men named Odette, Rand, and Sullivan; they sawed the spruce logs into stout lumber and built two flat-bottomed, shallow-draft boats, twenty-seven feet long: the *Yukon Belle* for London's team and the *Belle of the Yukon* for the other. The Lake Lindemann watershed would soon be denuded of trees, as during this year and the next more than 7,000 boats, rafts, and flats that defied categorical description set off down the lake. Many would sink of their own accord or be dashed to pieces in rapids, the drowned bodies of their crews surfacing in calmer eddies downstream.

The first blizzard of the year was roaring by the time the boats were loaded, and then rowed and sailed down the length of the lake. With Arctic winter fast approaching, they began gambling on dangerous shortcuts to save time. Lake Lindemann emptied through a whitewater chute that connected to the lower Lake Bennett; the experience of outfits up to that point was that it was safer to portage gear down the stream bank and careen down the rapids in an empty boat; London's and Rand's groups bit their lips and shot through fully loaded. For their first major risk, luck was with them and they emerged onto the stillness of Lake Bennett, silently passing the wreckage of the less fortunate. They were favored by a hefty south wind as they traversed the lake and another rapid outlet to Lake Tagish, and on then to Lake Marsh. They realized just how fortunate they had been in their progress when, on Lake Tagish, they were hammered by crosswinds at the aptly named Windy Arm, and they saw two other boats near them founder and sink, their crews splash about for a moment and then slip beneath the surface. Thompson called on London to beach and camp for the night, but if oyster pirating had taught London anything it was how to sail at night, and they pressed on.

The outflow of Marsh Lake was into the majestic, powerful 50-Mile River, as much as a quarter-mile wide and promising an easy stretch to navigate. Halfway down its length that proved to be a lie, as the banks rose to sheer rock walls and narrowed to a width of only eighty feet. The entire volume of the river ripped through the Box Canyon with such force that a ridge of water six feet high or more had formed down the middle. Beaching the *Yukon Belle* amid scores of other craft whose crews had determined to spend time portaging around the fearsome obstacle, London surveyed the canyon and—not surprisingly for him—decided that he could run it, despite the presence halfway through the canyon of a vicious whirlpool where the walls widened just enough to split the current. Still, running the canyon would take only a couple of minutes, measured against a two-day portage. It seems astonishing that the other men would place their faith in a twenty-one-year-old who seemed to have the confidence that he could defy any force of nature, but he had gotten them this far, and they acquiesced. As at Lake Lindemann, he did not show the canyon the respect of unloading the boat and running through it empty; overloaded and sluggish, he would take her through as she was. Leaving Tarwater ashore and placing Goodman and Thompson on the oars with Sloper in the bow, London lashed the steering oar down securely, they pushed off, intending to ride the Ridge down the middle of the stream well clear of the vertical walls. Other Klondikers gathered on the shore and the cliff tops to watch the daredevils, some yelling encouragement; once they were swept into the Box Canyon their fate was sealed, for good or ill.

The hardest thing about the Ridge was initially getting on top of it. London steered for it with all his might, and Sloper with the bow paddle pushed for it, sometimes just when the *Yukon Belle* would make a great upward heave, leaving him slashing at thin air before soaking him with a downward plunge. They just gained the crest as they entered the canyon, but then slipped off, Sloper breaking his paddle and London leaning on the steering oar until it cracked. The *Belle* began to turn her beam to the current and they approached within six feet of the sheer wall that would splinter them, but London managed to force her back up onto the rushing crest, just in time to encounter the whirlpool. For someone as classically read as London, the moment must have seemed like something out of Homer—Scylla and Charybdis, the choice of death between the crushing cliff face or the whirlpool. Still, he managed to skirt the swirling funnel of water, leaned on the steering oar to push the boat back up on to the Ridge and down to smooth water. Sensible men would have not pushed their luck further, but London had become friends back upstream with a team headed by a man named Rett who had brought his family with him. With little apparent thought London walked back up the length of the canyon and took their boat through as well.

After the terror of Box Canyon, two miles on loomed the even more dangerous White Horse rapids, where most of the crews banked their boats and pondered again whether to push their luck. The following year, entrepreneurs started a freight company that portaged the Klondikers and their gear around the danger, which was the first commerce that began the town of Whitehorse, destined to become the capital of Yukon Territory. But at the time London and his company were there, it was raw rock and water. Similar to Box Canyon, the White Horse rapids had at their center a raised chute of water, this one dubbed the Horse's Mane for its spray, and it also embraced a whirlpool. This one, however, lay where the main channel was thrown from the right bank to the left by a raised reef of rocks, which was incalculably more dangerous.

The *Yukon Belle* entered the Horse's Mane dead center, bucking high over mountainous waves before plunging her square bow deep into water that poured into the boat. Then, again, she turned sickly, presenting her beam to the current just as they approached the whirlpool. London bellowed to ship oars, intending to maneuver only with the steering oar. Briefly he fought the suction before realizing his mistake, then steered through a whole circuit of the swirling water, gaining the speed that would break them free. Up in the bow Sloper, who had broken a second paddle, was certain they would crash, and he leapt out onto a projecting rock, then as the boat made its circuit he realized what London was doing and leapt just as neatly back in. London heaved the *Belle* out of the whirlpool and back up onto the Horse's Mane, which they rode through to still water.[6]

Eventually the 50-Mile River widened out into Lake Laberge, later immortalized by the fictional cremation of the actual local character Sam McGee. It was September 25, a thick blanket of snow covered the ground, and blizzards were coming harder and colder. Three times in three days London's group set out to traverse Laberge's forty-mile length, driven back each time by stout north winds and waves that froze even as they broke over the freeboard. Other groups of Klondikers were admitting defeat and preparing winter camps to hunker down until spring, as it was plain that the lake was on the brink of freezing, even though the river below would continue to run. Again London assumed leadership, declaring on the 28th that unless the others were content to winter there on Lake Laberge, they would cross and stop for nothing. They sailed that day and all through the night; by morning they emerged onto 30-Mile River. Looking back, they beheld a thin sheet of ice flattening the surface of the lake.

For all intents and purposes, the mouth of Lake Laberge is the head of navigation on the Yukon proper, and fed by such brawling torrents as the Teslin and Big and Little Salmon rivers, the sheer weight of stream gave them a well-deserved smooth run downstream, after all this still in company with the *Belle of the Yukon*. For some time they had been meeting discouraged Klondikers heading back the way they came, bearing woeful tales that there was not enough food in Dawson to last through the winter, and the whole of the gold-mining area was already staked out. If that was true, they might as well try their luck where they were, so at mid-afternoon October 9 the *Yukon Belle* slipped onto the bank of Split-Up Island, near the mouth of the Stewart River, to make winter camp; her sister paused to take on Tarwater and continued the eighty miles to Dawson. London and his partners found shelter in a cabin that had once been manned by the Alaska Commercial Company, and the next morning unloaded the boat and began organizing the camp. On the 11th, Jim Goodman, the only one with any mining experience, explored a small nearby stream called Henderson Creek, and when he returned he showed around the tiny flecks of gold he had panned.

First thing the next morning, London, Thompson, and two other prospectors who had fallen in with them left camp for three days in the same watershed. When they returned, London was jubilant at having found his own little showing of gold; although Thompson later wrote that London actually came back with iron pyrite—"fool's gold"—he probably did actually find a smidgen of the metal he had come for. On this same October 15, John London died at home in Oakland, confident to the last that Jack would triumph. Perhaps Flora had discussed the literary possibilities with him, for Eliza later told Jack London's second wife that the long-dying man said not once, but often, "Jack is going to make a success out of the Klondike—whether he digs it out of the grassroots or not."[7]

On the 16th, London, Thompson, and the two newcomers, Charles Borg and Emil Jensen, packed tents, blankets, and food for three weeks, and launched the *Yukon Belle* for the two-day trip on to Dawson to register their claims. They beached on the south bank of the Klondike and rode the ferry across into Dawson City, a beehive of a frontier boomtown that, during the course of the gold rush, mushroomed from fewer than 5,000 people to more than 20,000. In the inflation of the boomtown, breakfast cost $3.50; it took $5 for a pound of tomatoes and $30 for a gallon of milk. Most of the Americans wintering in Dawson were still *cheechakoes*—tenderfeet—who had not actually done any mining and were living expensively off their grubstakes. There had been little mention of alcohol during all these long weeks on hiking and rafting, but once again a man among men, London and his companions visited one of the many saloons. In it London chanced across two fellow Californians, the brothers Louis and Marshall Bond, whose father was a judge in Santa Clara. They had a cabin in the town and invited London's group to pitch their tent next to it. With his partners securely in possession of Henderson Creek, London felt little urgency to file the claim right away, but he did so on November 5.

Of much greater interest to him were the Bond brothers, both Yalies, and young men with whom he could have an intellectual exchange. During one frozen, lamp-lit bull session in the Bonds' cabin, the talk passed to socialism. Various of the company made their ignorant stabs at it; one got it mixed up with anarchism. "Then," according to Marshall Bond, "from out of the shadow of the lamp, from the blur of beard and cap, came a quick-speaking, sympathetic voice. He took up the subject from its earliest history, carried it through on a rapid survey of its most important points and held us thrilled. . . . This was my first introduction to Jack London." Admitting that he had been educated into a goose step of conventionalism, he found London's independent intellect a blast of fresh air.[8] Of equal interest to London as having the Bond brothers to talk to was their massive, woolly dog, Jack, half collie and half St.

Bernard, with whom he bonded and whose fond memory he would recall in a future year.

With the Yukon just starting to freeze—it was a disquieting notion that these brutal conditions had actually been a mild beginning to the winter, and the river was freezing later than normal—London started back to the Split-Up Island cabin on December 3. It was a hard trek back up to the Stewart River, for the foot traffic and dog sleds had not yet packed the snow smooth on the trail, but it was a winter hike that later furnished the setting for his classic short story "To Build a Fire."

With no Yale men to counter him, London began opening intellectual fire on his cabin mates, who were badly overmatched. Another Klondiker who was one of a growing group who wintered on the island, one W. B. "Bert" Hargrave of Colfax, Washington, first met London at such a moment.

> His cabin was on the bank of the Yukon, near the mouth of the Stewart River. I remember well the first time I entered it. London was seated on the edge of a bunk, rolling a cigarette. He smoked incessantly. . . . One of his partners, Goodman, was preparing a meal, and the other, Sloper, was doing some carpentry work. From the few words which I overheard as I entered, I surmised that Jack had challenged some of Goodman's orthodox views, and that the latter was doggedly defending himself in an unequal contest of wits. Many times afterward I felt the rapier thrust of London's, and knew how to sympathize with Goodman.

Winter, however, would have been colder without the intellectual fire, and London never rubbed his partners' noses in their ignorance. "Though a youth," concluded Hargrave, "he displayed none of the insolent egotism of youth . . . [but] the clean, joyous, tender, unembittered heart of youth."[9]

Having visited the saloon in Dawson, there was no other mention of London in association with alcohol at the Split-Up Island bivouac, save one. Emil Jensen's partner needed an operation, without which he would die, and a foraging expedition to nearby camps, including ransacking the packs of a medical doctor, produced neither chloroform nor ether. Upon being told that a liberal consumption of whiskey would at least dull the pain, London produced a bottle from his packs and said, "Take it and welcome." In later days, when London was famous enough for his drinking to come in for censure, Jensen defended him as sober and kind. Jensen, however, had the luck to know London when he was engaged in hopeful work and good companions; unlike on the Oakland waterfront, he had no need to drink on the Yukon.[10]

Winter in the Arctic is shut-in time, with ample opportunity to talk during long hours wrapped in their bedding, and time to consider the present and the future. London did make various forays eighteen miles out to their claim on Henderson Creek to prospect. There he sheltered in an abandoned dugout, reflecting on what he had gotten himself into, and on what kind of future he could expect when he returned.

Common among the miners during the winter was the "Klondike Plague," scurvy, brought on by a diet limited to bacon, bread, and beans. Easily preventable as it is with fresh vegetables and fruit, if left untreated scurvy can become lethal. By May London was showing all the symptoms: flaccid skin, bleeding gums, and loose teeth (although what irked him more than scurvy was the lack of sugar in the staples; his voracious sweet tooth had not been placated in months).

Even worse, the sense of high adventure with which he had begun was supplanted by daily drudgery. He was cold, lonely, and increasingly frustrated as the vaunted gold proved elusive, and now he was getting sick. Since reading Nietzsche he had been enamored of the Superman, but now had to confront his physical limitations and what they meant for his future: he could not be a Work Beast much longer. If he tried he would end as one of the hopeless wretches he encountered on the road, one of the lame tramps who desperately wanted to work but could not. He must find a way to earn his living with his mind. In the *Call*'s literary contest he had bested the best Berkeley had to offer, eight of his stories had been published in the *Aegis*, and since then he had applied himself ruthlessly to the study and use of language. The dugout on Henderson Creek became his frozen crucible, in which his determination to become a writer finally hardened, to learn to do it professionally, no matter what it took. Having concluded this, he scrawled some portentous graffiti onto the log beside his bunk:

JACK LONDON MINER AUTHOR JAN 27 1898

The miner half of his self-assumed identity came to an unexpectedly rapid conclusion, for London's scurvy had become acute. Back down on Split-Up Island, the extended confinement caused tempers to run short among his partners; London ran afoul of Sloper when he used the latter's ax to chop ice to melt for drinking water. He swung too hard, striking rock beneath the ice and seriously dulling the blade. In the North this was a serious matter, and Sloper's abuse was so severe that London took up residence with a nearby camp, which included "Bert" Hargrave and a medical doctor, B. F. Harvey. Like London, Hargrave had an appreciation for the cross-section of humanity among whom they found themselves. In later years he provided a short list of the Klondikers who shared Split-Up Island. One was a Texan named Peacock, who beat the odds and actually became wealthy from Yukon gold; another was Elam Harnish, sardonically known by his sobriquet of Burning Daylight—another name that would appear in a later London tale.[11] Examining London's advancing scurvy, Dr. Harvey gave strident advice to leave for home at the first thaw, which would begin at any time. In preparation, London's partners and others who had taken up residence on the island began dismantling the cabin that housed London and his partners, lashing its logs together into a raft to carry him down to Dawson.

❧ ❧ ❧

The spring thaw on the Yukon is an event of unstoppable power. London and Dr. Harvey watched the enormous blocks of ice rise and heave with cataclysmic explosions and slowly move downstream. Where their edges caught the bank they gouged out huge chunks of soil and rock, tumbling mature trees into the torrent, and when the ice would jam downstream the surging river would rise and rise until it would finally float them and carry them on. It took hours for the Yukon to run clear and within its banks. Upstream the Stewart River was still frozen and would cause similar deadly conditions on the river, but London's need for medical attention was so grave that the raft was launched with Harvey and London on it.

In Dawson London found potatoes to eat, a rich source of vitamin C and fast relief for scurvy. He also found the hospital run by a Father Judge, who administered as well as he could, but he urged London, if he valued his life, to get back to civilization. London and Harvey got $600 for the logs of their raft, and London procured a small boat in which he meant, as though he had not tempted fate enough, to descend the whole length of the Yukon—1,500 miles.

Loading in supplies and two traveling companions named Taylor and Thorson, they pushed off from Dawson on June 8, bound ultimately for St. Michael's, on the south shore of Norton Sound, an inlet of the Bering Sea. For long stretches they passed the wide marshes lining the Yukon, in which mosquitoes awakened by the spring thaw emerged hungry, causing London and his companions endless grief. They slept under netting but were badly bitten nonetheless; one morning when London awoke in misery from them, Taylor "swore that he has seen several of the largest ones pull the mesh apart & let a small one squeeze through."[12] The mosquitoes had to be braved, though, to obtain the goose eggs that formed a large part of their diet. They also consumed ducks raw, which may explain London's penchant for them in his later famous years. Still suffering, no longer able to straighten his right leg but able to limp on his toes, London rested as much as he could, and even sketched some thoughts about the previous months—the first of a long career writing about Alaska and the Yukon. Ten days brought them to Anvik, a settlement on the south-flowing Yukon right before it swings west and enters its vast delta. There the Episcopal missionary provided London with vitamin C–rich canned tomatoes and fresh potatoes, "worth more to me at the present stage," he wrote, "than an El Dorado claim."

Eight days more—June 26—brought them into the Yukon's vast delta, where at last they confronted an element of danger. St. Michael's lay up the northernmost channel, which was a minor outlet. If they picked the wrong channel they could wind up being ejected into the Bering Sea with but little prospect of being found. With considerable trepidation they picked a route, which put them into the choppy sea near Point Romanoff, an easy sail from St. Michael's. In this isolated water London met the man he called the most interesting he had yet encountered in the Arctic, a French-Italian priest named Robeau, whom they took into their boat because his kayak was in danger of foundering. A Jesuit and highly educated, which won him London's sympathy right away, he had devoted his twelve years in Alaska to preparing a written grammar of the Inuit language. Bemused, London listened as Robeau rhapsodized on the Inuit language, as "moods, tenses, articles, adverbs, etc., fill the air." For once he felt as a complacent capitalist must feel when he held forth on the advancement of the proletariat.

In St. Michael's London found a steamer that was willing to sign him on as a coal stoker in exchange for passage to Port Townsend, Washington. Eight days out, however, weakened by the scurvy, London seriously burned his hand at the boiler he was feeding and was excused from duty thereafter. Those eight days' wages at least financed a steerage berth from Port Townsend to San Francisco.

Back in Oakland he discovered that his family had been through some wrenching changes. His stepfather had died nine months before, and Flora had reduced her lifestyle, moving into a smaller place on Foothill Boulevard. London's stepsister, not his beloved Eliza but the younger Ida, had developed into a wild child, married young and separated, and now had deposited her little boy, Johnny Miller, with Flora to raise. And galling as it was, Flora seemed to have found the maternal instinct to take care of the boy, with affection that she had never shown Jack.

There was no money and bills were due. Now he was responsible for the family, and he had brought back gold dust worth $4.50. This time, however, Jack London refused to just stare bleakly at the prospect of becoming once more the Work Beast. In the frozen vastness of the Arctic he had sworn to himself to become a writer, no matter what it took. And that was what he meant to do.

7 ❧ THE ASPIRING WRITER

One of the hardest things was to face Eliza. She had fled the family woes and was on a camping trip when he returned to Oakland. As much as Jack yearned to see her again, the joy of their reunion would not be unalloyed. She had allowed him to risk money from her and Captain Shepard's business, she had placed a mortgage on her house, and as if that weren't enough, she had paid for her father's funeral while he was gone. And now London had to admit that he had come back broke.

All John London was able to bequeath to his stepson was a good mackintosh that was worth $15. Jack was stricken by news of his death but, desperate for cash, he pawned it for $2. He also hocked his own bicycle and his watch; one friend from the waterfront traded him a dress suit bundled in newspapers for an assortment of his personal odds and ends. He needed the suit, but far more than that, he needed the $5 the pawn shop paid for it. As he'd been with sports cards and kerosene tins, he was still a canny trader.

There was simply no work, even for a Beast. He registered at five different employment agencies, he held out his services in three newspapers, but there was nothing doing. Willing as he was to trade on his handsome looks, he was unable to land any modeling jobs. Scurvy gone, he was strong again but found no success with any of the advertisements he answered seeking an aide to the elderly infirm. Finally in early August he pawned his pinch of gold dust and headed to Nevada for more prospecting but returned in defeat again. All was not yet lost in the Yukon; he had pulled out of his mining claim and come home rather than die from scurvy, but his partners had promised to write him if it turned productive. If there were gold to return to, he would end up a wealthy man yet. But he certainly could not count on it.

Always in the back of his mind was the desire to write, to publish, and when he wasn't looking for work he was writing like mad. After what he felt was relentless preparation, London decided it was time to put his work to the test, and wrote his first query letter on September 17, 1898, to the editor of the *San Francisco Bulletin*.

> I have returned from a year's residence in the Clondyke, entering the country by way of Dyea and Chilcoot Pass. I left by way of St. Michaels, thus making altogether a journey of 2,500 miles on the Yukon in a small boat. I have sailed and traveled quite extensively in other parts of the world and have learned to seize upon that which is interesting, to grasp the true romance of things, and to understand the people I may be thrown amongst.
>
> I have just completed an article of 4,000 words, describing the trip from Dawson to St. Michaels in a rowboat. Kindly let me know if there would be any demand in your columns for it—of course, thoroughly understanding that the acceptance of the manuscript is to depend upon its literary and intrinsic value.
>
> Yours very respectfully,
> Jack London

The rejection was swift, penciled beneath London's query. "Interest in Alaska has subsided in an amazing degree. Then, again, so much has been written, that I do not think it would pay us to buy your story. Editor."[1]

Less than a week later he tried again, with a political piece titled "The Devil's Dice Box." It too was turned back, first by the popular illustrated monthly *Collier's Magazine* and then by several others, until it finally resided in London's file of "retired" pieces he had lost hope of selling.[2] He tried poems; he had mastered the classical forms and could fill any template of rhyme and meter with fluffy metaphors or histrionic tragedy. He tried essays and short stories; in a week he completed a serial of over 20,000 words that he submitted to *Youth's Companion*, but it, too, was rejected.

He had read a news piece indicating that for published work, an author could expect a rate of at least $10 per 1,000 words; using the same calculus with which he correctly estimated his ability to pack his gear across the Yukon, he grandly figured that he could live comfortably on the $600 per month he could earn by writing just 3,000 words per day. He had no idea that very few writers ever produce 3,000 sellable words per day. As a sailor London had proven that he could navigate either San Francisco Bay or Lake Laberge under the black of clouds or a new moon, but as a writer he was discovering that to labor in the dark, with no hint other than reading the popular magazines for what editors might buy, got him nowhere. The pennies that he was spending for stamps, both to make the submissions and include return postage for the rejected pieces, seemed like a fortune.

He renewed his friendship with the Applegarths but Mabel, once his muse and his porcelain ideal, was increasingly proving herself to be her mother's daughter. Cautious and conventional, she was sympathetic toward his desire to write but discouraged him from doggedly pursuing it. When he mentioned to her that the U.S. Post Office was about to offer the civil service examination, she leapt at the chance to steer him toward that safe harbor. It was not what he wanted to hear, and a pall descended between them just as Mabel began to feel she might actually fall in love with him. His friendship with Ted Applegarth became the new focus of his visits, and Mabel did not take well to being relegated to the sidelines. It took an incident—she cleared their chessboard of its pieces in anger at being ignored—for her to realize, from his measured response, that she had lost him. Their friendship remained, however, and to spare her feelings London maintained the pretense of courtship.

Then came the first spark of interest in his writing that might prove her wrong about his literary chances. Oakland's Fifth Ward Republican Club sponsored a political essay contest, which he won along with $20 in prize money. It was enough to give him more hope, but not enough to change his circumstances. Bowing to reality, on October 1, 1898, he took the civil service examination so he could have a secure job as a mail carrier, still hoping against hope that literary success would rescue him from committing to further day labor. He passed that crucible of anxiety endured by all young writers, of waiting with bated breath for the postal delivery, only to hear nothing, good or bad, from anybody. And like most young writers, he endured the humiliation of not getting paid. "Everything seems to have gone wrong," he confided to Mabel. "I have'nt [sic] received my twenty dollars for those essays yet. Not a word as to how I stood in my Civil Service Exs. Not a word from the *Youth's Companion*, and it means to me what no one can possibly realize."[3] He had submitted a serial titled "Where Boys are Men," of 3,000 words in each of the seven chapters, to *Youth's Companion*. After they rejected it, London learned one more nuance of literary journeymanship: the pieces were accepted the next year by *Youth and Age*, but they were never actually printed.

He was gruesomely organized in recording his submissions, every rejection slip filed, every penny for postage stamps logged. What a blessing it would have been if he could have endured the frustration in privacy, but Flora saw every packet that crossed their threshold, and Eliza heard about each one. Mabel tried to help him, but her best advice continued to be that he give up, once going so far as to remind him of his duty toward the security of his family. Mabel had become perhaps his closest confidante, but in daring to refer him to a sense of "duty," she fouled a tripwire that set off a detonation—all his past resentments and his present frustrations poured out in a torrent of recrimination.

> I was eight years old when I put on my first undershirt made at or bought at a store. Duty—at ten years I was on the street selling newspapers. Every cent was turned over to my people. . . . I worked in the cannery. I was up and at work at six in the morning. I took half an hour for dinner. I took half an hour for supper. I worked every night till ten, eleven and twelve o'clock. My wages were small, but I worked such long hours that I sometimes made as high as fifty dollars a month. Duty—I turned every cent over. Duty—I have worked in that hellhole for thirty-six straight hours, at a machine, and I was only a child. I remember how I was trying to save money to buy a skiff—eight dollars. All that summer I saved and scraped. In the fall I had five dollars as a result of absolutely doing without all pleasure. My mother came to the machine where I worked and asked for it. I could have killed myself that night. After a year of hell to have that pitiful—to be robbed of that petty joy.

> How often, as I swept rooms at High School, has my father come to me at work and got a half dollar, a dollar, or two dollars [sometimes] when I did not have a cent, and went to the Aegis fellows and borrowed it.[4]

And apart from all this, when he returned from the Klondike he had done everything he could think of to sell himself as a Work Beast again. Writing was all that was left for him; his first choice was now his last, by default and by desperation.

London's night, however, passed its darkest point before dawn. To the venerable *Overland Monthly* he had submitted a short story, "To the Man on the Trail," a cleverly ambiguous title that sounded like it might offer advice to novice Klondikers, but which actually repeated a toast at a Christmas gathering in a Yukon cabin. The story might as well have depicted his own previous Christmas at Split-Up Island. The host, the Malemute Kid, is preparing a dubious punch of whiskey, brandy, and pepper sauce when the gathering is interrupted by the arrival of an exhausted passing stranger, whom they bed down and speed on his way the next morning, moments before the Mountie pursuing him also stops at the cabin. The Malemute Kid renders the lawman no aid, and only by demanding of a Jesuit who would not lie—even named Father Roubeau—does the Mountie learn that his quarry mushed out not fifteen minutes before. The men curse themselves for helping an outlaw, when the Malemute Kid wises them up, saying that what the stranger stole was only what his victim had stolen from him. It was an inevitable first London piece, combining the Yukon with the quest for fairness in a cheating world.

At the lowest moment of reading rejection letters and sending manuscripts back out to second and third and fourth choices, London received a letter from *Overland Monthly*. The editors were overstocked in accepted manuscripts, it said, but they thought it was a fine story, and if he would take $5 for it, they would publish it next month. Therein lay another lesson for the novice writer: if it was good enough to publish, and publish in a journal that had hosted Mark Twain and Bret Harte, why would they pay him only an eighth of a penny per word? But $5 was nearly a week's wage for a Work Beast, and he accepted. Then came the next lesson: waiting on the check. For months. And months.

Then London extracted another letter, from one H. D. Umbstaetter, editor of a nickel per copy monthly magazine of short stories called *The Black Cat.* They would pay him *forty dollars* to publish his submission, "A Thousand Deaths." They found the piece wordy, however, and wanted to cut it in half. London did not argue. They could cut it in half twice, he responded, if they would just pay promptly. A dozen years later, London wrote an introduction to a hardcover collection of stories from *The Black Cat* called *The Red Hot Dollar*. In it he recounted the sale of "A Thousand Deaths."

> Everything I possessed was in pawn, and I did not have enough to eat. I was sick, mentally and physically, from lack of nourishment. . . . I was at the end of my tether, beaten out, starved, ready to go back to coal-shoveling or ahead to suicide. . . . I had once read in a Sunday supplement that the minimum rate paid by the magazines was ten dollars per thousand words. But during all the months devoted to storming the magazine field, I had received back only manuscripts. Still I believed implicitly what I had read in the Sunday supplement.

He went on to recount the sale of "To the Man on the Trail" to *Overland Monthly,* and his despair at learning that the pay rate was vastly less than what he had been led to believe. But then the offer from *The Black Cat* had come that same afternoon. "Literally, and literarily, I was saved by the 'Black Cat' short story. . . . The marvelous and unthinkable thing that Mr. Umbstaetter did, was to judge a story on its merits and *to pay for it on its merits.* Also, and only a hungry writer can appreciate it, he paid immediately on acceptance."[5]

Years after selling "A Thousand Deaths," it was apparent that London still believed in its literary merits. For an early effort it was a curious amalgam of experience and imagination. Its opening is reminiscent of London's own near-drowning in the Carquinez Straits during his Fish Patrol days, but the story quickly evolves into a tale of twisted science. Some of its elements show the mark of the beginner: that the mad scientist who rescues a drowning sailor does not recognize his own son is a heavy imposition on the reader's credulity, and then ultimately it proves irrelevant to the story. However, the science-fiction plot, that the scientist has discovered the secret of reanimation and perfects it by repeatedly killing his captive son, is actually quite effective. The setting allows young London to fully deploy his ruthlessly bulked up—not to say "supererogatory"—vocabulary in perhaps the only way that is not pedantic and annoying. And certainly the rescue of a flailing sailor from San Francisco Bay by someone who proves to be a monster was a motif famously recycled years later in *The Sea-Wolf*.

In recalling the dark days before Umbstaetter and *The Black Cat* came to his rescue, London may have been venting a bit of hyperbole with the claim that he had thought of suicide, but his old friend Frank Atherton did not think so. He had come up from San Jose for a visit and found London so despondent that he lengthened his stay until he felt assured that London would not harm himself. Indeed he stayed so long that London missed his own trip down to San Jose to spend Thanksgiving with the Applegarths. He had written of suicide to Mabel as well. "As long as my mother lives, I would not do this; but with her gone tomorrow, if I knew that my life would be such, that I was destined to live in Oakland, labor in Oakland at some steady occupation, and die in Oakland—then to-morrow I would cut my throat. . . . You may call this foolish effervescence of youthful ambition . . . but I have had my share of toning down."[6] What propelled him out of contemplating suicide, he told Atherton, was a visit by a young lady friend of his, also despondent and threatening to kill herself. As he reasoned her out of it, he talked himself out of it as well. "I am going to stick to my writing," he told Atherton, "and the publishers are going to accept it whether they like it or not. And some of these days they'll be glad to . . . pay me a good price for it; you just wait and see." Yet another lesson of the aspiring writer: the helpless yawing from hopelessness to manic self-confidence.[7]

Doubtless Jack London missed his other friends. Eliza's stepson Herbert had enlisted to fight in the Spanish-American War, and Fred Jacobs of the Oakland library had enlisted in the Hospital Corps, leaving London to keep Jacobs's fiancée, Bess Maddern, company and go on bicycling excursions with her. In later years, the conflict between the United States and Spain endured more critical scrutiny as an act of American imperial expansion at the expense of a crumbling former power. At the time, however, patriotism was fervent, and London had little difficulty justifying it within his growing socialist doctrine. To him the war seemed "but a stroke against monarchy & for political democracy. . . . [It] is easily apparent that political democracy must come before industrial democracy—and there it is, perfect political & industrial democracy combined are really what?—Socialism."[8]

Rather than worrying about the war with Spain, London was more concerned that at this moment socialists were taking a drubbing in world opinion over the assassination of the beautiful Empress Elisabeth of Austria-Hungary. She had been killed by an anarchist, not a socialist, but the distinction was too fine for the appreciation of most. "Poor woman it was not her fault for she was born so," he wrote; she was merely the doomed exponent of a doomed political system. But London had become increasingly aware that to the average American indoctrinated with the ideals of patriotism, socialists, communists, and anarchists had all become lumped together into a bomb-throwing, vaguely Slavic cartoon that was inaccurate, and out of which they needed to be educated.

By the holidays he was gloomy once again, writing to Mabel on Christmas Day that the rent was due on his typewriter—he had finally rented one rather than wear out the Shepards'—and it would have to go back at the end of the month. "About the loneliest Christmas I ever faced—guess I'll write to you." Christmas was a season that exalted family ties, but his family had always been small and difficult. Now he was coming up on twenty-three, when many his age were settling down with wives and children; when he stopped to ponder it, he was lonely for it. "The ways of the gods are inscrutable—and do they make and break us just for fun? . . . [The world] is like a great Chinese puzzle—in every little community are to be found the Islands of the Blest, and yet we know not where to look for them. And if we do, our ticket in Life's Lottery bears the wrong number."[9]

While London wished his friends a happy New Year, the tally of his six months since returning to Oakland measured his small sale to *Overland Monthly* and his more substantial sale to *The Black Cat* against the receipt of forty-four rejections. After the first of the year his mood hardly improved when he endured yet another rite of passage: the rejection letter that many new writers receive containing the friendly and well-intended, but still intrinsically insulting, suggestion that he try to make his living at another trade. It came from *Youth's Companion*, and like many young writers, London retreated into a legalistic defense against specific criticisms. To the charge of exceeding the specified length in the pieces submitted, he responded, "Five of my seven chapters were within fifty of three thousand words; one exceeded that number by one hundred and fifty; and another sank to about twenty-six hundred." He wondered if his double-spacing had led them to miscount his wordage. What he, like nearly all in this circumstance, simply could not face was the intimation that he simply wasn't good enough; and what the publishers for their part could not recognize was that being a writer was not just something he wanted to do, increasingly that was who he was, and he could no more excise that from his being than he could amputate a limb. "Some day I shall hit upon my *magnum opus*," he vowed. "And then, if my struggling expression at last finds tongue, I will not have to go to the poor house because my muscles no longer work. And if not—well, so be it."[10]

In Alaska he had physically endured a similar Sisyphean struggle, packing and hiking nearly thirty miles for each mile actually accomplished—only to be confronted at the end by the spirit-killing sight of the Chilkoot Pass. Just as he was undergoing the same frustrating repetitiveness in the quest for publication, the ultimate challenge to his determination confronted him: on January 16 he received the results of his civil service exam. He had sailed through it with the impressive score of 85.38 out of 100. According to his local postman, he had an excellent chance to be appointed an extra man at $45 per month, and then in a few months to be made a regular carrier with a monthly salary of $65. Fate had offered him a cruel bribe. He had just turned twenty-three. Kelly's Army and then Alaska had left him with a marked distaste for walking, but delivering mail was nothing compared to shoveling coal, the wage was more than double, the work was permanent, and he dared not lose sight of his obligation to support his mother and nephew. All he had to do was forswear a literary career and relegate it to the status of hobby. It nearly tore him in half.

Into the breach, unexpectedly, stepped his mother. Whether she recognized that he had been laboring for the family since the age of ten, or whether she saw how desperately he wanted to succeed as a writer, or whether her gambler's hunch told her that if he succeeded, she could at long last recover her social station, as the mother and sponsor of a great writer, that she had spent her life striving for—probably it was a combination of all three—Flora told him he could forgo the opportunity with the post office. She had gained a small pension as the widow of a Civil War veteran, and combined with the income from the piano lessons, they would get by somehow. Taken aback and profoundly grateful, London prevaricated when the offer from the post office came, trying to win the concession that he could pass up the first opening and still be in line for the next one. An offended postmaster ended that possibility with a huff, declaring that the offer was good for once only. In a temper he told the postmaster to forget it, and Jack London's die was cast as an author, or nothing.

With publication of his first stories also came—unbidden but welcome—his first fan letter, praising "To the Man on the Trail." It was from a young man named Cloudesley Johns, the postmaster in the lonely, tumbleweed-studded outpost of Harold, California, near the western edge of the Mojave Desert.

"Dear Sir:—" London responded. "What an encouragement your short note was. . . . It's the first word of cheer I have received (a cheer, far more potent than publisher's checks)." Virtually any cheer would have been worth more than the $7.50 London received for the story, of course, but the surprise and joy that any writer receives with the first fan letter was not lost on him.[11]

Only with further communication did Johns confess his real aim—he wanted advice to help with his own beginning efforts at writing. He sent London a story for his evaluation, and London offered good advice: "Keep yourself wholly out of the story—I noticed a number of 'I's. They jar. Let it be all third person." "Don't permit repetition (it is sometimes allowable, but rarely) . . . in four words, 'waves' appears twice—change to billows, anything else." "Strike out 'of which we can have no conception'—while you cannot elucidate the why or how . . . you clearly do conceive the possibility of such a thing." All was given with the assurance of someone who had been publishing for twenty-three years, not someone who was twenty-three years old.[12]

Their correspondence lengthened and warmed; they met; Johns was a year older than London, intense and handsome, with dark eyes, a cleft chin, a shock of thick black hair, and, on occasion, a luxurious handlebar moustache that could have been an advertisement for a barbershop quartet. Northern California was an oasis for Johns; his own sun-baked town of Harold, at the northern base of the San Gabriel mountains where the Southern Pacific Railroad crossed the Fort Tejon military road, had already seen its heyday a few years before when it boasted as many as five buildings, then declined when the railroad moved the yard for its booster engines to flatter ground a few miles north.[13]

As they became better friends London met Johns's family and took a special shine to his grandmother, Mrs. Rebecca Spring. She had once been in the circle of the great Bostonians of American literature. For London, who had figured out that he was illegitimate and had no family heritage of his own, to hear her personal recollections of Holmes and Emerson and Longfellow was to hear, saga-like, the story of his own tribe. It was a clan into which he had insinuated himself, and to which, by his own daring, he now belonged. His friendship with Johns lasted the rest of his life.

Then there was more encouragement, the sale of a short story to another periodical, a local literary weekly called *The Wave*. Across from the University Club on Sutter Street was the newly rented photographic studio of the German émigré Arnold Genthe. A highly educated classicist, he had come to San Francisco employed as the tutor of a baron's son, took up photography so he could send pictures home to his family, and he gained fame for his naturalistic portraits that were a stark contrast to the high, formal poses that people were used to. After opening the studio in 1898 he became a sensation, photographer to the famous and the glamorous. Early in Genthe's career, a handsome young man entered the studio and handed him a note from John O'Hara Cosgrave, editor of *The Wave*. It read, "Please make a picture of bearer. He has written a rattling good story for *The Wave* and I feel sure he will be heard from in the future." Genthe looked up and saw a visage created for the camera. He "had a poignantly sensitive face," wrote the artist. "His eyes were those of a dreamer, and there was almost a feminine wistfulness about him. Yet at the same time he gave the feeling of a terrific and unconquerable physical force." Genthe was challenged to capture that on film, and his pictures of London are among the most revealing ever taken.[14] It was the beginning of a durable friendship.

While his fiction submissions were finding their mark with increasing frequency, London's ardent political views never strayed far from his heart. As a socialist he was somewhat obligated to be a pacifist as well, and in 1900 he placed an essay titled "The Impossibility of War" in the *Overland Monthly*. In preparing it he did enough homework to quote this general and that war minister, and dutifully recite the technological advances in both artillery and small arms, and the staggering cost of naval competition. It is his conclusions, however, that still strike home and make one wish that the bemedaled martinets who marched their cannon fodder out of the trenches in World War I had taken some heed of it: "Future wars must be long. No more open fields; no more decisive victories; but a succession of sieges fought over and through successive lines of wide-extending fortifications. . . . A condition of deadlock will inevitably result. . . . Since infantry can no longer drive infantry from a fortified position, the artillery [will] come to be greatly relied upon . . . and the side that advances, advances into extermination."[15] From military considerations he segued into the economic and social repercussions of future war: the loss of confidence in securities markets, currency collapse, loss of farm production leading to starvation, and, waiting at the end, revolution. And so it came to pass for the imperial houses of Germany, Russia, and Austria-Hungary.

Jack London's growing bibliography increased his profile among a clique of writers, artists, socialists, and bohemians in San Francisco, collectively known as The Crowd. It was a natural group for London to be drawn to, including his socialist mentor, Frank Strawn-Hamilton, and Jim Whitaker, who had continued London's tutelage in boxing and fencing. It was in The Crowd that London finally began meeting and socializing with people who made for natural allies, not wharf rats for whom he had to buy drinks to blend in, or high school swells he felt pressure to impress. The Crowd quickly assimilated him, and he formed friendships that profoundly influenced him for the rest of his life.

In December 1899, at a lecture by Austin Lewis at the Turk Street Temple, Strawn-Hamilton introduced London to a fetching, slender young brunette who would play a large role in his life in the coming years. Her name was Anna Strunsky; she was almost twenty-one, born in Babinotz, Russia, the fifth of six children in a Jewish family who immigrated to New York and then settled in San Francisco. Her maternal grandfather was a rabbi, her father owned a profitable liquor business, and she lacked only a semester to graduate from Stanford. She was more brilliant than beautiful, but for London at almost twenty-four, to meet a woman who could duel with him intellectually as well as engage him emotionally was a fascinating novelty. Doubtless they had heard of each other before; she was as famous for her outspoken socialism in San Francisco as he was in Oakland, and they both had ambitions to be authors. "We shook hands," Anna remembered, "and remained talking to each other. I had a feeling of wonderful happiness. To me it was as if I was meeting in their youth LaSalle, Karl Marx or Byron, so instantly did I feel that I was in the presence of a historical character."[16]

One of the most prominent members of The Crowd, socially if not artistically, was the poet George Sterling. Seven years older than London, Sterling was tall and impossibly pretty, but not photogenic. Few pictures captured the essence of him, first because of his penchant for exaggerated aesthetic poses, but more important because his was a face, like the marble busts of Alexander the Great, best seen in movement. He was London's height but more athletically built, sloe-eyed looking down a long and aquiline nose, with a lower lip that tended to pout although he smiled easily. He was originally from Sag Harbor, in the eastern part of Long Island. His father had converted to Catholicism when George was seventeen and George converted with him; at Saint Mary's College in Maryland, he considered a life in the priesthood but did not pursue it. He went west to work in an uncle's real estate office, where he met and married Caroline "Carrie" Rand. Imbued with a poet's nature, he was dedicated to beauty in any form, but his writing tended to block up without the stimulus of sharp sensation to release his creativity. It was to this need that those around him ascribed his affinity for saturating tactile experiences—the sting of cold surf, the danger of dizzying cliffs, and amorous physicality. "We all of us did know that George required the stimulus of sex to have a releasing effect on him," wrote one of The Crowd. "We knew, and lived in a kind of terror what it might bring on Carrie . . . for whom we all had the tenderest affection."[17] Considered a "mystical, rum-drinking humanitarian . . . poet of austere exoticism," Sterling wrote without much notice until he was discovered and championed by Ambrose Bierce, "Bitter Bierce," the famously unpleasant old columnist of the San Francisco *Examiner* and minion of William Randolph Hearst.

Despite the paltry $5 he received for "To the Man on the Trail" from *Overland Monthly*, London found a champion in that journal's editor, Ninetta Eames. Following his first story in January, she published "The White Silence" in February, "The Son of the Wolf" in April, and five more through the course of the year. Eames's sponsorship allowed London to focus his writing on the topic he knew best—as when the main character of "Son of the Wolf," Scruff Mackenzie, takes an Indian wife to alleviate the loneliness of the prospecting life—and concentrate his energy on deepening his narrative voice instead of casting about for imaginative ideas. His work and her guidance were vindicated when the *Overland* stories were compiled and published in book form as *The Son of the Wolf* by Houghton-Mifflin, a front-rank publisher, in 1900.

Ninetta Eames invited him to lunches, for which she paid, brought him into her home near Berkeley, and introduced him to her niece and goddaughter, Charmian Kittredge, who had been doing some of the editing on his stories, for which she self-deprecatingly referred to herself as the assistant sub-scissors.

Charmian (a Greek name that she shared with the lady-in-waiting of Cleopatra) was five years older than London, accustomed to culture and nice clothes, and to polished, well-educated friends. Her aunt's literary prominence placed her in The Crowd, but Charmian's affinity for more popular culture led her to prefer its fringes.

Upon meeting London at her aunt's house just as he was leaving an appointment with a copy of Boyd's *Composition* Eames had lent him, she was struck equally by his beauty and his clothes—"shabby bicycle trousers and dark gray woolen shirt. A nondescript tie, soft bicycle shoes and a worn cap." For his part he noticed that she was not shy and not pretty.

"So that's your wonderful Jack London," she sniped when he had gone.

Eames stood her ground. "With genius, clothing doesn't matter."

Her faith in him paid off when *Son of the Wolf* hit the bookstores, and London finally savored the sweet revenge not tasted by every starving artist: window-rattling reviews. From coast ("These stories are realism, without the usual falsity of realism"—*New York Times*), through the interior ("It is to be doubted if Kipling ever wrote a better short story than 'The Son of the Wolf'"—*Kansas City Star*), to coast ("You cannot get away from the fascination of these tales"—San Francisco *Chronicle*) he triumphed. It was all heady praise for a young man who wore "shabby bicycle trousers."

Charmian joined them for lunch soon after at Young's in San Francisco, where she took greater note not just of his long-lashed blue eyes, but that "there was about his feature a chastity, an untried virginity of expression that seemed greatly at odds with . . . his rather dubious career."[18] Like everyone who met him and wrote about him during his youth, she was captured by his openness and his questioning, as though he were looking, she wrote, for something he had never known.

On another visit to the Eames house, while Ninetta was interviewing Jim Whitaker for an article about London, Charmian took him into her den and showed him her books and curios. She learned that he had never learned to dance. He rhapsodized at the mention of Kipling. They shared an affinity for Thomas Hardy; he recommended *Jude the Obscure*, which she had never read, and he borrowed *Tess of the D'Urbervilles* with a promise that he "had a conscience about books" and would take good care of it.

Of all The Crowd, though, it was the alluring Anna Strunsky who most captured London's attention. His attraction to Mabel Applegarth began to fade, and the intellectual sympathy between London and the brilliant young Russian served as the prelude to a powerful physical attraction. It almost reached the pitch of romance. London's longing for a home life had grown into a void, and in desperation, he proposed to Anna. She was a passionate and vital creature, but her life had been strangely sheltered—her response to him was to blush and turn away, really for no more reason than that was what good girls did in novels. London knew how to take a woman, but he had no idea how to court one; he took her hesitation for rejection and let the matter drop, his soul crushed.

London had also been spending time with his former math tutor, Bess Maddern, who was bereaved with the death of Fred Jacobs. He had taken a fever on his way to Cuba and became one of the many casualties of the Spanish-American War that had nothing to do with battle. She was brilliant at mathematics but quickly retreated into irritation when the conversation turned to unknown subjects. London was gregarious; she was a quiet homebody. What they had most in common was a love of bicycling, and during their long trips together they found themselves amiably attracted.

With the matter of his love for Anna in awkward limbo, he decided to marry Bessie with little thought to future happiness. Two romantic disappointments, first with Mabel Applegarth and then with Anna, were enough to convince an impatient young man that mutual passion was too much to hope for in a marriage. Bessie was presentable, her family was reasonably well off, she would make a good mother, and they got on well together. That was enough. He did not love her, and she knew it; she was too heartsick over losing Jacobs to know what her feelings were, but she believed he could come to love her in time. London had made a lunch date with Charmian Kittredge, which he broke with a polite, typewritten note, announcing that rather than lunch, he and Bessie would be married that day—April 7, an auspicious day for new beginnings, as it was also the publication date of *The Son of the Wolf*.

Eames was no shrinking violet herself, a veteran of San Francisco's days of free love and flouting convention, just as was his mother. "Heaven and earth!" she exclaimed. "The boy must be crazy to dream that marrying in cold blood is living life!" The nuptials were exchanged politely, they vacationed on bicycles. Flora London had found some hope for her own future as his literary sponsor, and she was shocked and embittered when the new couple moved in together, not with her, but into a two-story house on East Fifteenth Street. It took only a short while to conceive their first child, a daughter named Joan, born in the house three days after London's twenty-fifth birthday.

During the waning months of 1901 London's good-natured sparring with Anna on the nature of love blossomed into an idea for a book. In this new work, a collection of letters, London would take the voice of Herbert Wace, arguing that marriage should not be based on physical love, which was a chimera that promised a false future. Rather it should be predicated on enduring qualities of respect and companionship, of compatibility as potential parents, and other qualities that were recognized by the mind, not the heart. Anna would take the voice of an older father figure whom they named Dane Kempton, and contend passionately for the opposite view, that romantic heat was the soul and sustenance of a successful marriage.

It was divinely ironic that London proposed the new book while sailing on the *Spray*, a small sailboat he had acquired, with both Bessie and Anna—Bessie, whom he had wed in an amicable but passion-bereft partnership of the very kind he would advocate in the new book, and Anna, to whom he was attracted as though by gravity itself, whom he would have married had she not demurred at the critical moment only because she thought she was supposed to. Being modern and bohemian, they both felt no compunction about discussing the new book within the full hearing of Bessie, ever the companionable sport.

London had now known Anna for two years and had fallen increasingly under her spell: her high small Tatar eyes and hint of a Russian accent, her natural wasp waist never bound by a corset, her incandescent socialist brilliance. The more they framed and edited their letters with an eye toward publication, and the more London contended persuasively for platonic marriage, the more his relationship with Bessie, ironically, crumbled. Unseasonable rains flooded the cellar of their house on Fifteenth Street, and London moved the family into the large and aptly named Villa Capriccioso of his sculptor friend Felix Peano. London adored the eccentric house with its round windows and tiny hidden staircases; Bessie loathed it. The Crowd came to depend upon "Wednesday at Jack's," and London lived for his weekly open house for his friends; Bessie abhorred them. He was full-blooded and highly sexualized; she according to him could barely tolerate mating. "She's devoted to purity," he told George Sterling and Joseph Noel. "Every time I come back after being away from home for a night she won't let me be in the same room with her if she can help it. . . . When I tell her morality is only evidence of low blood pressure, she hates me."[19] There was friction between Bessie and his mother, which Flora cultivated and tried to capitalize on. Somehow London managed to work on *A Daughter of the Snows* for McClure's, another mainstream publisher that began courting his work, while living in Peano's strange villa, and he finished it after a brief move to a large, fashionable house he couldn't afford on Bayo Vista Avenue.[20]

In the heat of completing what they titled *The Kempton-Wace Letters,* London invited Anna to stay with him and Bessie until they finished. "During the first few days of my stay Mrs. London was very cordial and manifested great interest in our work," said Anna a couple of years later, "but, after a stay of five days, I became convinced that, for some reason, Mrs. London had begun to dislike me."[21] In this reminiscence Anna neglected to mention that on one occasion Bessie had returned home unexpectedly to find her and London editing the manuscript with her sitting in his lap. When Anna packed up and left a few days later, Bessie was generous enough to affect regret that she was leaving so soon.

As London's situation became financially as well as emotionally untenable, his friend Sterling, poet and bohemian at heart but a real estate agent in the real world, offered him the rent of a rustic bungalow in the Piedmont Hills overlooking Oakland. Not coincidentally, it neighbored the Sterlings' own home. Redolent of happier rural days when his stepfather was still alive, London pounced on it. "We have a big living room," he wrote first fan Cloudesley Johns,

> We could put the floor space of almost four cottages into this one living room alone. The rest of the house is finished in redwood, too, very comfortable. We have also the cutest, snuggest little cottage on the same ground with us, in which live my mother and my nephew. Chicken houses and yards for 500 chickens. Barn for a dozen horses, big pigeon houses, laundry, creamery, etc., etc. A most famous porch, broad and long and cool, a big clump of magnificent pines, flowers and flowers and flowers galore, five acres of ground.

London expected no intention to ever leave, he said, unless a mob showed up and burned him out.[22] Bessie too approved of the Piedmont bungalow, and their relationship improved to the extent that they conceived a second child toward the end of January, but their widening incompatibility was becoming too great to bridge.

As London and Anna finished *The Kempton-Wace Letters* by correspondence, the salutations of his letters to her graduated from "Dear Anna" at the beginning of 1901, to "Dear, dear Anna" in May, "Dear You" in October, and finally for the first time "Dear, dear you," on January 5, 1902: "You look back on a tumultuous and bankrupt year; and so do I. And for me the New Year begins full of worries, harassments and disappointments. So you? I wonder?"[23]

8 ➳ THE MUCKRAKER

In 1898 Jack London had returned from the Klondike with the resolution to turn himself into a writer. What he discovered was that turning one's life was like turning a large ship: one might put the wheel hard over, but it takes some distance for her to answer the helm. After three fierce years, however, he had done it. His first book had appeared to ecstatic reviews, he was working on his second, *The Kempton-Wace Letters,* with Anna, and had undertaken a third, expanding his Yukon motif into a novel called *A Daughter of the Snows.* He had won the acceptance of the brightest intellectuals in San Francisco, married, and become a father. He was struggling financially, as most writers do, and he bore the literary badge of romantic entanglements, but that he had started up the literary mountain was undeniable. What he needed now was a breakthrough; Ninetta Eames had gotten him noticed, but now he needed a mentor with a larger profile than hers to set him on the national stage.

At first London did not recognize what a godsend, for both his obscurity and his poverty, had arrived at the very close of 1901, a letter from one of the United States' leading publishers, George P. Brett of Macmillan & Co. More than thirty years before, Brett's father, George Edward Brett, had been a London book distributor when he was hired by the company's founder, Alexander Macmillan, to open an American branch of his publishing house. Thereafter the New York address of 63 Bleecker Street became a mecca for leading American authors. Brett brought his son into the business in 1874 as a sales representative when he was only sixteen, and by the time he took over the reins of the American branch upon the senior Brett's death in 1890 there was no phase of the publishing industry he had not mastered. With the American book-buying market having come to rival that of Britain, the younger Brett negotiated a large degree of operating autonomy from the parent company, leaving him free to acquire books by American authors on American topics. An omnivorous and perceptive reader, Brett had followed the serialization of London's Alaska tales, both collections of which, he could not help but notice, came from different publishers. The Alaska stories, he wrote to London, "represent very much the best work of the kind that has been done on this side of the water." If London had any book manuscripts to show, Brett wanted to publish him, now and in the future.

London answered promptly and politely. "I have a novel, but McClure, Phillips & Co. are to publish it. . . . However, I have a series of Klondike short stories under way. Forty thousand words are done, and I have about ten or fifteen more thousand words to do to complete the series, which I call by the general title, *Children of the Frost*." If Brett cared to see them, he would be happy to send them.[1]

The Kempton-Wace Letters was now almost ready to show, as London's Herbert Wace was judged to have lost the debate when his sweetheart rejected his suit and cast him off on his platonic and self-sufficient own. London was doubtless satisfied with this ending, because what he had really been contending for were the principles on which he had married Bessie, and that union had by now degenerated into hell on earth. Anna Strunsky divined as much, later writing that both in their conversations and in the book, he had argued his case for platonic marriage "so passionately as to again make one suspect that he was not as certain of his position as he claimed to be." Early in May, Anna visited the Piedmont bungalow and London told her that his marriage was hopelessly broken and asked her again to marry him. In the oddly voiced third person of her memoir, Anna recalled of her refusal that she told him, "It was one thing to be in love with him when he was free like herself," but now that he had a wife and child, she did not think it possible to finally capture what they once almost had. London, however, pressed his suit, and "with a tumult of joy in her heart . . . she promised to marry him."[2] Within a couple of weeks she changed her mind, however, explaining that she did not love him enough to begin married life by crushing the marriage of another woman. London was still reveling in having finally wrung it from her that she loved him, and he would not take this new tone as a final refusal. For the moment he resumed his role as affectionate friend and co-author in polishing *The Kempton-Wace Letters*.

In truth he dared not give up on Anna, because not only was his marriage broken beyond repair, but he was afraid that his career was beginning to founder as well. Brett did ask to see the collection of stories comprising *Children of the Frost*, but although working furiously London was $3,000 in debt, and he had mined his literary Klondike bare of ore with his completion of *A Daughter of the Snows* and these new stories for Macmillan. He had been correcting the novel's proofs and was heartsick to discover that even to his own eye it read like hackwork, by turns flat and melodramatic. He had gotten ahead of himself. He had sold himself as a novelist and discovered, too late, that the forces that pull a novel are vastly larger and more complex than those for a successful short story. He wasn't up to it yet. "It is terrible to doctor sick things," he wrote to Anna. "Every batch seems the worst till the next batch comes along."[3] McClure Phillips & Co. did not find the manuscript very compelling either, but they were able to sell it to Lippincott's for more than they had paid for it, and as poor as London judged the work, he reaped $165 for the difference.

What he needed was a new turn entirely, and this salvation arrived about July 16 when he received a telegram from the American Press Association, inquiring into his interest in traveling to South Africa to interview military officers who had fought in the Boer War, which had just ended.[4] His recent *Overland Monthly* piece on "The Impossibility of War" had cited various engagements from that conflict, and he was a good candidate for the job. It was an offer that answered many needs, escaping Bessie not least among them; he wired his acceptance immediately, packed that night, and boarded a train for New York the next day. Cameron King, a comrade and mutual friend of Anna's (and, unknown to London, a competing suitor), saw him to the station.

"The Desert, Nevada," he wrote Anna the next day. "Dear, dear You:—Just a line to let you know that all is well, that I am exceedingly warm, that the train is wobbling, and that I am thinking of you." The sentiment may have been true as of that moment, but there was a second reason the train had been rocking: London had suddenly found a powerful release for his pent-up frustration with Bessie. As he later wrote to a confidante, "You remember when I started for South Africa. In my car was a woman traveling with a maid and a child. We came together on the jump, at the very start, and had each other clear to Chicago. It was sexual passion, clear and simple. . . . There was no glamour of the mind, not even an overwhelming intoxication of the senses. Nothing remained when our three days and nights were over."[5] The recipient of this naked honesty, intended as a warning of the ease with which the sexual beast within him could be set free, was Charmian Kittredge, the very modern niece of *Overland Monthly*'s Ninetta Eames.

On arriving in New York, London checked in at the American Press Association and was crestfallen to learn that his assignment had been canceled because the generals who were to have been his interview subjects had already dispersed from the war zone. With his passage to England already purchased, however, he began casting about for another project. His ship, the White Star liner R.M.S. *Majestic*, did not sail for another week, and while staying at the press association he received a forwarded letter from John Spargo, who was on the editorial board of a socialist monthly called *The Comrade*. Spargo solicited an article on how London had become a socialist, to which he amiably agreed, but advised that he could not tend to it until he returned from abroad several months hence. Meanwhile, that new English project had begun to form in his mind. "I may do some writing of the London slums," he added, "possibly a book, though as yet everything is vague & my main idea is to get a vacation."[6]

As this new thought developed, he tried it out on his new benefactor, George Brett at Macmillan, where the seed fell on ground more fertile than he knew. Macmillan had been founded by adherents of "Christian Socialism" and had published reformist books since its inception; Brett himself had begun acquiring for Macmillan the works of Jacob Riis, the pathblazing Danish-American social reformer, wooing him away from his previous publishers Scribner's Sons and Century. Riis's 1890 exposé of the New York slums had spurred that city's police commissioner, Theodore Roosevelt, to improve conditions. Brett had published Riis's autobiography the year before and was just bringing out *The Battle of the Slum,* to which London's examination of the homeless paupers in England would likely make an effective companion. Encouraged, London wrapped up his affairs at the American Press Association and enjoyed a brief reunion with his first fan and fast friend, Cloudesley Johns. He had ridden the rails to New York to sample life there as a starving artist, which was proving more precarious than he had anticipated; London lent him $10 and headed for the pier.

He had traveled aboard steamships before—as a coal stoker aboard the *Umatilla* after the debacle with Kelly's Army, and on *City of Topeka* en route to Alaska—but they could not have prepared him for the sight of the R.M.S. *Majestic.* She was the pride of the White Star Line and one-time holder of the Blue Riband, the trophy for setting a speed record in crossing the Atlantic, a feat that she accomplished in five days and eighteen hours. The former oyster pirate and sealer regarded her gleaming white honeycomb of superstructure rising above the beetling black hull, stretching nearly six hundred feet long beneath two towering yellow and black funnels. She was powered by two gigantic engines that swept her 1,500 passengers through the water at over twenty knots. London the socialist, however, saw something much more. By the turn of the century the great Atlantic liners, each new one larger and faster than the last, had become indelible symbols of Western industrial capitalism, but they also embodied its hypocrisy. Their reputations were made by hosting the vacationing wealthy in opulent salons and staterooms, but their operating expenses were paid with deep black bellies full of steerage-paying immigrants headed to the New World—a few to find opportunity, and the rest to be chuffed like human coal into the boilers of capitalist exploitation, as London himself so very nearly had been.

On his first full day at sea, London wrote a letter to Anna Strunsky, "Dear You:—I meet the men of the world . . . in Atlantic liner smoking rooms, and, truth to say, I am made more hopeful for the Cause by their total ignorance and non-understanding of the forces at work. They are blissfully ignorant of the coming upheaval, while they have grown bitterer and bitterer towards the workers. You see, the growing power of the workers is hurting them and making them bitter while it does not open their eyes." With some of his temper vented, the rest of the note was a love letter: "my love, my dove . . . there are many To-morrows, and we will make them all To-days." Anna was to give a lecture that day at Pacific Grove. "Possibly you are speaking at this present moment. Well, good luck be with you, comrade. I know you will do well."[7]

❧ ❧ ❧

He went to England armed, his egalitarianism girded with a copy of George Haw's 1900 *The Plaint of Overcrowded London*, an exegesis of the conditions endured by the city's poor. After landing at Liverpool and reaching London, he first checked in with the Social Democratic Federation, a contact that Anna had arranged for him, and the group loaded him down with papers and pamphlets full of facts and figures to work into his book. He rented a room at 89 Dempsey Street, Stepney, in the East End—the poverty-ridden Whitechapel area of Jack the Ripper infamy. This room became his refuge, a place where he could get dry and warm, and write up what he observed.

For ten shillings—about $2.50—he purchased a suite of used clothes in which he could blend in with his lower-class subjects, for whom he affected to be a stranded American sailor down on his luck. This was a role that he adopted easily; not only was he himself a sailor, knowing the vocabulary and able to tell tales of Japan and the Bering Sea, but beached American seamen were hardly an uncommon sight in London. British shipowners would hire British crews for the "duration of the voyage," which meant that as the vessel tramped cargo from Dakar to Buenos Aires and so on around the world, they did not get paid until they returned to their home port, which might not be for two years or more. Shortly before returning, officers would make a point of treating them so badly that some of them would jump ship in America, saving the owners a bundle while needing only to pay a spot wage to American sailors to round out the crew and bring the vessel home—thus stranding the American sailors in England. It was a perfectly believable pose for London, to say nothing of a vivid indictment of the way unregulated capitalism was practiced.

"Am settled down and hard at work," he wrote Anna on August 16. He had thought he was steeled against whatever he might find, but what he discovered were scenes straight out of darkest Dickens. "The whole thing," he wrote, "all the conditions of life, the intensity of it, everything is overwhelming. I never conceived such a mass of misery in the world before."[8] He saw poor women by the score fingering through butchers' scraps for fat and gristle; he saw appalling tenement rooms whose only heat in winter was a single gas jet governed by a heavily locked coin meter. In such rooms he was demoralized by the sight of tightly wrapped corpses of children and toddlers, stored on a shelf until there was money saved for a service. He met the streetwise who, when they could manage a penny for breakfast, bought a cup of tea in some tatty coffeehouse, which they drank so slowly that when no one was looking they could devour what others left on their plates. ("It's surprising, what some people leave," one assured him.) He saw urchins reaching up to their armpits into mounds of rotten fruit discarded by markets. As he worked he annotated his copy of George Haw, blocked off paragraphs whose assertions he could verify, and penciled its margins with supporting examples of the horrors he witnessed that passed for everyday life, and data on the mortality rate of the poor.[9]

In the sharpest conceivable contrast to the life into which he had immersed himself, the city—indeed the whole empire—was gearing up for the coronation of King Edward VII. After the long, dour widowhood of his mother, Queen Victoria, it would be the first crowning of a monarch in six decades. The capital burgeoned with royal relations of the sixty-year-old "Uncle of Europe," commemorative memorabilia were on sale everywhere, the main thoroughfares and even by-lanes were elaborately decorated, the atmosphere electric.

The anticipated celebration also had an ugly underbelly, however, and it was one upon which Jack London intended to cast a harsh spotlight: the suppressed muttering of discontent. While part of the new king's inheritance was the imperial throne of India, a twelve-year-old boy named Keshava, long before he became celebrated as the Indian nationalist Dr. Rashtra Rishi Hedgewar, wrote, "It is an utter shame to partake in the . . . coronation of a king who has enslaved our Bharatmata."[10] Similarly, James Connolly, the socialist and Irish nationalist, wrote a vituperative column referring to the coronation as "this saturnalia of tyranny," an event to which socialists in their minds' eyes also "hasten thither in order to offer to King Edward, in the name of ourselves and our class, the only homage we owe him—OUR HATRED." Connolly perceived that the ceremony was not only about tradition and values, it was about subterfuge. The coronation was "not merely . . . a huge parade of pomp and magnificence, cloaking the festering sores of that slave society on which it is built—but [it has] also become an elaborately contrived and astutely worked piece of propaganda, designed to captivate the imagination of the unthinking multitude," who would thus be led to discredit socialists who were working to alleviate the conditions of the lowest class.

The Social Democratic Federation would undoubtedly have given London a copy of the Connolly piece, for it was written to spoil the original date of the coronation, June 26. (The ceremony had had to be postponed because of the king's sudden appendicitis on June 24, and was re-set for August 9.) Standing with the throng in a steady rain in Trafalgar Square while awaiting the procession, London and his pauper fellows caught no more than a glimpse of the golden coach as it creaked and rumbled by, a glimpse of the king within, his fat gray brow weighted with several pounds of jewels in the form of the Imperial State Crown. Beside him was Queen Alexandra, by all accounts one of the most beautiful women in the world, her swan's neck barely accommodating the high choker of massed diamonds almost as brilliant as the crown matrimonial designed especially for her.

London looked around at the toothless and the bedless, those who had every reason to despise this royal symbol of their oppression, and to his horror they threw their grimy caps into the air and lustily cheered their new monarch. This was not what he had come to England to see, and it did not fit the conclusions he had already drawn for *The People of the Abyss.* London acidly quoted the song of the day, once in standard English and again a few pages later, for literary effect, in the Cockney dialect of his companions:

Oh, on Coronation Day, on Coronation Day,
We'll have a spree, a jubilee, and shout, Hip, hip, hooray,

> *For we'll all be very merry, drinking whisky, wine and sherry.*
> *We'll all be merry on Coronation Day.*[11]

There was, however, one very practical reason to be merry, which London chose not to write about, and that was that some 450,000 people were being fed in street banquets. (Ironically, this was the same number estimated to be homeless in the East End.) While the royal party was fêted on trout with caviar and hollandaise sauce, and Jambon d'Espagne à la Basque, the humble masses were fed such stout yeomen's fare as beef and onions stewed in beer.[12] Still, it was food, and better food than they were used to, but to describe feasting in the streets would not have served the purpose of *The People of the Abyss*.

That London omitted such an extenuating circumstance did not alter the essential truths of his book, but neither can it be claimed that he went to Britain as an objective journalist. As a literary leader at the cutting edge of the "muckraking" age, he went to expose and decry those inhuman conditions he already knew existed, not to determine whether they existed. To that end, London was keenly aware of the metaphorical power of the coronation, so much so that although he spent ten chapters of *The People of the Abyss* leading up to it, the actual event took place only three days after he arrived in England.[13]

Later in the week, just like the seasonal migrant workers in America, he traveled down to Kent to pick hops, only to discover that this annual ritual was thrown out of kilter by bad weather and a late harvest. "At Dover," lamented one newspaper, "the number of vagrants in the workhouse is treble the number there last year at this time." No sooner did the hops ripen than the crop was devastated by hailstorms, stripping the flowers from the poles and pounding them into the dirt, leaving the pickers with double or more the amount of labor to earn their shilling for seven bushels.

As little as London had seen of England to cheer him, the weather was equally depressing. "Been in England 11 days," London wrote sardonically to Cloudesley Johns, "& it has rained every day. Small wonder the Anglo-Saxon is such a colonizer."[14] Another few days of sampling London homeless life and he sat to write George and Carrie Sterling: "How often I think of you, over there on the other side of the world! I have heard of God's Country, but this country is the country God has forgotten that he forgot.... Actually, I have seen things, & looked the second time in order to convince myself that it was really so." The poor stooped to pick rotten apple cores out of the gutter and bite into them; the old and the sick who used to work still wanted to work, but as no one would hire them they walked and wasted until they died quietly. Many sought to hasten the day, and threw themselves into the Thames or closed themselves in a room with a gas jet; those who failed were hauled into court and remanded to jail, for attempting suicide was a crime. London attended court sessions and heard a magistrate upbraid one poor wretch for being rescued.

On August 21 he wrote Anna, "Dear, dear You:—Have not received a letter from you since I arrived in England—all of two weeks now, plus voyage of eight days. On receiving this, again address mail in care of American Press Association.... Have book 1/5 written & typewritten.... Am rushing, for I am made sick by this human hell-hole called London Town. I find it almost impossible to believe that some of the horrible things I have seen are really so."

He then plunged back into what he now called the Abyss—a term originally applied to the East End by the British socialist and Fabian, H. G. Wells. Saturday he stayed out all night with the homeless ones in the rain, walking the streets. One of the few good things that might happen while walking all night was to encounter a do-gooder from the Salvation Army, some of whose volunteers walked abroad at night to distribute breakfast tickets, redeemable Sunday morning at the Salvation Army barracks near the Surrey Theater—which for many meant a walk that took up most of the rest of the night. They started gathering outside the door before dawn; those who could find stoops to sit on were soon fast asleep, until a policeman came by and rousted them out. A city ordinance prohibited them from sleeping in the parks or in public at night, although the police looked the other way during the day as long as they stayed out of sight. "But the policeman passed on," London wrote, "and back we clustered, like flies around a honey jar."

The door to the barracks opened at seven-thirty and the men were admitted in stages, those with tickets first and those without at nine, and they were herded into a courtyard, where they were kept standing a further two hours, wedged in so tightly that some fell asleep standing up. London estimated there were seven hundred, their massed body odor so foul that he nearly retched, and when they were finally allowed to sit they were presented not with food, but with hymns and a sermon. This he found a waste of effort, not just because the famished men cared more at that moment about grub than salvation, but because they were already "too inured to hell on earth to be frightened by hell to come." The freshest of them had been there four hours, and most much longer, when each man was given a paper packet with his breakfast: two slices of bread, a wedge of cheese, a mug of "water bewitched" (thin, weak beer or punch), and a small plug of what might have been raisin bread or fruitcake. The portions were sufficient only to exacerbate their existing hunger. After eating, London caused a minor disturbance by asking to leave, unaware that entering the compound had committed him to hear the entire service. "The idea! The idea!" huffed an orderly. It was then nearly noon, and London explained that he needed the breakfast to strengthen him to look for work, which surely was the most important thing.

He was referred up the scandalized chain of command. "Oh, you 'ave business, eh?" grandly mocked a Salvation Army adjutant. "It's a man of business you are, eh? Then wot did you come 'ere for?" He was finally taken to see the major, who rather than letting word get around and give other mendicants any ideas, let him leave quietly. On this stint he was out thirty-six hours either working or looking for work or for food before returning to his room at 89 Dempsey Street. He bathed, shaved, and slept fifteen hours straight before rising to write down the images still in his mind.

By the end of the day he had written, typed, and revised 4,000 words of the new book. At one o'clock in the morning he did open a letter from Anna, who had almost become the muse for whom he wrote—to read a withering broadside rejecting his proposal of marriage and telling him to leave off further expectation of intimacy between them. In all of Jack London's meticulously preserved correspondence, this letter is missing, surely destroyed in his distress and anger. Anna later recalled of it that she had tried to communicate her cool disinterest, but then "in the middle of a page came her words like a torrent of tears."[15]

Judging from the fractured pain of London's reply, Anna had learned that Bessie was pregnant again, after he had given her to believe that relations between them were over. "Please remember that I am worn out & exhausted," he replied to her, "and that my nerves are blunted with what I have seen and the suffering it has cost me." Therefore, he warned her, his reply might seem colder than it would if he were in a calmer state of mind. But after this little prevarication, he lit into her: "You are ever quick to harshness. You are one of the cruelest women I have ever know[n]." He recounted the arithmetic of Bessie's conceiving a child as having taken place before the time when he told Anna the marriage was over: London had declared his love for Anna and asked her to marry him in early May. Becky London had been conceived in late January and was born October 20. "Shall I tell you what I have been guilty of? Not of lying, but of keeping my word." The rest of the long letter makes little sense without hers to compare, but his shock and pain are still palpable.[16]

Back in California Anna read his reply, and years later related to her daughter that the force with which his pen had bit into the paper made her fear that he might harm himself.[17] Her remorse was swift, but his knowledge of this would have to await several arrivals of the mail boats. Thinking his flame extinguished, London determined to try to save his marriage, and wrote an endearing if insincere letter to Bessie, enclosing a photograph of him in his stranded-sailor guise to share with baby Joan. And though his muse had rejected him, the work still had to be completed and he waded back into the Abyss.

Jack London's complaint with the British system of aid to the poor was not just that it was appallingly bad. His greater complaint was that it was the capitalist labor market itself that had sidelined workers into idleness and then made no provision to keep them alive with anything like dignity. London did acknowledge that some of the city's well-to-do harbored a soft spot for the needy, but as often as not their acts of charity were worse than useless. He cited the case of a woman whose job was the manufacture of artificial violets, for which she was paid three farthings per gross—about one and a half cents for every 144 flowers. For her daily wage of nine pence, less than twenty cents, she had to fold and twist 1,726 of them.

For the elevation and recreation of her and those like her, one group of concerned citizens mounted an exhibition of Japanese art prints, hoping, according to their mission statement, to inspire them with yearnings for the beautiful, the true, and the good. "When the people who try to help," wrote London, "cease their playing and dabbling with day nurseries and Japanese art exhibits, and go back & learn . . . the sociology of Christ, they will be in better shape to buckle down to the work they ought to be doing in the world. . . . They won't cram yearnings for the Beautiful & True & Good down the throat of a woman making violets for three farthings a gross, but they will make somebody get off her back."

That was a telling choice of words: *the sociology of Christ*—not the gospel or the passion. With his religion as with his socialism, London believed in the principles but would not ally himself with the dogmas of any particular sect. What he looked to was the effect of the doctrines, and in the Bible it was unmistakable to him that the life of Christ was about sociology, about comforting the downtrodden and stinging the complacent, about the practice of justice and mercy in everyday lives. To him, Jesus's pronouncements on the treatment of the poor were the most unambiguous in the book.

He made his way to Whitechapel Workhouse, whose grim brick edifice had loomed over Charles Street (now Vallance Road), Spitalfields, for sixty years. Because London was applying for aid as a transient pauper and not for residency, he was shown on around the corner to the Casual Ward on Thomas Street (now Lomas Street).[18] The workhouses whose horrors Dickens made famous had been around since late in the reign of Elizabeth I but had been systematized and regulated only since an amendment to the Poor Law was passed in 1832. Like most aid to the poor that is conceived by deeply conservative and unsympathetic governments, actually aiding the poor was second in importance after ensuring that that aid was so odious and dehumanizing that almost no one would actually resort to it. The conditions London found in 1902 would have been even worse, had it not been for earlier crusades led by the nation's leading medical journal, the *Lancet*, and a famously meddlesome nurse named Florence Nightingale.

London had tried twice before to gain admittance to Whitechapel Workhouse, without success, as it was full. Most workhouses could accommodate between 150 and 300 indigents; Whitechapel was one of the largest in the country, with a capacity of 600.[19] The door was customarily opened at six in the evening, and though he joined the line at three, he was number twenty, and they were admitting only twenty-two on that night. A dozen more were in line after him, hoping against hope that some in front of them would leave. London had a chance to talk to the first in line, a laborer called Ginger (British slang for a redhead) who had been employed by a fishmonger until he was given too heavy a crate to carry and herniated his back. One charity hospital let him rest for four hours, rubbed Vaseline on his back, and packed him off. He was treated similarly at a second one. "But the point is," London wrote indignantly, "the employer did nothing, positively nothing, for the man injured in his employment." Now Ginger's effective working life was over, and his only future was the workhouse, or starvation on the street.

At least getting food in the workhouse lacked the prayers and hymns of the Salvation Army. Immediately on being enrolled he received what he at first thought was a brick but proved to be a small loaf of bread. Ushered farther on down into a cellar, he also received three-quarters of a pint of corn gruel in which to dip it. Salt was scattered on the tables for the men to dredge their bread through. At seven the men were stripped and taken to bathe, two tubs of water for twenty-two of them (although this was against health regulations in most cities). The previous user handed his towel to London, who saw as the man turned away that his back was pocked with open sores. London bathed and dried minimally, and all were issued blankets and workhouse uniforms before trooping back upstairs to sleep.

In the morning he took a photograph of the dormitory where homeless people slept—a high corridor with windows down both sides, both walls lined with what appear to be ballet barres coiled with rolls of canvas, one after the other. Down the center of the corridor two more iron railings ran parallel, with a narrow passage between them. At night the canvas beds were unrolled from the outer rails and fastened to the inner ones, creating hammocks. The strips of canvas were eighteen inches wide and nearly touched each other, so that when one man shifted his position during the night it created a ripple of disturbance to the end of the hall. Such disturbances were incessant because the hammocks did not hang level, but from high on the wall to low at the aisle, so that one slid down as he slept. At the lowest point they were about eight inches off the floor; after finally drifting off to sleep, London awoke at the six a.m. breakfast call to find a rat on his chest.

Of the work actually done in a workhouse, had it been in a prison it would have gone under the heading of "hard labor." Breaking granite into rubble was a principal occupation for the men, or else "picking oakum," unraveling the fibers of scrapped hemp rope, which were sold to manufacturers to mix with pitch and used for caulking wooden boats. Needlework was a common task of poor women, and since the workhouses were all the country had in the way of shelter for elderly indigents, surviving photographs depict vast halls of white-capped old women bent over their toil. The wage they received, even by the standards of the Abyss, was so small that London overheard one younger woman urging another to sneak away with her to life as a streetwalker rather than this. He asked another woman on the outside if she thought she might end up in a workhouse. "Gawd blimey if I do," she spat out. "There's no 'ope for me, I know, but I'll die on the streets. No work'ouse for me, thank you, no indeed!"

The work London drew was considered light duty: cleaning the sick wards in the workhouse hospital across Thomas Street. Reforms enacted in 1867 had mandated removal of regular inmates into separate buildings so they would not be disturbed by the screams from the sick and imbecile wards. London and several others were convoyed to the hospital to scrub floors and empty garbage cans of fouled bedding and bandages. "Don't touch it, mate," one of the regulars advised him. "Nurse says it's deadly."

Enrollment in a casual ward obligated one to stay two nights and a day, but London bolted, although leaving without permission was punishable by up to two weeks in jail. He continued undercover for the next four weeks, submerging himself in the East End for days at a time before retreating to his room to bathe and write. Still affecting his stranded-sailor guise, he nearly betrayed himself once by paying for a meal with a gold sovereign, prompting close questioning by the "Cockney Amazon" proprietress as to where he had obtained such an extravagant fortune—the coin's denomination was one pound sterling.

In his writing London made heavy use of the statistical data provided him by the Social Democratic Federation, finding that the raw numbers of the government's own studies concerning the economy, population, food portions, disease, and mortality were in and of themselves every bit as eloquent—and damning—as the anecdotal instances he could augment them with. And during this month his correspondence settled back to a normal tone with Anna Strunsky. "What rot this long-distance correspondence is!" he wrote her on September 28. "About the time you are receiving harsh letters from me, I am receiving the kindest letters from you." Of her explosion over Bessie's pregnancy and his explosion in return, he explained, "You have never had the advantage of seeing a prizefighter knocked out . . . but should you have seen such a man, panting, exhausted, dazed, bewildered, terrific blows landing upon him from above, below, and everyside—then you would understand my condition when I received that frightful letter from you. My arms flew about madly, blindly, that is all. And I am sorry. I should have taken the knock-out clean & not put up any defense."[20]

With *The People of the Abyss* completed, London's long-cherished goal of a continental vacation found itself competing with an overwhelming desire to return home. He limited his Grand Tour to three weeks in France, Germany, and Italy. Delayed by a train wreck in La Spezia, he fell in with a Frenchman who offered to take him sailing in the harbor. They visited an Italian warship and became friendly with the boatswain, who obtained shore leave and showed them the town. "Both he and the Frenchman were revolutionists," he wrote later. "Birds of a feather, you know—and by three in the morning there were a dozen of us, singing the Marsellaize (spl?) and clashing with the police."[21]

After this adventure it was high time to return, and London touched foot on the dock in New York on November 4, looking more like one of his East

End subjects than America's premier ascendant author. "He wore a wrinkled sack coat," recalled a friend who met him at the pier, "the pockets of which bulged with papers and letters. His trousers bagged at the knees. He was minus a vest, and his outing shirt was far from immaculate. A leather belt around his waist took the place of suspenders. On his head he wore a dinky little cap."

One of his first stops was to see George Brett at Macmillan and ask the loan of $150 to get home and back to work. As soon as he returned to California in mid-November London was back in harness, filing a sycophantic puff piece on laying the cornerstone of the Hearst Memorial Mining Building for the San Francisco *Examiner*, which not coincidentally Hearst also owned. Most writers venture cautiously into a career by keeping the day job, but London had committed himself irrevocably to the life of an artist, having concluded that not to do so would inflict catastrophic psychological damage upon himself. He had lived all the incarnations of the Work Beast that he intended to. As he approached his twenty-seventh birthday, with multiple households dependent on his efforts, he must write whatever he could sell, and he knew it. But in Brett and Macmillan he saw the opportunity for relief from drudgery such as praising Hearst, a chance for a supportive publisher with whom he could build a relationship and a history. After careful drafting and revising, London typed out a risky nine-page letter to Brett. "Now, concerning myself and the work I wish to do, I should like to have a good talk with you. The hurry and bustle is over with . . . and I think I can say what I wish to say somewhat more coherently than I could when I was rushing through New York.

"In the four months I have been away, my stock of articles and stories has been disposed of to the magazines; so I return home without these assets, without income, and with nothing before me but to sit down and write up another stock. . . . Of course, this means the work of months." Brett, he noted, had been kind enough to take an interest in his career and wanted to consider his future books, and London wanted to write books. However, "the returns from a book, from the moment of beginning the first chapter, do not arrive for a year or two, but the tradesmen's bills arrive the first of each month. . . . I have no income save what my pen brings me in the magazine and newspaper field. . . . We live moderately. One hundred and fifty dollars per month runs us, though we are seven, and oft-times nine when my old nurse and her husband depend upon us. Now, if I am sure of this one hundred and fifty dollars per month, I can devote myself to larger and ambitious work." London described six books that he had in mind, including *The Kempton-Wace Letters* and *The People of the Abyss*, and asked Brett for an advance-stipend of $150 per month for a year to see him through the whole program of six titles.

"Once I am in a position," he concluded, "where I do not have to depend upon each day's work to keep the pot boiling the next day, where I do not have to dissipate my energy on all kinds of hack, where I can slowly and deliberately ponder and shape the best that is in me, then, at that time, I am confident that I shall do big work."[22]

Brett's artful angling had landed the most promising writer in the country, and he telegraphed his acceptance to London immediately to ease the young author's mind before sending a longer letter with the contract. That document contained the important revision that London take two years to produce the six volumes. "I hope," wrote Brett, "that your work from this time on will show the marks of advancement which I found so strong in your earlier books. But which is not so marked in the last volume or so, these showing signs of haste. There is no real place in the world of literature for anything but the best a man can do."

It was an observation with which London had no trouble agreeing; he had concluded that *A Daughter of the Snows* was hopeless even as he corrected its proofs—an estimation that time has done nothing to alter. To be fair, *Daughter* was a first novel. Ninety-nine writers in a hundred enjoy the blessing that their first novels never see light of day. Especially when conceived with "literary" pretensions, they are inevitably clumsy and didactic, with the characters acting as megaphones for their creator's philosophy—all of which could be truly said of London's first effort. By the standards of the day it was publishable—Lippincott's had found it so—but judged by what people came to expect of Jack London, it was at best a student effort. London had mastered the language, but not the art. As London defended himself to Brett, however, he had written the novel more than two years previous, and the juvenile stories in Century Co.'s *The Cruise of the Dazzler* dated from even earlier. London had no control over when they would be published, and that both volumes appeared at the same time Brett published *Children of the Frost* was just bad luck all around, and "gave rise to a feeling that I had become unduly prolific and was turning out regular machine stuff." With the financial security now afforded him, London was certain he could perform up to Brett's expectations.

Brett was impressed with *The People of the Abyss*, but unknown to London he sent both it and *The Kempton-Wace Letters* to an outside reader, English professor G. R. Carpenter at Columbia University, for evaluation. Carpenter recommended turning down both books, the latter for being overwrought and not believable, and the former for being brutish and distasteful—which was to say, modern; this represented the usual reaction of polite pedants to the arrival of American naturalism. Brett, however, had invested too much effort in London to cut him loose so soon. Shrewd publisher that he was, he followed his own instinct and accepted both books for publication, but with a few suggestions for *The People of the Abyss*: that London be more specific on the health hazard of white lead production (one of many lethal occupations whose deaths and disability he described in the book), that he make a firmer connection between poverty and crime, and that he end the book on a note more positive than the relentlessly depressing narrative of the whole. Finally, doubtless in agreement with Dr. Carpenter's observation that this was "scarcely the thing" for Macmillan's English division to publish, Brett suggested that the author mute any direct criticism of the new king.

"I think your idea is excellent," London answered concerning a more hopeful last chapter, and promised to communicate further on the other suggestions.[23] He must have approved them as well, for the finished book contains only the brief glimpse of Edward VII that London himself had, his crown described as "flashing" within the coach although it was pouring down rain. It also contains a bloodcurdling description of the symptoms of lead poisoning that inevitably befell workers who ground carbonated lead for paint, including the case of one young woman who was fired for missing work once she fell ill.

She obtained a position at a second company, where she worked until she dropped dead at her station. (Meaningful health regulations were not enforced in the white lead industry until 1929.) London's solution to providing a more hopeful last chapter was ingenious, arguing not kindness or morality or even justice, but efficiency. Recapitulating arguments he had made in his 1900 *Cosmopolitan* essay, "What Communities Lose by Competition," he introduced a comparison between society in England and society as practiced among the Inuit of the Yukon delta. The former society enjoyed an average per capita wealth of some £350, the latter only about £2, yet the Inuit prospered or suffered as a community. In England, even in times of the greatest plenty, there was a large segment of the population who never had adequate food or clothing or shelter or fuel. That, he alleged, was inefficient. "If this is the best that civilization can do for the human then give us howling and naked savagery. Far better to be a people of the wilderness and desert, of the cave and squatting place than to be a people of the machine and the Abyss."[24]

The People of the Abyss was a success both in the marketplace, where it sold a solid 20,000 copies, and among critics. According to the Boston *Herald*, the book was "an eloquent arraignment of civilization, a book which stirs the blood, takes away the appetite, and opens the door to socialism." London by now subscribed to an author's clipping service, and the reviews he assembled in his scrapbook were salve to his socialist soul. His effort was similarly endorsed by the *Cavalier:* "There are others whom cold and lifeless statistics are powerless to stir . . . who will be moved by the new and living meaning Jack London has given those statistics. These will not be alarmed by the conclusion of timid readers—'such books will make socialists of everybody.'"[25]

When *The People of the Abyss* was released in Britain, however, the reaction was largely hostile, although civilly expressed, drawing upon that inexhaustible national store of reserved disdain. What they could not declaim as falsehood, they faulted for style. "He has written of the East End of London as he wrote of the Klondike," sniffed the *London Daily News*, "with the same tortured phrase, vehemence of denunciation, splashes of colour, and ferocity of epithet. He has studied it 'earnestly and dispassionately'—in two months! It is all very pleasant, very American, and very young."[26]

"If I were God one hour," London retorted, "I'd blot out all London and its 6,000,000 people, as Sodom and Gomorrah were blotted out, and look upon my work and call it good."[27]

A copy of the book came into the possession of George Wharton James, a prolific California writer who had begun developing a friendship with London. The English-born James had gained a reputation as an admirer and photographer of American Indians, and he wrote lovingly of them and of California natural history. He was London's senior by eighteen years but still a physical specimen, as London wrote approvingly of him as a "gorgeous, splendid man." London inscribed the copy of *The People of the Abyss* to James, "God's still in his heaven, but all's not well with the world. Read here some of the reasons of my socialism, and some of my socialism. Walk with me here, among the creatures damned by men and then wonder not that I sign myself, Yours for the Revolution, Jack London."[28] Indeed, as a document of manifesto and the reasons for manifesto, the book lost none of its visceral impact over the next century. Even allowing for the author's predisposition toward the subject and his artful sequencing of events, *The People of the Abyss* was a milestone both in social reform writing and in its naturalistic treatment—in short, muckraking.

And now, what to do next? His literary barrel was empty, but when he had written his brave proposal for a multi-book contract to Brett in November, the first concern London expressed to him was his desire to put the Alaska motif to rest. "In the first place, I want to get away from the Klondike. I have served my apprenticeship at writing in that field, and I feel that I am better fitted now to attempt a larger and more generally interesting field."[29] One ghost of his Alaska memories, however, had continued to haunt him: during his stay in Dawson City, he had pitched his tent next to the cabin of Louis and Marshall Bond. London adored animals, and he had fallen in love with their enormous dog, Jack. He also felt badly for the way he had treated a dog in his earlier short story "Diable—A Dog." (The title was changed to "Bâtard" when it was collated into *The Faith of Men*.)

For a last visitation to the North, he began a new story, about a loving California family pet named Buck, kidnapped, mistreated, and mischanced into forced survival in the Alaska wilderness. He intended it as a 4,000-word short story, but for the first time in his life, a muse seized his hand—no struggle for technique or searching for the right word, as for the first time the artist shaped characters and events swiftly and with the confidence of his craft. It is a signal breakthrough for every author when a story writes itself for the first time, and he arose, shaken, not with a short piece but with a novel. He settled on the title *The Call of the Wild.*

9 ⁂ THE WAR CORRESPONDENT

After his scarifying adventure investigating *The People of the Abyss*, London did not neglect his previous commitment to John Spargo of *The Comrade* to prepare a statement on how he had become a socialist. England had sharpened his sensibilities, he wrote, but his conversion had happened many years before, on the road first with Kelly's Army and then tramping on his own.

> I had good health and hard muscles. . . . I loved life in the open, and I toiled in the open, at the hardest kinds of work. Learning no trade, but drifting along from job to job, I looked on the world and called it good, every bit of it. . . . I was healthy and strong, bothered with neither aches nor weaknesses.
>
> And because of all this, exulting in my young life, able to hold my own at work or fight, I was a rampant individualist. . . . I could see myself only raging through life without end like one of Nietzsche's Blond Beasts, lustfully roving and conquering by sheer superiority and strength.
>
> As for the unfortunates, the sick, and ailing, and old, and maimed, I must confess I hardly thought of them at all, save that I vaguely felt that they, barring accidents, could be as good as I if they wanted to real hard. . . . I was as faithful a wage slave as ever capitalist exploited.
>
> Just about this time . . . just turned eighteen, I took it into my head to go tramping. . . . And on this new Blond-Beast adventure I found myself looking upon life from a new and totally different angle. I had dropped down from the proletariat into what sociologists love to call the "submerged tenth," and I was startled to discover the way in which that submerged tenth was recruited.

> I found there all sorts of men, many of whom had once been as good as myself and just as Blond-Beast; sailor-men, soldier-men, labor-men, all wrenched and distorted and twisted out of shape by toil and hardship and accident, and cast adrift by their masters like so many old horses. . . . And I confess a terror seized me. What when my strength failed?

The harder he had worked at a dime an hour, he realized, the lower into the social pit he'd slid. London's concept of socialism as it evolved was never the socialism of the slacker. He did not oppose the finer things in life, indeed he wanted them for himself, and once he determined to work with his brain instead of his back, he had labored mightily to obtain some luxuries for himself. But everyone, he believed, should have an equal opportunity for the good life, which the current system of labor exploitation rendered manifestly impossible. Fortunes gained by sweat and brilliance were acceptable; fortunes gained by capitalizing on the desperation of others were not. And he felt little loyalty to the political system that sanctified the existing economy. In the article for Spargo, London bitterly recounted his imprisonment in Buffalo, where he "was nabbed by a fee-hunting constable, denied the right to plead guilty or not guilty, sentenced out of hand to thirty days . . . and put to work under the eyes of guards armed with Winchester rifles." After that experience, he wrote, people need not wonder why "some of his plethoric national patriotism simmered down and leaked out the bottom of his soul somewhere."[1]

He saw the cycle: physical labor was leading him only to the bottom of the indigents' pit. He learned it from the men with whom he camped and rode the rails. He had gone tramping for adventure and met men who were forced into it because their strength had given out. In their desperation and hunger he saw his own future, and swore an oath: "May God strike me dead if I do another day's hard work with my body." That was when he turned all his faculties toward becoming a writer. Five years after making that commitment, such eventual ruin seemed highly unlikely, for mighty news was coming in: *The Call of the Wild* was a smash hit. The sales, as well as the reviews, were extravagant.

The story recounts the adventures and transformation of Buck, half St. Bernard and half sheepdog, the pampered pet of a kindly judge's family in

Santa Clara, California. Kidnapped by the gardener and sold into the Alaska sled-dog trade, Buck is thrust into a world of savagery. Traded to a series of owners who represent various faces of the white man in the North, Buck learns to survive in a world where dogs, when not in harness, are left to work out their rivalries and dominance by themselves. Eventually he is owned by a trio of Americans who have no business in the North, a woman named Mercedes and her husband and brother, whose joint incompetence kills off their dog team one by one. Buck is taken from these foolish *cheechakoes* by John Thornton, a manly master to whom Buck can devote himself and be fully requited.

Buck's affections are divided, however. Life at the edge of the wilderness exerts a pull on him, in the proximity of wolves calling him to revert to his most primitive state. When Yeehat Indians kill Thornton and loot his camp, Buck slaughters them and gives himself over to his destiny as master of wolves.

Dark and bleak, yet weirdly credible, *The Call of the Wild* stunned the public like a one-two punch. By telling the story from Buck's point of view, London struck to the late Victorians' soft heart for anthropomorphic animal tales, while his own skill for riveting narrative made them believe the story while their guard was down. Not for nothing had he been taking boxing lessons from Jim Whitaker.

One reader stricken by the story was London's high school acquaintance Georgia Loring. She had grown up to marry Frederick Irons Bamford, the reference librarian in Oakland, who had picked up where Ina Coolbrith had left off as London's literary coach. Leery of London before, Georgia Bamford was so converted by the woolly tale that she pronounced herself ready to forgive even his vehement socialism. "How could he do it? By what magic of words could he make me feel that the dog was no longer a dog, but a fellow creature with all the feelings of a human being? . . . No book that I have read seems to have exerted the same power over me. I shall never forget it."

Left breathless by *The Call of the Wild,* Georgia Bamford could hardly wait to read *The People of the Abyss,* having seen the laudatory reviews. Her newfound esteem for London abruptly evaporated, so shocked was she that he could find such people a fit subject for commentary. "I could see no reason for such a book; it served no purpose and was not literature."[2] It was an early manifestation of a phenomenon that haunted London's whole career, then and for the rest of his life: the audience who craved entertainment did not care to read about the troubles of the world. He could bountifully satisfy what they wanted, but they refused to listen to what they needed to hear, and what he needed to tell them.

One effect of the runaway success of *The Call of the Wild* was London's full assimilation by his peers in San Francisco. His extraordinary output reversed the valence of the attraction between London and The Crowd: where he had once desired to be accepted by them, suddenly he had achieved recognition beyond any of them, and The Crowd courted him with an even greater fervor. His publication of one volume of short stories in each of the years 1900, 1901, and 1902, in addition to *A Daughter of the Snows*, gave him rank above the others, except the legendary Ambrose Bierce and the poet Joaquin Miller. The year 1902 also saw publication of *The Cruise of the Dazzler*, an action tale based on his own oyster-pirating youth on San Francisco Bay, and in which the title boat was an iteration of his own sloop *Razzle Dazzle*. The effort won him recognition as an author for juvenile readers. It was an extraordinary output.

For the newly hailed hero, the most visible effect of his new popularity was the final strain it put on his dying marriage. In February 1903 London's first fan, Cloudesley Johns, arrived for a visit at the Piedmont Lodge procured for the Londons by George Sterling; they played good hosts and he suspected no troubles, but the rift was all but complete. That summer, London moved Bessie and the girls for the summer up to Wake Robin Lodge, a property in Glen Ellen, north of the Bay Area, that had several rental cottages; it belonged to *Overland Monthly* editor Ninetta Eames, now his friend and frequent publisher. When boyhood friend Frank Atherton, now with a wife and baby, visited him, he found London flying kites—a hobby he had acquired and to which he was passionately attached. With six kites in the air, London talked Atherton into taking over the lease on the bungalow, and later moved Atherton's family into a flat with him on Telegraph Avenue in Oakland.

One measure of his deep personal misery in the wake of separating from Bess was that after they were all settled into the apartment, London took Atherton on a tour of the old bars, imbibed to his limit, and resumed the oyster pirate's habit of buying rounds for the house—and buying affection with them.

London also began laying plans to take some mistress out on the *Spray* to release some long-pent-up tension. He had no idea who it would be—there was Blanche Partington, witty, attractive, cultured member of The Crowd; or there was Ninetta Eames's niece Charmian Kittredge, who was a bit horse-faced, but she had a good figure and was wonderfully intelligent—he didn't care who it was.

As he was acquiring supplies for the excursion, his eye out for any female he could importune into accompanying him, his design fell, with him, in a brutal tumble from his buggy that strained, sprained, or extensively skinned both arms and both legs. As it happened, Bessie had asked Charmian to take some things down to Oakland to Jack, which she did. London was in a sour humor; he and Charmian had a short conversation, mostly about what he did not like about her, at the end of which he kissed her. Charmian Kittredge, who like London was the offspring of parents who had dabbled in free love, was no wallflower. Over the course of a couple more visits they discussed, rationally, their growing animal attraction to one another. More than that, London found himself falling in love—a concept he had once argued against.

Around The Crowd but not of The Crowd, Charmian had much to recommend her to London's notice. She was intelligent, and forthright and articulate in expressing her opinions. She was a horsewoman and a concert-quality pianist. She had a sharp editorial eye, having helped her aunt Ninetta in editing the *Overland Monthly*—in which capacity she developed almost unbelievable speed and accuracy on a typewriter. She could be refreshingly earthy in a society where women were expected to be prudes, and she had a rich sense of humor and a keenness for daring and adventure that he found remarkable in a woman. She was altogether different from both the brilliant but repressed Anna Strunsky and his increasingly distant and carping wife. The physical affair that ignited was rich and lusty, but London also found himself sharing his feelings honestly and fully with a woman capable of bearing them. To Charmian's misfortune, however, they opened their relationship just as he fell into the clutches of a dark, tenacious depression, what he later called his Great Sickness, and her strength and commitment were tested almost from the beginning.

The admiration of friends, the political sympathy and reassurance of comrades, the romantic possibilities that beckoned him outside his mummified relationship with Bessie, were all elements of happiness that had, in the main, eluded him up to this point. When he found, to his bewilderment, that once he had them they did not make him happy, the discovery caused him to examine—closely, earnestly, honestly examine—what it was he wanted from life. Early in July 1903, he tried to articulate in a letter to Charmian what he had concluded. He wrote that in previous years he had tried to explain it to other women he had loved, and been rewarded with their passionate anger:

> Shall I tell you a dream of my boyhood and manhood?—a dream which in my rashness I thought had dreamed itself out and beyond all chance of realization? Let me. I do not know, now, what my other loves have been, how much of depth and worth there were in them; but this I know, and knew then, and knew always—that there was a something greater that I yearned after, a something that beat upon my imagination with a great glowing light and made those woman-loves wan things and pale, oh so pitiably wan and pale! . . .
>
> For I had dreamed of the great Man-Comrade. I, who have been comrade with many men, and a good comrade I believe, have never had a comrade at all, and in the deeper significance of it have never been able to be the comrade I was capable of being. Always it was here this one failed, and there that one failed until all failed. . . . It was plain that it was not possible. I could never hope to find that comradeship, that closeness, that sympathy and understanding, whereby the man and I might merge and become one for love and life.
>
> How can I say what I mean? This man should be so much one with me that we could never misunderstand. He should love the flesh, as he should the spirit, honoring and loving each and giving each its due. . . . A man who had no smallnesses or meannesses, who could sin greatly, perhaps, but who could as greatly forgive.[3]

It was a breathtaking thing for a man to entrust to the woman he had been seriously courting, but Charmian, guided by an unerring sense of navigation that steered her to prove herself wiser than her predecessors, accepted his dream. His next letter to her was awash in relief. It had always been his fate, he wrote, for good or ill, to be able to win love easily. In consequence he had theretofore easily won the love of shy, innocent, sweetly silly little girls. "But YOU, YOU who are so much more, who know life and have looked it squarely in the face, who are open-eyed and worldly wise . . . that YOU should love me . . . Pride? Oh, if you could but know the pride I take in this!"[4]

The man who had awakened this long-dormant dream, though it had remained painful in its long dormancy, could only have been George Sterling—brilliant, sympathetic, impossibly beautiful, old enough (six years older than London) to be a mentor and yet young enough to be the soul mate he now admitted he had always pined for. London could survey his whole life of acquaintances, from wharf rats and hoodlums to men of the sea to overeducated tramps to *cheechakoes* and frostbitten prospectors, and realize that Sterling alone held the potential to embrace a soul as vast and complex as his own. But how to voice such incendiary feelings? How to even probe whether such a deep relationship was possible? London chewed the matter over for only a few more days before, just as *The Call of the Wild* hit the bookstores, trusting Sterling with a letter no less remarkable—and risky—than the one he had written Charmian: "You know that I do not know you—no more than you know me. We have never really touched the intimately personal note in all the time of our friendship. I suppose we never shall. And I speculate and speculate, trying to make you out, trying to lay hands on the inner side of you—what you are to yourself, in short. Sometimes I conclude that you have a cunning and deep philosophy of life, for yourself alone, worked out on a basis of disappointment and disillusion . . . and then it all goes glimmering, and I think that you . . . are living your life out blindly and naturally. So I do not know you, George; and for that matter I do not know how I came to write this."[5] It was the kind of letter that most men, if they had dared write it at all, would have read over, wadded up tightly, and buried in the wastebasket. But something impelled London to trust Sterling with the whole matter; if ever he was to give his dream a chance, it must be now.

Sterling was charmed. He welcomed the intimacy of the suddenly most famous writer in America. And as their once-cordial friendship deepened into something much more, there was an outlet for all of London's easy affability, his sincerity, and his inquisitiveness, to which Sterling responded with all his wit and verve. Sterling began editing London's daily output and demonstrated a keen skill and dedication. London began calling him the Greek, on account of Sterling's classical beauty; Sterling began referring to London as Wolf, an endearment previously reserved only for Charmian. For the time being, it seemed as though London's dream might have finally become a reality. On Christmas Eve, the Greek presented him a volume of his new collection of verse, *The Testimony of the Suns and Other Poems.* He inscribed it, "To our genius, Jack London. Here's my book. My heart you have already. Piedmont, Cal., Dec. 24th, 1903."[6]

For all the felicity of their literary interlude, the real world now intruded, an unwelcome guest with bills to pay, and an estranged wife and two daughters to support, in addition to still contributing to his mother's needs. *The Call of the Wild,* though it made Jack London a household name, did not make him rich. George Brett had not been convinced of its marketability, and instead of the usual royalty contract had bought it for a $2,000 lump sum, with the promise of extensive publicity. Neither he nor London foresaw the phenomenon it would become, and had there been a standard royalty contract, London would have gained wealth commensurate with even his powerful imagination. But the author was not dissatisfied with the lump payment. "I do hope you'll make a strike on that dog story," he wrote Brett at the time, "for you have been such help to me that I want to see you getting some adequate return."[7]

Celebrity though he now was, London needed work. *The Call of the Wild* had been written outside the six-book sequence once outlined to Brett; not so the great sea novel that was the principal topic of his first big proposal. Originally he had intended to call it *The Mercy of the Sea,* but as its main character

Wolf Larsen began to dominate the story, it evolved into *The Sea-Wolf.* Much of the composition took place on a folding camp stool at a portable writing desk in the woods surrounding his rented cabin at Wake Robin Lodge, where he sought refuge after finally separating from Bessie; the rest he wrote onboard the *Spray* during several weeks on a cruise with Cloudesley Johns, who came up for one of his regular visits. The story was scheduled to begin serialization in *Century* in January, but the serial would not conclude and the book, with its royalties to tap into, would not be published until well into the fall. He needed work immediately, and at that opportune moment the job of war correspondent presented itself.

The early 1900s were militaristic in any event; high officers were lionized and news of wars and imperial conflict were followed closely. The obsession only increased after the United States helped itself to an empire following the Spanish-American War. During the spring of 1904 a new conflict drew the world's notice. In the Far East, the storied "Hermit Kingdom" of Korea, no longer virile enough to maintain a separate existence, had become a contested hors d'oeuvre for the imperial appetites of Japan and Russia. It had been just over thirty years since Japan's wealthy lords had overthrown the burdensome shogunate and restored the emperor. In that time they amazed the Western world with the speed with which they gained the modern industrial muscle that they were now keen to flex. Russia was just beginning to grow into its vast geography and had recently developed a Pacific port at Vladivostok, though it was iced over for much of the year. Anxious for an ice-free port, they had pressured a weakened China into leasing them Port Arthur, on the Liaotung Peninsula at the head of the Yellow Sea, and west of Korea. Japan had controlled the peninsula through a puppet king since whipping China in a war in 1895, and felt threatened when the Russians began building a railroad spur across Manchuria to consolidate their hold on the port.

Increasingly it looked like war between Japan and Russia. William Randolph Hearst, who had relished his role in whipping up public opinion in favor of the Spanish-American War, prepared to send correspondents to the Orient, even as other Western journals also began lining up reporters to cover the conflict.

Jack London was courted by *Harper's*, *Collier's*, and the New York *Herald*, but Hearst, for whose San Francisco *Examiner* London had taken many assignments, made him the best offer.

In a rush to sail, London hurried *The Sea-Wolf* to completion, assigning to Sterling and Charmian his literary power of attorney to edit the manuscript as they saw fit to get it into production, serialized in *Century* and published by Macmillan. He also arranged with Brett to send his monthly stipend to Bess, their estrangement notwithstanding. London packed the manuscript off to Brett on January 6, 1904, and most of The Crowd saw him off the next day as he embarked for Yokohama aboard the S.S. *Siberia*, brawny new workhorse of the Pacific Mail Steamship Company.

American built with two black oval funnels towering 108 feet above the deck, the *Siberia* was the class of the Pacific Mail fleet—fifty feet shorter but a thousand tons heavier (and therefore five knots slower) than the *Majestic*, which had taken him to England a year and a half before. She boasted first-class accommodations for three hundred, including on this passage much of the American and some of the British press corps dispatched to cover the impending bloodbath. So expectant were the reporters of recording carnage that they began referring to themselves as the Vultures. A couple of them would become London's lifelong friends. Special among these were Robert L. Dunn, who was to cover the war for *Collier's* after they were unable to procure London, and Dunn's photographer Jimmy Hare, and Ed Winship, who with his wife, Ida, later became frequent guests at the ranch London would later own.

During the week's crossing to a stop in Honolulu, London celebrated his twenty-eighth birthday by coming down with a savage case of "la grippe," probably influenza. He passed the siege not in his cabin but mostly in a deck chair, delirious with fever for a day. "Oh, how my bones ache, even now," he wrote Charmian. "And what wild dreams I had!" Apart from the illness, the trip was enjoyable. "The weather is perfect. So is the steamer." Traveling on Hearst's bank account, the angry socialist did not find the classy accommodations too unbearable. "Sit at the Captain's table, and all the rest—you know."[8]

His lingering illness did not prevent London from taking a dip at Waikiki and attending a concert at the Hawaiian Hotel during their brief layover, but soon after resuming the voyage something worse than the flu befell him. While taking part in a deck sport that involved broad-jumping from a height of three and a half feet, his left foot landed on a piece of wood the diameter of a broomstick. He fell, rupturing the tendons in the inner ankle and spraining the outer ankle so badly he was immobilized for nearly three days.

Even in pain, he was a favorite of the press corps, and his stateroom was filled with well-wishers from six in the morning until eleven at night. "As a rule there were three or four," he wrote Charmian, "and very often twice as many. I had thought, when the accident happened, that I should have plenty of time for reading; but I was not left alone long enough to read a line." On the third day Percival Phillips, the correspondent for the London *Daily Telegraph*, began carrying him on deck for some fresh air each day, and by the sixth day he was scooting about on crutches, albeit painfully. A gale had begun to blow, giving him a chance to admire his ship's seakeeping qualities. "*Siberia* is behaving splendidly. . . . I hope war isn't declared for at least a month after I arrive in Japan—will give my ankle a chance to strengthen."[9]

Once in Tokyo, the Western reporters were bivouacked in the Imperial Hotel to await the Japanese government's arrangements to transport them on to Korea. They were joined by the dean of American war correspondents, the rock-jawed Richard Harding Davis, who had covered conflicts in Latin America and the Balkans, and who most recently had reported on the Spanish-American and Boer wars. Davis was also a popular author of stories for boys, a station he shared with London, and the two struck up a congenial rapport.

Japan may have seemed quaint and exotic to ethnocentric Europeans and Americans, but the Japanese military was years ahead of their Western counterparts in the art of railroading journalists. While treating the newsmen with exaggerated hospitality, the military liaisons came up with excuse after roadblock after feigned misunderstanding until it was clear to all that the Japanese had no intention of allowing them near the front.

The deceit dawned on them slowly. "Our experience with other armies had led us to believe that officers and gentlemen speak the truth," wrote Davis highly, "that men with titles of nobility . . . do not lie. In that we were mistaken." London's assessment was simpler. The Japanese, he later told Charmian, "settled the war correspondent forever—and they proved that he is a dispensable feature of warfare."[10]

The first to figure out that the press corps was being sandbagged was *Collier's* Robert Dunn. "Politely the War Office gave permits but refused to sign them, beguiling us with promises and banquet speeches about international brotherhood. All we got was secrecy and censorship and propaganda."[11] Suspecting that the Japanese were about to strike the Russians without the formality of declaring war, Dunn abruptly disappeared from the Imperial Hotel to make his own way to Korea. In a flash, London reached the same conclusion and followed suit. Although Japan had controlled Korea in effect since winning the Sino-Japanese war of 1895, they maintained the fiction for diplomatic reasons that Korea, "ruled" by its own emperor, was an independent country. Unless they wanted to give the lie to that subterfuge, they could not forbid Western journalists from going there, once the reporters escaped their official clutches in Japan itself.

Hearst was paying him to cover the war, and that was what he meant to do. London spent the entire day of January 28 bound for Kobe, some two hundred miles to the southwest, in a train car whose interior temperature he read to be forty degrees. He boarded an express train, traversing the country to its southwestern extremity at Nagasaki on Kyushu Island, where he hoped to catch a steamer across to Korea, but no transport was available there. He had to backtrack to the town of Moji, on the north shore of the island, where he intended to catch some form of passage across the Sea of Japan. Like any tourist with time on his hands, he began to take in the sights. Unknown to London as he snapped idle photographs—peasants and merchants, four coolies carrying a large bale of cotton, children playing—Moji was a fortified area, on the strategic strait that separated Kyushu from Honshu, and the Japanese were vigilant to the threat of espionage. Russians were white; London was white, and the spectacle of this white man snapping off pictures left, right, and center resulted in his rapid and unceremonious arrest.

London sent an urgent cable to Dick Davis in Tokyo, who was famous for his entrée into and skills among the diplomatic crowd. As a result, even as London was arraigned in the Kokura District Court, rescue was on its way in the form of the American minister, Lloyd Griscom, who would spring him from the Shimonaseki prison. The local authorities quickly became aware that London was not a spy but as a matter of saving face, London was convicted of espionage and then sentenced only to a small fine and loss of his camera. His old insistence on justice, however, would not allow him to let go of the camera, and he protested vigorously. Griscom obtained an appointment with Foreign Minister Baron Jutaro Komura, who insisted that under Japanese law, weapons used in a crime became government property. With a lusty twinkle, Griscom asked Komura whether, if he could name one exception to that rule, the innocent London's camera would be returned. Komura, who was a graduate of Harvard Law School and did not think he was in over his head, agreed, at which Griscom triumphantly said, "Rape." Komura issued the order.

London surmised that something important must be brewing, for the steamship *Keigo Maru*, on which he was to sail to Korea on February 8, was commandeered at the last moment by the Japanese government to carry troops. He was put off the ship and just had time to break into a full run, lugging his trunk, for a small steamer that was just casting off lines, bound for Fusan. He was taken aboard but got drenched in rescuing his trunk from a plunge into the icy bay. Fusan (now Pusan) was Korea's principal port, on the southeast coast directly opposite Moji, about 150 miles across the narrowest part of the Sea of Japan. In crossing, they passed the top entrance of the Strait of Tsushima, where a crushing Japanese naval victory over the Russians would settle the conflict later in the year. At Fusan, London switched to a puffing little steamer no larger than the *Sophia Sutherland*, which headed south and then west around the tip of the Korean peninsula to Makpo, so badly overloaded that she limped into the port listing thirty degrees to starboard. There this vessel, too, was seized by Japanese authorities, leaving London well short of his ultimate destination of Chemulpo, the former name for Inchon, the port and gateway to the major city of Seoul.

Now all but certain that action was about to commence, London chartered a local junk to continue up the west coast, but instead entered a different danger that he was lucky to survive. London, his crew of three Koreans, and five

Japanese passengers, each group mutually unintelligible to the other two—set off in a blasting February storm of ice and snow. The crew brought the boat into the little port of Kun San minus a mast and with a broken rudder, but still floating. Treated that night as a celebrity in the town, London was stripped, bathed, and shaved by five local girls, while anyone who was curious—including the police chief and the mayor—peeked in for a glimpse of the white man. It was virtually the first and last congenial experience he had with Korean culture (except for once allowing a man to watch as he removed the upper bridge from his mouth before retiring—an act that quickly netted a crowd that dissolved in hysterics as they demanded encores of putting in his teeth and taking them out again).

No other junk being available, London chartered a sampan and continued his journey north up the coast into the teeth of the same wretched storm, only now in an open boat, with a Japanese crew that didn't understand a word he said. Lucky to have survived the last leg after the boat was dismasted and the rudder disabled, now he was even luckier to survive the exposure, sheltering only under rice mats in temperatures well below zero, with only a small charcoal box to warm themselves. But there is a language among seamen that needs no translation; they did not need to explain to him what they were doing and London watched with admiration as the sailors brought the sampan into a small port, riding the flood tide over an obstructing reef to enter the harbor. The Japanese had closed the port of Chemulpo to large ships, but London glided right in on his native sampan, and there found Robert Dunn, who wrote that when London landed, "I did not recognize him. He was a physical wreck. His ears were frozen; his fingers were frozen; his feet were frozen. He said that he didn't mind his condition so long as he got to the front."[12]

Upon their arrival in Seoul on February 24, London assembled a kind of household around himself, consisting of a Japanese interpreter named Yamada, a Korean valet named Manyoungi, and two young grooms to care for the three packhorses and two saddle horses he felt that he required to do his job properly. English-speaking Koreans were not as rare as one might think, for the country had been competitively evangelized for decades by both Catholic and

Protestant missionaries, but Manyoungi's formal dress as an English gentleman's gentleman, and his habit of addressing London as "master," began to take some of the starch out of London's socialism.

Robert Dunn's suspicion that the Japanese were preparing a surprise attack with no declaration of war was borne out on February 4, 1904. Frustrated by the lack of progress in negotiations, they struck not at Korea, but at Russia's naval base at Port Arthur in Manchuria to remove the Russian Pacific fleet from the contest at the beginning. Then they began disembarking four separate armies to consolidate their control of the Korean Peninsula. They defeated the Russians in repeated engagements, pushing the front so far north that Dunn and London, when they set out on a 180-mile trek to Ping Yang (now Pyongyang, the capital of North Korea), which they reached on March 4, that city was already well to the rear of the action. The Japanese army had closed the roads to all but military traffic, so the two Americans slogged along iced-over rice paddies. The Koreans treated them hospitably, but the reporters had to angle to enter a town before any Japanese troops in the area might arrive, on pain of having nowhere to sleep. When they did find a place, London and Dunn would catch one glancing at the other and burst into giggle fits at the sheer lunacy of what they had gotten themselves into. "If we ever meet again," London told him when they finally parted, "my memory will be your laughing at me and my laughing at you, and your knowing, and my knowing you know I am."[13]

Although London always maintained that the five months spent trying to cover the Russo-Japanese War were a wasted blank in his career, at the time he was living the adventure, he found it and the companionship of the half dozen or so other journalists who eventually straggled into Korea to be so vital and invigorating that he did not even have to drink. He had liquor in his kit, and in a certain city that he didn't name he took to visiting a certain woman daily for the subtlety of her cocktails, but in the field, once more a man among men, he shared his whiskey socially but had no trouble maintaining his sobriety.[14]

Dunn's and London's reward for showing the pluck and enterprise to have traveled as far as Ping Yang was to be nabbed by Japanese troops and detained by the Japanese Consul for a week. Upon their release they were sternly warned to return to where they came from; London and Dunn split up, the latter returning to Seoul to plead for permission to do their jobs, while London found his way to the fighting front in the far north of the country—for which he was apprehended and spent four days in military jail. As it turned out, the complaint against them for having too great freedom to travel had been lodged by the Western reporters still in the hotel in Tokyo, who were missing the story.

When the officials finally relented and agreed to let correspondents see something to report, a chosen delegation, which did not include such prominent reporters as Dick Davis, was brought over in a group and allowed to accompany General Count Tamemoto Kuroki's First Army and witness an assault from across the Yalu River valley. The Japanese had stacked the field with 50,000 troops to pummel 5,000 Russians, so there was little chance they would lose. "Believe me," London wrote to Brett, "it has all the appearance now (so far as we are concerned) of a personally conducted Cook's tourist proposition."[15] The reporters' vantage point was the walls of the hilltop Wiju Castle; no fighting was visible, although they believed they could discern the distant boom of field artillery. Intense vigil through field glasses finally revealed a muzzle flash, and with all focusing their attention on that point they were able to record the time between flash and boom, and calculated the battle to be raging some two and a half miles away. Their disgust only compounded when they learned that their viewing spot would not be repeated; their conducting officer had made a mistake—they were not supposed to have been allowed so close to the action.

Nevertheless, London saw enough to file stories with Hearst, albeit with a proportion of "filler" and ginned-up text that would have made Hearst, the master of yellow journalism, proud. "Perfect rot I am turning out," he confessed to Charmian on March 29. "It's not war correspondence at all, and the Japs are not allowing us to see any war." Watching a column of troops rumble by, with officers stopping in his quarters to shake hands and leave their cards, became

JAPANESE SUPPLIES RUSHED TO FRONT BY MAN AND BEAST, filed from Wiju on April 16. On May 1 he managed to cross the Yalu River into China, filing GIVING BATTLE TO RETARD ENEMY from the city of Antung. Mocking his own dispatches, he wrote to Charmian Kittredge, "IMPORTANT! ANOTHER VEXATION! Just caught five body lice on my undershirt. That is, I discovered them, Manyoungi picked them off. . . . Lice drive me clean crazy. I am itching all over. I am sure, every second, that a score of them are on me. And how under the sun am I to write!"[16] His change of clothes was watched by a Korean noble, who offered the use of his house, but now that other Western journalists had begun to trickle in, they were required to stay together where they were ordered.

There were now a total of fourteen Western reporters, including London, with the most famous of them, Dick Davis, still stuck in Tokyo, his temper souring. As the action moved north, their camp was moved to the Manchurian town of Feng Wang Cheng, where they were told little and allowed to do less. London's portion of the camp was distinctive, both for the American flags he always kept flying there, for his hospitality, and for Manyoungi, always cooking, mending, brewing tea, providing whatever London needed almost before he thought to ask for it.

While in camp, London had a favorite saddle horse named Belle, who had belonged to the Russian minister in Seoul. A sailor, London was not a natural rider, and he became an equestrian autodidact, picking up various clumsy habits and never learning to look comfortable in a saddle. He characterized Belle as a joy, and the only gentle riding horse in Korea. "I am my own riding teacher," he wrote to Charmian, who was an accomplished equestrian and who scandalized her proper friends by disdaining the ladylike sidesaddle; she rode astride a horse like a man—to London's admiration. "I hope I don't learn to ride all wrong. But anyway, I'll learn to stick on a horse somehow, and we'll have some glorious rides together."[17]

That London cared for his horses was undeniable. He could be enraged by cruelty to animals, and his exposure to the Asian cultural indifference to brute suffering was hard to bear. At one point, in company with Dunn, he witnessed a fully loaded packhorse hobble by on three legs, the off-hind leg being broken and strapped up to its belly. A soldier was pulling him along hard by the halter. "Look at that for cruel ignorance," London told Dunn. "God damn him." According to Dunn, the soldier heard them and answered in English. "'If leg don't touch ground, very soon mend.' And the little yellow brother laughed. We wanted to hit him but we didn't—it would have started an 'international incident.'"[18] Nor was the lame horse the worst he had to see. The Korean, he reported in one dispatch, "eats his dogs, not only when he is hungry but when he wishes to titillate his stomach with a delicacy." Old dogs, he wrote, were eaten as commonly as mutton was in the West, but puppies were a great delicacy. He must also have observed that the approved way to tenderize the meat was to beat the dog before killing it.[19] This was not the way to instill cultural appreciation in the author of *The Call of the Wild*.

Much has been written of the racism, both explicit and implied, in London's Korean dispatches. With the partial exception of Davis, the same could be said equally of any of the Western correspondents. They saw elements of Asian culture that contradicted their own Western notions of honor and decency and fair play, from obsequious dissimulation to sneak attacks without a declaration of war to animal cruelty. London's reporting, however, expressed it in ways more nuanced than is sometimes reported in his biographies.[20]

After the Japanese defeated the Russians along the Yalu River, and London and other reporters were shown a cell full of Russian prisoners of war, it was true that he felt a pang of racial sympathy for the jailed men whose eyes were, he wrote, bluer than his own. He did not write that it was unnatural or even unfortunate that soldiers of the Asian race had defeated and captured them; all he said was that it sharpened his realization that he had been living as a foreigner among an alien race. Moreover, his questioning of the tactics by which the Japanese had won the battle—they had suffered a thousand killed and wounded in a frontal assault on the enemy position when a simple flanking maneuver would have compelled the Russians either to surrender or be cut to pieces attempting a retreat—showed a grasp of the Japanese military philosophy that the United States would have done well to study a generation later.

As London appreciated, the Japanese outfought the Russians rather than outmaneuvered them. They did so to make their enemy lose face in the eyes of other Asian nations whose respect the Japanese intended to claim. "The Asiatic does not value life as we do. The generals of Japan have no press of populace at home to harp at the cost of victory, while they do have at home a press and a people clamorous . . . for splendid victory, and never mind the cost." Of the Asian performance in the battle, he wrote, "The Japanese never stopped nor hesitated. Twice they reinforced their line, advancing at the double across the shelterless sands, the while every gun of every battery worked at fever heat. . . . The Japanese are so made that nothing short of annihilation can stop them."[21]

That the Japanese were out to not just defeat the Russians but humiliate them was driven home not by London, but by a Japanese press attaché, who told him bluntly, "Your people did not think we could beat the white. We have now beaten the white." Even knowing that it was Russia who had brought about the conflict by demanding port concessions in Japanese-controlled Korea, London was chilled by the fanatical militarism he observed among the Japanese. "Henceforth," he wrote to Charmian, "I shall preach the Militant Yellow Peril." The Western press corps' ethnocentrism also perceived few correctives in a society even more racist than their own, a society in which they were guests but were also decidedly *egin*: barbarians, and there were lines that they were not to cross.

The reporters now assigned to the First Army were corked up in a grove of pine trees near a temple, under strict orders not to stray beyond carefully circumscribed boundaries. Life in the camp was not unpleasant once the weather began to warm—"In the afternoon, the call goes forth, and we (the correspondents) go swimming in a glorious pool—clear water, over our heads, plenty of it"—but it was impossible to cover the war from there. "I am at liberty to ride into headquarters at Feng-Wang-Cheng, less than a mile away," he fumed to Charmian. "And I am at liberty to ride about in a circle around the city of a radius little more than a mile. Never were correspondents treated in any war as they have been in this. It's absurd, childish, ridiculous, rich, comedy." He worried that his letters would be impounded by the censors, but they proceeded through the post, perhaps because they contained the welcome promise that he was going to quit the country. Unless Hearst could arrange for him to cover the war from the Russian side, which was unlikely, "as you read this I may be starting on my way back to the States, to God's country, to White man's country. At any rate, believe me . . . it would take many times bigger salary for me to put in another year in Japan." [22] London was also uncertain whether the photos he was taking would ever be seen. Lacking a development kit, he had to mail off the undeveloped film, which could easily have been seized by the censors, but for all the restrictions he was working under, London's pictures remain among the best visual documentation of the Russo-Japanese War and its environs.

Encamped at Feng Wang Cheng, London learned the position of the white under Japanese control to his cost when he socked a Japanese servant he caught trying to prevent his groom from obtaining his fair portion of fodder. The *mapu*, Korean horse grooms, relied on the Japanese army for forage for their correspondents' horses, and they applied for it weekly at the commissariat. All was in close proximity, and one day London overheard one of his *mapus* in a hot dispute with a Japanese whom he recognized as one he had seen stealing supplies from him before. He intervened, and when the man made a threatening feint, London punched him, once—"he fell right into it, and then down with a thud. And he went around whimpering in bandages for two weeks."

For a white to strike a Japanese, regardless of how low in station, was stunning, unthinkable. London was summarily arrested, and there followed another emergency cable to Davis, who was still fuming in Tokyo, awaiting his own travel documents, to intercede for him. This was a very serious matter—it was not out of the question that London might be executed for such an outrage. The case was heard by Kuroki's chief of staff, to whom it was explained that frontier Americans had their own version of *bushido*, the code of conduct governing samurai warriors, and that in London's culture, it was necessary to meet an insult with a physical blow. Davis, who was famous for his skill with powerful circles, managed to bring major diplomatic pressure to bear, and the disapproving squint from abroad may have been what influenced Fuji to forbear punishing London. Still, the incident set all the Western reporters on their guard for days; they armed themselves, alert to the possibility that one of the Japanese would attempt to vindicate their racial honor with a reprisal that doubtless would have met with the military's tacit approval.

By the time he was released, London was so exasperated that when another of the reporters, Fred Palmer, offered the palliative that London should at least admit the Japanese were brave in a charge, he blurted back, "so are the South American peccary pigs in their charges!" It was another remark that came back to haunt him, further coloring his reputation as a racist, but London had in fact already written in detail of the Japanese's impressive military prowess. They "are surely a military race," he testified in his dispatches. "Their men are soldiers, and their officers are soldiers. . . . Patriotism is their religion and they die for their country as the martyrs of other peoples die for their gods."[23] London's latter-day critics may be correct that there was a racist subtext to his observations, but of the factual truth of his reporting, the United States learned a generation later. (They might have done particularly well to study the Japanese tactic of opening a conflict with a sneak attack on distant naval bases.)

London's disgust with the whole venture had not eased by the time he determined to quit the enterprise. He filed a final sarcastic dispatch on June 2, JAPANESE OFFICERS CONSIDER EVERYTHING A MILITARY SECRET, in which he actually quoted from the correspondents' operating instructions: "For the present and until further notice the transmission of any dispatches . . . where wireless telegraphy is employed is forbidden. . . . From to-day and until further notice it is forbidden to take photographs or make sketches. . . . The necessary steps are being taken to see that this order is obeyed. It may be found necessary to enforce a still stricter censorship than that already existing." All the reporters in the camp, English, French, and American, signed a joint cable to all their papers protesting the impossibility of their situation and declaring their further attempts to cover the war futile. The Japanese censors, "by their usual Asiatic indirection," wrote London, "which involved the subtlest dialectics and discussion of things metaphysical, and concerning all things under the sun except the point at issue," made the telegram disappear.[24]

Even as London had gone to Korea without official sanction, he sought none in leaving on June 4; he stopped back in Tokyo, where he reconnected with Davis, presumably thanking him for the intercessions that retrieved his camera at Moji and possibly prevented his execution in Korea. "I liked him very much," wrote Davis, "he is very simple and modest and gave you a tremendous impression of vitality and power. He is very bitter against the wonderful little people and says he carries away with him only a feeling of irritation." Davis counseled that with time London would just remember the good things. Still, Davis was somewhat wistful that as a correspondent London had, by his initiative and courage, scooped the most celebrated war reporter in America. "I did envy him so, going home after having seen a fight and I not yet started."[25]

In returning to America, London brought home with him two acquisitions he could not do without: Belle, the mare who had formerly belonged to the Russian consul, and the very Westernized Manyoungi, who had become indispensable as his valet and aide, and who had agreed to continue in his employ.

The serialization of *The Sea-Wolf* had begun in January, and when London returned in midsummer he found himself at the center of a literary firestorm. Prose such as *The Sea-Wolf* had never been published; there was no mistaking that it marked a sea change in American letters. The polite manners of the Gilded Age were torn asunder in the brutal naturalism of a story about a milquetoast writer, Humphrey van Weyden, who is rescued from a collision and brought aboard the sealing schooner *Ghost*, only to be virtually enslaved as a cabin boy by the monstrous captain Wolf Larsen. The captain rules his ship by brutalizing his crew in scenes that shocked and terrified readers, even as Humphrey fell into a kind of morbid, sensualized thrall of his captor. The open-sea rescue of Maud Brewster, her and Humphrey's escape onto a desert island, and then their fresh confrontation with Larsen created a shock wave in

American literature. After the serialization in *Century*, all 40,000 copies of the book's first printing were sold before being shipped, as were the 15,000 copies of the second printing.

The critics were quick to recognize its importance. The Boston *Herald*, which had praised him so well for *The People of the Abyss*, took equal cognizance of *The Sea-Wolf*. The New York *Herald* hailed it as "a superb piece of craftsmanship."[26] *The Sea-Wolf*, however, had a serious weakness. Its depiction of life on a sealing schooner was as vivid and authentic as London's memory of the *Sophia Sutherland* could provide—even Larsen was based on an infamous sealing captain London had heard of during his seven months before the mast, Alexander McLean. The relationship between Humphrey and Maud, however, was stilted and prudish out of all proportion to the rest of the story, and indeed wrecked the story, especially for those critics who felt that once London had opened the door to honest, naturalistic narration, to retreat into polite convention where Maud was concerned was distracting and dishonest.

First in line among London's critics was Ambrose Bierce. To his protégé George Sterling he fumed that, while the creation of a stunning character like Wolf Larsen was an accomplishment Protean enough for any one man's lifetime, "the love element, with its absurd suppressions and impossible proprieties, is awful." At Macmillan, Brett also perceived the faults of *The Sea-Wolf* but published it without requiring any major revisions. It was a safe bet that the American public was more comfortable with violence than with sex, and in any event he still regarded London as an author-in-progress. In this era editors were content to nurture a developing author through flawed masterpieces.

While generations of English literature papers have been written on the strongly implied homoeroticism contained in *The Sea-Wolf*, only once, apparently, was London directly asked about that aspect of his characters. He received a letter from Maurice Magnus, an American travel journalist and one of the few openly homosexual writers of the Edwardian era. He was London's own age, and he was well known for a point of view—that the sexual impulse cannot be denied—that mirrored London's own. In London's writings, Magnus observed, London never articulated what became of the sexual imperative among men who found themselves together. "Do you evade that for the sake of Anglo-Saxon prudery of your readers?" Magnus inquired of him. "Tell me please." London had of course addressed the topic directly on point in private conversation, with Joseph Noel and others, to their shock, but his reply to Magnus was curiously sharp and defensive:

> I have always imagined Wolf Larsen . . . as "knowing" women—but I did not think it necessary explicitly so to state in my writing.
>
> You are certainly right. A certain definite percentage of men are so homosexual, or so nearly homosexual, that they can love another man more than they can love any woman. But then, I dare say, no homosexual man is qualified to say whether a fictional woman is real or not to a normally sexed man. . . .
>
> Surely, I have studied the sex problem even in its "most curious ways." I, however, have drawn men-characters who were sexually normal. I have never dreamed of drawing a homosexual male character. . . .

"I think I get your point of view," he concluded snidely. "Am I wrong? Do you get my point of view? Flatly, I am a lover of women. Sincerely yours, Jack London."

There was nothing in Magnus's inquiry that should have been interpreted as a personal overture requiring London to affirm his own heterosexuality. That he dismissed Magnus with such abruptness indicates either that he read the letter as such, or that he knew of Magnus's reputation and wanted no association with him, or perhaps that he felt vulnerable that the realization of his long-cherished dream in his special relationship with Sterling might become public knowledge and be misunderstood, or perhaps merely that in the spirit of those times, he could not afford to let even a rumor get started that he had created characters of ambivalent sexuality.[27] Then again, he may have been disgusted with his work, because pandering to "American prudes," as London himself called them to Brett, had indeed been a consideration in crafting Humphrey's chivalrous but unrealistic bearing toward Maud on the desert island.

The question of whether London's increasingly intense friendship with Sterling had any bearing on the homosexual undertones of *The Sea-Wolf,* or indeed with the surprisingly lyrical descriptions of male beauty, stripped and muscular, in the novel that followed it, a boxing tale titled *The Game,* exasperates defenders of his heterosexuality. And it is somewhat ironic that the issue was clouded just as London's sex life was about to be buffeted by a typhoon such as he had only witnessed on the Pacific.

10 ❧ THE LOVER

Jack London's dispatches from Korea, attacking what he perceived to be a dangerous and chilling streak of fanatical militarism on the part of the Japanese, were mainly greeted with hostility in the American socialist quarter. The ethnocentric tone in which he wrote them later fueled a charge of racism when seen through modern sensitivities. Still, even as London acknowledged that it was Russia who was the aggressor in this conflict, it took a world war a generation after London's death to vindicate his observations about Japan's culture of militarism.

American socialists may have been annoyed with him, but Hearst was pleased. London had been among the handful of American reporters to outmaneuver their Japanese handlers and reach the scene of action. Thus at twenty-eight, London had followed up the runaway success of *The Call of the Wild* with gripping war stories—sometimes when there was precious little material to grip with—read by a national audience in all the Hearst newspapers. For his efforts he was paid about $4,000, and now, for the first time in his life, he had real money.

But when he returned home in June 1904, accompanied by Manyoungi and Belle, his saddle mare, he found his personal life in greater chaos than ever before. The S.S. *Korea* had not even landed when London was served Bessie's divorce suit, filed in his absence, charging cruelty and desertion and outdatedly naming Anna Strunsky as co-respondent. She also had obtained a restraining order freezing his finances until her monetary demands were satisfied. Bessie made considerable theater of the step, and demonstrated that not without reason was she a cousin of the famous actress, Ibsen interpreter, and forerunner of Method actors Minnie Maddern Fiske.

Bessie had always hated entertaining The Crowd, but now she poured out her heart to any of them who would listen to her, especially Carrie Sterling. Any exaggerations she indulged in relating her grievances—for instance, that London and Anna Strunsky had made love in front of her—she regarded as merely paying back the pain he had caused her (although, again, in this era, the expression "making love" might as easily have referred to flirting as to anything more carnal). Another of her confidantes, whom she never suspected in the matter and whom she trusted more as a friend than the others, was Charmian Kittredge. Listening to bile she would rather not have heard, and knowing that it must all eventually land on her, Charmian fled the storm, staying with an aunt in Newton, Iowa, and determining to stay put even when London wired her the money for a train ticket to come home and meet him. When London returned to the United States as a literary superstar, the divorce action caused a sensation.

Reporters, to Anna's mortification, sought her out for a statement, and she obliged them. "Absurd is hardly a word strong enough to be used in regard to the silly stories about the love-making that went on before Mrs. London's eyes. Mr. London and I were very good friends, and we treated one another as such—no more. Besides, Jack London is hardly the man to make love to another woman in his own house. . . . The ridiculous part of the whole thing is the fact that my visit to the Londons' house occurred exactly two and a half years ago. . . . Since 1901 I have seen Mr. London but three or four times. Immediately after my visit to his home, I went to New York, and from there to London, and I have spent the greater part of my time since then in Italy, returning from Naples only four months ago."[1]

Flora London, eager to embrace the prospect of becoming once more the principal woman in her son's life after Bessie was out of the picture, also went public in defending him. "So far as Anna Strunsky is concerned, she was at our house several years ago, when she and Jack were finishing their book together. Her behavior was always that of a good friend to all of the family. I think there is no reason for the connection of her name to Jack's. . . . I can hardly believe that Bessie has made such charges. . . . He was loving, affectionate, and generous to a fault [to Bessie] during the first two years of that marriage. Then there began to grow a gradual coolness between them, due to her not understanding the needs of his literary work, and partly caused by the 'hero worship' of a lot of silly girls who wrote him letters and veritably dogged his footsteps whenever he left the house."[2]

London saw no help for Anna's reputation but to meet with Bessie and confess that there was another woman, but that it was Charmian, not Anna. They finalized the terms of their divorce, and the price of his freedom was to agree to build Bessie a house, which cost $2,175, and the lot for it another $1,500—wiping out the entirety of his Korean earnings from Hearst. London added a proviso about the house, however: Bessie could have it and live in it, unless and until she remarried—a reasonable-sounding condition at the time, but one that would cost Bessie dearly and cause new venom to issue in future years.

Making up for Bessie's cleaning out his bank account, London received another $4,000 from *Century* for the serialization of *The Sea-Wolf*. But between his own living; maintaining Bessie and his daughters, and his mother and nephew Johnnie Miller; and the largesse he had resumed toward Mammy Jennie, who had fallen on reduced circumstances, he was quickly back in debt. Bessie dropped the restraining order on his finances, but her sense of rage and betrayal now had a new target—Charmian—that lasted until the day she died. An interlocutory decree was issued on November 11, which finally set the clock running on the one-year waiting period before London and Charmian could marry. In the meantime, London set up a new household in a rented cottage at Ninetta Eames's property, Wake Robin Lodge.

Through several difficult weeks London consoled himself by reconnecting with The Crowd, the clique of Bay Area bohemians. They had a kind of godfather of whom London grew to be very fond in sixty-two-year-old Charles Warren Stoddard, a former editor of *Overland Monthly*, "a figure of tossed-back hair and long fingers forever busy with a cigarette, bridging the Bret Harte period to ours." They had corresponded as early as 1900, when London sent Stoddard a photograph of himself, "the most like, perhaps, or the most flattering. I don't know which," in acknowledgment of Stoddard's praise of *The Son of the Wolf*.[3] With his belly and white beard he rather resembled an American Victor Hugo; his universal reputation as gentle, kind, and empathetic belied the breath of scandal concerning his resignation from Notre Dame University, ostensibly for reasons of health but with whispers of attentions he had bestowed on certain students. Like London he cherished the dream of an intimate male companion, but unlike London he had lived this as a reality, having a close relationship with Robert Louis Stevenson, among others, and having corresponded with Herman Melville and especially Walt Whitman on sexual as well as literary matters.[4] Forty years before publication of *The Sea-Wolf*, Stoddard's stories drawn from his tour of the South Seas in 1864, when he was twenty-one, approvingly depicted fervent same-sex friendships with less obfuscation than the emotionally constipated desires of London's Humphrey van Weyden. During London's lengthy fret over whether to tell George Sterling of his feelings, he may have consulted Stoddard about it, for at the time of his careful overture to Sterling, he closed a letter to Stoddard, "With all the love in the world, & a man's love, Jack London."

Also prominent among The Crowd was the humorist Harry Leon Wilson, longtime assistant editor and then editor of *Puck*; he had cowritten a play with Booth Tarkington, with whom he would collaborate four more times, and had produced three light, funny novels in the preceding four years. Ray Stannard Baker brought more gravitas as a longtime staffer at *McClure's magazine*, and attracted to the circle social reformers such as Ida Tarbell and Lincoln Steffens. Tarbell was nearly fifty; her unflattering history of the Standard Oil Company permanently stained the reputation of John D. Rockefeller, but she rejected the relish of "muckraking" and insisted that her findings were balanced—never minding that Rockefeller had bankrupted her father. Steffens was ten years London's senior and even more radical in his political thinking, and had recently written an exposé of American political corruption, *The Shame of the Cities*. As a newsman Baker had covered the march of Coxey's Army, and the spotlight that London had beamed into London's East End by writing *The People of the Abyss*, Baker was plotting to do with American racism—a shocking first—a project that came to fruition as *Following the Color Line* in 1908.

The Crowd actually numbered more artists than writers, and one of the mainstays was the painter Charles Rollo Peters, whose moody, moonlit canvases led the other bohemians to dub him the Prince of Darkness. A native of San Francisco but a product of the Ecôle des Beaux Arts in Paris, Peters's work had been highly praised by James McNeill Whistler. His thirty-acre estate in Monterey, Peters Gate, was a frequent gathering place for The Crowd, whose members little guessed that his hospitality was bankrupting him. Another painter, Xavier Martínez, was a native of Guadalajara, a founder of the California Society of Artists, and soon to become the son-in-law of Jim Whitaker, London's mentor in boxing, fencing, and the class struggle. "Marty" to The Crowd, Martínez was artistically prominent but not financially successful, and when the bohemians gathered to dine at Coppa's in San Francisco, he could like as not be seen adding to a long mural of black cats to pay for his meal.

Soon to join The Crowd was Michael Williams, an "incomparable talker, Irish and fey, and destined, though none of us suspected it then, to become the editor of the most respected Catholic journal in America," the *Commonweal*. There was the winsome but interminably sad Nora May (but she called herself "Phyllis") French, whose poems lamenting the position of women in the American scheme of things won her notice from a small band of feminists but no wider fame. Among The Crowd she had a smorgasbord of unhappy affairs, her greatest heartbreak alleged to have come over the disinterest from one of London's favorites, Jimmy Hopper. "Jim Hop," London called him—stocky and muscular beneath a mop of blond curls, he had been a football star at the University of California. London first met him at the Cole Grammar School in Oakland, their friendship blossoming only in later years as Hopper established himself as a journalist and capable practitioner of short stories. Hopper was a favorite hiking companion of George Sterling, the latter "striding through the woods at a long-legged gait that few could follow, as one saw him often with Jimmy Hopper, Sterling's long figure always a little in advance."

The Crowd hailed from all over—Stoddard from Rochester, New York; Wilson from Illinois; Baker from Lansing, Michigan; Martínez from Guadalajara. The diversity created a fertile atmosphere for love affairs, for the comparison of ideas and experiences, and for commiseration on their surrounding society's indifference to the artistic and the brilliant. Like most bohemians, they had decided that the world was cruel and brutish, and each carried as an accessory of membership a vial of cyanide, so that when the world and its stupidity became unbearable they could exit at a time and place of their own choosing.

By far the most meaningful of London's friendships in The Crowd continued to be that with Sterling himself. At first London presented a problem for Sterling. London was the loudest and now the best-known socialist in the Bay Area, and Sterling owed what literary existence he had to Ambrose Bierce, who was virulently antisocialist, and who sometimes made good on threats to drop protégés who went down the road of social reform. A few weeks after receiving London's exploratory "I don't know you" letter, Sterling wrote to Bierce, then in the East, about him, couching the introduction in careful flattery: "I'm getting very fond of Jack London. When I first made his acquaintance, about two years ago, he was, through ignorance, a lukewarm admirer of yourself. Under my tutelage he has changed, and last week actually took up the cudgels on your behalf when [Richard Walton] Tully and his wife began a verbal assault upon you at a literary (?) gathering." Bierce's all-clear came a week later: "I'm glad you like London; I've heard he is a fine fellow and I've read one of his books—'The Son of the Wolf' I think is the title—and it seemed clever work mostly."[5] Bierce had already seen an article by London in *The Critic*, whose subject was Bierce's home turf, and in it London praised Bierce, to which he responded that the article was excellent and London "knows how to think a bit."[6]

London and Sterling had also spent a good deal of time together after London separated from Bessie and moved in with the Athertons, but much of it was juvenile—romping, drinking too much, and, according to Atherton, experimenting with drugs. "I well remember one night when they had been together. It was quite late when Jack came home. His eyes looked glassy . . . he was very quiet, retiring immediately. We didn't see him again until the next morning when he related his experience. . . . He and George had tentatively indulged in hashish."

"To one who has never entered the land of hashish," London said to his childhood friend, "an explanation would mean nothing. But to me, last night was like a thousand years. I was obsessed with indescribable sensations; alternating visions of excessive happiness and oppressive moods of extreme sorrow. I wandered through aeons of countless worlds, mingling with all types of humanity." When a shocked Atherton demanded an explanation of why he had done such a thing, London invoked the writer Marie Corelli, who, he said, "couldn't have written *Wormwood* if she hadn't drunk enough absinthe to experience all those strange dreams. . . . So you see in order to write intelligently one must have certain experiences that coincide with the subject."[7]

Sterling, however, came to be more than a partner in mischief. There was something about the handsome Greek that got under London's skin, something that fascinated him and attracted him and would not let him go. Back from Korea, though financially broken by Bessie, London was once again in the bosom of The Crowd. Late 1904 into 1905 was a halcyon time for the Greek and his Wolf. In the seamy parts of San Francisco they visited bars and Chinese prostitutes; at the Sterlings' camp near the rugged coast of Carmel they romped and skinny-dipped and bellowed from rocky crags. Sterling posed naked, his penis pinched demurely between his thighs, and London photographed him. Many pictures also survive of a minimally clad London in he-man poses; he was proud of his blond-beastly body and was not shy about showing it off. Unpublished nudes of him also exist, with nothing tucked demurely anywhere; one of the pictures later found a home tacked to the window frame by Charmian's desk, but whether they were taken by her or by Sterling is unknown.

Wolf and the Greek also found yet another venue in which to be playmates: London's celebrity had now grown to the point that he was invited to join San Francisco's Bohemian Club, which had been started in 1872 as a means for the city's creative element to mingle with the wealthy and powerful, and thereby benefit the arts, and artists. Their principal activity was an annual retreat in the northern redwoods for several days of impromptu plays and other general nonsense. London was energized by the intellectual atmosphere of the gathering; Sterling was already a regular, and after London first attended in 1904 he returned as often as he could.

Charmian eventually returned from Iowa to face the music, and it was not pleasant. Despite their long regard for Ninetta Eames and the *Overland Monthly,* The Crowd did not take to Charmian and felt that they had to do something to get her out of the picture. As a weapon, they turned to the charms of a vivacious young drama critic named Blanche Partington. She wrote for the San Francisco *Call,* the same newspaper that had published London's debut "Typhoon Off the Coast of Japan." Her father, John Herbert Evelyn Partington, had painted portraits of several of The Crowd, including Ambrose Bierce, and she was one of four talented siblings, a brother and three sisters, who acted, sang, painted, or wrote, and associated with The Crowd in varying degrees. Unlike London, Blanche was an anarchist, a point on which Bierce had warned Sterling away from her, and on which London would have engaged her in fierce but fun combat. She was, like Sterling, a Bierce protégé, whom the latter had recruited into the literary world only to bully her into his vision that art should be practiced only for art's sake—a point diametrically opposed to that of London, who increasingly believed that art that did not seek to reform or elevate was a waste of time. "You want to reform the world—poor girl," Bierce admonished her, "to rise and lay about you, slaying monsters and liberating captive maids." Declaring his disappointment, he threatened to withdraw his patronage if she could not focus herself on the quality of her writing and on that only. [8]

London was stung and angry that Charmian had stayed in hiding in Iowa even after he had sent her train fare to return and be with him. When they first opened their affair, she had pronounced herself game for her share of whatever scandal they might cause, and at that time he warned her in the plainest terms that he would hold her to it. She must prove herself seaworthy in the storm, and not retreat into feminine deceptions and at all costs, not hysterics. If she became hysterical around him, he swore she would find him unsympathetic and cold, although perhaps mildly curious about what she thought she might accomplish with such tactics. In his childhood he'd had quite enough, he said, of his mother's tantrums and feigned fainting fits, and he wanted no more of that. Charmian had held out to him both the woman-love, as he had termed it, that she could sexually offer and the masculine comradeship whose lack had caused his previous affairs to burn out. Her flight to Iowa and decision not to return even when summoned was a serious failure; he had been very frank with Charmian about his expectations, and she knew in a hurry that she had woefully blundered, if she meant to keep him. London proved susceptible to The Crowd's dangling Blanche Partington in front of him, and he responded by going after her "on the jump," as he would say.

Of The Crowd's scheme to force out Charmian with Blanche, George Sterling was part and parcel, even writing to Blanche, only partly in jest, suggesting a schedule by which they could divide London between them. If London had shared his long-secret dream with Sterling, as by now he certainly had, Sterling knew Blanche would never last and that he would become the central figure in London's affections. The intuitive Charmian divined exactly what The Crowd was up to and scratched in her diary, "Hell!" While squiring Blanche, he had not defended Charmian from either the sniping behind her back or the slights in her presence; it was one of the ways in which he was now testing her mettle. "My rule of conduct is for every man to stand on his own legs, and every woman too. I made Charmian stand on her own legs." Realizing that she was now on a kind of romantic probation, she behaved faultlessly; she did not attempt to hide her hurt, but rather than act the part of the vengeful harpy, as Bessie would have done, she twice offered to release him from their engagement.

London declined his freedom, and during the spring of 1905, The Crowd's intrigues against Charmian finally grated against his sense of justice. She and London began again, and as their affair blossomed London realized more clearly than ever that she was everything Bessie was not. She was lusty and enjoyed sex—or as she euphemized it, "lolly," and they quickly took to referring to each other as Mate Man and Mate Woman, terms that he had devised and used as long ago as the ill-fated *A Daughter of the Snows*. Charmian's sense of adventure was as fearless as his own, and her keenness for practical jokes was as game as his. She was fiercely intelligent and independent, and he had to learn how to relate to a woman he could neither con nor dominate. London relished the experience, however, and slowly she won him back. On May 10 he confessed his affair with Blanche; it was a painful interview, but cathartic, and served to let Charmian know she was still in the game.

As far as London's relationship with the rest of The Crowd was concerned, it would not be altogether fair to assert that the Wolf merely basked in the worship of the lesser members of his pack. There is no doubt that the San Francisco bohemians enlarged his artistic sensibilities in exchange for the increased artistic credibility his presence lent them. London came away from his involvement with Blanche with a more sophisticated appreciation of music, which stayed with him for life. (This at least worked to Charmian's advantage, as she was a virtuoso pianist.) But it was the lovely Greek who best repaid London's friendship with his critical appraisal. "At this time," wrote one of The Crowd, "one found him reading manuscript and proof for London with a meticulous interest that never flagged; his diction was irreproachable, and his feeling for the fall of a sentence and the turn of a figure particularly sensitive. The two of them used to talk over their literary projects with even exchange." London's photographer friend Arnold Genthe noted the same thing. "They would write all day in adjoining rooms and in the evening go over each other's work. Jack London in those days rarely gave a manuscript its final typing until he had submitted the drafts to Sterling, who had an eagle eye for careless writing."[9]

In one surviving earlier exchange, as he read through *The Call of the Wild*, Sterling challenged use of the words "penetrated" and "rippling" in the sentence "In the fall of the year they penetrated a weird lake country, sad and silent, where wild-fowl had been, but where then there was no life or sign of life—only the blowing of chill winds, the forming of ice in sheltered places, and the melancholy rippling of waves on lonely beaches." London stuck to his guns, but in a letter Sterling appealed the point to Bierce, who replied, "The passage that you quote from Jack London strikes me as good. I don't dislike the word 'penetrate'—rather like it. It is in frequent use regarding exploration and discovery. But I think you are right about 'rippling'; it is too lively a word to be outfitted with such an adjective as 'melancholy.'"[10] Of course, London had stood on the shores of cold northern lakes and observed how such rippling could magnify the sense of loneliness and melancholy, and they had not.

From late 1904 into 1905 there was plenty of work to edit, for London had long since established the rule, and he lived by it, doggedly, of writing 1,000 words every day, without fail, whether or not inspiration was upon him. He wrote a short piece, "The Story of Keesh," which was sold to *Holiday*, and an "Explanation of Socialist Vote in U.S." for the *Examiner*. Knowing of London's circumstances, George Brett sent him $3,000 against *The Sea-Wolf*'s earnings and stayed in close editorial touch as London vented a plume of his socialist steam in a volume of reformist essays that Brett published in April 1905 as *The War of the Classes*. The final essay in it was a reworking of "How I Became a Socialist," which he had written for John Spargo upon his return from England. He also produced a new novel, set in the world of boxing, called *The Game*, which came out in June. Then he turned his attention to a collection of short stories for juvenile readers. Just as *The Cruise of the Dazzler* recounted his days as an oyster pirate, this new one was drawn from the days after he joined the law, *Tales of the Fish Patrol*, published in September.

Sterling's editorial eye never faltered, and moreover it was Sterling who, to his credit, tapped into an entirely new vein of London's creativity, a sweet gift of expression that would have shocked the readers who even then were snatching *The Sea-Wolf*, which had finally appeared in book form in October 1904, off the bookstore shelves and shuddering over its savagery. London wrote a poem about Sterling; it was never published, but the Greek cherished it among his papers, perhaps his consolation prize for later losing the Wolf himself.

Entitled "George Sterling," so there would be no mistaking what it was about, it describes a beneficent gardener who manually and gently opens an iris bud that was having difficulty blooming. Serene in rhythm and propelled by a complex rhyming sequence, it shows to a startling degree what kind of poet London could have become, had he been free to follow his earliest natural childhood bent: gentle, loving, inquisitive, enthralled and enthralling.

Here was a side of London's creative wherewithal that readers of his muscular fiction and his angry socialism would never become familiar with, and Sterling had the satisfaction of knowing that it was he who had unfolded London's artistic edges. But Sterling, for his part, gained more than the satisfaction of mentorship from his intimate association with London, and he gained more even than validation, for despite his own formidable talent he must have been aware that he would be catalogued as a "minor" poet. Time spent with London was time away from the cold realities of his own life that were an artistic cruelty. Carrie was not shy about letting him know that he was a disappointment to her, and as she aged, all that remained of her former beauty was her bone structure. And then there was Bierce, who bossed him unmercifully; London gave Sterling the freedom of his deep sensuality, where Bierce projected his prudery to such an extent that, once on a canoe trip, he forced Sterling to jump in the river when Carrie rounded a bend unexpectedly because it was unseemly for Sterling's own wife to see him in a bathing suit.[11]

The possibility that London and Sterling might have become, or experimented with becoming, lovers was sensed early on. In her highly selective two-volume biography of London, Charmian (who later saw to it that any mention of morphine was omitted from his death certificate) was emphatic that he was too high and noble to have considered it. Later, the idea that their feelings for each other may have tapped into the sexual has proven more appealing to authors of Jack London literary criticism than to his leading biographers, who have been virtually unanimous[12] in their conclusion that both he and Sterling would have been livid at any hint of homosexual suspicion. And that is undoubtedly true, for the only frame of reference they would have had for homosexuality in that era were the effeminate, rouge-cheeked inverts London had seen lounging about the Flatiron Building, mincing and posing. According to the prevailing paradigm, if two men had relations, one must necessarily assume the role of a woman; Wolf and the Greek were nothing like that. London's relation of his dream to Charmian, however, characterizing his ideal male companion, explicitly embraced love of the body as well as love of the spirit. Nor is it realistic to think they were unaware of such sentiments elsewhere among the more effeminate men of The Crowd, whether on the part of the older Charles Warren Stoddard or the younger Michael Williams, with both of whom they maintained warm friendships. So if sometimes on their drunken pub crawls or amid their swimming and fencing and nude photography and poetry reading and shared confidences, there were moments when they stumbled across the discovery that love can be masculine on both parts, without either of them resorting to the pathetic feminized caricature that was the popular perception of the homosexual at that time, they would not have been the first to do so. Nor would they have been the first to conclude that the rest of the world would not understand it, and decide to keep it between themselves. London was never bashful about recommending the therapeutic value of recreational sex, and Sterling was equally forthright in his contention that orgasms liberated creativity. Although the most noted affairs of both men were certainly with women, it seems not improbable that Wolf and the Greek found time and circumstance for one another, but neither man ever committed to paper how deep their relationship extended.

❧ ❧ ❧

It was Charles Warren Stoddard who discovered the charm of Carmel-by-the-Sea, a hamlet on the coast southwest of Monterey, and very near the thirty-acre estate of Charles Rollo Peters. The Crowd was seized with the rapture, partly out of disaffection with mainstream society, partly out of a sense of their own superiority, and largely because of rent spikes caused by completion of the Hall of Justice near their San Francisco haunts, to relocate there and live as a colony of artists, free to inhale the purity of their own atmosphere.

The setting offered the inspiration of nature, and the privacy to pursue their lives and bohemian liaisons free from the scrutiny of lesser, conventional people. They adopted rules that were informal but strict. One of their first decisions was not to pave the lanes and encourage tourists with their horseless carriages. Mornings were for work; there was to be no socializing before noon. Most illumination was by candlelight; kerosene was permitted but frowned upon, and electricity was not allowed to intrude its harsh glare. Likewise there was no gas for cooking, and no stores in which to shop. Meals were prepared over fires, and lists of needed supplies were posted by the road so the Monterey grocers would know where to come out and deliver them—even as London's stepfather had once plied such a trade. Socially, there was to be no standing upon rank; ambitious beginners were treated with the same respect as the working professionals. It was an egalitarianism fueled at least in part by the presence of so many socialists, who happily shared food, drink, and rhetoric with such gusto that when the dour old capitalist Ambrose Bierce visited the group, he shook the dust from his feet as he left and vowed never to return.

Sterling, to wife Carrie's mortification, resigned from his uncle's real estate firm and resolved to live, full time, as a poet. Sterling built a house at their camp there—or rather it was provided for him by his aunt, Missus Havens. They called it the Bungalow, an oversized cabin on a hilltop, the focal point of which "was a large oblong room, with a large fireplace, a wide porch, and back of the house a ring of trees surrounded by skulls, and having in the midst a fireplace in the form of an altar."[13] Believing that the dream London had handed him of their indissoluble love was still in effect, Sterling reserved the neighboring lot for him, counting on living next to his Wolf. But it was not to be.

Even as they romped and read poetry together, London had been sinking deeper into his "long sickness," the depression that had begun to take hold of him before leaving for Korea. Dividing his time between Charmian and her people in Glen Ellen, and Sterling and The Crowd as they began relocating to their colony at Carmel, London felt torn in two. Eventually he must make a decision, and when London had to inform Sterling that he was going to establish his household near Charmian's aunt in Glen Ellen, Sterling wrote him an anguished letter on the death of their dream, and sounding out whether there might still be a chance for them. "No," London wrote him back, "I am afraid that the dream was too bright to last—our being near each other. . . . It's not through any fault of yours, nor through any fault of mine. The world and people just happen to be so made."[14]

To any man who ever failed to keep the love of another man, no more gentle reproof could have been possible. Elsewhere in the letter London described his current financial woes in detail—hundreds of dollars in doctors' and dentists' bills for Flora, Bessie, the two girls, Mammy Jennie, and his stepsister Ida Miller, who had spent five weeks in the hospital, and that was apart from "the several hundred dollars that Bessie's lawyer hooked me up for." His purpose, he explained, was to demonstrate to Sterling that there was still an intimacy between them. "You are the only person in the world I'd take the trouble for. The rest could go to the devil and I wouldn't care. But you, dear Greek, you I do want to know." But as for the idyll that they both once had envisioned, that dream would have to be put away. "If you don't understand now, some day sooner or later you may come to understand."

One thoughtful biographer has suggested that London would have loved Sterling completely if he had dared, but that his eventual choice of Charmian over him represented the same calm harbor that his choice of Bessie over Anna Strunsky had provided a few years before: social acceptance, safety from ridicule, and a refuge from his own passions, which he well knew could be tempestuous.[15] This view is consonant with London's habitual self-sacrifice in his desire to do the right things by others—his life-long support of Flora despite her manipulative shrewishness, and the generous allowance he settled on Bessie and the girls. It would also embrace London's active study of the subconscious, and his wariness of the consequences it could wreak on careless decisions.

London was aware that he had intellectual equals among the bohemians in San Francisco, in ways that Charmian could not compete with. But during the course of 1905 he also came to realize that he did not need other equal captains; what he needed was his Mate—one who loved and helped and understood and steadied him in ways that The Crowd could not compete with. George Sterling left London a more complete artist than he found him, but that service did not save him. Soon after London's gentle letter demoting the Greek's station in his life, Charmian could write in her diary, "So good to be going about publicly together—Jack and I. I've waited so long, so long."[16]

London himself was simpler in his assessment to Charmian that he had chosen her because she represented to him both man-love and woman-love. Indeed, therein probably lay the root of his "long sickness," his inability to force himself to abandon the dream once more after Sterling had come so close to actualizing it. Reluctant to put it away, but perhaps realizing that the only way left to fulfill his relationship with Sterling was to risk being relegated to the literary and social margin like Stoddard and Magnus, London saw in Charmian the best way out, and he took it. Even from a distance Bierce knew that Sterling was heartsick about something, but did not question him. "No," he wrote a correspondent, "George has not acquainted me with his trouble, and of course I have not asked him. Something about Jack London, wasn't it?" As time had passed, Bierce's earlier tentative approval of London had soured and withered until he was able to add, "I detest Jack London. He has a lot of brains, but neither honesty nor shame."[17]

Sterling seems to have passed through a crisis of his own, spending not all his time at the new bungalow in Carmel, but also living part time out of a room at the Bohemian Club in San Francisco, a safe nest from which he began pursuing a shadow life away from Carrie and her frustrated expectations. London continued an affectionate relationship with him, but on the understanding now that he and Charmian would be married as soon as his divorce became final. Wolf and the Greek went together down to Colma, just south of San Francisco, to cover the lightweight boxing championship for Hearst,[18] and they frequently made the rounds of bars when London was in the city. They became regulars at a trotline of taverns, where London gained more local fame for his consumption of "cannibal sandwiches" of raw meat and onions, or duck that had barely been passed over a flame before being pressed, and occasionally getting into fights. Both Carrie and Sterling's mother blamed London's bad influence for the beginning of Sterling's long, gradual breakdown, but in reality it was probably not London, but losing London, that was the beginning of his descent.

❧ ❧ ❧

Jack London opened 1905 by briefly evading his personal dramas with a trip to Los Angeles to lecture. First fan Cloudesley Johns had escaped both his poverty and his dusty village to a comfortable house and income in the city. For himself, Johns had worked out a stamp of socialism similar to London's own, one that demanded an equality of opportunity for everyone, but one that accepted a well-appointed life as a reward for hard work. He had begun hanging about the Socialist Party in Los Angeles, and through him they invited London to speak in Simpson Hall on January 8. (London did make it clear to his first fan that he would need to bring Manyoungi to prepare hot baths for him: "I never could stand a cold sponge." The socialist who had survived winter in a Klondike cabin was clearly evolving.)[19] One result of the flurry of body punches that London had landed on the book-reading public—to say nothing of his looks and his sensational divorce—was their curiosity to see him and hear him speak. This was an art he had begun honing on the street corners of Oakland, and now that he could make trade on his celebrity, he was anxious to tell the people what was wrong with the country. His Los Angeles speech was favorably reported by Julian Hawthorne, son of one of America's literary giants. "Upon his big, hearty, healthy nature is based a brain of unusual clearness and insight . . . his opinions are his own—independent, courageously expounded; with no trace of pose."

If London took his Los Angeles success as a harbinger of wider welcome for his message of social reform, however, he would have to absorb a cruel disappointment. At the end of January he was back home, invited to pick his own subject and lecture at the University of California at Berkeley, where he had been a student for only one semester. He chose the topic of "Revolution," perhaps forgetting this was the same class of people whose clothing he used to launder; they were unlikely to be interested in upending the social order. His Berkeley speech—logical, expository, persuasive—created enough converts among the students that a Socialist Club was started in his wake, but the coldness of his reception there and in other places only served to convince him the more strongly that a just society would never be voluntarily handed down by the class who would lose their privileged position in doing it. The hostility he encountered only helped him rest his case that justice must be taken by revolution. But as it happened in Berkeley, the day's worst gaffe was more lighthearted, when his accusation that literature was being taught using irrelevant texts was countered with a show that students were studying *The Call of the Wild*, and he accepted the loud laugh at his expense in good humor. The new Socialist Club, at least, was an idea that took. A national organization of collegiate socialists was formed in New York the following September, with London as at least nominal president and Upton Sinclair as vice president.

London was now famous enough that when he spoke, news of it extended far beyond the cities where he lectured. When word of his uncompromising viewpoints reached the East, he discovered how entrenched was the economic system he bid to destroy. Laudatory reviews of his stories were now mixed with attacks on his political views, which were widely held to be un-American and dangerous. He was also famous enough to generate news on another front: Charmian may have won London from the embrace of Blanche Partington, but she had known London since he was an impoverished nobody; she could not have prepared for the challenge, now that he was a national celebrity, that the press would be as interested in his private life as in his literary output.

She had to learn to ignore rumors of his infidelity. He had remolded his short story "Scorn of Women," published in his second book, *The God of His Fathers*, into a play, and he was interested in the actress Blanche Bates for the central role of Freda Maloof, a saloon dancer in Dawson during the Klondike rush. (London also discussed the role of Freda with, of all people, Bessie's cousin Minnie Maddern Fiske, and with the legendary Ethel Barrymore, who was initially interested, but by the time the play was published late in 1906 she had decided it was not right for her.) When London appraised Bates performing in another play three nights running, visited her in her dressing room, and hosted a dinner party for her, Charmian was left to read in the newspapers of Bates and London's romantic linkage and reputed upcoming marriage. Charmian knew of London's intense focus on the play, for she had been typing up his drafts, and she knew that he had also discussed the role with another actress, Mary Shaw, whom he had seen in *Mrs. Warren's Profession*. Thus her Mate-Man's denial was sufficient against the charge of involvement with Bates, but now there was a new shoal to navigate in their relationship—a meddlesome press in search of a sensation. She already well knew his randy nature, so she must either trust him or not, and she chose to believe him, assessing that he had not spared her feelings for a lie up to then, and likely would not start now.

London's rumored affair with Blanche Bates lent some spice only days later to his allowing the Oakland socialists to enter his name for mayor. He postponed campaigning, however, so that he and Cloudesley Johns could sail into the Sacramento delta on the *Spray* to write and recreate for six weeks. In doing so he left Charmian in charge of editing and correcting the manuscript of the essay "The Class Struggle," a component of the upcoming *The War of the Classes,* and forwarding it to the publisher. It was an imposition, to be sure, but also gave evidence of his trust in and reliance on her, which she was all too glad to have.

In early May 1905, just when London was agonizing over how to tell Charmian about his affair with Blanche Partington, he was in active ferment over a new novel. His Oakland mentor Fred Bamford was a crack reference librarian, and London wrote him for some preliminary information: "Can you find out for me the following: (1) When do wolves mate? (2) How long do they carry their young? (3) What time of year do they bring forth their young? All this data is for a new book I am beginning." It took Bamford the better part of a day to round up the answers, and ever afterward he related with pride that he had been part of the inception of *White Fang.*[20] Actually, however, the taproot for the book extended back to the previous December, when London was struck by, and made notes on, a piece he read in the San Francisco *Chronicle.* Local author Flora Hines Loughead had considered *The Call of the Wild* and reversed the process in "The Call of the Tame: An Antithesis," about the domestication of a wild wolf-dog. London always acknowledged that the weakest point of his artistry was inventing plots, but once an idea was planted, he could develop it with high panache. Loughead's article electrified him. The next day he dashed off a hasty, ebullient letter to Brett: "I'm dropping you a line hot with the idea . . . Not a sequel to *Call of the Wild.* But a companion to *Call of the Wild.* I'm going to reverse the process. Instead of the devolution or decivilization of a dog, I'm going to give the evolution, the civilization of a dog.—development of domesticity, faithfulness, love, morality, & all the amenities & virtues. . . . A complete antithesis to the *Call of the Wild.* And with that book as a forerunner, it should make a hit. What d'ye think?"

Brett, whose company had made a fortune on *The Call of the Wild* with their single $2,000 lump-sum payment, saw the possibilities in a heartbeat and responded with encouragement, but cautioned that the new tale should not be in any way an extension of the first. The break should be complete. Relearning how energizing it can be when author and editor are mutually attuned, London responded enthusiastically. "Yes, your idea . . . is precisely my idea. There must be no hint of any relation between the two. Even in title I had decided there should not be the slightest resemblance. I have figured on naming book after dog—*White Fang*, for instance, or something like that."[21] White Fang he was indeed, the offspring of a male wolf and female half-wolf, half-dog who eventually takes her pup back to the Indian village she abandoned. Abused by the other dogs in the camp, his lot a misery, White Fang's fate worsens when he is sold for whiskey money to a white tough named Beauty Smith and is trained for the dogfighting arena. Turned into a killer until he is bested and nearly killed by a bulldog, White Fang is rescued by Weedon Scott, learns kindness and how to respond to it, and is taken to California to live out his days as a pet. Although he agreed to make no similarity or reference to *The Call of the Wild*, the story ends with a curious symmetry to the first book, in saving the life of Scott's father, a judge.

By May London was deep in thought over the new story, and almost ready to begin. Instead of settling among the bohemian community as Sterling and others of The Crowd so dearly wanted, London continued working out of his cabin at Wake Robin Lodge. Charmian was with him, but careful now to observe social convention: she stayed in the main house, he in his lodge.

Gradually Charmian took over Sterling's duties as London's first reader and responder. Her eye was different from Sterling's, but it was a good eye even so. Sterling was a poet, alert to the impropriety of a word to the feel or meter of a sentence; Charmian's eye was more purely editorial, reading for general flow and cohesion. She believed in London's gift as completely as Sterling, but she was slower to intrude herself into his work. Doubtless she would have written, and later did write, in a vastly different style—more erudite and grammatically clever—and there were hints that she wished he had written, as Ambrose Bierce demanded from his protégés, with more thought to artistic purity. "Never was I able to wring from him any worship of art for art's sake," she lamented, "although he strove for art . . . [and] attained art, high art at times." But London was adamant that he did not care to be weaned from his conclusion that "I no more believe in Art for Art's sake theory than I believe that a human and humane motive justifies the inartistic telling of a story."

Between the two of them, he was the stylistic pioneer, and she had the good sense not to contest him on points of style that he had already put to rest in his own mind. "Long hot afternoons of typewriter dictation under the trees sometimes got on our mutual touchy nerves," she recalled. "I might unwittingly start disputes in which I had no chance against the assault of his logic." Occasionally she felt herself on the verge of tears, but stifled them when she remembered his cold warning against feminine hysterics.[22] In time they worked more smoothly together; indeed they were a formidable team. Her aunt's husband, Roscoe Eames, was a secretarial entrepreneur who had developed an unconventional but efficient form of shorthand that she had mastered, and she was an ace typist, reaching well over a hundred words per minute on her Remington No. 7 typewriter, newly purchased especially for her role as amanuensis to America's most popular author. These skills in addition to her sharp editorial instincts made her a vast help in his work.

And they had fun. In an era in which nearly all photographs were formal and stiffly posed, in most of the photographs of them they mug and pose and grimace over their work, often in full laughter. When she typed the final versions of his countless letters, she reserved the option to temper his tendency to hyperbole with her own corrections. "It's warm, nay, hot," London wrote Fred Bamford late in the summer of 1905. "I am dripping sweat. Charmian, who is hammering the typewriter, says she is *dribbling* sweat! (Didn't either, Mr. B.—C.K.) And we're going swimming; and after that, when it gets cooler, to drive an unruly cow up to the ranch."[23] To prove her gameness she even boxed with him. She stood in and took her licks, and occasionally landed a shot of her own, one occasionally drawing blood from the other, an occasion for praise and solicitous inquiry. It would have been a high price for a woman to pay for a man, had Charmian not understood the nature of sport and been keen to compete. One did not box, she allowed, without the expectation of getting one's blood up and thinking it healthy to do so. She also noted that he never took cheap shots at her and never landed punches on any "feminine unmentionables." In further fairness, London always freely admitted her superiority at her own sport, riding horses, and made sure that she knew how much he wished he could match her grace in the saddle.

They loved each other madly, but they slept apart. She suffered from insomnia, and he thrashed in his sleep and might rise to read or write or light up a cigarette at any hour. He smoked and suffered the smoker's cough; she did not smoke, but quickly learned that it was a sensitive subject with him that she was not to press. In any event, his divorce would not be final until the following autumn, and some heed still had to be paid to convention. As satisfying as it was, however, for him to finally have a partner whose libido matched his own, Charmian was also alert to the fact that emotional intimacy still eluded him as his depression approached a crisis. Throughout the spring and summer she had acted as his typist and secretary, sparring partner and bedmate, but emotionally he had held her at arm's length or more.

And to be sure, his "long sickness" held their relationship hostage even as it gave him no peace with George Sterling. It turned out there were multiple reasons he had been distant from her. He felt guilty about his involvement with Blanche Partington. He also grew discouraged when the body of which he was so proud began letting him down. He had developed his flat feet marching with Kelly's Army, and he had nearly died of scurvy in Alaska, but now he suffered symptoms that all but convinced him that he had bowel cancer and that his long climb out of obscurity was headed toward a cruel joke with his early death. Treatment, when he finally sought it, showed nothing worse than hemorrhoids, which were corrected with minor surgery. But neither of those reached into the root of his depression. Where members of The Crowd each kept a vial of cyanide, London kept a pistol, but once he actually began weighing suicide, he disposed of it when he could no longer guarantee that he wouldn't use it.

Nevertheless, he was not beyond reach. He and Charmian went riding daily, her body conforming elegantly to the movements of her horse and he bouncing helplessly up and down in his saddle. As they explored the tracts around Wake Robin, the country around Sonoma Mountain quickly came to have a particular effect on him that went beyond its being scenic. Perhaps for the first time in his life, he felt peace there. They explored one small ranch property that was for sale. About forty acres of it had once been cleared for a vineyard, now fallow. The remaining ninety acres began on the southeast with a forested defile along Asbury Creek, crossed the Valley of the Moon, and spread up hills covered with majestic stands of timber on the flank of Sonoma Mountain. It took his breath away and he put up a $500 option to purchase it. He described it to George Brett as "the most beautiful, primitive land to be found in California. There are great redwoods on it, some of them thousands of years old . . . there are great firs, tan-bark oaks, maples, live-oaks, white-oaks, black-oaks, madrono and manzanita galore. There are canyons, several streams of water, many springs, etc. . . . for the last two months I have been riding all over these hills, looking for just such a place." London asked Brett to forward $6,500 of royalties, pointing out that they had already been earned by *The Sea-Wolf*. The place had to be saved, lumbermen were already on the property when he snapped it up, and he must pay the balance or lose his $500 option. "Arrange it any way you wish," he insisted, "every moment counts."[24]

Brett found a way to comply, and London thus acquired the first tract of the Beauty Ranch that occupied him for the rest of his life, writing Sterling that he was throwing out an anchor so heavy that all hell could not get it up again. It was a signal moment for him, not just because it gave him a retreat to enjoy with Charmian, but it gave him as well a whole new set of themes to develop in his writing. London had begun his literary career with the terror of nature and steeped it in the cruelty of people one against another. Now for several months he had basked in the fierce and steadfast love of a woman he deeply respected, and now for the first time he realized the redemptive power of nature, the ability of the land to heal itself and those on it. Perhaps it might even heal him.

The effect showed in his writing. In a sense, *White Fang*, on which he was hard at work and in which the application of love and kindness healed the savagery of its subject's early life, also healed the bleak ending of *The Call of the Wild*. Only several days before writing Brett for the money to complete purchasing the ranch, he had completed a story, "All Gold Canyon," that was radically different from his previous work in feeling and lyricism and sense of wonder, in which a wild gorge heals itself after the incursion of rapacious miners.[25] The story opened a hopeful theme that he amplified in many later works, but this first appearance of it escaped Charmian's intuition; indeed she was almost convinced that she had lost him. She and Aunt Netta both had been urging him to stay indefinitely at Wake Robin but he declined. He wanted to go sailing; the *Spray* was moored at Napa, and Charmian sadly accompanied him toward there on horseback, through the forests of Nunn's Canyon with its multiple bridges over a tumbling stream. On this trip the land's cure finally, inexplicably, took; his mood lightened and then rocketed. He exulted in the landscape; he accounted that he had received a $350 prize for the short story "A Nose for the King" in a contest sponsored by *The Black Cat,* and he asked her to buy him a horse with it. At the top of a grade he stopped and laid a hand on her shoulder. "You did it all, my Mate Woman. You've pulled me out. You've *rested* me so. . . . Something wonderful has happened to me. I am all right now. Dear My Woman, you need not be afraid for me any more." At last she knew that their kiss goodbye was not the end, and "there was that in his eyes which brought tears to mine. But it was the happy rain of a new day. . . . I turned and retraced the road, hardly able to contain myself."[26]

FLORA CHANEY LONDON
Reproduced by permission of the Huntington Library, San Marino, California

Jack London's mother was a free-loving nonconformist, a spiritualist who earned most of her living by holding séances. Both her physical growth and emotional state were damaged by a childhood fever; she was brittle, demanding, manipulative, and unloving. London once called her a devil, but kept her on a stipend until he died.

JOHN LONDON
Reproduced by permission of the Huntington Library, San Marino, California

Jack London was eight months old when Flora married his stepfather, a Civil War veteran partially disabled by lung disease. He worked to the limit of his ability, but was repeatedly ruined by Flora's pushing him into financial overextension. He was kind and attentive to his stepson, who adored him.

JOHNNY LONDON,
AGE 8, WITH ROLLO
Reproduced by permission of the Huntington Library, San Marino, California

At eight, Jack had his first set of store-bought underwear, but it was the end of his childhood. When not studying at the Cole Grammar School, he was soon throwing newspapers morning and evening to help with the family income, and on weekends setting pins in a bowling alley and working on an ice wagon. Remembering these years bitterly, he called himself the Work Beast.

HICKMOTT'S CANNERY
Courtesy Oakland Public Library, Oakland History Room

At fourteen, Johnny London—now "Jack"—got a full-time job stuffing pickles into jars for ten cents an hour, at least ten hours a day and usually more. This rare photo of Hickmott's interior was taken some years after his stint there, but shows the exposed machine belts that occasionally caused serious injuries.

JACK LONDON WITH KELLY'S ARMY

Reproduced by permission of the Huntington Library, San Marino, California

After spraining both wrists shoveling coal at a railway power house, London learned that he was replacing two men, each of whom earned more than he did. He quit in a rage, and while recuperating joined the Commonweal of Christ's march on Washington for a federal jobs program. Later tramping landed him in jail in Buffalo, but he also met educated men who introduced him to socialist principles. (London is just visible in the lower right corner.)

IN YOKOHAMA

Reproduced by permission of the Huntington Library, San Marino, California

Filled with library-book visions of the romantic world beyond Oakland, London finally got to travel at seventeen, as a boat puller on the sealing schooner *Sophia Sutherland*. Eagerly taking shore leave in Japan, he was deflated to learn that Yokohama was a prosaic and largely Westernized city.

INA COOLBRITH
Reproduced by permission of the Huntington Library, San Marino, California

A divorcée and estranged granddaughter of Mormon founder Joseph Smith, Oakland's librarian recognized the secretiveness of family strife in Jack London. A published poet at thirteen, she also recognized his talent and love of books, and guided his reading regimen for years. He idolized her.

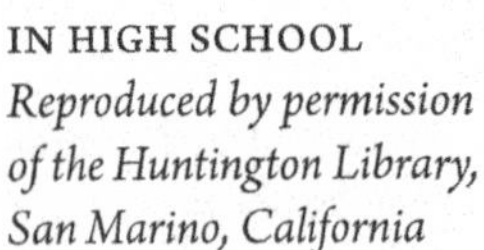

IN HIGH SCHOOL
Reproduced by permission of the Huntington Library, San Marino, California

Returning to Oakland, London finished his secondary education, even though he was much older than the other students. Some mocked him for earning his keep as the janitor; others were fascinated by his raffish life and admired his writing in the school magazine.

DRESSED FOR THE YUKON

Reproduced by permission of the Huntington Library, San Marino, California

With money borrowed from his loyal stepsister Eliza, London left for the Alaska gold fields only ten days after news of the strike arrived in California. He went with no thought of mining for literary material. Sick of poverty and hopelessness, he went to find gold.

DEAD HORSE GULCH

Courtesy the Alaska State Library; Asa Baldwin Photos, ASL-P71-344

Many Klondikers took horses to Alaska to do their hauling, only to discover a murderous climate, vicious terrain, and no forage. London loved horses, and was appalled by the rampant cruelty and abuse. Dead Horse Gulch, on the way to the gold region, was only one ravine where exhausted animals were discarded.

KLONDIKER CAMP

Courtesy F.H. Nowell, John Urban Collection; Anchorage Museum B64.1.26

The disorganization of the Klondike gold rush approached total chaos. London prepared better than most, taking with him books on the geography and exploration of the far North.

CHILKOOT PASS

Courtesy the Alaska State Library; Eric A. Hegg Photos, ASL-P124-04

The exit from Alaska to the gold fields of the Canadian Yukon lay atop Chilkoot Pass, a trek three-quarters of a mile long, upward at a forty-five-degree angle. The daunting sight made many would-be prospectors go home. London traversed the climb many times, hauling up his half-ton of gear in hundred-pound stages.

ANNA STRUNSKY

Reproduced by permission of the Huntington Library, San Marino, California

Refugees from Czarist pogroms in Russia, the Strunsky family settled in San Franciso and prospered. London was fascinated by Anna's brilliance, her free spirit, and the ferocity of her political views. But there were ways in which she was sheltered, and when Jack proposed marriage she hesitated. He took this for rejection, married another, and they were left to negotiate their love for each other on more difficult terms.

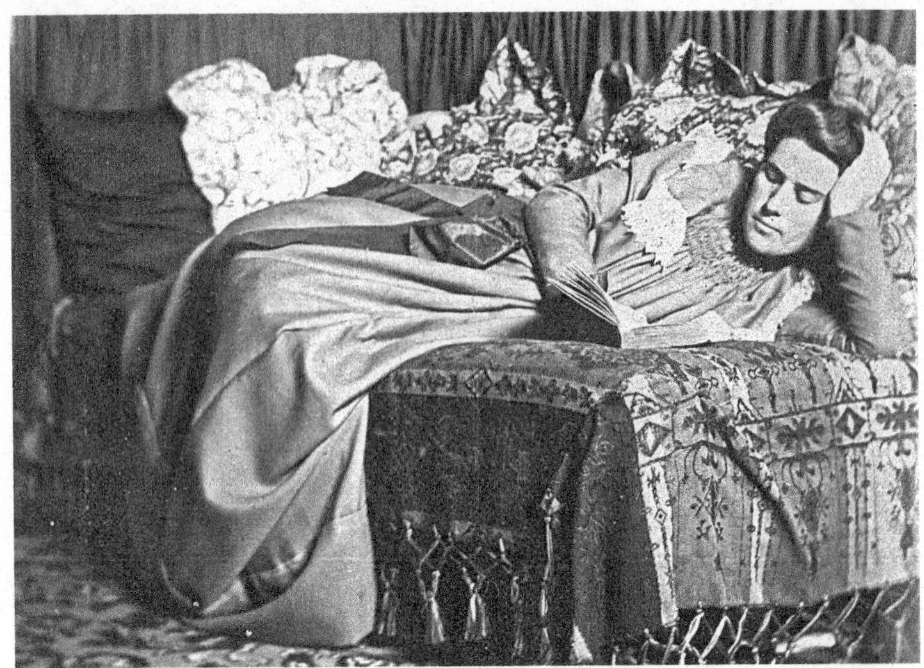

BESS MADDERN LONDON

Reproduced by permission of the Huntington Library, San Marino, California

London's first marriage was doomed from the start. They didn't love each other, but agreed that their compatibility would make a good home for children. He loved company and entertaining, she preferred seclusion. He was full-blooded and sexual, she could barely tolerate the act. His desertion turned her into a vengeful harpy.

BECKY AND JOAN

Reproduced by permission of the Huntington Library, San Marino, California

London's two daughters were born in rapid succession, even as his marriage was foundering. With no frames of parental reference from his own childhood, London was an unsuitable father, alternately berating and spoiling the girls.

R.M.S. *MAJESTIC*
Photographer unknown, public domain

As a sailor London was enthralled by the R.M.S. *Majestic*. When she went into service she was the largest and fastest ship in the world. As a socialist, however, he was repelled by the Atlantic liner's role in trafficking impoverished immigrants to the United States, to be chuffed like human coal into the boiler of capitalist exploitation.

IN THE EAST END OF LONDON
Reproduced by permission of the Huntington Library, San Marino, California

London took a large number of photographs while researching *The People of the Abyss*—tramps, workhouses, homeless people sleeping in parks—that are now an important document of Edwardian England. He is seen here in his undercover guise as a cast-off American sailor, down on his luck.

IN TROUBLE IN KOREA

Reproduced by permission of the Huntington Library, San Marino, California

On assignment as a war correspondent for Hearst Newspapers in 1904, London spent much of his time covering the Russo-Japanese War trying to outwit Japanese press handlers, who were intent on preventing Western reporters from learning anything meaningful. His determination often landed him in trouble with the Imperial Army.

A FEW OF THE CROWD AT CARMEL

Reproduced by permission of the Huntington Library, San Marino, California

Sharing an intellectual moment on the beach are (from left) London's best friend George Sterling, whom London called The Greek on account of his classical beauty; Southwest chronicler Mary Austin, who adored Sterling and was jealous of his intimacy with London; London himself; and his childhood friend who became a capable short story writer, Jimmy Hopper.

THE ARTIST AS A YOUNG MAN

Reproduced by permission of the Huntington Library, San Marino, California

Impressed with London's literary talent, a magazine editor sent him to the great photographer Arnold Genthe to make a portrait. Genthe was captivated by the mixture of dreaminess and determination, femininity and steel, and he took a remarkable series of pictures.

WOLF AND THE GREEK

Reproduced by permission of the Huntington Library, San Marino, California

London was an autodidact, and occasionally misunderstood the principles of philosophy that he taught himself. He was captivated by the image of Nietzsche's "blond beast" and erroneously believed him to represent the super race. He often struck poses to show off his own physique, but as he aged, his growing belly was harder to conceal.

CHARMIAN KITTREDGE
Reproduced by permission of the Huntington Library, San Marino, California

Brilliant but not particularly attractive, Charmian was the first woman London knew whom he could neither con nor dominate. She was literate, modern—including honest about her enthusiasm for sex—an adventuress and a practical joker. At their first substantive conversation alone, London catalogued the things about her that he didn't like, and then kissed her.

THE REMINGTON #7
Reproduced by permission of the Huntington Library, San Marino, California

Charmian was not welcomed into London's crowd of San Francisco bohemians, where beauty was as important as brilliance. London, however, had the good sense to recognize her love, her intelligence, her editorial eye, and the fact that she took shorthand and could pound out a hundred words per minute on her Remington #7 typewriter, which she purchased to process his secretarial work.

SNARK LEAVING HONOLULU
Reproduced by permission of the Huntington Library, San Marino, California

London alienated much of America's socialist community by lavishing $35,000 on his yacht *Snark*, and he tried to make amends with lectures in Hawaii and Tahiti that were coldly received. He was not against work or having luxuries; he was against exploiting others to obtain luxuries. His enchantment with the rich and gentle native Hawaiian culture led him to reexamine the "racialism" with which he had long been comfortable.

RIDING ON THE RANCH
Reproduced by permission of the Huntington Library, San Marino, California

Charmian was an expert equestrienne, but London taught himself to ride in Korea and was always ungainly in the saddle—a sailor on horseback, as one observer characterized him. Disillusioned with American society, London increasingly withdrew to his Beauty Ranch, where he practiced progressive agriculture and husbandry.

CHARMIAN AMONG MELANESIAN NATIVES
Reproduced by permission of the Huntington Library, San Marino, California

There was a very good reason that Charmian went armed when ashore in remote corners of the South Pacific: head-hunting and cannibalism were still a way of life. Furious with American critics who accused him of exaggerating the danger, London could name names of those who had hosted them, and were later eaten.

ELIZA LONDON SHEPARD
Reproduced by permission of the Huntington Library, San Marino, California

London was eight years younger than his stepsister Eliza, who helped raise him. Their relationship of love and trust was one of the most stable and enduring of his life.

NEUADD HILLSIDE
Reproduced by permission of the Huntington Library, San Marino, California

London's lifelong love of horses reached its zenith when he acquired this stunning shire stallion, whom he proudly showed off to visitors. The animal's sudden death was a terrible calamity.

ON THE PORCH OF WOLF HOUSE
Reproduced by permission of the Huntington Library, San Marino, California

Built of lava blocks and redwood in the style of the great Western hotels, christened Wolf House by George Sterling, a sinkhole of his earnings but a labor of love, the enormous lodge burned to cinders the night it was finished. London feigned philosophical calm, but he never recovered.

TOGETHER AT THE END
Reproduced by permission of the Huntington Library, San Marino, California

Charmian was deeply wounded by London's infidelities, but understood his nature, accepted his contrition, and appreciated the tenacity of his love for her. She remained fiercely loyal to him long after his death, and shaded her two-volume biography to soften his harsher aspects.

11 ❧ THE CELEBRITY

Jack London originally rode to literary fame on the trio of *The Kempton-Wace Letters, The People of the Abyss,* and *The Call of the Wild,* published in rapid succession. Since then, amid a steady production of articles, juvenile stories, and reportage, it was *The Sea-Wolf* that had kept public attention riveted on him. Now it was time for his maturing voice to consolidate the laurels won early on.

Publication of *The War of the Classes* in April 1905 underscored the national news coverage he had been garnering for his increasingly outspoken views on social reform. Its collected essays, old and new, summarized his characteristic revolutionary message that seemed less and less popular. But backed by George Brett and his long history of publishing social reform, he hoped that with room to clarify and expound, his message would sound less threatening.

While some found it incongruous that the country's loudest socialist traveled with an obsequious Oriental valet, London became increasingly provocative in his rhetoric. Following up the lecture at Berkeley with another at Stockton, and then in giving one passionate speech during his ensuing campaign for mayor, he vented his frustration that audiences, while they admitted his intelligence and fire, rejected his political views. At one point he even ventured to insult his audience: "You are ignoramuses. Your fatuous self-sufficiency blinds you to the revolution that is surely, surely coming, and which will as surely wipe you and your silk-lined, puffed up leisure off the map." No longer merely the "boy socialist" of Oakland, London made his first public foray as a bona fide celebrity, and he made a mess of it.

Brilliant as he was at preaching to the socialist choir, as a representative to the general public he was an unalloyed disaster. What eluded him was the fact that the kind of stem-winding barnburner of a speech that would galvanize an audience of radicals was exactly the wrong tack to take with nonpolitical laymen he might have persuaded, but whom instead he alienated and alarmed. In the election, he quadrupled the tally he received four years earlier, to 941, but he still finished only third. Worse, he lost any possibility of winning over converts; SOCIETY CLOSES GATES ON YOUNG AUTHOR, noted the Los Angeles *Examiner*—as though being debarred from the company of those he had been calling "drones and parasites" was a punishment.

Some observers, such as a now thoroughly disenchanted Ambrose Bierce, believed that London's increasing shrillness was a publicity stunt to hype sales of *The War of the Classes*, which indeed went into a third printing within a year.[1] Even if this had been London's intention, the ploy backfired, because newspapers that were increasingly hostile to him found him a more tempting target to misquote or attribute out of context. During one presentation he allowed that in the United States people such as himself were free to argue to the extent of their energy to persuade a majority to accept peaceful reform, while in countries such as Russia that freedom did not exist. Therefore, he said, "I think and speak of the assassins in Russia as my comrades." Only that last sentence, however, became the money phrase, the hot quote for which London was widely excoriated, as its context was left in the auditorium. In an even starker example, London cited the case of abolitionist General Sherman Bell on the eve of the Civil War, who had so famously declared, "To hell with the Constitution!" London expounded that if conditions existed in which the Constitution sanctioned outrages and protected their perpetrators, then that phrase would be appropriate. That was too meticulous a distinction for most of the journals, and the whole discussion was reduced to JACK LONDON SAYS TO HELL WITH THE CONSTITUTION, and the San Francisco *Newsletter* maintained that he should be tried for treason.

Nevertheless, *The War of the Classes* sold in amazing numbers, solidly profitable for Brett—and an eloquent testimony that not every reader in the United States was as content with the status quo as the newspapers claimed even as they panned it. In Europe, where there was even less social mobility than in America, and where there had been a spate of anarchist unrest, the book was an even greater sensation.

As London attempted to grow into his celebrity, Charmian became increasingly indispensable to his work. She took dictation and typed; they boxed and rode and fell even more in love. London's awakening from his "long sickness" that Charmian had witnessed after their ride through Nunn's Canyon was his final surrender. He had been negotiating it for weeks, settling it in his mind that he could live without the ultimate male companion of whom he had always dreamed. One thing that helped him to this conclusion was his noticing, when associating with The Crowd in San Francisco as they prepared to relocate to Carmel, that their wit and repartee and disdain for workaday society was underlain by a persistent gloom. On the artists' wall at Coppa's restaurant, where they often congregated, a member of the circle transcribed a line from sad Nora May French, in script inverted and reversed: "I have an idea that all sensible people will ultimately be damned." Whatever its source, whether a suspicion that they were not as brilliant as they pretended, or a more generalized sense of alienation from the majority culture that all artists feel, they were fixated on youth, beauty, brilliance—and doom.

London noticed that this sadness also affected their work: they didn't actually do much. It took time and physical separation from them for him to realize that he was cut from fundamentally different cloth. *The War of the Classes* was his eleventh major opus, *The Game* his twelfth, and the juvenile-oriented *Tales of the Fish Patrol* followed in September. Now he was preparing a new collection of stories for Macmillan to include "All Gold Canyon" and seven others, he would publish *Moon-Face and Other Stories* the next year, and *White Fang* was on deck. His spiritual if not physical lover George Sterling was seven years older, and he was still trying to put together only his second volume of poems. From the standpoint of simply being able to write, life with Charmian made vastly more sense.

She took $250 of London's prize money from the *Black Cat* contest and, as he requested, bought him a horse. It was named Washoe Ban, a dazzling chestnut thoroughbred of chiseled conformation and eyes as liquid as his own. London was at Wake Robin recuperating from his surgery when Charmian led him out to see him, and London's heart melted at the sight of the magnificent animal. For once it seemed as though his life was on track. He and Charmian would marry when he was free, and he now owned the nearby tract of which he had written Brett. Of course, saving those oaks and redwoods from the lumberman's ax took every dime he had, especially after he bought the previous tenant's stock and ranch equipment as well, and hired a foreman named Werner Wiget to run the place. That one of America's leading socialists was now a stakeholder in the American dream spoke eloquently to the peculiar concept of socialism that he had developed. He took a backseat to none in his insistence on equality of opportunity and dignified treatment in the workplace, but to him socialism was not about banning wealth; it was about banning wealth accrued by exploiting others.

London had made his commitment to Charmian, but getting The Crowd to accept her looked to be a campaign of Napoleonic proportions. They had already tried to wreck the pair with Blanche Partington, to which Charmian's brilliant response was to make a friend of her and acknowledge with a smile that she couldn't blame any woman for loving Jack. She then left London to stew in discomfort over what the two women might talk about when alone together. Blanche, for her part, never again gave Charmian reason for jealousy.

Sterling had opposed admitting Charmian into The Crowd, but faced ultimately with the prospect of losing his Wolf or sharing him, he chose the latter. In fact, it was Sterling's wife who presented the most immovable obstacle. In the matter of Charmian, Carrie had been a consummate hypocrite; on Charmian's few visits to San Francisco, Carrie had welcomed her warmly and hosted her generously, leaving Charmian with no clue what was being whispered behind her back. Carrie's own marriage to the Greek had become a nest of tensions. Dour by nature and increasingly bitter about Sterling's preference for writing poetry over making money, and probably more aware than The Crowd knew of Sterling's serial infidelity (for which she and Sterling's mother blamed London), she was more than willing to believe anything that Bessie claimed of Charmian's having wrecked her home. Carrie went so far as to write to London requiring his statement of Charmian's conduct in the matter before she would accept her.

For a man who was famous for not making excuses for himself, London's reply was astonishing for its patience and detail. While the Londons lived in the Piedmont bungalow, before his trip to England, "Charmian was often at the house. There was not the least iota even of flirtation between us. During that time I was tangled up with Anna Strunsky." As his marriage became unbearable, "I made up my mind to go to pieces. . . . I was going out on the *Spray* to have a hell of a time, with any woman I could get hold of. I had my eyes on a dozen women." He thought of Charmian in this connection. "I was not in love with her, had never even flirted with her." His illicit design crashed when he fell from a wagon and was injured badly enough that he could not take the boat out at all. Charmian delivered him some supplies to take to Bessie and helped him pack. They had half an hour together, during which London realized that he loved her. After they parted, he wrote her a letter, asking to see her; they rendezvoused and admitted how powerfully they were attracted to each other. "Bessie was jealous and suspicious at that time. She feared every woman. She was jealous of the nurse-girl, jealous of everybody. Going through my wastepaper basket constantly, piecing torn shreds of letters together, etc., etc." One letter that she reconstructed was from Charmian, but as it was typewritten she could not identify the source. London warned her of this, and over the telephone Charmian declared that she would be game for her share of the trouble.

Carrie, London challenged, had wronged Charmian in alleging that she had broken up the London household. "I don't consider it a crime for any woman . . . to attempt to cut out a man from under the guns of another woman. . . . It happens in this case however . . . that Charmian is absolutely Not Guilty. It makes your mistake more egregious in-so-far as you have made that mistake public. And public you have made it, because already, and for weeks past, the gossip has been dribbling back that The Crowd dropped Charmian because Charmian broke up the London household."

Rather than concede the issue Carrie replied with a pointed cross-examination, to which, again, London replied patiently and firmly, refuting her points in a lawyerly and sometimes blunt way. He avowed his continuing friendship for her but conceded nothing. Carrie seemed to allow the matter simply to drop.[2] If George Sterling needed to be reassured with evidence that he still mattered to London, he needed look no farther than these patient, time-consuming, and detailed letters intended to stay on his wife's good side, notwithstanding her turning into a sour old gossipmonger. In an earlier year Sterling had written a note to Blanche Partington suggesting a schedule by which they could share London; now after his demotion and he had awakened from the dream, Sterling could recognize and be grateful that Charmian was, in fact, sharing him, or at least was shrewd enough not to attempt to leash the Wolf. So now to atone for Carrie's rudeness, Sterling journeyed to Glen Ellen with flowers and a new poem to extend his friendship to her.

London had made it amply clear that settling his affections on her was predicated on her ability to provide him both a woman's love and a man's companionship, and the test of her willingness to do so was not long in coming. Midsummer 1905 found London reading Joshua Slocum's *Voyage of the Spray*, a memoir of his global travels in a thirty-five-foot sloop, ill-equipped and probably lucky to have survived. He was reading in the presence of Ninetta's husband, Roscoe Eames, who was nearly sixty and a recreational sailor of many years' standing. Suddenly London posed a question to Eames: if Slocum could sail the world in a thirty-five-footer with bad gear, why couldn't they do it in a forty-five-footer with better equipment and more company aboard? Like schoolboys the two wove a fabric of mental circumnavigation, until suddenly London turned to her. "What do *you* say, Charmian?—suppose five years from now, after we're married and have built our house somewhere, we start on a voyage around the world."

Charmian had failed one test and was not about to fail again. "I'm with you every foot of the way," she stated. And then she went him one better: why wait? He was the one who was always saying they were all dying cell by cell, they weren't getting any younger (and she was five years older than he), they would likely never want to travel more than they did right then, and there was little use in building a house just to leave it. London "growled facetiously" that she had hoisted him by his own petard—and she knew she had passed. Thus was born the almost two-year odyssey of planning and building the *Snark*—a vessel named for the mythical creature sought by a mismatched and hapless crew in Lewis Carroll's lugubriously funny "The Hunting of the Snark: An Agony in Eight Fits." Still making his output of a thousand words a day, the *Snark* came to so dominate the rest of his attention—sketching the vessel, envisioning the voyage—that Charmian finally began teasing him that he had lost all his ambition.

Despite the pummeling that he was taking in the press for his espousal of socialist reform, London was increasingly convinced that he had, indeed, set his place at the literary table. On one of his rides with Charmian on Belle and Washoe Ban, they visited the hot springs at Agua Caliente and made the acquaintance of Captain H. E. Boyes and his wife, proper English folk who kept a proper English cottage and maintained close ties to home. In happy surprise, Boyes showed him a letter from Rudyard Kipling praising London highly and asking whether Boyes had ever met him. London, who as a much younger artist had copied out by hand whole pages of Kipling just to catch their music, was undone.[3] Later in the summer, he and Charmian attended the premiere of a play called *The Great Interrogation* by one Ada Lee Bascom, pen name of Mrs. George Hamilton Marsden. Based on a Jack London story, the play was a rousing hit. As the drama critic for the San Francisco *Examiner* reported, tumultuous cries for the author led to London being discovered in a twenty-five cent seat, and he was all but pushed onto the stage to share the acclamation with Bascom. "The man that can talk the ears off a thousand Socialists," noted the *Examiner*, "who is at home on any rostrum from the cart to the curb, was obviously 'rattled.'" London modestly deflected the praise to Bascom, but the reviewer judged that the story and much of the craftsmanship were his.[4]

High summer was also the busy time for Roscoe and Ninetta Eames, for Wake Robin Lodge was a working tourist court, and their most famous residents proved to be something of a draw. In the afternoons, after reaching their daily quota of a thousand words, London and Charmian would often mingle with the tourists at Sonoma Creek's swimming hole. Strangely for a man whose own small daughters had come to play little role in his own life, London frolicked almost domestically with the children of others, teaching them swimming or boxing and reading to them afterward. Charmian was already thirty-five; if they were going to have children of their own, their marriage could not come too soon. After months of stewing over his planned inversion of *The Call of the Wild*, London finally began *White Fang* soon after his mother and nephew arrived. He had considered the piece for so long that progress on it was swift, composed mostly not in his Wake Robin cabin but at his writing table in the trees nearby, with a great woolly dog named Brown Wolf lying at his feet. The story ran about twice the length of its predecessor, with much of the difference consisting not of more complex plot, but of social and evolutionary theory on which London now felt ordained to evangelize rather than letting the story do it for him.

A new controversy began swirling about his writing as *The Game* entered serialization in *Metropolitan* magazine. Some boxing aficionados claimed that its ending, in which the protagonist is killed when his head strikes the canvas floor of the ring, was not credible, and it took an intervention by the world lightweight champion, Jimmy Britt, to settle the criticism in London's favor.

Even as London scaled back his relationship with Sterling, the two of them went to Colma to witness Britt defend his title against Danish challenger Oscar "Battling" Nelson. Britt had defeated him once before on points, but in this bout "Bat" Nelson attacked relentlessly while Britt, who landed whole volleys of punches that had no effect, was beaten to a pulp, finally knocked out in the eighteenth round in a fight that some observers called the most gruesome and desperate they had ever witnessed. Britt might have called *The Game* "an epic on pugilism," but London's reporting on this fight was almost singularly bad. Now that he had come through his "long sickness," it was almost as though the fevered visions of his principal themes—socialism, evolution, raw nature—were racing around in his head like bats about to fly the belfry. At one turn Nelson was an abysmal brute, a fighting animal to Britt's mere thinking animal, at the next turn Nelson was a gaunt proletarian with nothing to lose, and Britt a complacent, sporting, "beautiful as men go" representative of the bourgeoisie seeking to protect what he had accumulated.[5] Whether because he was edgy being with Sterling after their recent tension, or perhaps because they had been out drinking or smoking hashish, the verbose and repetitive piece was a caricature of his now-mature style and, once written, was well left behind.

News reports of London's more radical-sounding lectures, and the brisk sales of *The War of the Classes*, prompted the Slayton Lyceum Bureau to offer him $600 per week to undertake a lecture tour across the country, to begin in late October. While it was time away from the beautiful new ranch, and time away from Charmian, who for convention's sake could not travel with him, it was a badly needed infusion of cash to outfit the new place and to lay the five-ton iron keel of the new ketch in which they would sail the globe. In a move he would come to regret, he entrusted the vessel's construction to Charmian's Uncle Roscoe, who proved himself almost stunningly wasteful and incompetent.

The itinerary that the Slayton Lyceum Bureau arranged for him, far from being a sensible progression of stops, had him backtracking and crosshatching all over the Midwest before ever heading east. Sometimes he gave a lecture every other day, but usually it was every day: entrained for Kansas City on October 18, he progressed 300 miles northeast to Mt. Vernon, Iowa, near Cedar Rapids, then 150 miles farther east to Chicago, before heading 500 miles back west to Lincoln, Nebraska, then 250 miles back to Iowa, then 400 miles southeast to Indianapolis, back west to Illinois, back east to Ohio, and back west to Wisconsin. Even though he was attended by the ever-discreet, ever-attentive Manyoungi, it was a brutal zigzag of a tour.

The former boy socialist wanted to deliver jeremiads on the injustice in the world and the coming revolution, but quickly discovered that people, when not curious to hear about Alaska, were more interested in him and his much-reported love life. While he obliged them with stories of the Klondike, and tramping, and Japan, he doggedly returned to his socialist theme, reverting to methods that had worked well in *The People of the Abyss*; he personalized large-scale injustice to the level of the suffering individual, named and identified. "On a pile of rags in a room bare of furniture and freezing cold," he intoned to one audience, "Mrs. Mary Gallin, dead from starvation, with an emaciated baby four months old crying at her breast, was found at 513 Myrtle Avenue, Brooklyn, by Policeman McCommon of the Flushing Avenue Station." Her three other children, ages two to eight, looked at the policeman like ravenous animals who might eat him.

The American public was willing to read about the Cockney flower girl who was paid one and a half pence for twisting together 144 artificial violets—after all, it appealed to their nationalistic feelings of superiority. To tell such stories about the United States, though, just made most people mad. The pattern developed that wherever he held court, London delighted local comrades, enlightened some of the open-minded, alienated most, and netted generally negative press coverage.

Exactly one month on the road, he happened to be in Elyria, Ohio, on November 18 when he learned that his divorce from Bessie had become final. He had a travel day before his next speech in Lake Geneva, Wisconsin, on the 20th, and he wired Charmian to meet him on the 19th in Chicago to be married. That being a Sunday, some strings would have to be pulled; London promised the exclusive story to the Hearst papers, one of which, the *Chicago American*, had a city editor who arranged for a justice of the peace, and they were finally wed. The Hearst paper got the exclusive, but the non-Hearst papers ran with a different story (which turned out not to be true) that in Illinois divorced persons could not remarry for a year after their final decree, and that London was a bigamist. Half amused and half annoyed, London declared that he would marry Charmian in every state of the Union if he needed to.

They planned on a honeymoon in Jamaica, but the S.S. *Farragut* would not sail from Boston until two days after Christmas, so Charmian got to experience life on the lecture circuit for another month: Chicago and other cities in Illinois and Indiana before visiting her relatives in Iowa, who had sheltered her during the hailstorm of Bessie's divorce action. Then the newlyweds headed east; London had time to visit New Brunswick, Maine, to speak at Bowdoin College, before making himself very prominent in Boston. He spoke not only at Harvard but at both of the city's most famous venues, Faneuil Hall and Tremont Temple, before taking ship with wife and manservant.

The *Farragut* was one of four new banana boats acquired by the United Fruit Company that had originally been built for the Navy, able to deliver 35,000 bunches of bananas and fifty-three passengers each time she docked. One of the perquisites of fame was having instant friends wherever he might visit, and with his imminent arrival splashed across the Jamaican papers, once the *Farragut* tied up at Port Antonio the Londons were taken in tow by the local literati, led by the prominent poet Ella Wheeler Wilcox. While there, London gave an interview to the *Western Comrade* in which he vented his building frustration with American complacency and insistence that all was well in the face of the plain want and poverty to the contrary. Identifying himself with the workers of the world despite the cushion of his lifestyle, he called himself a fairly good artisan. "The only reason I write is that I am well paid for my labor. . . . I always write what the editors want, not what I'd like to write. I grind out what the capitalist editors want, and the editors buy only what the business and editorial departments permit. The editors are not interested in the truth; they don't want to tell the truth. A writer can't sell a story when it tells the truth, so why should he batter his head against a stone wall?"

After a month of critical beatings for his lectures on revolution and socialism, such sentiments were understandable but could well be read as unfair to George Brett at Macmillan, who had gone above and beyond the call of editorial duty in developing America's literary enfant terrible. Brett, however, was probably not uppermost in his mind as London fashioned these comments for a readership of comrades.

For a month, he and Charmian lived a Caribbean idyll. They were wined and fêted as celebrities, they were squired around plantations, they rode horseback over Jamaica's scenic Blue Mountains, and then they leisurely hopped a succession of small tramp steamers. They docked at Santiago, Cuba, and took in San Juan Hill, then visited Key West and Miami, shopping and sightseeing, exploring the Everglades and visiting an alligator farm, then Daytona Beach and Jacksonville. London was slated to give a lecture to the Intercollegiate Socialist Society (ISS, the student group that had been formed in the wake of his California lectures) on January 19, 1906, at New York's Grand Central Palace, and their ship moored just in time. The five-minute ovation he received from the eager audience—some students but mostly laborers—gave him a rousing welcome home. Learning that London was in New York, Dr. Alexander Irvine, pastor of the Pilgrim Church in New Haven, Connecticut, hurried down to ask if he could work in an additional lecture at Yale. As vociferously as it was denounced by industrial barons who had a stake in exploiting the working class, socialism a century ago was also widely approved by progressive clergy as an avenue toward social justice, and Irvine was one of New Haven's most prominent socialists.

London agreed, and preparations raced ahead. A Beaux Arts–style poster of London by Max Dellfant was plastered all over the Yale campus the morning of January 26, and Woolsey Hall was packed to its capacity of 3,000 for the event. Keenly aware that he was in the lion's den of American capitalism and that many in his audience were the sons of some of the country's most offensive robber barons, London stood at the edge of the stage, speaking quietly, almost gently, but clearly, for two hours to a silent hall. "It was probably the straightest thing they had ever heard," reported the local newspaper. "It was truth by the chunk." Before the talk his pending arrival had caused such controversy that the professors were reduced to pleading with the students to hear him out fairly. After the talk, the students shanghaied London to a dormitory and crowded in until there was no escape, clamoring for more. "He is very gentle," wrote the reporter. "He speaks softly in conversation, but the boys were conscious that behind the gentle voice was the heart and nature of a lion."[6]

Even more gratifying than his open-minded reception at Yale was London's discovery that his recent notoriety was beginning to bring new disciples out of the woodwork. In New York he was contacted by the vice president and chief organizer of the ISS, an ardent young comrade named Upton Sinclair, and they had lunch. Almost three years younger than London, Sinclair had just completed an exposé of the Chicago meatpacking industry that he called *The Jungle*, which was published later that year and caused the national outrage that London, who gave the book a laudatory review, had been able to raise only with his preaching and his love life. The two became friends until London's death, although principally by correspondence because Sinclair, a teetotaler from Baltimore, loathed alcohol and would not keep company with drinkers. London's literary gift was multifaceted, and his attention was divided among fiction, nonfiction, and drama; Sinclair's was not, and he went on to far surpass London as a muckraker airing the dirty linen of the American economy and society. In New Haven, London had also been approached by a somewhat nervous student named Sinclair Lewis, editor of the Yale literary magazine and a protégé of Upton Sinclair who had worked on the latter's experimental commune. Just short of turning twenty-one, Lewis was in some awe of London, but as he recalled, "The great man was extremely friendly to the skinny, the red-headed, the practically anonymous secretary."[7] Their paths would cross again soon in California, and they too became friends for life.

All too soon London, Charmian, and Manyoungi were back on the road to lecture in Chicago, St. Paul, and North Dakota. However, the bad press London had received for his political views and his hasty marriage caused some sponsors to cancel his appearance, creating gaps in the schedule; there were also reports of his books being removed from library shelves, justified by his alleged moral turpitude. Happy together but exhausted, London and Charmian felt no guilt in calling off the tour early and returning to California in early spring 1906.

* * *

As well paid as he was for the lecturing, and even with *White Fang* a hit (although rather less so than *The Call of the Wild* had been), there was still no rest for the most famous writer in America, as the need for money was constant. Partly because of Roscoe Eames's poor management and partly because London insisted on purchasing only the finest materials, construction of the *Snark* was running so over budget and behind schedule that the local press had begun referring to the enterprise as "London's folly." In addition to his own and Charmian's expenses, and meeting the upkeep of Bessie and the girls, now he bought a comfortable two-story home with Ionic pilasters at 490 Twenty-Seventh Street in Oakland, into which he moved his mother, with a stipend of

$60 a month, his nephew Johnny Miller, and Mammy Jennie. All he asked in return was that a bedroom be kept free for him and Charmian as their pied-à-terre when they were in Oakland.

Once home, it was time to reconnect with The Crowd, whose members were dividing their time between their old haunts in San Francisco, where rents had exceeded the ability of most of them to stay, and the arts colony they were organizing in Carmel. The idea of artists and writers living in proximity to one another, allies in empathy and creativity, was compelling enough to attract outsiders, who had to be vetted for suitability to admit into the circle. One of the more remarkable figures to descend on Carmel was Lewis, the tall, gaunt, young scarecrow of a writer. Nine years younger than London, he was consummately ambitious and so pompous that his Yale classmates had joked that he was the only man on campus who could fart through his mouth. But he brought with him one magical possession that made him a locus of attention. Michael Williams, the Irish poet and regular of The Crowd, recalled that "Lewis brought a trunk with him to Carmel . . . that became locally famous and a thing of wonder to the writers there, most of whom were six-days-a-week loafers, and mere Jock o Five Dreams compared with the new arrival. For that trunk was packed with a veritable card index of a fiction manufacturer. . . . There were clippings galore, news stories that might be the source of fiction plots; there were innumerable sketches in words of persons, places, happenings recorded by Lewis himself. . . . There were dozens, scores, hundreds of possible plots for novels, short stories, plays. Once he sat up all night with Jack London in George Sterling's bungalow, going through the plot file." London, far from feeling threatened by the newest and most genuine talent to show in Carmel, bought several plot ideas from him.[8] London was always frank in admitting that the invention of stories was his weakest point, although he could "everlastingly elaborate"—a confession that could be verified by a survey of his Alaska stories, and a few heated claims of plagiarism from earlier writers. London was also aware that while Lewis was entrained across the country, though he was not yet reduced to tucking himself above wheel trucks as London had done, he still could not afford passage in a sleeper and crossed the country in carriage cars. Paying Lewis $5 or $10 each for a small sheaf of plots provided new material, helped Lewis with some cash, and according to Williams, no more reduced Lewis's store of ideas than removing two cups of water from a pond.

Another newcomer at Carmel who was particularly keen on meeting London was Mary Hunter Austin, an interpreter of Southwestern life and literature who had been heaped with critical praise for her *Land of Little Rain*, published in 1903 when she was thirty-five. Like Nora May French, she was a discovery of C. F. Lummis of *Out West* magazine, but the force of her style and determination to be noticed made her a success, whereas French's career never caught fire. On her first visit to San Francisco, in that year, she had attached herself to George Sterling with all the force of a repressed matron yearning for attention and affection before her advancing age made moot the possibility. There were occasions when Austin and London found themselves in the same circle of discussion, and the liberated bohemians felt free to discuss virtually anything, including sex. To Sterling's well-known belief that sex released creativity, London's contribution was that what the men responded to was the apparent need of women to prefer "the tenth share of a man of distinction to the whole of an average man."

In response the highly independent Austin snapped, "I never needed a love affair to release the subconscious in me!" There is no note of the subject having been pursued further, but Austin's abrupt dismissal of therapeutic sex would have struck some present as divinely sour grapes, for she was not attractive. It was well gossiped by then that on her introduction to San Francisco in 1903, she had been taken to dine at Coppa's restaurant. The new venture of an immigrant chef from Turin named Giuseppe Coppa—The Crowd called him, with suitable fun, Papa Coppa—quickly became a favored haunt of the leading bohemians because of the low prices and heaping portions. They earned their keep, however, for customers were drawn by a wall of whimsical caricatures of the bohemians by such artists as Maynard Dixon and Gelett Burgess as well as Xavier Martínez. The decor featured distinctive black cat decorations and a facsimile of a rotund man displaying a witty motto: PASTE MAKES WAIST. The artistes welcomed Mary Austin to the table but then in coded under-the-table footsie decided not to invite her into their circle. She was brilliant enough, they allowed, but she was ugly.[9] In the three years since, whenever she was in San Francisco she became a frequent companion of Sterling, who genuinely admired her writing and continued to introduce her to his contacts. In 1906, she determined to move to the area, and with the friendship of Sterling and London, the rest of The Crowd were cornered into accepting her.

Austin had enormous appreciation for Sterling's aesthetics but considered him too closely tied still to Ambrose Bierce, and she once became irked with him for being reluctant to introduce her to his mentor. Sterling was afraid she might inadvertently reveal how close he and the Wolf had become, and Bierce had come to vigorously disapprove of London. Once she met him, Austin disapproved of Bierce, who cooled his relationship with Sterling over the latter's embrace of London's political views. "We were not, at Carmel, inclined to the intellectual outlook," she recalled, "except that there was a general disposition to take Jack seriously in respect to the Social Revolution." Sterling had little political inclination of his own, which made it easier for him to defer to the views of his Wolf.

London and Mary Austin did not start off well together; at one session he held forth on the merits of Darwinian evolution, which she shrugged off, not being very impressed that, apparently, he was just learning of it. (That was unjust; it was on his mind because he had been working on *Before Adam*, a novel with protohuman characters.) For his part, London challenged her claim to psychic powers, which resulted in a hot argument one night at the Sterlings' bungalow. With these and their initial collision over the issue of sex and creativity, Austin admitted that she and London "had to shake down a bit" before working out the kind of friendship they would have,[10] and how they would share Sterling's affections. Eight years older than London, she was homely and opinionated and arrogant, and to the perception of those around them she was jealous of the time Sterling spent with London. After she moved to Carmel, the rest of The Crowd learned that her eccentricities more than qualified her for acceptance among even the stranger of them—she sometimes dressed as a Native American princess and preferred to do her writing in a tree house—but London did not let The Crowd's derision define his own response to her. He knew from their machinations against Charmian that they had a shallow and catty side, and eventually Austin and London settled into a collegial, lifelong friendship.

For her part, Austin pronounced herself fascinated by his interaction with Sterling. "They were new to me, Jack and George . . . a source of endless intellectual curiosity. They were, for instance, the first two men I had known who could get drunk joyously in the presence of women whom they respected. For in the outlying desert regions where I had lived, this was not done. So I gave myself to discovering what the others got out of it." She also had genuine respect for London's writing; she was aware of his self-deprecating admission that he bought story ideas from others such as Sinclair Lewis, but did not believe that he needed them. "I have always suspected that Jack's buying of plots for short stories from any writer with more plots than places to bestow them was chiefly a generous camouflage for help that could not be asked or given otherwise."[11]

The Crowd's doubts about Austin's psychic powers may have been given an overhaul after she arrived in San Francisco on April 17, 1906, to confer with a publisher about her novel *Isidro*. She was to stay at the Palace Hotel, with its famously elegant Palm Court, but once there she telephoned her brother and half a dozen others that she was terrified by a premonition that the hotel was about to collapse. Most soothed her, telling her she had merely been working too hard and to get some sleep, but her friend Kitty Hittell invited her over to spend the night, which Austin accepted.[12] At a quarter past five the next morning San Francisco was shattered by a massive earthquake, and the Palace Hotel was consumed in the first day of the firestorm.

At Glen Ellen Charmian, habitually a late sleeper, had a less theatrical premonition, awakening with a start about five a.m., wondering what could have disturbed her so. She had just lain back down when the tremor struck, first a sickening few lurches, followed by a pause. "Then it seemed as if some great force laid hold of the globe and shook it like a Gargantuan rat." They had houseguests, the Norwegian landscapist Johannes Reimers, whose counsel London had sought about plantings for the ranch, and his wife. All gathered in the living room, comparing their observations of having seen the surrounding trees "thrash crazily, as if all the winds of all quarters were at loggerheads." From Aunt Netta's lodge, London and Charmian ran to a barn they rented at the nearby Fish Ranch, where they found that their spooked horses had broken their halters. Willie, the stable boy, swore to them that he had seen the enormous madrone tree by the barn lay down and stand up again, "which was less lurid than many impressions to which we listened that day."

Within a half hour London and Charmian were mounted, riding for the Beauty Ranch. From its height they made out two distant columns of smoke, one in the direction of San Francisco, the other toward Santa Rosa, which was also devastated by the quake, but that news was overshadowed by the destruction of San Francisco. London wondered aloud whether the city had been swallowed by the sea, or whether the Atlantic might be even then lapping at the other side of the Rockies. Their attention was diverted by the loss of their new barn; London had ordered stone walls two feet thick, and only from the ruins learned that he had been cheated by the workmen: the walls had only been faced with stone and filled with rubble.[13]

Remarkably, the quake had not distorted the railroad tracks, and as quick as they could they left for Santa Rosa, and on seeing the damage there went on to San Francisco. For most of his life London had endured a recurring nightmare of wandering through scenes of desolation and horror at the end of the world, and their walk through San Francisco during the fire seemed almost the very realization of that fear. Several times they were nearly trapped by the flames as London snapped photographs, when he would spy the last route of retreat from the advancing wall of fire. Charmian recalled a man being carried on a stretcher, in extremis, his back broken, and she was aware as their eyes met that she was the last woman he would ever see. They saw the Fairmont Hotel ignite as they made their way up Nob Hill; there was no water pressure with which to fight the fire, and they felt the ground shake as army troops under General Funston dynamited buildings in the path of the flames to create a firebreak. They spoke to one wealthy man named Perine; in shock that his mansion and his life's memories were about to go up in flames, he gave the Londons a tour of the house and his fine things, and he asked Charmian to play the piano. She demurred, but London urged her on. "Do it for him," he whispered. "It's the last time he'll ever hear it." No sooner had she started than Perine was overcome by emotion, and they left him to his doomed elegance. On the stoop of another house that was not in danger they slept fitfully until daybreak.

The next day they found the ferry still running, and crossed over to Oakland to rest at the house London kept for his mother and to take in what they had seen. Perine was only one of thousands who lost everything that day, including friends of theirs. Most of The Crowd had relocated to Carmel and escaped the worst of the devastation, but Arnold Genthe lost his photographic studio; Ina Coolbrith lost her home. After leaving the Oakland library in 1893 she had moved to San Francisco, renowned as one of California's leading literati, and indeed the first female member of the Bohemian Club. Soon after, in a remarkable show of affection, California's leading writers subscribed construction of a new house for her on Russian Hill. London himself wrote her an affectionate remembrance, recalling her praise of him for checking out the book about Pizarro: "If you only knew how proud your words made me. . . . I was raw from a ranch, you see. But I stood greatly in awe of you—worshipful awe. . . . No woman has affected me to the extent you did. I was only a little lad. I knew absolutely nothing about you. Yet in all the years that have passed I have met no woman so noble as you." Remembering also that that was when he had bricked off his artistic nature behind a wall of drinking and brawling, he concluded, "I am all iron these days; but I remember my childhood, I remember you; and I have room in me yet, and softness, too, for memories."[14] Almost alone in a sea of ruins, Coppa's and the rest of its block on Montgomery inexplicably survived. Rendering his restaurant unapproachable by the mounds of debris, however, Giuseppe Coppa decided to close, serving a "Last Supper" that was understood to also close San Francisco's bohemian age.

Having surveyed the cataclysm, London told Charmian that he could never write about what they had seen, that it beggared description. He was, however, the best writer to witness the destruction, and when *Collier's* offered him a celebrity's wage of 25 cents a word for an account of the event, he wrote "The Story of an Eyewitness," one of the starkest and most vivid glimpses of a city brought to its knees.

A few weeks later, London and Charmian saddled up Fleet and Washoe Ban for a two-week ride through Northern California, for a short vacation that would allow them to take in how well the area had ridden out the earthquake. Soon after this trip something far worse than the earthquake befell them. London and Charmian returned from running errands in Oakland to the news that Washoe Ban had entangled himself in a barbed-wire fence and mangled one of his legs to the bone. They knew from a singled horrified look that he would have to be destroyed. London had once witnessed a botched attempt at putting down a horse, and the agony of it burned into his memory. He told his foreman Wiget he would do it himself if he had to, but he didn't want to. Knowing London's great love for the chestnut thoroughbred, the horse that had cemented his love for Charmian, Wiget said no, he would do it. London instructed him to place the bullet in the center of the X drawn from left ear to right eye, right ear to left eye. He and Charmian held each other in a hammock near the house, waiting on the gunshot, and when it came, both wept fully.

The survival of the fittest: it was a shock that strong, deep-chested Ban could come to such an end. This tragedy gave a painful turn to London's work on what in some aspects was his most daring novel to date, *Before Adam*, serialized in *Everybody's* before publication in book form in February 1907, only three months after *White Fang*. The narrator is a young boy who, when he sees a caged lion in the circus, reacts with primordial frenzy because the cat awakens in him a latent racial memory of the Tawny One, the terror of his kind, who were the cave people. In this novel primarily of atavism, London marshaled the forces of evolution, modern psychology, and what was known at the time of anthropology to reconstruct the wanderings of the boy's distant ancestor Big-Tooth and his tribe, and their struggle to survive in a world of terrifying beasts and protohumans called the Tree People.

The unexpected combination of storytelling ability with the Darwinian theory that had fascinated him since his student days created a sensation as much in the scientific community for transforming their dry lectures into high drama, as it did in literary circles for its inventiveness. A noted anthropology professor at Yale actually began using it as a textbook, while the *New York Times* marveled at this "romance of the unknown ages, of the creatures that may have been . . . all endowed with poignant reality." It was perhaps London's most fiercely imaginative novel and sold an astonishing 65,000 copies, yet it is virtually forgotten today.

❧ ❧ ❧

When London chose Charmian over Sterling, it turned out there was wisdom in the selection beyond settling his emotional quandary over where to place his primary love and loyalty. By choosing Glen Ellen over Carmel, he also chose productive work over pretentious indolence, for the bohemians of the colony on the coast began suffering a widespread onslaught of what one observer called "Carmelitis." Outsiders and newcomers noticed right away the tendency toward procrastination and outright laziness. They might have established a rule that no socializing took place before noon so they could work, but that did not mean much work got done. London's thousand-word daily output, corrected and now typed by Charmian, would not have thrived in their artsy atmosphere.

Outing Magazine began the serial publication of *White Fang* in May 1906, continuing until October, when Macmillan brought out the book. George Brett was ebullient over London's effort in the novel, which he found "to be a much better knitted piece of work than any other long story that you have written, and to show a clear advance in your art." He especially found it an improvement over *The Sea-Wolf*, which he finally allowed himself to criticize for losing interest at the end, in the fatuous propriety of Humphrey and Maud on their desert island. Some critics disagreed with Brett over *White Fang*, charging that to reverse the process described in *The Call of the Wild* showed a lack of originality. When Bach wrote a fugue, however, the inversion of the subject was an expected part of the form, and even so *White Fang* proceeded naturally from *The Call of the Wild*. It also, unknown to the critics, issued from London's newfound optimism that came from acquiring the Beauty Ranch at Glen Ellen and the end of his "long sickness." "I am an evolutionist," London answered the critics. "I have always been impressed with the awful plasticity of life and I feel that I can never lay enough stress upon the marvelous power and influence of environment."

The robust sales of *White Fang* established that his critics did not have nearly as wide a reach as he did, although London had done much to resuscitate his own reputation after returning from the controversial lecture tour with the publication of a moderate and sincere piece in *Cosmopolitan* titled "What Life Means to Me." He had written it in Newton, Iowa, the previous autumn, resting with Charmian and her relations. In it he retreated from none of what he had lectured the country, but in clear prose he described his beginnings in the working class, his imagination of what it must be like to live "on the parlor floor" of society, and his rise to fame. Upon meeting the rich and powerful, however, he found moral decay he had never imagined. "I met men who invoked the name of the Prince of Peace in their diatribes against war, and who put rifles in the hands of Pinkertons with which to shoot down strikers in their own factories. I met men incoherent with indignation at the brutality of prize-fighting, and who, at the same time, were parties to the adulteration of food that each year killed more babies than even red-handed Herod had killed." In explaining his socialism as simply his reaction to discovering corruption and moral bankruptcy at the heart of capitalism, "What Life Means to Me" brought *Cosmopolitan* more requests for reprints than it had ever received before.[15]

Doubtless some of the critical brickbats were hurled less at *White Fang* than at London himself, with whom the jingoistic press was becoming increasingly annoyed for his socialist preaching. A few months after its appearance no less a personage than President Theodore Roosevelt weighed in on the novel, accusing London of "nature faking." "London describes a great wolf-dog being torn in pieces by a lucivee, a northern lynx," he carped. "This is about as sensible as to describe a tom cat tearing in pieces a thirty-pound bull terrier. Nobody who really knew anything about either . . . would write such nonsense."

It was a signal moment, for the former Oakland wharf rat to have occasioned the notice of the president of the United States, but the criticism was reprinted with something approaching glee in the newspapers that found London so objectionable. Embarrassingly for them and for Roosevelt, however, the president must have only been told the story and not read it for himself, because he had the facts exactly backward. "The President is evidently a careless reader of my stories," London answered. "He has rushed into this criticism all twisted around. . . . My story was about the wolf-dog killing the lynx and eating the body."[16] Unaccustomed to being gainsaid, Roosevelt fired off a hot letter to the editor of *Collier's*, which had printed London's reply, but let the matter drop with a huff.

The essential lesson for London from *White Fang* was that his Alaska motif had finally run its course. He had survived a winter in the Yukon and knew that its cold and its dangers were relentless; indeed his adventures there should have killed him three or four times over. His writing about it, however, had become equally relentless, and he had exhausted readers' interest in the frozen North. What he needed was a new subject entirely, and with the *Snark* finally nearing completion, that need would be filled presently. Worn out from a stint of hard production, he needed a rest before undertaking what would surely be a physically taxing small-boat voyage across the Pacific. So in February 1907 London and Charmian descended on Carmel for a sojourn of several days, which so electrified the bohemian community that they suspended their "rule" that all were forbidden from doing anything but work before noon.

Since relocation to the colony had been hastened by the great earthquake, The Crowd had devolved into two more or less distinct sets: they called themselves the Eminently Respectables, those such as Mary Austin, the MacGowan sisters, and photographer Arnold Genthe, who worked hard and were sociable when time permitted, and the merely Respectables, the more convivial who enjoyed the good life and whose output suffered for it—Sterling, Jimmy Hopper, Lucia Chamberlain, Fred Bechdolt, Xavier Martínez, and others.[17] All were congenial in the evenings, though, and the real society took place usually on the beach, usually over feasts of fresh abalone. On one particular occasion as night approached, Hopper was taking a photograph of Sterling, who had scaled a cliff in his bathing suit and stood, posed as a Poseidon with a trident. Mary Austin was communing with her Indian princess alter ego, standing on the beach in beaded buckskins, her arms raised to the western twilight, chanting what sounded like Browning: "'Tis a Cyclopean blacksmith striking frenzied sparks on the anvil of the horizon." London, who had been gorging on an abalone steak, decided to bring her down a tone. "Hell!" he bellowed at her with fork in hand. "I say, this sunset has guts!"[18]

For such cookouts on the beach at Point Lobos, Sterling had composed a piece of nonsense doggerel he called "The Abalone Song," complete with its own trite little tune, although it could also be sung to "Yankee Doodle." The Crowd regularly bawled it out over roaring beach fires:

Oh, some folks boast of quail on toast, because they think it's toney;
But I'm content to owe my rent and live on abalone.
Abalone! Abalone! Abalone! Abalone!
I'm content to owe my rent and live on abalone.

Oh, Mission Point's a friendly joint, where every crab's a crony,
And true and kind you'll ever find the clinging abalone.
Abalone! Abalone! Abalone! Abalone!
True and kind you'll ever find the clinging abalone.

Some live on hope, some live on dope, and some on alimony,
But my Tom Cat and I get fat on tender abalone.
Abalone! Abalone! Abalone! Abalone!
My Tom Cat and I get fat on tender abalone.

Oh, some like jam and some like ham, and some like macaroni;
But bring to me a pail of gin and a tub of abalone.
Abalone! Abalone! Abalone! Abalone!
Bring to me a pail of gin and a tub of abalone.

There were over a dozen verses[19]; others of The Crowd contributed their own until there were said to be more than ninety. Very likely the song was sung doggedly while preparing the feast: Sterling and Hopper dove for them at the foot of the cliffs, after which the abalones had to be pounded for an hour to tenderize them, and then boiled for another hour or more before grilling. Throughout the revelries, Austin kept her perspicacious eye, when not appraising Sterling's near-naked body, on London. She noted that he was "sagging a little with the surfeit of success . . . making him prefer the lounging pitchwood fire or the blazing hearth." His magnetism, however, was undiminished, and Charmian had to remain vigilant. Austin may not have conceded the "biological necessity" of women to prefer sharing a man of distinction, but as she saw plainly enough, "Women flung themselves at Jack, lay in wait for him."[20]

Such women were soon to run out of chances, however, for the *Snark*, hampered by both Roscoe Eames's incompetence and by materials shortages occasioned by San Francisco's rapid rebuilding, was finally ready for her sea trials.

12 THE SAILOR

Seven years before, in June 1900, Jack London had written to The Crowd's senior statesman, Charles Warren Stoddard, to acknowledge a compliment to his writing. He was also somewhat familiar with Stoddard's own career. "You have been down in the South Seas, haven't you?" he wrote. "That's where I've always longed to go, and somehow never made it." His rounding of the Hawaiian Islands on the *Sophia Sutherland* and shore leave in the Bonin Islands "only served to make me hungry ever since."[1]

He first mentioned the possibility of a long ocean voyage to Charmian during their year of waiting for the divorce from Bessie to become final. Although she was becoming more secure in their relationship, there were moments when he could be abrupt and domineering with her, even mean. Thus, there was a certain determination to the unending cheer and helpfulness that visitors to Wake Robin so noticed in her during summer and fall 1906. She loved her Mate-Man, to be sure, but beyond that she believed in him, to the point of ploughing past his increasingly evident shortcomings, knowing that when he was done being sharp or nasty to her, he would come right again. She came to depend upon it.

The journalist Joseph Noel left a telling vignette of his stay as a houseguest at Glen Ellen. As with all guests, he arose and Manyoungi served him breakfast without a peep from his hosts. Mornings were when London did his writing and he was not to be disturbed. London called Noel upstairs at about eleven o'clock, where he was still in bed, a large walnut four-poster, Noel wrote, "of the kind affected by captains of windjammers." London was sitting against large pillows with pages of manuscript about him on the bed. Cigarette butts were mounded in a saucer on the nightstand, and Noel noticed a green-shaded reading lamp and a decanter of scotch surrounded by glasses. As the two drank whiskey, Charmian entered with a cheery "Good morning," and fetched away the morning's work to type.

> I drink a second drink. So does Jack. Manyoungi comes in with two cups of coffee. Manyoungi is an obsequious mind-reader. Before you know it he has everything you want at your elbow.
>
> Between sips of the coffee Jack asks his bodyservant for a certain portfolio. The boy brings it, opens it, and places the bundle of new notes on the quilt in front of the master. . . . I hear the steady click of a typewriter touched by expert fingers. "That would be Charmian typing off the morning's work," I say. Jack nods. There are pages from a book in the litter. Having arranged them to his satisfaction, he reaches up and, with the old-fashioned wooden clothes pins, fastens them in little bundles to a clothesline strung across the bed. . . .
>
> Charmian comes in again. Altogether it is hardly ten minutes since she picked up the last page of Jack's longhand script from the bed. She is back with the whole thing finished. "If we do as well tomorrow with this story as we did today, we'll have something great," she says with quiet enthusiasm. You feel the enthusiasm.
>
> "What do you mean by that we?" Jack snaps. The enthusiasm evaporates.
>
> "Well, I just mean . . . "
>
> "Don't mean it. Get busy with these."
>
> He gives her a sheaf of notes scribbled with a pencil. She leaves to copy them off. For a moment her eyes differ but slightly from Manyoungi's. There is a beaten look in them.

When Charmian joined them downstairs she was cheerful again, London's shortness with her having been shrugged off. "A thousand and twenty-one words today, Mate," she said. Noel called it bookkeeping in paradise.[2]

It could not have been long after Noel's visit that Manyoungi, too, finally had enough of his hauteur and asked to address him as "Mr. London," as the other employees did. London refused, insisting on being addressed as "Master."

"Would God care for a beer before retiring?" Manyoungi asked coldly.

"No, Manyoungi, I don't want anything from you." He was fired the next day. According to Charmian, although this might have been one of the more rose-tempered pages in her biography, what grated on Manyoungi was not London's arrogance, but the impending world voyage. He did not want to go, and he got his wish.

London's short temper might have stemmed in part from the fact that, oddly for a man who was about to cruise the globe in a $30,000 yacht, his literary attention had been focused on some final broadsides at the capitalist system he was leaving behind. One was an essay, "The Somnambulists," which was largely a recapitulation of the revolutionist essays from the preceding year. The robber barons who were exploiting labor and keeping workers in penury to produce shoddy goods and adulterated food were, he wrote, oblivious to the havoc they were wreaking in the lives of the have-nots. "He will bribe . . . a state legislature for a commercial privilege; but he has never been known, in all his sleep-walking history, to bribe any legislative body in order to achieve any moral end, such as . . . child labor laws, pure food bills, or old age pensions." Child labor had been much on his mind, anyway. Unable, to his distress, to accept an invitation to make a tour of the American South and investigate factory and mill conditions there, he instead wrote "The Apostate," a memory of his own days of wage slavery in the jute mill. It was published in the landmark September 1906 issue of *Woman's Home Companion,* which wielded considerable influence in the eventual passage of a national Child Labor Act.

As if these were not enough, he also undertook a new novel, *The Iron Heel.* Just as *Before Adam* imagined Paleolithic life as humanlike drama, this story looked ahead to a bleak future, when a revolt of the workers, led by a Londonesque Ernest Everhard (named for London's Michigan cousin), has been crushed by the oligarchy. Now for their punishment, they are forced like slaves raising a pyramid to build the city of the oligarchs' supremacy, which was completed, significantly, in 1984. *The Iron Heel* found itself in the middle of a genre tradition: London probably got the idea from William J. Ghent's *Our Benevolent Feudalism* (published in 1902 by Macmillan),[3] which had gotten the idea from an earlier article in the *Independent. The Iron Heel,* in turn, was later read by a British socialist writer named Eric Arthur Blair, who under his pen name of George Orwell took his own shot at the concept in *Nineteen Eighty-four,* published in 1949.

The Iron Heel suffered from haste (London wanted to turn it in before leaving on his voyage and stay out of debt to Macmillan) and shrillness. It contained not so much dialogue as staged dialectical prophecy. As with his more intemperate stump speeches, the book was cheered by socialists but received coldly by the more patriotic press. Despite its lack of art, the novel had its greatest influence abroad and was praised by Anatole France and Leon Trotsky.

It was impossible to meditate daily on injustice and maintain a sunny disposition for Mate-Woman and visitors, and as problematic as his relationship with his mother had always been, the timing could have been better for Flora London to come up for a stay. Still worse, she also brought London's step-nephew Johnny Miller, Ida's boy, who was now twelve, with whom Flora had bonded in a way that had always eluded her with her own son. Between family and the sojourning tourists, Flora recovered some of her long-lost gregariousness, and London seems to have enjoyed himself, but he could not warm to Johnny. Beyond any innate jealousy he felt, his own stunted childhood made it virtually impossible for him to relate intimately to any child who was not, as he had been, a Work Beast. It was the only time his mother was known to have seen the Beauty Ranch; apparently the visit was cordial and pleasant, but she never went back.

Many of The Crowd also began making the trip up to Glen Ellen, especially George Sterling, often with Carrie, who managed to swallow her disapproval of Charmian and keep the peace. Also there were Jimmy Hopper and Arnold Genthe, the ever-funny Harry Leon Wilson, Xavier "Marty" Martínez, and Jim Whitaker, who continued his boxing and fencing practice with London. The Partington siblings also came, including Blanche, although Charmian had neutralized any threat she might pose. Between Wake Robin and the new Beauty Ranch, there was plenty of space to indulge London's juvenile passions for flying kites, often several at once, and blowing soap bubbles. With no home yet of their own, the Londons lived in an annex of Wake Robin Lodge, and visitors batched in the cabins on the property. Despite his workload, London also hosted friends from his days as a war correspondent, Richard Harding Davis and Ed Winship with his wife, Ida. To Charmian's growing disapproval, Glen Ellen also became a stopping place for tramps who had known her husband when he was riding the rails. Many of them were still down and out, and while sometimes diffident about doing so, usually asked for a handout. Although perennially strapped for cash himself, London almost always handed over a few dollars.

His financial burdens weighed him down, to the point that he began referring to meeting the monthly bills of his own, Bessie's, and his mother's households as his "Monthly Miracle." His requests to George Brett for further draws against his future work were less and less certainly worded, and indeed his long-suffering editor finally had to tell him that he would be charged interest on future advances. To keep on the positive side of the royalty balance, London hurried up two more short pieces, reminiscences of his days as a hobo—memories that London's visiting tramp friends could have earned their handouts by helping him to recall. These he collated with previous tramp pieces and offered to Brett as *The Road*, a combination memoir of his months riding the rails and exposition of tramping as an American subculture created by capitalist abuse of workers. Brett was less than enthusiastic but published it anyway: while it could be argued that *The Iron Heel* had expanded the book-buying market to include many angry have-nots, they were not the core of the book-buying audience. The reviewers and mainstream readers who were mortified by *The Iron Heel* were not likely to well receive a book that rhapsodized about life as a hobo. Even *The Iron Heel*, though, made money and increased their profile abroad, and London had become Macmillan's keystone. *The Road*, when it appeared in November 1907, was a flop, and Brett learned first the cost of publishing a book against his formidable instincts and second that London was not infallible. While their correspondence remained cordial even in their occasional disagreements, London as he aged grew progressively less amenable to editorial guidance, something that he had taken gladly with *The People of the Abyss* five years before. Mentorship was Brett's specialty, and the combination of London's increasing financial demands and decreasing popularity strained their relationship. Placing that at risk would be dangerous indeed.

Along with London's other financial obligations, now there were improvements to make on the ranch as well. At first London had told Brett he did not think to ever make a profit from the place, but ownership and exposure to the land nourished the transformation that had bonded him to Charmian. Nature, rather than the uncaring cosmic power of "To Build a Fire," was now a healer and provider, and like Voltaire's Candide, London perceived his rest in chopping his wood and making his garden grow. Hiring Werner Wiget as foreman had been the first step, and during the fall he finished the first major construction, the barn, making certain of the two-foot-thick stone walls this time. It was a massive structure with half-timber upper works supporting a forty-ton tile roof with long, low slant dormers front and back. London had not been exaggerating when he told Sterling that his ranch would anchor him permanently, and the barn was only the beginning. Johannes Reimers, the landscape architect who had been there when the great earthquake struck, had visited since, and the two planned the initial landscaping around the site for a future house, an image of which began to coalesce in London's mind as a rustic castle of lava rock and redwood on a monumental scale.

Ranch and house would have to wait on the voyage, however. Sailing had always been his renewal, and now every shuttle across San Francisco Bay made him ache more and more to disappear into the Pacific. He had been paying Roscoe Eames $50 per month to oversee construction of the *Snark*, which, in fairness to Charmian's lazy and excuse-making uncle, was not an easy job. There were literally hundreds of vendors to deal with to obtain the best materials, and being a good socialist, London directed that Roscoe use only union labor. He and Charmian were in the San Francisco shipyard often; almost obsessively they photographed the growing lattice of ribs that curved out and up from the five-ton iron keel. As the boat took shape, Charmian realized what a confined world they would inhabit as they circled the globe. One photo of the skeletal interior she captioned, "Where are we going to put it all?"[4]

The forty-five-foot ketch was finally launched and brought to Oakland for her fitting out. During November 1906, London and Charmian relocated to their pied-à-terre in the house he maintained for his mother so he could ride herd more closely over the vessel's ballooning expense. The Crowd took advantage of their proximity to descend for cards or to hear Charmian put her new Steinway "B" through its paces. Flora was happy to be once again in the center of the action, but she did not approve of Jack and Charmian boxing with each other, and scolded them once when their roughhousing cracked the redwood door of the dining room. London would have been far more put out over delays in fitting out his boat had it not been for the daily lunches on "10-Minute Duck"—wild mallard or canvasback, barely cooked before pressing—at his favorite restaurant, the Saddle Rock. He loved the dish so much he published a recipe.

Before lunch came the daily thousand words; after lunch a trip to the shipyard to try to correct whatever had gone wrong that day. The *Snark* would not be just any boat; she would be state-of-the-art. Her two collapsible masts would allow her smoothly under the bridges on the Seine so they could dock in Paris; they planned to explore the Yellow River in China and the St. Lawrence Seaway, through the Great Lakes to Chicago, thence down the Mississippi to New Orleans. Below deck, London's cabin was in the port bow, Charmian's in the starboard; midships was the main cabin, with an ultramodern head with flushing toilet abaft the main cabin on the starboard side, the galley to port, where cool refreshments would be guaranteed by an ice maker. Roscoe was also provided a smaller cabin next to a seventy-horsepower motor that would keep them going through calms and up canals. The stern was ballasted by a thousand gallons of gasoline. And somewhere they must find room for four hundred books, a phonograph, and five hundred records. Visually, she was as sleek and sporty a boat as Oakland had ever seen, and designed to be fast: twelve knots under full sail, eight knots under engine power.

Most of The Crowd were on board when London nosed the *Snark* through the Golden Gate for her sea trials on February 10, 1907. The weather was blustery but not dangerous, the sails bellied in the wind and took them twelve miles out. Hardly had he dreamed of such a perfect boat; her two-masted rigging, which he had designed to mimic the English fishing boats of the Dogger Bank, made her handle almost as if she had a responsive intelligence of her own—although most of the guests got seasick. Ever since they had known London they had heard his sea tales but had never seen him in action, and they were impressed. To editors who wrote darkly that sailing a small boat to Hawaii expressed nothing less than a death wish, one replied that the *Snark* might sink, but London, never. Then the delays resumed, and the Londons returned to Glen Ellen—only to learn that Brown Wolf, the big dog that had supervised the composition of *White Fang*, had died during the winter and Wiget, knowing how they felt about him, had not the heart to inform them of it.

Turning his thoughts to crewing the vessel, London determined to take Roscoe along to run the boat, despite his demonstrated inability during her construction. He did not want to do it himself, needing to meet his quota of one thousand words per day output on the myriad new topics and ideas that inevitably would come to him during the voyage. He had needed for a long time to enlarge his repertory from Alaska and tramping and socialism, and hoped their seven-year circumnavigation would give him grist for the rest of his life.

The rebellious Manyoungi had been replaced by a young Japanese of a rather serious and somewhat religious bent, Paul Tochigi, who would serve as cabin boy. Other crew would have to be sought out, and it must have been partly for the publicity value that London put out word nationally that he was taking applications. The imagined size of his supposedly shrinking audience was corrected by the avalanche of responses, many offering money—a lot of money—just to be taken along. From every corner of the wide world, wrote Charmian, applications came from "doctors, lawyers, beggarmen, chiefs, thieves, multimillionaires, sailors single and in crews, poets, historians, geologists, painters, doctors of divinity," and the whole cross-section of humanity. In one letter that they lingered over with gusts of laughter the applicant asked to be taken along because he found respectable people tiresome![5]

One who read the announcement of the intended voyage was a twenty-two-year-old in Independence, Kansas, a clerk in his father's jewelry store. Martin

Elmer Johnson was tall and cocky, "blond-beastly" in London's own parlance, and eaten up with unfulfilled longings for adventure. He had actually traveled some already; he had been to England and lived a little reality of the stranded American sailor depicted in *The People of the Abyss*. But the real adventure he ached for was limited to his imagination. In his dreams, "I breathed strange airs; I engaged in remarkable pursuits; by night, unfamiliar stars and constellations glittered in the sky." Greatly magnifying his experiences and his skills, he wrote London an impassioned appeal to take him into the crew.

"I knew that my letter was one of a host of letters," wrote Johnson later, "I knew that among those who had applied must be many who could push far stronger claims than mine." Johnson was right; among the other applicants was a renowned chef. What London could see in Johnson, however, that he could not see in others, was, in short, himself at a younger age—bright and able and eager, but languishing for want of an opportunity. "Capacity of cook," London telegraphed him. "Also do trick at wheel. Twenty-five dollars per month. Can you cook. What is your weight. Telegraph reply."

Of course he could cook. "Try me," responded Johnson, who then quit the job in his father's jewelry store and went to work in a friend's restaurant to learn how to cook. "I shudder as I think," he recalled, "what weird messes I may have served up to my friend's customers" as he learned his way around a kitchen. Nevertheless he prevailed upon his father to write to London separately, attesting to his cooking skills and his character. Probably unknown to Martin, his father added that he did not want him to go but couldn't stop him.[6]

With further correspondence London was pleased with his choice, writing Johnson buoyantly, "Oh, if you have a bad temper, don't come, for it'd be the only one on the boat! Incidentally, if you like boxing, I may tell you that all of us box, and we'll have the gloves along. You'll have the advantage of us on reach." He also explained that Martin would, like everyone on board, have to turn his tricks at the wheel. Encouraged by how beautifully she handled on her trials, however, he wrote that the vessel would largely steer herself.

The last to join the crew was a young Stanford man named Bert Stolz, as mate and engineer, but whose only qualification was that he had once lived in Hawaii. London, who with his growing belly, flat feet, and recovery from hemorrhoids was as aware as Mary Austin that he was no longer the physical specimen he once was, took Stolz on as a general hand to make up the difference in what he could no longer do himself.

Once the *Snark* put to sea, London intended to pay for the seven-year voyage by filing stories from remote points of the globe. Like any astute freelancer, he planned to write about different aspects of the trip for different, noncompeting magazines, whether news, politics, fiction, or travelogue. This scenario, however, became as star-crossed as trying to outfit the vessel herself, and as the intended sailing date approached London was still scrambling to finalize contracts. *Cosmopolitan* had apparently understood that it would be his exclusive outlet and at one point suggested that London rename the boat *Cosmopolitan*. London replied lightly that if they cared to pay for the vessel, they could have all eight syllables of "Cosmopolitan Magazine," and he would sell subscriptions in their ports of call. Otherwise, "boats, like horses, should have names of one syllable. Good, sharp, strong names, that can never be misheard." *Cosmopolitan* had it wrong, however; London had also been negotiating with *Woman's Home Companion*, *Everybody's*, and others. In fact, John O. Cosgrave, who had been one of London's earliest champions at *The Wave* in San Francisco eight years earlier, had become managing editor at *Everybody's* after *The Wave* went under. He did London more good service in this new position and had just agreed to buy the serial rights to *Before Adam* for a handsome twelve and a half cents per word.[7]

When *Cosmopolitan* learned that London had been dealing with other periodicals, they put out furtive word that he was not to be trusted. In a hot letter to the magazine on November 18, London pointed out that he had received no response to any of his three latest letters to them, and "it would be much fairer, and certainly more logical and trouble-saving, to answer my letters instead of blatting around New York City charging bad faith on my part." He also had the acumen to remind them that he expected to be paid separately for the photographs he would send back (as indeed is standard freelance practice) and he had already spent a considerable sum on cameras, lenses, film, and developing equipment. Even as he pressed *Cosmopolitan* for fast clarification of their relationship, he wrote Arthur Vance of *Woman's Home Companion*, "For two cents I'd throw up the whole proposition and let everybody sue my mortgaged ranch for what they could get. . . . *Cosmopolitan* has been so superlatively mean that I am sure of one thing and that is I will do my very best work for *Woman's Home Companion*."[8]

At her christening, the deck of the *Snark* was jammed with the well-wishing Crowd—Carrie and George Sterling, she dressed to the nines and he alternately displaying his Greek profile to the camera and fixing his eyes on his Wolf. For a christening ensign, Jimmy Hopper merrily donated his blue-and-gold University of California football jersey. No one was present, however, when in the dark on the eve of her sailing, two large lumber scows drifted into the sleek vessel and squeezed her between them, staving in one side slightly and bowing out the other. The extent of the damage would not be known until she was at sea, but that day was postponed yet again when some unpaid tradesmen had the vessel impounded by the sheriff. This was on a Saturday, and to London's fury he could do nothing about the bills until Monday. Not until April 23 were they free of the land and all its hooks; they hoisted Jimmy Hopper's jersey, and with cheers from the docks and whistles from the harbor London pointed her through the Golden Gate.

After downing their first dinner, Tochigi played a sad melody on his flute, cut short as first he and then Charmian rushed up on deck, leaned over the rail, and made the heaving sacrifice of seasickness. It proved to be an omen.

The only thing that went smoothly the first several days was London's teaching himself navigation. Roscoe Eames had previously told London that he could navigate, but his total befuddlement by the charts and instruments said otherwise. From San Francisco the *Snark* sailed south along the coast, not venturing into the trackless ocean until London practiced with the sextant and studied logarithms until he felt confident that he could keep them on course. In his memoir about the voyage he downplayed his quick study. "Any young fellow with ordinary gray matter, ordinary education, and with the slightest trace of the student-mind, can get books and charts, and instruments and teach himself navigation. . . . Seamanship is an entirely different matter; it requires years. . . . But navigation by observations of the sun, moon and stars, thanks to the astronomers and mathematicians, is child's play."

The *Snark* headed west; early on the sea was rough, the buffeting that the *Snark* took was frightful, and moving about on deck was downright dangerous. "Never for a moment could we let go of one hold without being assured of another," wrote Martin Johnson. "I have seen many acrobatic feats, but nothing resembling in mad abandon the double handspring Mrs. London turned one day when her hand missed its hold and she landed down the companionway in the middle of the table, on top of a dinner which I had just cooked, and which Tochigi was serving." Charmian's memory was that she landed at the foot of the ladder. "Above us, Martin eyed me suspiciously, and ventured tentatively, 'Now, in Kansas, in my family, the women cry when they hurt themselves like that.' No, I shed no tears—then. But when I was alone at the wheel, under the stars, I wailed right womanly."[9]

"We didn't discover all our handicaps at once," recalled Johnson. Thus they were well out to sea when the full extent of their predicament became clear. The boat was leaking dangerously. The two lumber scows in San Francisco Bay had crushed her into a bean shape; the hull leaked, the bulkheads leaked—most of their three months' provisions were spoiled by either sea water or gasoline leaking out of the ruptured tanks—cabbages, beets, turnips, carrots, fruit—much of it had to be pitched overboard. Her lopsided shape also made her sluggish to steer; the sea anchor was ineffective, and she would not heave to. The main engine of seventy horsepower had dismounted itself from its plate and lay useless. The toilet stopped working. The five-horsepower engine ran the pumps constantly, but the cabin that they sucked out during the day sloshed knee-deep by the following morning. After several days the galley floor buckled from the water pressure, and Johnson took to wearing thigh boots to cook the meals. Eames was driven from his cabin by gasoline fumes, which collected so thickly down below that the crew feared striking matches. Their frame of mind was not aided by the discovery that the *Snark*'s lifeboat was in no better condition than the mother vessel.

Johnson began the voyage with the fearless daredeviltry of a young London, but during the terror of his second storm at sea he finally expressed despair for their survival. London tut-tutted this and remarked that he figured they were no more than two miles from land. "Where?" asked the incredulous Johnson. "Straight down, Martin," he said. "Straight down." Eventually they mastered the worst of the problems and reached a kind of working routine; one photo of hundreds taken on the trip shows London contentedly at the wheel, a book open between his hands. Twenty-seven days after leaving San Francisco London's navigation proved itself worthy. They passed through the Kaiwi Channel, rounded Diamond Head, and slid into Pearl Harbor, accompanied by two tugboats.

Access to the mail brought the chance for a quick missive to George Brett, confessing that he was hard up and confused as to where they stood with each other. But he outlined several projects he had in mind for Macmillan, including a collection of short stories about sharks. "I have already gathered much material for work in the future, down here in the Hawaiian Islands."[10] Sensing that London could replay all of his previous Alaska success with new tropical material, Brett responded by sending him $5,000 and a contract for 1908, which London quickly signed and returned with a note of fulsome thanks.

London had entrusted Ninetta Eames to run his business affairs in his absence, and there was a barrage of affectionate but busy and incredibly detailed letters to her. In addition to keeping his books straight and forwarding such supplies as camera film, she also had to manage his submissions, of which he had always kept meticulous records. In one case he informed her that he had sent a short story, "The House of Pride," to *Collier's*, with her address as the return. If they turned it down, he advised her of his next twelve choices, in order; it finally sold to *Pacific Monthly*, which was the eleventh on his list. He also undertook an equally vigorous correspondence with Wiget that showed London's increasing involvement in the minutiae of the ranch.

Aunt Netta's management of London's business affairs was simple compared to the family tangle in which they found themselves: Roscoe Eames, with whom London's patience had almost exhausted itself, wrote a vituperative letter to

Charmian, and London finally turned him out with equal name-calling, "you . . . hopeless, inefficient, wretched creature." Netta had had her own problems with Roscoe but felt obligated to advocate for the devil, explaining to London that he had always reacted poorly to disorder, but even then if his rest had not been so regularly disturbed, he might have made a better job of it. London was incredulous, citing as only he could whole paragraphs of Uncle Roscoe's dereliction that had cost him thousands in discovering that "he is no more a sailor than I am an Egyptian dancing girl." For her part, Netta had been left in the role of dealing with Flora, whom she found to be the last degree of shocking. "That woman is a horror in flesh and blood. I never saw her like. . . . She is horrible, horrible—full of mean innuendoes about the ones she depends upon for her living. . . . Sometimes I feel like choking off the allowance you make just to see her wriggle. . . . I never saw so utterly hopeless a woman. No redeeming trait in her." "Let me tell you right now," London answered, "that you have not seen one thousandth part of the real devil that she is." That London and Aunt Netta could deal with the worst that the other's family had to offer, and remain affectionate and trusting, was a testament to the durability of their long friendship. She swore he could not truly be the offspring of "that ungrateful hag," and he allowed that in marrying Roscoe, "now for the first time I appreciate what you have endured."[11]

Fortunately, Honolulu was about more than work. The Londons were celebrities as much there as anywhere among the American population, and for weeks they enjoyed the social whirl, keeping company with the best the city could offer, including Acting Governor Jack Atkinson and Honolulu newspaper publisher Lorrin Thurston, who had been attorney general in the government of Queen Liliuokalani but had conspired in her 1893 overthrow. For much of her time under repair the *Snark* was careened, so they could not have remained on board in any event; London and Charmian first stayed in a rented tent cabin of four rooms near Waikiki Beach. It was the property of the Seaside Hotel, whose manager, Fred Church, had been a Klondiker and whom London knew well. Subsequently the Londons were lent a romantic, forest-sheltered waterside bungalow with a pier extending over its narrow beach, property of local artist Thomas Hobron, for the remainder of a stay that embraced five months in all. The writing quota never slackened, and during a brief sojourn with Thurston, London began a major new novel, autobiographical, about a sailor and would-be writer named Martin Eden.

On June 2 London got it into his head that he would attempt surfing. He knew of it from other authors, including Mark Twain, who maintained that only native Hawaiians could master such death-defying esoterica. London acquired a board and attempted for an hour to position himself on a wave, when he was spotted by Alexander Hume Ford, an American-born adventurer who had been on his way to Australia when he tarried a week in Hawaii to see if he could learn surfing, and had dedicated himself to it ever since. He was in the process of founding the Outrigger Canoe Club and applying for a grant from the estate of the late Queen Emma Kaleleonalani to preserve surfing on boards and in canoes as a national heritage. He lectured London clearly and precisely on what he was doing wrong—exactly the kind of discourse that London gave on subjects on which he was knowledgeable, and he listened raptly. Riding a wave was not a question of brute strength, for even the winsome Princess Kaiulani, late uncrowned heiress to Hawaii's throne, had been an expert surfer. It was timing, and balance, and understanding the physics of the wave. They waded out together and London mounted Hume's board. At the right instant Hume gave him a powerful shove, and an electrified London rode the wave all the way to the beach. "From that moment," he wrote, "I was lost."

Perhaps never had he been so completely captured by any discovery he had made. Describing surfing in "The Royal Sport," his prose reached an ecstasy heretofore unknown to him. First he described how puny and insignificant one feels observing the majestic waves.

> And suddenly, out there where a big smoker lifts skyward, rising like a sea-god out of the welter of spume and churning white, on the giddy, toppling, overhanging and downfalling, precarious crest appears the dark head of a man. Swiftly he rises through the rushing white. His black shoulders, his chest, his loins, his limbs—all is abruptly projected on one's

> vision. Where but the moment before was only the wide desolation and invincible roar, is now a man, erect, full-statured, not struggling . . . but standing above them all, calm and superb, poised on the giddy summit, his feet planted in the churning foam, the salt rising to his knees, and all the rest of him in the free air and flashing sunlight, and he is flying through the air, flying forward. . . . He is a Mercury, a brown Mercury. His heels are winged, and in them is the swiftness of the sea.

He could not help himself; he surfed, and surfed, and surfed, until the tropical sun nearly killed him. A doctor was sent for the next day, who pronounced him the worst case of sunburn he had ever treated. London was bedridden for four days, and a week and a half later he was still pained by enormous blisters. But he was still positively giddy from the experience. "Please," he begged Charmian through swollen lips, "don't let me laugh; it hurts too much." The experience may have contributed to the skin maladies that plagued him through the rest of the tropics, but his writing about surfing in the subsequent *The Cruise of the Snark* introduced the sport to the world and helped to preserve a Hawaiian patrimony. It was a turning point also in his depiction of native peoples. His exposure to Hawaiians led him to depict them with an identity and a dignity that marked a departure from his previous espousal of a kind of sympathetic racialism.

With the worst of the *Snark*'s disabilities now under repair, it was time to fix the crew as well. Roscoe had been sent back to Glen Ellen, and two abortive attempts were made to replace him, the first put forward by George Sterling and summoned to Hawaii at London's expense, and then one found locally. Both were as bad as Roscoe. Finally London hired a professional mariner, Captain James Langhorne Warren, who proved suitable. Tochigi, beloved as he was, could not tolerate more seasickness and quit, later to attend an Episcopal seminary. To replace him as cabin boy London hired a merry young Hawaiian Japanese, Yoshimatsu Nakata, who remained in the Londons' service for several years. Finally, Bert Stolz received a letter from his mother, insisting that he return to Stanford. London had once written of him critically that he was as hopeless a shirk as Roscoe, but accepted his manly apology that he had allowed himself to come under Roscoe's sway. During their time together, Stolz confided that his real reason for coming to Hawaii was to visit his father's grave. When Bert was six, Oahu County Sheriff Louis Stolz had been shot and killed by a leper who, rather than be separated from his young wife, fled into the mountains, evading capture and exile to the colony on the island of Molokai. London could not have found better plot material in Sinclair Lewis's trunk of clippings.

He must have heard the story of Molokai, of its leper colony and its humble Father Damien, long before from Charles Warren Stoddard, who visited the island and its remarkable priest more than once and wrote of them in his Hawaii dispatches. (Stoddard was also not shy about recalling his return to Molokai to resume a sexual affair, to the mortification of the missionaries, with a young Hawaiian boy who lived outside the colony.) And London was reminded of the lepers again when, at a dinner party they gave, one of the guests was the president of the Board of Health, Lucius Pinkham. He had been as zealous in his efforts to remove the stigma from the leper colony as London had been for his socialist cause. "It is time to cease crying 'Unclean, Unclean,' to the lepers," Pinkham had written, "and refraining from painting dark pictures for literary or sensational effect, thus making segregation more cruel than necessary."[12] If he could get London to visit the island and write favorably of the colony, that alone would accomplish more reform than he could ever do, and he pressed his case vigorously. In this he was backed by another new acquaintance of the Londons, the influential Lorrin Thurston. Intrigued, London agreed to visit the mysterious place.

They went over on the interisland *Noeau* on July 2. The lepers' primary settlement on Molokai was Kalaupapa, and its superintendent was a man who could help Pinkham's cause with London. John Devine "Jack" McVeigh was a stocky French Canadian of privileged background; in his youth, while seeing the world in the charge of a tutor, he disappeared in Hawaii and went native, eluding capture when relatives came to bring him home. He had been superintendent for five years, during which he transformed the place from an open-air detention camp of drunkenness and despair into as modern a town as it could be. For two days the Londons visited with the residents, practiced with them at their rifle range, and interviewed their doctors at length, and on the Fourth of July McVeigh arranged for the native-style celebration of random antics in fright-masks to pass by the Londons' door so they could take pictures of them and the town's two brass bands. London visited with an Anglo patient, a former mariner, who enjoined him to describe the place accurately, not the terrifying hellhole that the world's press made it out to be. They also visited the grave of the remarkable Father Damien and heard his story from nurses who had worked with him.

The sojourn on Molokai changed London. The journalist in him prized truth above preexisting assumptions, and as Johnson wrote in his memoir of the voyage, "When we were sailing along the windward side of Molokai on the *Snark*, Jack had pointed to the island, and said it was the pit of hell, the most cursed place on earth. But he never spoke so after his visit. His eyes were opened."[13] Immediately London sat down to write "The Lepers of Molokai" and submitted it to *Woman's Home Companion*, the journal that had struck such a blow to alleviate child labor. Although he wrote the piece as a favor to his Hawaiian hosts, the article was also true and just and served a purpose; when Lorrin Thurston read the text he called it "a value to Hawaii that cannot be estimated in gold and silver" and swept the Londons off to vacation with him on Maui. When the article was published in January 1908, it was greeted with equal approbation both in Hawaii and on the mainland. (Thurston's enthusiasm turned to scorn two years later when he learned of London's fictional story "Koolau the Leper," based on the tale Bert Stolz had told him of his father. In it the grotesqueness of the deformities caused by the disease is somberly portrayed, and the pain that the removal policy created among its victims drives the plot. The Londons were long gone, but in his newspaper Thurston raged that London was "a sneak of the first water, a thoroughly untrustworthy man and an ungrateful and untruthful bounder."[14])

On Maui, the Londons were housed at the 50,000-acre Haleakala Ranch, 2,000 feet up the flank of the volcano. A going business concern since 1888, the ranch had been hugely improved by Louis von Tempsky. The ranch's manager since 1899, von Tempsky was a polo player who could engage London on his love of horses. He also had tales of family adventure to rival London's own, being the son of a Silesian nobleman and soldier of fortune who had rented his services all over the world, including the Maori War in New Zealand. During a stay of several days, London and Charmian journeyed up to the lip of the crater, threaded dizzying paths on sure-footed mountain horses beneath roaring waterfalls on the windward side, and later got a close look at ranch operations. Von Tempsky had two daughters, Armine and Gwen, who were imps after London's own heart, mischievous, pretty, teenage tomboys. On one excursion up the mountain he and the girls engaged in a lusty combat; in lieu of snowballs they flung over-ripe, egg-sized raspberries at each other. When they came down they looked like they had been machine-gunned. Sixteen-year-old Armine accompanied them riding, and upon finding Charmian an expert horsewoman turned over her spirited mount, Bedouin, whom no other female had ever ridden. London himself, she noted dryly, rode like a sailor. She ventured a step too far, however, when she confessed to the famous Jack London that she wanted to be a writer and asked to show him some of her effort. As he did even with his own daughters, he criticized her in the same tone as he would an adult and ran the risk of crushing her adolescent dream. But he was always precisely honest. Most of it, he said, was "clumsy, incoherent tripe." She preferred to hear his comment that there was "a streak of fire" in it that, with a lot of hard work, could lead her to success.[15]

After Maui they reconnected with their new friends before being spirited off to the Big Island, to Holualoa on the Kona Coast. Riding in the highlands, they could see in the distance the *Snark* being run to Hilo on her new trials by Captain Warren. On September 1 London lectured in Hilo, something that he seldom did on a trip that was meant to gather material for stories, through islands where people were far too content to want to hear about socialist justice. Nor ought he to have expected a sympathetic hearing from Hawaii's American elite, an avaricious business clique who had overthrown the constitutional monarch, Queen Liliuokalani, on the grounds that she was "bad for business."

That he persisted in lecturing at all may evidence a conscience guilty for having abandoned American socialism to make his voyage.[16]

Faced with the need to assemble the crew, London had already engaged Captain Warren and Nakata. He promoted Johnson to engineer and hired a Japanese cook, Tsunekichi Wada, and Stolz was replaced with another able youngster named Hermann de Visser. There was time yet, however, for one last purely Hawaiian adventure. Given a tour of a sugar plantation, they learned that the cane was grown in the highlands, and then sent down for processing by being tied in bundles and loaded into flumes to be floated to the mill. There was a local sport of riding bundles of cane at startling speeds down the flumes, across unbelievably spindly aqueducts hundreds of feet above canyons. Once on, there was no getting off; photographs of the Londons and their hosts shooting the flume on a bundle of cane show them all laughing hysterically.

London left instructions to forward his mail to Tahiti, and newly crewed the *Snark* hoisted her sails on October 7, 1907, and made for the Marquesas Islands, 2,000 miles more or less southeast. It was a voyage that previous generations of mariners claimed could not be sailed because of contrary trade winds. Once at sea, however, it was a trip that had to be made, because all of the boat's engines broke down. Judging the breezes carefully, London found the thin boundary of variables between the northeast trades and the doldrums and inched his way forward. It took nearly two months, but on the night of December 6 they anchored at Taiohae Bay. It fulfilled a childhood dream; after reading Melville's *Typee* London had longed to meet that race, and when he did it provided another lesson in the awful plasticity of existence. Amid monumental stone foundations that proclaimed a mighty civilization, he found the few hundred remaining Typeans struggling against consumption, leprosy, and elephantiasis.

Five hundred miles to the southwest lay Tahiti. Christmas Day 1907 was spent fighting a storm before reaching Papeete, where a pile of mail awaited, in which the greatest discovery was that Aunt Netta had botched his affairs beyond remedy. She had changed banks without telling him, so he had written hot checks in Hawaii; she had spent $1,000 on living quarters for Wiget and doubled her own salary; and when the newspapers printed the rumor that the *Snark* was lost at sea the bank foreclosed on his mother's house.

There was only one thing to do: suspending their trip for a month, he and Charmian trudged aboard the S.S. *Mariposa* for a twelve-day voyage to San Francisco, a reunion with The Crowd, and a flurry of deals to shore up his affairs before returning to Tahiti on the same vessel. They were gone a month and a day. In further exploring the Society Islands the *Snark* was almost capsized by gifts of fruit and fish and pork. There were further changes in crew, although Captain Warren was forgiven some theft and kept on for the time being. They rode the trades 1,500 miles west to Samoa. At Pago Pago they stayed with the governor and trekked up a mountain to pay their respects at the crypt of Robert Louis Stevenson, and they visited his villa, which was closed but they peeped in the windows. London's remaining attempts to lecture on socialism were not amiably received. In Tahiti the French authorities had made sure the only venue made available to him was the burlesque hall, and police spies were spread through the audience; Pago Pago was little better.[17] Still, though he was politically checkmated, his creativity was liberated. Stories poured from him, many now with South Seas themes, and Charmian hammered away at her Remington. There may have been a time in his career when he could not think of new things to write, but now he was overloaded.

After repairs in Fiji, where Captain Warren and some other crew were replaced, it was on to the Solomon Islands, where they arrived on October 27, 1908. Nine months since the emergency run to San Francisco had flown by. On Guadalcanal the Londons ensconced themselves at Penduffryn, the island's largest copra plantation, as the guests of its owners. As they explored the Solomons, most of their decisions were pleasant ones: what to do with a beautiful but exhausted pigeon that flopped onto the deck one day at sea (London expended some of his last gasoline to carry it to the nearest island, an act that moved Johnson deeply); what to do with the daughter of a Malaitian chief who was gifted to the boat's new captain (she was left at a mission); what to do with a bouncing Irish terrier that took up with Charmian and wouldn't leave (they kept her, named her Peggy, and installed her as ship mascot).

There were troubles, too, in the form of well-known tropical scourges: yaws—skin eruptions caused by a spirochete related to syphilis, nonsexual but capable of a destructive tertiary stage if left untreated—malaria, ngari-ngari. Most worrisome, two fistulas opened in London's rectum. Also of concern, a skin condition began affecting London's ability to perform even simple daily tasks, his hands and feet swollen and peeling. They pressed on with side trips while based at Penduffryn, determined not to have their fun spoiled by tropical diseases.

London also got them lost once, in the open ocean south of the Solomons and several hundred miles east of Australia. He intended to take his bearings when they reached Lord Howe Island, but despite days of anxiety could not find it, and he discovered to his shock that he had left the chart at their base on Guadalcanal. Through most of the voyage it had been London's determination and good humor that saw them through troubled times, but this time it was young Johnson who saved the day. "Lord," he opined, "Howe did we miss that Island?" Howling (or, perhaps, Howe-ling) over the worst pun they could remember, it set off a contest of "Lord, Howe?" puns to which even Nakata, shivering with malaria, contributed. London reworked some tables and they raised the island two days later.

Cruising the Solomon Islands, London gained sober insight into the primitive state of that part of the world. Although the natives might lavishly welcome armed white colonial masters, just beneath the surface lay the opportunism to scavenge them if the chance presented itself. London learned this to his horror when the *Snark* rammed her beautiful raked prow onto an unseen reef. "The minute before we struck," he wrote the Greek, "not a canoe was in sight. But they began to arrive like vultures out of the blue. Half of our sailors held them off with rifles, while the other half worked to save the vessel. And down on the beach a thousand bushmen gathered for the loot. But they didn't get it, or us."[18] Photographs of Charmian, laughing bravely among natives, also show a revolver prominently holstered on her hip. As London wrote,

> This is just about the rawest edge of the world. Head-hunting, cannibalism and murder are rampant. Among the worst islands of the group day

> and night we are never unarmed, and night watches are necessary. Charmian and I went for a cruise on another boat around the island of Malaita. We had a black crew. The natives we encountered, men and women, go stark naked, and are armed with bows, arrows, spears, tomahawks, war clubs, and rifles. . . . When ashore we always had armed sailors with us, while ten men in the whale-boat, laid by their oars with the bow of the boat pointed seaward.

All this gave London much to think about in his evolving synthesis of the nobility of non-Western, non-technological cultures, as he had so favorably described the Hawaiians' cultural evolution, the lack of which he was seeing in the Solomons, and how they might alter his innate belief, abiding even while eroding, in white superiority.

When the mail caught up with him the Western world came rushing back in two letters from Bessie, one written the previous March and the second in July, with news of her intention to marry her longtime friend Charles Milner, and requiring a modification of their divorce agreement, under which if she wed again she would lose the house London built for her. If he would not agree, she threatened, she would decline the marriage and be miserable. In reply London wrote a veritable testament in rebuke. "Why, my dear child, I don't care a whoop in high water whether you get married a second time or not. I should like to see you happily married for your own sake, but I regret that I cannot genially contribute money to finance that second marriage. . . . I have always done better by you than I agreed to do. I have always given you more than was laid down in the letter of our contract." He threw up to her the untruths contained in her divorce allegations and subsequent lies and gossip, all of which he would see made public if she tried through the courts to get the house, and he let her know that he was sending carbon copies to everyone even remotely connected with the matter to hold her in check. His temper with her was undoubtedly made worse by realizing that his own finances were crumbling and that his political sentiments were costing him popularity in the United States.

Beneath all, his books were the engine that financed his life—the voyage with its expenses, the ranch with its expenses, and his allowances to his mother, his old nurse, and his ex-wife and their children. The American economy was in the grip of a recession, and between that and his slumping popularity over his political views, the well was running dry. "I have had a big slump in all my book-sales in the States, partly due to the panic and partly due to my socialism, and I am so pinched that I scarcely know where to turn." As one act of economy, he would soon have to suspend their voyage to generate faster work, and he was cutting Bessie's allowance from $100 per month to $65—which if she found too great a hardship, she could mortgage the contested house.[19]

At Penduffryn, London's skin malady worsened, his hands swollen to twice their normal size and peeling so badly that he wrote that in places there were seven layers of skin in various stages of exfoliation, and his toenails had swelled as thick as they were long. Suddenly he was seized with the terror that he might have contracted leprosy from his too-free association with the residents of Kalaupapa. Preparations were made to get on a commercial passage to Australia, and a hospital. Ten days later the ship docked in Sydney, where London was relieved for his skin condition to be diagnosed as nothing more serious than bad psoriasis. He did, however, need surgery to close his two fistulas, which was successfully carried out on November 30. London was always depressed when his once-hard body let him down, and the following week he and Charmian made the painful decision to abandon the around-the-world cruise. They sent Johnson back up to the Solomons to fetch the *Snark*, in company with a licensed mariner named Read, to bring her down and prepare her for sale.

Recuperating in Sydney the day after Christmas 1908, London was able to file a remarkable piece of sporting reportage for the New York *Herald*. He was ringside for the celebrated heavyweight title bout between defending champion Tommy Burns of Canada and the flashy African-American challenger, Jack Johnson. The bout had a fascinating backstory that revealed a clear division between London's alleged racism and his chops as a reporter. In the early twentieth century, blacks often boxed publicly and professionally but were not permitted to contest for the world championship. The phenomenally gifted

Johnson challenged this bar, but the previous world heavyweight champion, Jim Jeffries, refused to fight him and retired undefeated. The title passed to Burns, but Johnson followed him all over the world, often taunting him from ringsides. When Burns went to Australia to defend his title against another challenger, Johnson pursued him, and Australian referee and fight promoter H. D. McIntosh persuaded Burns to meet Johnson in the ring.

The bout was held in the outdoor stadium at Rushcutters Bay, attended by at least 20,000, and London estimated twice that figure or more. As Australian film director Raymond Longford shot continuously from an adjoining platform, Johnson administered a bloodcurdling beating, laughing at his opponent and the crowd alike, winning by a technical knockout when police stopped the fight in the fourteenth round. In filing his story, London admitted his natural tendency to desire the white man to win, just as, he said, had Johnson been a spectator he would have wanted the black man to win. But as he had in Korea before and would do again in Mexico, London lay his personal sentiments aside to report on the fight as it was and even chastised other white members of the press for belittling Johnson's victory:

> Johnson was too big, too able, too clever, too superb. He was impregnable. His long arms, his height, his cool-seeing eyes, his timing and distancing, his footwork, his blocking and locking, and his splendid out-sparring and equally splendid in-fighting, kept Burns in trouble all the time. . . . He was smothered all the time. . . .
>
> Because a white man wishes a white man to win, this should not prevent him from giving absolute credit to the best man who did win, even when that best man was black. All hail to Johnson. His victory was unqualified. It was his fight all the way through, in spite of published accounts to the contrary. . . . In spite of much mistaken partisanship, it must be acknowledged by every man at the ringside that there was never a round that was Burns's.

A Martian landing among them, he wrote, would have asked why Burns was even allowed in the same ring with Johnson.[20]

Three weeks into the New Year the Londons were based in Hobart, taking in the austere beauty of the Tasmanian National Park while coming to grips with the reality that they could not continue the *Snark*'s cruise. Rather than write all their friends and contacts separately, he prepared a mimeograph for all, explaining that among his operation, malaria, and other tropical afflictions, it was just too dangerous for him to continue.

> There are many boats and many voyages, but I have only one body; and after waiting and watching my condition carefully all these months, I have prescribed for myself my own climate and environment, where always before my nervous equilibrium has been maintained.
>
> Not only would it be foolhardy for me to attempt to continue the voyage in my present condition, but it would be practically impossible. At times this mysterious malady so affects me by its physical reactions as to make me helpless—physically helpless. . . .
>
> There is nothing more to say except this, namely, a request to all my friends. Please forego congratulating us upon our abandonment of the voyage. We are heartbroken.[21]

London was awaiting the *Snark*'s arrival from the Solomons, and his intention was to sell her and be home within three months. This was confirmed in a letter to Aunt Netta the following day, advising that because of the sale she need not pay the California taxes on the vessel and specifying other small measures to economize, including not renewing magazine subscriptions.

A month later they were back in Sydney, health largely recovered, and London was again feisty on the point of Bessie's intention to marry and keep the house. "When I get home I'll make things warm for her," he wrote Eliza. His intention to sell the *Snark* hit a snag when she went overdue from the Solomons, and as the watch lengthened he began to fear that the vessel, never seaworthy, had sunk.[22] When she finally glided into port on March 3, Charmian was heartbroken to learn that Peggy had not survived the trip. London later memorialized the dog in *Jerry of the Islands*, a loving tale of a feisty

Irish terrier whose penchant for chasing natives with snapping abandon winds up saving the life of his master from a headhunter. Published posthumously under Charmian's supervision, its depiction of unrelenting savagery on the part of South Sea islanders was doubtless an exponent of London's irritation with critics who clucked that he was overstating the dangers of fraternizing with primitives.

With grief, the *Snark*'s salvageable gear was removed and she was consigned to Justus Scharff Ltd. for sale. London funded Johnson, the only remnant of his original crew, to continue at least another leg of adventure before finding his way back to Kansas. Johnson let it slip that he intended to write a book about their travels, at which Charmian jotted in her diary, "Haw! Haw!" Her experience with one determined man should have led her to take him more seriously. Not only did he complete *Through the South Seas with Jack London,* it was better than her *Log of the Snark* and he beat her to press by two years—doubtless part of the reason she attacked the book as presumptuous and inaccurate. Indeed, along with the muckrakers, Martin Johnson became an important Jack London literary legacy. Like London he married a fellow adventurer, Osa Leighty of Chanute, Kansas, in 1910, and the two garnered wide fame as coauthors and filmmakers, especially of their exploration of interior Africa.[23]

On April 7, 1909, London and Charmian commenced a circuitous journey back home, signing aboard the tramping 5,200-ton collier S.S. *Tymeric* as purser and stewardess, respectively.[24] Charmian spent most of the passage in her cabin, shivering with malaria, nursed alternately by London and Nakata, but by the time they docked in Guayaquil, London had wrapped two more stories and a new novel, *Adventure,* which Macmillan brought out early in 1911. They surveyed the Andes, and in Quito they took in a bullfight, which London found so revolting that he excoriated the so-called sport in "The Madness of John Harned." Then it was aboard the S.S. *Erica* to Panama, quarantine, and passage on the S.S. *Turrialba* to New Orleans, where ever-helpful Eliza wired him enough money to post a bond to spring Nakata out of immigration detention and get home.

Entrained from New Orleans to Oakland, with Nakata safely recovered, the Londons stopped at the Grand Canyon for a look. They reached Oakland on July 21, 1909, after an absence of twenty-seven months, to a boisterous welcome from The Crowd—meals at the Saddle Rock, attending the theater, and a chance encounter with the captain of the *Tymeric,* whom they spirited away for a homecoming at Beauty Ranch.

13 ❧ THE RANCHER

During London's absence, Aunt Netta had not been shy about looking to her own comfort from his income, but the bad intent of her mismanagement should not be overstated. She had sold *Martin Eden* for $9,000 and was able to present London with a ranch more than twice the size he had left. As opportunities had presented themselves, she purchased two small adjoining tracts of 9 and 24 acres, and the 127-acre La Motte Ranch. London now owned nearly 400 acres, enough for a proper, and profitable, working ranch. In fact, only one parcel stood in the way of his owning all the land from Asbury Creek to Netta's Wake Robin, and that was the Kohler-Frohling tract of 700 acres that reached up the east flank of Sonoma Mountain. Planted mostly in Tokay vines, its winery had been wrecked in the 1906 earthquake, and there were still stands of timber on it, watered by three creeks. It would be a steep purchase, but the vision of a contiguous, harmonious working property inspired him to set his sights on it.

The appearance of *Martin Eden* in September 1909 marked a comeback of sorts for Jack London the literary artist. Neither travelogue nor diatribe, it told the largely autobiographical story of a young sailor who wanted to be a writer, who struggled and succeeded, only to have the fruits of success turn sour in his mouth. Characters throughout the tale are transparently modeled on the real people cast throughout London's own life, and they have provided English students with generations of term papers on who they really were and how heavily they were fictionalized. But London certainly revisited his earliest literary roots in engineering the story, for Martin Eden's eventual plunge from the ship's porthole is heralded with a quote from Longfellow—"A single step and all is o'er / A plunge, a bubble, and no more"—that he had used in his earliest efforts while at Oakland High School.

The irony of London's comeback novel was that its meaning was universally misinterpreted. "I must have bungled it," he wrote to Sinclair Lewis, "for not one reviewer has discovered it." He expressed the same bafflement to Blanche Partington and, later, to Mary Austin. *Martin Eden* was analyzed as praise of Nietzsche and individualism, when in fact he meant it as a torpedo fired into the side of Nietzschean philosophy. Eden the character, he wrote to Blanche, "was unaware of the needs of others. . . . He worked, strove, fought for himself alone. And when disillusionment came, when love, fame, the worthwhileness of the bourgeoisie—all things—failed, why there was nothing left for him to live for." Seen another way, both Jack London and Martin Eden had suffered the "long sickness" of Nietzsche; London had survived, and Eden had not. *The Call of the Wild, White Fang,* and *The Sea-Wolf* were more popular than *Martin Eden,* but the latter book came to enjoy greater respect among succeeding generations of writers, who can so easily fall prey to the same disaffection and sense of futility. As a cautionary tale, *Martin Eden* probably did more good than London ever knew.

In his own life, what gave him purpose and direction was less and less his own writing, although he continued his thousand words per day, good ones or bad ones, for his income. More and more he lived for Beauty Ranch, and as he had hoped, he began to recover the health ravaged by months in the tropics. While his formerly frightening skin disorder had already been diagnosed as no more than a bad case of psoriasis, any lingering fears of leprosy were dispelled when he came across an army medical treatise, *Effects of Tropical Light on White Men,* by Lieutenant Colonel Charles E. Woodruff. Near the equator, it explained, the ultraviolet range of the sun's rays was more intense than in northern latitudes, and Caucasian skin slowly cooked in it. His disfigured hands would improve. What worried him now were his kidneys. Besides abusing them with years of heavy drinking, he had done them more damage than he knew by taking mercury chloride for the yaws he suffered from in the South Pacific.

He was depressed as much as debilitated by his maladies. He still occasionally affected he-man poses in bathing suit or underwear, trying to hold in his growing paunch but no longer fooling himself that he was the specimen he once was. It was time to settle down, build up the ranch, and start a family with Charmian. At thirty-four, he knew he had best get on with it. They had been living in the annex of Wake Robin since 1906, and now they were planning to move into the old winery's cottage on their original purchase—a move not actually accomplished until 1911. Beyond that, his thoughts returned to that high slope above Asbury Creek that he and Charmian had selected, and which Johannes Reimers had long since begun landscaping to be ready for his mighty house. In a way, it had been forming in his mind since he was a child, when he boasted to his stepsister Eliza that one day he would live in a house, one room of which would contain nothing but his books, and now he meant to do it, for his library was scattered in boxes all over the ranch. This house would have a library nineteen feet by forty, with a spiral staircase up to a study of equal dimension. In their present circumstance there had never been room to entertain The Crowd, or even more than a few visitors at a time. Nearly a decade before, London had written Anna Strunsky of the almost helpless pleasure he took in entertaining. "I have the fatal faculty of making friends, and lack the blessed trait of being able to quarrel with them. And they are constantly turning up. My home is the Mecca of every returned Klondiker, sailor, or soldier of fortune I ever met. Some day," he added, "I shall build an establishment, invite them all, and turn them loose upon each other. Such a mingling of castes and creeds and characters could not be duplicated. The destruction would be great."[1] In the contemplated new house he planned to be able to seat fifty for dinner.

Slowly, determinedly, ideas became sketches; he engaged architect Albert Farr of San Francisco and sketches became blueprints. It was to be a colossal four-story castle, the spaces of the first floor nestled among monumental pylons of purple-brown lava blocks quarried from ancient volcanic flows there in the Valley of the Moon, with upper works of redwood framed by lava chimneys and topped by a massive tile roof. The porte cochere would be framed with redwood trunks, still clad in their bark, approached along a reflecting pool. The ground floor would host grand entertaining: a kitchen, a dining room, and a party room eighteen feet by fifty-eight. Stairs led up to the parlor floor, with a vast, two-story living room the same size as the party room, surrounded by a balcony that led to guest rooms; London's own bedroom would be an aerie on the fourth floor. Sight was never lost, though, that the house would be the beating heart of a working ranch. There was a gunroom, root and wine cellars, and a milk room.

When George Sterling saw the plans he immediately christened the place Wolf House, an apt name not only because it would be the lair of the Wolf and his Mate, but because the architecture masterfully evoked the great tourist lodges of the western wilderness. The cost would be phenomenal and it would be a project of years, but thanks to the $9,000 Aunt Netta had obtained for *Martin Eden*, and then the *Snark* sale for $4,500 (about 15 percent of the boat's construction cost), not to mention his backlog of manuscripts written during the voyage, there was enough to begin.

Charmian did her part, conceiving a child in late September or early October 1909; husband and wife were overjoyed, and anticipation for the addition to the household was keen. Boy or girl, London told visitors, he was having a baby with his Mate-Woman and he truly had no preference for the child's sex—although those who knew him well believed he ached for a son.

From April 30 through May 2, 1910, the ranch had a distinguished houseguest: Emma Goldman had been on a lecture tour, promoting anarchy through thirty-seven cities in twenty-five states, organized by her lover and traveling partner, Ben Reitman. Across the breadth of the country she got a fresh taste of America's devotion to conformity and hatred of anything that smacked of less than jingoistic patriotism. She learned to appreciate surprises, as when she was defended by the newspaper in Denver, and she reveled in some of life's more sublime ironies, as in Reno, when women who were in town to obtain quick divorces successfully demanded that she be put out of their hotel because of her espousal of free love. She had not seen London since his days as the Boy Socialist in 1897. She had, however, read and admired his books; in San Francisco she sent him a note inviting him to attend her lecture. "Dear Emma Goldman," he shot back. "I have your note. I would not go to a meeting even if God Almighty were to speak there. The only time I attend lectures is when I am to do the talking. But we want you *here*. Will you not come to Glen Ellen and bring whomever you have with you?"

Charmed, Goldman spent three days at Beauty Ranch with Reitman and her attorney, E. E. Kirk, and was fortunate enough to behold the Londons at, apparently, the height of happiness. Charmian was now great with their keenly expected child, and London was overflowing with verve and intellect. Goldman was now forty-one, and while London was thirty-four she saw him, perhaps because of their respective stations in their political movements, as a full generation younger than herself, but she admired the flowering of the promise she had first marked in him in 1897. "How different was the real Jack London from the mechanical, bell-button socialist of *The Kempton-Wace Letters!* Here was youth, exuberance, throbbing life. Here was the good comrade, all concern and affection. He exerted himself to make our visit a glorious holiday. We argued about our political differences, of course, but there was in Jack nothing of the rancour I had so often found in the socialists I had debated with. But, then, Jack London was the artist first, the creative spirit to whom freedom is the breath of life."

Goldman appreciated that London admitted the virtues of anarchy, but he maintained staunchly that society was not ready for them and must pass through a period of socialism before people could responsibly undertake to live without laws or authority. "In any case," she wrote, "it was not Jack London's politics that mattered to me. It was his humanity, his understanding of and his feeling with the complexities of the human heart." She chose not to mention that they also suffered one of London's practical jokes. Playing on the reputation of anarchists as bomb-throwers, London once left on Reitman's dinner plate a little red book entitled *Four Weeks, A Loud Book*. When Reitman opened it, it blew up with a huge bang. "They're such soft people, anarchists," London later said to Charmian, laughing, "when it comes to actual violence—and when they try to do it, they usually make a mess of it because they're dreamers. . . . He must have thought it was a bomb, for he went positively green."[2]

Charmian too was aglow during the visit, although Goldman feared she was exerting herself too much for her advanced pregnancy. "Charmian hardly rested," she wrote, "except after dinner, when she would sew on the outfit for the baby while we argued, joked and drank through the wee hours of the morning."[3] London tolerated his differences of opinion with Goldman over anarchy with what was, for him, a mild tone. As he confided to Charmian, "The anarchists whom I know are dear, big souls whom I like and admire immensely. But they are dreamers, idealists. I believe in law . . . you can see it in my books—all down in black and white." Charmian was equally taken with Goldman and presented her a lace handkerchief as a keepsake of the sojourn.

Emma Goldman departed with her suite, never guessing the extent to which Charmian labored to create that illusion of effortless domestic bliss, when in fact life on the ranch could be anything but. Indeed, the preceding months had not been easy ones; the boys had been drinking too much, especially George Sterling, who had been making himself obnoxious on a punch he mixed from Amer Picon liqueur, with London usually getting equally inebriated to keep him company. At one point Charmian's forced projection of happiness crossed an unseen line, and London barked at her to stop making him love her in public. Even he felt the excess of this rebuke and apologized with a baby grand piano, a Steinway she had long pined for.[4]

Other visitors during this season included London's childhood mate, Frank Atherton; his first fan, Cloudesley Johns, who came to show off his new wife and remained for a month; the tramp calling himself "A No. 1" from London's days of riding the rails; minor literary figures such as editor Lem Parton; and the remarkable Lucy Parsons, an anarchist and founder of the International Workers of the World.[5] Those close to the Londons were sure that Charmian wished many of them would go away but, doggedly gracious, she never let on. Instead, she abided by forming a couple of creative alliances, the first with Carrie Sterling, she who had been so against admitting Charmian to The Crowd, and who had grilled London in stunningly nosy letters demanding to know details of their relationship before the divorce from Bessie. Mary Austin had written of the care they had all taken to shield Carrie from George Sterling's serial infidelities, but eventually they failed, and Carrie was now unexpectedly learning about life in humiliation. In a brilliant maneuver Charmian extended her friendship to a former enemy and was rewarded with genuine affection—even as was the case with her second alliance, with her former rival Blanche Partington.

Soon after Goldman's visit, London saw the opportunity to complete the ranch and moved to strike: the seven hundred acres of the Frohling winery's exhausted soil would cost some $26,000, but it connected London's two existing tracts and was a perfect candidate to be resurrected by his renewed zeal for the land. He didn't have the money—the *Snark* was for sale in Australia and he had been answering queries about her particulars, but there had been no taker. Then he remembered George Brett. "It is a long time since I've written to you for a lump of money in advance," he wrote on May 5, pointing out that Brett now had six manuscripts in hand awaiting publication, the best candidate of which was the novel *Burning Daylight*. The New York *Herald* had paid $8,000 for the serial rights to this saga of an honest but somewhat naive man undone by Wall Street sharks, on whom he ultimately takes his revenge, which London said indicated a healthy book sale. He needed $5,000, but he regarded his present prospects as so good that he hoped not to ask for such a favor again.[6]

While expanding the ranch, he also divested himself of one small tract. Ninetta Eames finally had enough of the woebegone Roscoe and divorced him, uniting herself instead to Edward Payne, with whom she had been in business. London gifted her with a sunny meadow of seventeen acres. But for the rest, 1,100 acres, cleared and able to produce, or else untouched and scenic, which was of equal though different value, therein London saw his future. "In a few years," he wrote in his journal, "this valley will prove what I have said. Men will learn that by modern methods more reward can be brought from ten acres of land than in the old days could be obtained from two or three hundred."[7] He sought and received advice from the famous Dr. Luther Burbank, the horticulturist who lived in nearby Santa Rosa. Burbank was already celebrated for developing a superior potato before he moved to California from Massachusetts in 1875, and now the ever-busy old man managed thousands of simultaneous cross-breeding experiments. One of them was a spineless cactus, which London began growing on his ranch. The crop that ended up exciting him most, however, was eucalyptus.

Many American investors at the time were excited about the prospects of importing Australian eucalyptus, a species of gum tree, to replace eastern hardwoods that had been depleted for furniture and other manufactures. The pitch was that the eucalyptus grew fast, did not need rich soil, and would provide quality hardwood in less time than replanting American species. California farmers flocked to the opportunity, and London looked at the scrubby hillsides of the old La Motte place now on his ranch and saw dollar signs. In one season he planted 16,000 eucalyptus trees, notwithstanding that they had to be watered for the first two years and it was two hundred feet down to the nearest creek. Still strapped for cash, he extracted from his files a letter of December 1, 1909, from the Fuller & Johnson Manufacturing Co. of Madison, Wisconsin, which had sought to draw near his name and fame with a demonstration of one of its engines on the ranch. London now asked for an engine and pump, using for a credit reference his entries in *The Dictionary of American Authors* and *Who's Who in America*. He planned to plant 25,000 more gum trees the next year, and wrote Brett, "If I could get you out here and tell you the profits of eucalyptus-growing, you'd quit the publishing business." He was wrong on that last point. Like most speculative bubbles, the craze for growing gum trees soon popped, and California was left with countless groves of eucalyptus with little marketable value. By that time London had planted several times his original acreage, but he took the collapse in stride, realizing that he had stabilized his soil while giving himself what would, in time, become beautiful groves to ride through.[8]

London's improvements to the ranch extended well beyond the venture in eucalyptus trees. To complement the huge barn completed after the earthquake, he began planning an equally sturdy blacksmith shop and two substantial grain silos, the first in California to be built of concrete blocks. He began planning a large-scale swine operation, centered on a state-of-the-art rock enclosure and pens capable of housing three hundred animals. Dubbed the "Pig Palace," it became a showpiece of the ranch and, London expected, would contribute to the income stream.

❧ ❧ ❧

After five days in the hospital, Charmian underwent a cesarean section to deliver a daughter, Joy, on June 19, 1910, but the baby was fatally injured in the difficult extraction and expired after a day and a half. The shock to both father and mother was profound, but during her subsequent weeks in the hospital Charmian slowly came to terms with the loss of her daughter. "I am a mother," she wrote a friend. "I bore a child—but there is not a child. . . . How much better that my arms never nested her, seeing she was to go so soon. She is more a child of the imagination, and must always remain so."[9] Charmian was so devastated she had to be sedated, and a heartsick London went to meet Joseph Noel at the Tavern Café for a drink. London had previously agreed to report for the New York *Herald* on what was being billed as the fight of the century, between Jack Johnson, the reigning heavyweight champion who was, to the mortification of a racist country, black, and former champion Jim Jeffries, recalled from retirement to put Johnson back in his place. On the way to meet Noel, London purchased some copies of Jeffries's autobiography, one for himself and three for friends. When London entered the bar its owner, Tim Muldowney, thought the colorful books were posters warning against social diseases, and he told London not to post them; London, in no mood to mess with, told him off. Muldowney began throwing punches and ejected London from the bar. London filed assault charges, Muldowney filed counter charges, and the police judge, George Samuels, released both men until a trial date of July 8, when he hoped they would be in better condition to testify.

The issue was still hanging over London's head when he left town to cover the upcoming prizefight. It was slated, meaningfully, for July 4, and there was unprecedented national anticipation. Johnson, from Texas, had reigned as undisputed heavyweight champion since pummeling Tommy Burns in Australia. White supremacists in America were mortified and infuriated, and eventually persuaded Jeffries to come out of a seven-year retirement to take Johnson down. Promoted as the "Great White Hope," Jeffries shouldered the burden even knowing that he was too old, too fat, and too out of condition to win. London himself accepted the job because the fight would be in San Francisco and close to home, but after a legal wrangle it was moved to Reno. After the loss of their daughter London was reluctant to make the trip, but Charmian, still in the hospital, as she would be for several weeks more, sensed his need for a change of scene, and sent him on his way. The national buildup to the bout was so keen that London had agreed to file stories for ten days before the actual event, reporting on the principals, their training camps, the mood of the city—building what in a later time would be called "hype."

The match, when it took place, was even more of a slaughter than Johnson's fight with Burns, and London's reportage of the historic event was similar to what he filed from Australia. Accepting in himself that he had personally wanted Jeffries to win, he deconstructed the rounds accurately and without bias, recounting both the taunts directed at Johnson from Jeffries's handlers and trainers, and the cries from the audience of 20,000, "Don't let the negro knock him out!" Johnson answered everything with a smile and banter. At the beginning, Jeffries refused to shake hands, which London criticized. From the first round, when Jeffries's trainer would insult him, Johnson would smile, and land a punishing flurry on the Great White Hope, until they recognized the pattern and kept quiet.

It was obvious to London from the start that Jeffries had no chance. "What he failed to bring into the ring with him was his stamina, which he lost somewhere in the last seven years. Jeff failed to come back. That is the whole story." He saw clearly, setting hype aside, that Johnson outclassed Jeffries in every way: "There is nothing heavy or primitive about this man Johnson," wrote London. "He is alive and quivering, every nerve fiber in his body and brain, withal that it is hidden, so artfully, or naturally, under that poise of facetious calm of his. . . . His mind works like chain lightning and his body obeys with equal swiftness." London did not rank it as a great fight. "Faster, better fights may be seen every day of the year in any of the small clubs in the land." Nevertheless, "Johnson is a wonder. No one understands him, this man who smiles. . . . And where now is the champion who will make Johnson extend himself, who will glaze those bright eyes, remove that smile and silence that golden repartee?" Of all the white reportage on the Johnson-Jeffries debacle, London's, though he admitted joining in the widespread hope that a white champion would come forward, was fair and honest.[10] He managed not to mention that he had wagered $4,000 on Jeffries, and lost.

Back in Oakland, London had to stand trial over the bar fight with Muldowney, at which he expected to be vindicated and to see Muldowney convicted of assault. In court on July 8, Police Judge Samuels quietly dismissed all charges and let both go. London was enraged, first because that was how he usually reacted to manifest injustice, second because he was being deprecated in the national press as a drunken brawler, and probably spurred also by the desire to prove to Charmian that he was not culpable in the affair. He asked Noel, a journalist friend to whom he had assigned dramatic rights to *The Sea-Wolf*, to poke around. What he said he discovered was that Muldowney's bar was owned by Judge Samuels, and London went off like a skyrocket. He might have to accept such treatment as a penniless tramp in Buffalo, but Jack London the author demanded fairer treatment at the bar of justice than at the bar of the Tavern Café. He penned an open letter, widely published, in which he threatened Samuels. "Entrenched in your miniature high place, under the sacred panoply of the law, with behind you the policemen's clubs, the city prison cells, and the right to punish for contempt . . . you elected to bully me. Someday, somewhere, somehow, I am going to get you legally, never fear. I shall not lay myself open to the law. . . . But get you I will . . . and I shall get you to the full hilt of the law." The judge responded, also in the newspapers, tut-tutting London's temper. He "received a fair deal . . . and was not mistreated. . . . This young man has long been known as an obstreperous youth. . . . He is an Oakland boy, and is still a boy—a foolish boy, at that."[11] The only satisfaction

London actually got from the matter was Samuels's being turned out of office at the next election, and he sluiced his venom into a short story, "The Benefit of the Doubt," for which the *Saturday Evening Post* paid him $750—well enough earned for his black eye.

As the time approached for the Bohemian Club's annual summer High Jinks, Charmian felt able, cocooned among friends and family, to encourage London to go and have fun. This event, however, promised more drama than those in previous years.

After a long residence in the East, Ambrose Bierce had moved back to California in 1910, which left his protégé George Sterling in a stew to keep him from finding out how close he and London had been. While London remained as popular as ever among The Crowd, Bierce had been nursing an ever-growing disdain for London that passed the boundary of hatred but seems to have stopped short of insisting that Sterling choose between them. London had managed to avoid confrontations with him by not attending gatherings when he was warned that "Bitter Bierce" would be there, but at the 1910 High Jinks they were sure to meet. "Damn Ambrose Bierce," he wrote to Charmian. "I won't look for trouble but if he jumps me, I'll go him a few at his own game. . . . If we meet, and he's introduced, I shall wait & watch for his hand to go out first. If it doesn't, hostilities begin right there."[12]

Secluded among the redwoods on the Russian River, where amicable sociability between the wealthy and the creative sets was the whole reason for the gathering, warfare somehow did not break out. Bierce and London were once seen drinking at the same campfire with Sterling and Arnold Genthe, after which Wolf and the Greek conducted Bierce safely back to his tent through some dark forest, but beyond that, the confidence was kept.

With the *Snark* gone and sailing still in his blood, London acquired a graceful thirty-foot yawl called the *Roamer,* in which he intended to make one of his periodic explorations of the inland delta. She was forty years old and cost only $175, tall and lateen-rigged to catch every breath of wind, with an unusually large cabin for such a small boat. When Charmian was recovered enough, they were out for weeks with Nakata and a new cook named Yamamoto, renewing their closeness and recovering themselves after their trauma.

February 1911 brought an inquiry close to his heart. Henry W. Lanier was secretary of Doubleday, Page & Company; in addition to its line of books, Doubleday also published *Country Life in America* and wanted London to write an article about sailing one's own boat. London responded with a brief summary of his open-boat experience, from the flatboat on the Des Moines River with Kelly's Army, to the trip down the Yukon, to the frigid sampans off the coast of Korea, to the *Snark*. The project went into his hopper, but work was not rapid.

He and Charmian worked in a visit with his old friend Felix Peano, the sculptor in whose eccentric Villa Capriccioso he and Bessie stayed for a while when they were married. He was now living in Los Angeles, and during the trip the Londons also visited Catalina Island and witnessed a new land speed record set by racer Barney Oldfield. Later the year reached highlight as London harnessed four horses to his Studebaker wagon for a tour of Northern California and Oregon. With Nakata attending them, it was a restful and joyous vacation, unhurried, not knowing the next day's route until inquiring of local bar patrons the conditions of the roads ahead and the locales for the best fishing. With several side trips and sojourns, including ten days on a friend's houseboat near Eureka, the four-in-hand jaunt lasted from June 12 to September 5. The only nuisances were the pestering of reporters in seemingly every town, and the regularity of London being asked to speak publicly. In too good a humor to rise to any bait, he eschewed socialism as his topic and spoke on everything from comparative climates to horse driving.

Nevertheless it was a working vacation. He maintained his quota of a thousand words per day, and in 1911 London published more short stories than in any other year, nearly thirty, in addition to the novel *Adventure,* with its vivid descriptions of Melanesian headhunters. There was also a potpourri of stories on various themes in *When God Laughs,* and two volumes of South Seas stories and reminiscences, *South Sea Tales* and *The Cruise of the Snark*. It was a protean output, even for London. In fact, 1911 would have been an ideal year, had it not been for souring relations with Bessie, who wanted more money and used his occasional visits to his daughters to press the issue, resulting in royal battles in front of the girls. In one incident that came to have a life of its own in retelling, during a visit to Bessie's house London asked his younger daughter, nine-year-old Becky, if she did not trust him to take care of her no matter what a situation looked like, then pretended to pitch her through a closed window. He accidentally swung her too close to it, cutting one foot badly enough that he carried her across the street to the hospital. Becky remembered the incident lightly, but her older sister, Joan, embellished it bitterly, portraying him as drunk at the time.

❧ ❧ ❧

As the year drew to its close, several factors led London and Charmian to plan a visit to New York. As both London and Brett had hoped, the cruise of the South Pacific had engendered a whole new London franchise, which now he had in mind to expand further. During 1910 and 1911 he added to his fiction possibilities by purchasing fourteen more of Sinclair Lewis's story ideas, but more important, a new novel had begun to come to him, a mutiny on a full-rigged sailing ship, the likes of which he had never sailed and which were fast becoming extinct. He had also begun thinking about an autobiography, not a bland memoir but one that plumbed the reasons for his lifelong relationship with alcohol. Prohibition had long since become the most widespread political cause célèbre in America, and as he meditated on the topic dispassionately, he found himself somewhat surprised to be coming around, tentatively, to the point of view that alcohol should be banned. But whatever political opinion he eventually came to, an explanatory but somewhat repentant memoir from a writer of such prominence could be a massive seller. *John Barleycorn,* he was thinking to call it; he had done a lifetime of research on drunkenness already, and perhaps it was merely rationalizing to believe that a visit to New York would allow him a final exploration of new depths not yet explored.

On an unrelated matter, London needed to investigate a financial boondoggle in which he had involved himself to the extent of mortgaging Flora's house again, a new process for producing three-color lithography. When local printers had pronounced the technique a breakthrough, London raised money himself and recruited his friend Noel to pitch in. With modest capital in hand, they moved the inventor, a man named Miller, to New York to start developing his Millergraph. In a case of life imitating art, in this case the Wall Street skullduggery of *Burning Daylight*, stock was issued, with London's name at the head of the company to attract investors, all of whom lost money when the printing process, which was truly good, lost out to competing advances in lithography. London had felt railroaded by correspondence from the company's supposed managers and wanted to get to the bottom of why the company was failing. Then, too, as accommodating as Brett had been over the years, London had begun to feel, as highly successful writers sometimes do, somewhat like a captive of one house, and he wished to make some new contacts. Thus the plans were laid to spend some weeks in New York, and then to board a tall ship to return home via an old-time sail around Cape Horn, with the vessel eventually docking in Seattle.

They departed Oakland by train on December 24 and arrived in New York on the second day of 1912. There they were met by F. G. Hancock, a correspondent who had supplied London with newspaper and magazine clippings for enough years to have developed a friendly rapport. Hancock installed them in his apartment at 40 Morningside Park East. Tending straight to business, London had some hope of working out a publishing agreement with Doubleday, Page & Co., for which he was writing "The Joy of Small-Boat Sailing" for its *Country Life in America* magazine. Doubleday agreed to publish a collection of his stories, *A Son of the Sun*, which came out in May. But a week after his arrival the company secretary, Henry Lanier, waived off a long-term agreement, with a note that Doubleday feared it would not be able to do London's books the justice that a writer of his stature deserved. This was a danger sign to any writer that his stature was not what it used to be. "Hell," London wrote in response, "I haven't started to write yet."[13] London also made a four-day trip to Boston to see what he could arrange with Houghton-Mifflin, but nothing was doing there, either. Back in New York he struck a deal instead with Century for six books, dealing with W. B. Parker, an editor to whom he had submitted manuscripts back in his grim and starving days as a beginner. Dependable Eliza was now managing his literary affairs in his absence, as well as the ranch, and London sent her specific instructions on the dispatch of completed manuscripts while he was at sea—specifics he would not have had to tell an experienced editor such as Aunt Netta, such as making sure to send the typewritten manuscripts, not his handwritten drafts. She could, he wrote, expect advance money of $1,000 per month for six months, keeping some in reserve should he and Charmian arrive in Seattle without funds the following summer.[14]

At Macmillan Brett was correct and professional during London's flirtation with other publishers, offering to advance him money—which he had been asked to do enough times in the past, God knew—while he was in the city. Brett's politeness under pressure was the best way of getting his wayward author home again. London declined for himself but asked Brett to keep available $1,000 on his account that Noel might need to disentangle the Millergraph business.

With his affairs returned to a sort of order, there was time for society. One friendly face of The Crowd was in town, Arnold Genthe, and London and Charmian reciprocated the California visit of Emma Goldman. Of keener interest, however, was his reconnection with Anna Strunsky. Since their warmly remembered romance she had traveled and lectured as far as Geneva in support of socialists in Russia, and she had married a good comrade, William English Walling. Oddly for one who had argued for passionate marriage in *The Kempton-Wace Letters,* she was not particularly attracted to her husband and procrastinated consummating their relationship for some months. Charmian felt no qualms about the reunion, for Anna was another former rival with whom she had not just made peace, but become friends, which was as much Anna's doing as her own.[15]

In New York, however, Charmian was often left alone in Hancock's apartment, as London left on drinking expeditions with Noel and others, such as Michael Monahan, the editor of *Papyrus,* a small literary journal. Sometimes there were incidents that made it into the papers. Jack and Charmian London were far too public a couple for him to carouse at night without her and not excite comment, but he took no cognizance that she found this deeply humiliating, and the two months in New York were, for her, hell. "The city reached into him," she wrote, "and plucked to light the least admirable of his qualities." And he had warned her already that he intended to souse to his limit on this trip, to plumb his personal depths for material that he would use in the new *John Barleycorn* memoir.

I know my man, she kept telling herself, having no choice but to trust the vivid distinction he had always drawn between his deep love for her and the mere sexual adventuring to which he had always been drawn. And as she knew, "I had never yet waited in vain to welcome back the sane and lovable boy." She hearkened back to another warning he had given her early in their marriage: "Don't forget what I have been and been through. There may, mark, I only say *may* come times when the temptation to 'drift' . . . will stick up its head, and I may follow. I have drifted all my life—curiosity, that burning desire to *know*." She was forced to accept that this was such a time, "but I knew my man, and, content or not, waited." When he was sober he was loving and attentive, and sometimes referred jokingly to what he called his "pirooting," but it made the experience no less galling for Charmian, who sometimes had to learn from newspapers or from gossip "the story of a hard-fought game of cards . . . or a weird experience of one sort or another with some nameless waif he had elected to trot around with."[16] Three such nameless waifs, actresses of color, were riding in an automobile with London when it was involved in an accident from which he emerged banged up and with glass in his mouth. All refused treatment and hurried from the scene before it could be publicized.

Once, after losing patience with London on the subway Charmian snapped at him to keep his house in order, to which he replied with a chilling defiance that he would do as he pleased. What got Charmian through it was the knowledge that she would soon have him all to herself again on that long voyage back to California. The exchange ended with her muttering aloud that she longed for that tall ship that would take them home. It proved to be the *Dirigo*, a four-masted bark of 3,000 tons. She was departing from Baltimore, and before sailing the Londons paid their respects to the grave of Edgar Allen Poe—London in a newly shaved head, a prank that left Charmian truly and earnestly furious to the point that she refused to be seen with him unless he wore a hat.

Maine-built and named for the state's motto, "I Lead," the *Dirigo* was among the last of a majestic breed, a tall ship indeed rigged with skies and royals above single topgallants and double topsails. A sweeping 312 feet long, 45 feet in the beam, and drawing 25 feet of water, she rose in the ways the same year that London was hunting seals in the Bering Sea, and for the eighteen years since she had hauled bulk cargo—coal, sugar, case oil—to and from every corner of the planet—Shanghai, Honolulu, Rio de Janeiro, Delaware, Liverpool—her six- to nine-month voyages managed to pay for themselves because she could disgorge 5,000 tons of cargo at a destination.

She was not, however, rated for passengers, so the Londons and Nakata signed aboard as crew although their passage cost him $1,000. They came aboard with a new member of the family, a barely weaned fox terrier they named Possum, a $10 purchase from a pet store and a far cry from the shaggy wolf-dogs with which London had come to be associated, but soon rooted deep in their affections. The journey did not begin well for Charmian, as she was nearly devoured by bedbugs until her bunk was thoroughly cleaned. However, the long days at sea restored much of their strained relationship. Her lovable boy had indeed returned to her, and Charmian ventured to ask him whether, in New York, he would have preferred her to have withdrawn from him and given him totally free rein. "No," he said, "you did exactly as you should have done. If you had left me, I don't know *what* I should have done." Once again, Charmian had charted the right course to keep him, without buoy or lighthouse. It was a needed comfort for her because, as she had signed aboard as stewardess, she wound up nursing the *Dirigo*'s captain, who was in the terminal stage of stomach cancer.

The towering storms of Cape Horn had been the stuff of literature for centuries, and as the *Dirigo* made her run through the Straits of Magellan the Londons were treated to an unforgettable and truly dangerous tempest. The bulk of the voyage, however, was like a second honeymoon. In the mornings he wrote and she typed; they worked and loved harmoniously, and they conceived a second child. Of all the ships London ever boarded, the *Dirigo* was the most evocative and he sucked in all her atmosphere, talking extensively to the crew; she provided the setting for his last sea novel, *Mutiny of the Elsinore.*

London spent much of his time in the mizzen-top, a dizzying perch in which to read, reflect, and let the fresh salt air cleanse New York and its liquor out of his system. For all the hell he had put Charmian through in his deliberate plunge to the bottom of the bottle, he made good use of it, doing extensive preliminary work on *John Barleycorn.* He also thought about his emergence from the "long sickness," and what the ranch and the countryside meant to him. It allowed him to write an optimistic and bucolic finish to *The Valley of the Moon,* completed ten days before the *Dirigo* completed its nearly five-month voyage, docking in Seattle on July 26. For four days the Londons kept company with *Snark* veteran Martin Johnson and his new wife, Osa, before boarding a much more conventional vessel, the steamer *City of Puebla,* and regaining Oakland on August 2. Operating out of their pied-à-terre in Flora's house they made a hurried reacquaintance with favorite restaurants and theaters for three days before returning to the ranch.

Oddly for one who believed himself to be increasingly tied to the land, London left almost immediately for the 1912 High Jinks with the Bohemian Club. Only four days after he left, Charmian suddenly miscarried the son he had wanted so badly. There were complications, and the necessary surgery that followed ended the possibility of their trying again. The only positive was that it happened when she was in Oakland to visit the doctor, and where she stayed to recuperate. Had it happened in the isolation of the ranch the outcome might have been far more grim. A devastated London wrote her from back at the ranch:

> Dearest Love-Woman and Mate:—
>
> I have just received your Monday night telegram; got word to Eliza who is starting immediately for Oakland; and called up 490 and talked to grandma.

> I am so sorry; yet my gladness is vastly greater, in that you are all right.
>
> I have never loved you, and all your dear things here about the house, more.... I wandered about the rooms and breathed your atmosphere, & felt so lonely.
>
> Dear, dear woman!
>
> Mate Man

He then made an attempt to cheer her up with ranch chatter—the mosquitoes were just about gone—and news of the present visitors, Frank Strawn-Hamilton and the socialite Laura Grant, Charmian's close friend.[17] Losing a second child, however, made those close to the couple wonder if the tragedy might not strain the marriage beyond saving.

Charmian was back at the ranch two weeks later, coping as best she could, determined not to seem weak or soggy, and as always, keeping her darkest fears to herself. Autumn visitors to the ranch included an Australian pianist they had befriended during the *Snark* cruise, Laurie Godfrey-Smith, whom London took out on the *Roamer*. The year 1912 had been productive for him; he was receiving top dollar for his short stories, of which ten appeared during the year. Three books were published as well, including a compendium of a dozen short stories, *Smoke Bellew Tales*, for Century. This volume he regarded as a potboiler and not his best work, despite their popularity, and he declined to continue the thread despite entreaties from the serializing magazine. The two books finished during the year, however, *The Valley of the Moon* and *John Barleycorn*, were works that he was proud of and had great hopes for. London fulfilled his obligation to Century: ten more stories collated as *The Night Born* in February 1913, including his indictment of bullfighting, "The Madness of John Harned"; the novel *The Abysmal Brute* was published in May of the same year; and the book that achieved the most lasting note, his life seen as a struggle for temperance in *John Barleycorn*, released in August 1913. After their publication, however, he returned to Macmillan to handle *The Valley of the Moon* in October. The patient Brett was waiting to take up the reins of his prized author again with gentlemanly correspondence, and remained London's publisher from then on, the reward well earned.

It seemed as though London had recovered his literary voice and popularity, and his sales internationally were strong. Both the Prince of Wales and the Crown Prince of Germany were fans; he received expressions of admiration from such renowned foreign writers as Joseph Conrad, the Polish-born British adventure author of such works as *Heart of Darkness*. In a letter written in his calligraphic but difficult hand, Conrad took "immense satisfaction" in hailing London as "an accomplished fellow craftsman and brother in letters—of whose personality and art I have been intensely aware for many years."[18] Even with such admiration for his books, London poured ever more of himself into the ranch. For a time, "Jack's Monthly Miracle" seemed to happen with less desperation, and there was money left for improvements. He began a dam to impound one of his creeks to form a small irrigation lake, and Wolf House rose on the heights above Asbury Creek, a fantasy of lava buttresses and redwood ramparts. He had always loved horses, and the sudden violent death of Washoe Ban had caused him sharp pain. On March 5, 1913, a new horse arrived at the ranch more remarkable than any he had seen. His name was Neuadd Hillside, not a riding thoroughbred but a shire stallion, a draft horse of colossal proportions whom London began hiring out for stud fees.

In April London was in Los Angeles for talks about rendering his stories into motion pictures. Previous ill-considered agreements that he signed resulted in tangled and acrimonious relations with the Balboa Amusement Company, but when he emerged victorious from the legal actions with his copyrights in hand, he came away with a potentially powerful new source of income. He did decline to act in any of the films, however, and Hobart Bosworth had agreed to portray Wolf Larsen in a feature film of *The Sea-Wolf*.

Laid low by appendicitis later in the year, London was on a downward track that was becoming pronounced; at age thirty-seven, he was bloated and in increasing chronic pain from flouting his failing kidneys with alcohol and a far too rich diet of virtually raw duck. And then there was agonizing pyorrhea, which necessitated pulling all his remaining upper teeth. To his daily intake of alcohol was added morphine to deaden a growing roster of pains, and a certain unspoken knowledge that there would be no good outcome, but he did not significantly alter his habits.

❧ ❧ ❧

Through the summer the spectacular Wolf House crept toward completion, and Charmian began detailed planning of the interior decoration. Through the third week in August the heat was intense, the house was on the verge of occupancy, and workmen inside were wiping down the floors and woodwork with linseed oil. At the conclusion of the workday on August 22 they piled the rags on the floor before departing. The foreman suggested they take them outside, but it wasn't done. London and the foreman regarded the house that evening with satisfaction.

At two o'clock the next morning, London awoke to Eliza shaking him violently. Wolf House was on fire, fully ablaze by the time he, Eliza, and Charmian hitched a team and got out to the site, and there was no water with which to fight the fire. It burned to the ground, leaving the monumental lava pylons rising starkly against the sky. As there was no mortgage on it, he carried no insurance.

Arson was the immediate thought. The house had been considered all but fireproof; the bark of the redwood pillars was naturally fire retardant, as was the roofing paper under the tiles. For the huge structure to be so fully involved in the fire before it was even discovered pointed to multiple sources of origin. London had recently fired a workman for slacking and insolence; he might have done it. The socialist press was scandalized that their former champion would even consider living in such a baronial mansion; one of them might have done it. Even James Shepard, who had been entangled in a vicious divorce from Eliza, was mentioned. An investigation would have accomplished little, however, for with the exception of the lava block walls that now formed a towering ruin, the house was in ashes. Subsequent experimentation proved at least the possibility that the blaze could have begun with spontaneous combustion of the linseed cloths, but the burning of Wolf House, and the staggering financial loss it represented, will always be a mystery.

As Wolf House went up in flames, London wept fully but only briefly before, as he did with his deepest agonies, internalizing it. He suffered a devastation so complete that he appeared at first to handle it philosophically. But he was a changed man by October 5, 1913, when he was in San Francisco to watch the seven-reel motion picture of *The Sea Wolf*, the first feature film in the United States—or it would have been, if the previous copyright holder had not emerged from its suit against London with the right to finish its version of the story, having only to call it by another title. Thus *The Sea-Wolf*, curiously, was the subject of both of the first two feature motion pictures.[19]

Insects and bad weather had ruined much of the year's agriculture on the ranch; London had gotten over that; he had borne the loss of a son and the possibility of starting any family with Charmian; he had survived appendicitis and endured the loss of Wolf House, and the unremitting slide of rotten luck caused him to reevaluate his ambitions and scale them back to something no more grand than reconnecting with his daughters. He visited them at Bessie's house and offered them the chance to live on the ranch with him. It never occurred to him that he was too late.

"Almost the entire population of the world consists of little people," he urged in a letter to Joan. "Here and there are a few of the big people. It is a hard proposition to put up to you at your age, and the chances are that in deciding on this proposition . . . you will make the mistake of deciding to be a little person in a little place in a little part of the world. You will make this mistake because you listened to your mother, who is a little person in a little place in a little part of the world, and who, out of her female sex jealousy against another woman, has sacrificed your future for you. . . . On the other hand, I offer you the big things of the world; the big things that big people live and know and think and act." It was important, he continued, that she act now, in her formative years, because if she grew to adulthood under her mother's tutelage, she would not be able to prevent "this malformation of you, this wizening and pinching of you into the little person—you may be able to charge this directly to your mother's conduct in influencing your conduct, because your mother is so small, so primitive, so savage, that she cherishes a sex hatred for a woman who was bigger than she to such an extent that her face is distorted with passion while she talks about it."

Even allowing that in the early twentieth century, children were expected to perceive and behave as miniature adults—and Joan at twelve was old enough to expect few indulgences—and even allowing that London himself had few parental reference points, his October 11 letter to her was staggeringly cruel and unreasonable. Indeed it reads less like a letter and more like one of his abstract literary compositions with the emphatic repetitions that so marked his style, and its adult content, repeatedly charging her mother with "female sex jealousy," was stunningly inappropriate for a girl of Joan's age. While there were ways in which London was never a child, there were also ways in which he never grew up, and this outburst was childish and self-indulgent even for one who had suffered the recent losses that he had. It was left to twelve-year-old Joan to assume the adult role in the exchange, but it took her more than two weeks: "Well, Dad, I've read over your letter, read it twice carefully. . . . I am satisfied with my present surroundings. . . . I resent your opinions of my mother . . . she is a good mother, and what is greater, in this world, than a good mother? . . . And now, Daddy, since we have thrashed this question out together, may we not leave it? I have nothing more to say in the matter. . . . Please, Daddy, please let me feel that this is the last of these awful letters you force me to write to you; it hurts me so to write them, and yet, you demand these kind of answers and I can only write them."[20]

Ironically, it took a girl no older than Joan herself to make London see the faults of his attempt at parenting. One of their Glen Ellen neighbors and occasional guests was Earl Rogers, who with the possible exception of Clarence Darrow was the most famous criminal defense attorney in the country, and who in fact had successfully defended Darrow in his own jury-tampering trial over the 1910 bombing of the *Los Angeles Times* building that killed twenty-one people. On one occasion, Rogers's daughter Adela (familiarly addressed as Nora) saddled up and went for a ride in the early morning. London and Charmian habitually worked in the mornings and never saw their guests before lunch, so Nora was startled to shortly see London galloping after her. He led her to a secluded glen, where they dismounted and he led her around the site, saying he meant to build a house for his first wife and their two girls, and asked her what she thought of the idea.

When Nora expressed her doubts that it would work out, London argued his case about Joan as frankly—typically for him—as though he had been addressing an adult. "I ask her to give me a chance to make her know me. Is that too much?"

Nora was uncomfortably pinned, but she took him on. "Not too much," she answered, "but it may be too late. If my father had gone off and *left* me—when a person has showed you they can live without you for years and go all over the world, it isn't so easy to believe all of a sudden they can't live without you any more. . . . You have to think about Joan as she is, the way she has grown up. She's made a choice, she had to. I don't think she can be expected, the way you treated her, to understand you the way I do Papa."

London stared at her, dumbfounded, and Nora realized he was accepting what she had said. "He was not like most of the grown-up people I had known," she wrote, "who were only interested in their side. He reached out to understand even when, as it did now, it had to hurt and anger him." The awkward moment was broken when Charmian and Earl Rogers rode up. London asked Rogers, "Can a man adopt a godchild when she's half grown?"

Rogers thought he was bantering, and responded that that was the best time, because there was no telling how an infant might turn out; saints and pickpockets were equally troublesome. "I have decided to adopt Nora as my goddaughter," said London.

"Charmian looked at me quickly," recalled Nora, "her eyes narrowed to golden slits, she swung down and came and kissed me and said, 'I shall be godmother.'"

As Rogers and his daughter rode away, he clarified to her that he was not fond of Charmian, but he felt sorry for her. Nora began struggling to fit the pieces together, that although London loved Charmian he missed and needed his family. Nora believed that Charmian was unaware that London was weighing an idea to bring them all up to the ranch, but that she felt the failure of losing their own baby, she sensed the threat, the perennial possibility that she might lose him, and "her claws went in and out and her ears went flat back like a mountain lioness."[21]

Jack London had been through much in the preceding two years, and had dragged Charmian through it with him. And even now she still had to wonder how secure her position was.

14 ↠ THE JADE

London's frequent sorties from the ranch into Oakland often included visits with Johnny Heinold, who had renamed his saloon the First and Last Chance and had presided over it, usually with a fat stogie in his mouth, since opening in 1883. London never failed to give Heinold an inscribed copy of each book as it came out. "He always found time to come around here and have his little two-finger drink and bring me his latest book with his name writ in the front," Heinold later recalled. Away from the pressures of the ranch and its debts, London's open-handed ways reasserted themselves. Heinold was with him one Fourth of July when they passed a cluster of children staring at fireworks for sale in a store window. London asked them where their fireworks were, and they responded that their parents had no money. "He took them kids into the store," recalled Heinold, "and when they came out you couldn't see 'em for fireworks."[1]

The Oakland waterfront was sometimes where London would happen across men he had known from the tramping life, hoboes past and sometimes present, or seamen, or Klondikers, usually down-and-out. At one point he even met French Frank, now a very old man, from whom he had bought his oyster raider the *Razzle Dazzle* when he was fifteen. French Frank's ire over losing Mamie the Queen of the Oyster Pirates now gone, they posed together, beaming, for a photograph. To Charmian's dismay he would often bring such derelicts home for dinner, a decent sleep, breakfast, and a dollar to see them on their way. Sometimes they made their own way out to the ranch, almost always to be made welcome.

Generosity to those he had known, he seldom begrudged. It was the demands of his literary position now that taxed him. It was ten years now since he had rocketed to fame with *The Call of the Wild* and *The Sea-Wolf*. In his decade as leader of America's literary pack, he had been challenged and snapped at by traditionalists who hated the new naturalism in writing, by capitalists who hated his socialism, and by socialists who thought his expansive lifestyle inconsistent with the principles he espoused. His popularity had waxed and waned, and just as that of the wolf who battles his way to lead the pack discovers that there is nowhere to go from there but down, London's vigor began to decline. He was now thirty-seven, and his health was in alarming decline, as the years of abusing his body with alcohol, cigarettes, and raw meat, and the aftereffects of tropical diseases, all began to manifest themselves with aches and pains that would soon mature into rheumatism and uremia and kidney stones.

Still, his celebrity brought a never-ending correspondence from complete strangers who wanted something, offered something, needed something. They wanted his endorsement of their inventions and patent medicines. Impoverished artists needed grubstakes. Half tired and half exasperated, he groused to one friend that in an average year he was offered the chance to buy into a hundred gold mines. Requests for help in getting something published, either by reading and offering advice or even publishing it under his own name, arrived close to daily, as did pleas to "furnish college educations to orphan boys, endow old ladies' homes with libraries . . . and contribute to every bazaar that was ever got up by a ladies' aid society." And those were in addition to letters from socialists calling his attention to wrongs that they wanted him, particularly, to expose. He answered their letters daily to the bottom of the stack, although it ate into his life force to do it. A few he could help, but precious time was lost each day excusing himself from "the flotsam and jetsam that swamp this ranch ten-deep year in and year out and all the time."[2]

At least he could indulge in some laughs at people who impersonated him for whatever lark or advantage they could get out of it. London was astonished to receive a letter written with easy familiarity from a total stranger, and answered, "I am not so much surprised at receiving a letter from a dead man as I am from receiving a letter from a live man whom I have never met and who knows me as well as you know me, and who has eaten and slept with me as often as you have eaten and slept with me. . . . This man you traveled with made believe he was Jack London. Your letter makes me very curious, and I should be hugely delighted if you would kindly take the time to give me further information about this namesake of mine." He also, predictably, invited him to the ranch. "I always have the grub and hard liquor, and the latchstring is always out."[3]

Losing Wolf House was not his last adventure with fire, as the next month a blaze that roared down Sonoma Creek threatened the town of Glen Ellen itself. London rushed ranch hands to the town and assumed direction of fire brigades that saved the town; for his efforts, he was hailed as a hero. That was quite enough excitement, and he soon boarded the ever-comfortable old *Roamer* for a cruise of the inland waterways. He was still producing his thousand words per day and had been nursing one particular project, recruiting different magazines to sponsor him in a stint of travel writing about great tourist destinations of the world. It would serve the same purpose as the aborted *Snark* voyage, but with the luxury of being a paying passenger. The first installment would be about Japan, which he had not visited since his days before the mast on the *Sophie Sutherland*. Those plans were put on hold, though, when he learned that his affairs in New York, both with the Millergraph lithography process and with Joseph Noel over dramatic rights to *The Sea-Wolf*, had so fouled themselves that there was no escaping a second trip there, in February 1914. He returned nearly $4,000 poorer for clearing the copyright, which was at least a moral victory, for he had been sued for $40,000.

In addition to the literary output, celebrity brought ancillary opportunities that he used to boost his income, such as lending his name to commercial products. Still handsome, he was featured as a model when Royal Tailors of New York and Chicago bought a full-page ad in *Cosmopolitan*, a journal in which he had frequently published. It was *John Barleycorn* that provided one likely opportunity. The book appeared in 1913, the last of his contracted six with Century, with a leering, bleary-eyed London on the jacket. Aside from being the first recorded use of "pink elephants" as the prototypical hallucination of a drunk, the volume was an assessment of his drinking and his life. London's own friends were taken aback that he could look so honestly in the mirror; his friend Upton Sinclair reviewed it as "assuredly one of the most useful, as well as one of the most entertaining books ever penned." In his memoir, therefore, London's correlation of alcohol with the search for male bonding gives the surest testimonial of what he had long ago confessed to Charmian of his need for a deep and unshakeable Man-Love.

More visibly, a nation in the grip of the Prohibition movement was ready to embrace a sinner come to self-realization, and an Arizona prohibitionist visited him at Glen Ellen with the novel proposition that grapes from the ranch be pressed and sold as nonalcoholic juice instead of to a winery. Lending his name to a product that served a popular cause was intriguing and made sense from every direction; Tom Wilkinson of the International Press Association in San Francisco, an investor, drew up documents creating the Jack London Grape Juice Company and forwarded them for London's signature. A few days later, however, London's enthusiasm for the venture was sidetracked by another new writing opportunity.

In the years following 1910, news in the United States was increasingly distracted by a tumultuous civil war in Mexico. The three-decade-long dictatorship of Porfirio Díaz was brought down in 1911, but his successor, Francisco Madero, was no sooner in place than Madero's army chief, Victoriano Huerta, seized the government and had Madero killed. Huerta's fellow conspirators, Emiliano Zapata, Venustiano Carranza, and Francisco "Pancho" Villa, then turned on him and on one another in a free-for-all that by 1914 was as bloody as it was confusing. Intricately entwined in it all was American capital investment, which had replaced the political colonialism of Spain with its own economic overlordship.

The United States opposed the Huerta regime, and early in April the U.S. Navy landed marines in the Mexican port of Vera Cruz on the reediest of pretexts to ensure that arms shipments intended for Huerta were interdicted. Fighting appeared likely, and on April 16 *Collier's* contacted London with a head-turning offer of $1,100 per week, plus expenses for himself and Nakata, if he would go to Mexico and report on the mayhem. Sensing a chance to expound upon the class struggle in an underdeveloped and colonially victimized country, London agreed, provided the publication would pay expenses for his Mate to go as well. His terms were met, and the three left the next day for Los Angeles to board a train for Galveston, Texas, there to board ship for Vera Cruz.

There was one issue he wanted settled before leaving the country. His misadventures with Noel, with the Millergraph, and with Balboa Entertainment had given him good evidence that he needed to be more watchful and bloody-minded when it came to business. From Galveston he sent Eliza the batch of papers concerning the grape juice company, with explicit instructions to have them read by a lawyer to ensure that he was in no wise liable for any debts incurred by the venture. If the existing agreements did not leave him clear, she was to insist on new papers being drawn up. "Also, pledge no grapes from our ranch to the Company, unless said grapes are paid for in cash in just the same way as you sell grapes to a winery." He had had quite enough of good-naturedly trusting people who could take advantage of him. (He was wise. The company did go under, he was sued for part of the obligation, and he was found not liable.)

In Galveston, London encountered unexpected opposition. The expedition to Mexico was under command of Major General Frederick Funston, the same whose demolitions had prevented more of San Francisco from burning than actually did after the earthquake. Funston had been angered by an article he read that had appeared under London's name, which he regarded as unpatriotic and insulting to the military. "Young men:" London's article read, "the lowest aim in your life is to become a soldier. The good soldier never tries to distinguish between right and wrong. He never thinks; never reasons; he only obeys. . . . If he is ordered to fire down a crowded street when the poor are clamoring for bread, he obeys."[4] The incensed Funston would not take London's suite on any ship in his command.

In Japan ten years before, officers more clever than Funston at railroading the press had not been able to keep London out of Korea, and he was not discouraged now; he counterattacked on two fronts. First he went over Funston's head and out of his branch of service, and received an offer from the secretary of the Navy, Josephus Daniels, of passage on a destroyer if he could not find another way. Second, he wrote a disavowal of the objectionable piece to the editors of the Houston newspapers and repeated to the editor of the *Army and Navy Register*, explaining that parts of the article were quoted from his novel *The Iron Heel*, but he had nothing to do with it, and "it was one canard of a thousand canards that at one time & another have been circulated about me." Besides, he offered in a last line of defense, no less a journalist than the great Richard Harding Davis would state that "London couldn't have written it, because it's bad English."[5]

London was still awaiting a decision when fighting erupted in Mexico, resulting in the deaths of nineteen American servicemen. With Funston mollified, London shipped out on the U.S. Army transport *Kilpatrick*, with Charmian following a day later on the *Atlantis*. The *Kilpatrick* would be the first ship to unload soldiers once they reached Vera Cruz, and there were three other troop ships with her, escorted by three torpedo boats and joined by the pre-dreadnought battleship *Louisiana*, all steaming in line ahead; it was slow going, as one of the transports had engine trouble. On board with London were four other war correspondents, including the veteran Davis, who had saved London's camera and possibly his life in Korea ten years before. Sitting with them on deck one day was a green "cub" reporter, working feverishly on a dispatch. They asked him what he found to write about before ever landing, and he answered cheekily, "Well, maybe I see things you fellows don't see." The teasing he took from the older hands after that was ruthless.[6]

In Korea ten years before, London had strained every fiber and provoked the Japanese authorities to get to the front of battle. He wisely did not do so now. Although he had turned only thirty-eight, his he-man myth was becoming harder to maintain, and his hale appearance increasingly was held together only by the ferocity of his constitution. Tropical Mexico was infamous for savaging the health of gringos, and having once been laid low by a host of tropical maladies in the Pacific, London did not need another lesson. (Davis, too, suffered, writing that he quickly lost eight pounds in humid heat "that would sweat water out of a chilled steel safe.") Then, too, in Korea there had been recognized national armies and something resembling organization to the Japanese handling (albeit manipulating) a press corps. Mexico was nothing like that. There the choice was among roving bands of murderous brigands, and the danger inherent in contacting and reporting on them had only the year before claimed the life of someone London knew well. Both the experience and reportage of war had long been a staple of Ambrose Bierce, London's longtime literary critic and social scold. "Bitter Bierce" at seventy-one had gone to Mexico to report on Pancho Villa, disappeared, and was never heard from again.

What London found in Mexico threatened his ideals in ways they had not been challenged before, and forced his socialist sympathies to give way to the hard gaze of the journalist on the ground. At the opening of the Mexican Revolution he had written some pieces praising the peonage for rising up against their oppressors, but now the outrage of his dispatches revealed the writer still at the height of his powers, who had needed only the proper goading to set a record straight.

> I, for one, cannot comprehend how it is germane whether Madero was a patriot or a grafter; whether Huerta is a heroic figure of an Indian or a lunatic black Nero; whether Huerta murdered Madero. . . .
>
> What I see, with all this talk of little things filling my ears, is a torn and devastated Mexico, in which twelve million peons and all native and foreign business men are being injured and destroyed by the silly and selfish conduct of a few mixed breeds. I see a great, rich country . . . being smashed to chaos by a handful of child-minded men playing with the tragic tools of death made possible by modern technology. . . .
>
> From garret to basement the dwelling of Mexico is being torn to pieces. . . . The stay at home American listens to the slogans uttered by the various leaders of this anarchy and makes the mistake of conceiving the leaders in his own image and of thinking that "Liberty," "Justice," and a "Square Deal" means the same to them as they mean to him.
>
> Nothing of the sort. In the four centuries of Spanish and Mexican rule, liberty, justice and the square deal have never existed. Mexico is a republic in which nobody votes. Its liberty has ever been construed as license. Its

> justice had consisted in an effort at equitable division of the spoils of an exploited people. . . . And so it is with all the rest of the bombastic and valorous phrases in the vocabulary of the Mexican. . . .
>
> These "breeds" do politics, issue pronunciamentos, raise revolutions or are revolutionized against by others of them, write bombastic unveracity that is accepted as journalism in this sad, rich land, steal payrolls of companies and eat out hacienda after hacienda as they picnic along on what they are pleased to call wars for liberty, justice and the square deal.[7]

Back in the United States, London was excoriated by the socialist organizations as a traitor to the cause, and indeed his Mexican dispatches have also caused some London biographers no little consternation. They have rightly taken note that in Mexico, apart from two days' riding with rebel troops, London did not venture into the hinterlands of insurgency, but accepted the hospitality of the capitalist-run estates. But this does not defeat his point. London saw that there was not one obstacle to social justice in Mexico, but two: the traditional exploitative ruling class was bad enough, but even worse was the bemedaled parade of cynical martinets who lived high by spreading death and ruin, while claiming to advance the cause of the impoverished peonage. If anything set London off it was hypocrisy, in this case that of the avaricious generalissimos claiming to care for the suffering peasants while laying waste the country that fueled the outrage of his Mexican dispatches. If London had been incorrect in this assessment, then his Mexican reportage could be written off as bought propaganda, but Mexico's experience, from then to the present hour of warring drug cartels, shows that his ire was not misplaced at all.

Dick Davis perceived the same elements as London. "I hate to say it," he wrote, "but I *like* these Mexicans. . . . They are human, kindly; it is only the politicians and bandits like Villa who give them a bad name. But, though they ought to hate us, whenever I stop to ask my way they invite me to come in and have 'coffee' and say, 'My house is yours, señor,' which certainly is kind after people have taken your town away from you and given you another flag and knocked your head off if you did not salute it."[8]

In the relative safety of Vera Cruz Charmian was able to mingle and socialize with war correspondents and military officers. London had received fan mail from sailors for years, and now he and Charmian were entertained in high style aboard the American warships. In one of the first serious articles that London had ever written, "The Impossibility of War" for *Overland Monthly* that got him sent to England to write *The People of the Abyss,* London had given an apocalyptic view of the future of combat. Now he got an up-close view of how accurately he had predicted the evolution of the technology of death. In Vera Cruz the lumbering old U.S.S. *Louisiana* was joined by the most modern battleships of the new dreadnought concept, the *Arkansas* and the *New York,* each mounting a dozen twelve-inch rifles that could rain seven tons of high explosives down upon an enemy with each flaming broadside. The Londons were in Mexico only a month before he was laid low with acute dysentery and evacuated on the transport *Ossabaw* back to Galveston.

By the third week in June they were back on the ranch, and able to watch the firestorm of ire that his Mexico pieces raised among the socialists who had memorized their slogans—as indeed he long had done—but knew nothing of conditions in Mexico. Disillusioned that his comrades were more interested in their rhetoric than in learning the truth, it was the beginning of the end for him as a participant in that faction.

Progress on the ranch also drew his attention away from the cause that once anchored his existence. Part of his heart had burned to a cinder with Wolf House, but as he and Charmian settled back into their cottage at the old Frohling winery, he was able to witness the healing and productive renewal of cared-for land. The new lake was stocked with fish; that acreage still in brush now had Angora goats on it, there were Jersey cows in the meadows, he had settled on the Duroc breed to raise in the circular stone Pig Palace under construction, and ripening crops rose toward the sun. But he could not heal himself, and increasingly he took opiates for the pain of his failing kidneys. He tried valiantly to keep his fate, the death hovering nearby that he had long referred to as "the Noseless One," at arm's length, although he still ate voraciously of rich rare duck and drank too much.

John Barleycorn, as Charmian took to euphemizing his consumption since that book's appearance, occasionally got the better of him. One of his favored cronies these days was Earl Rogers, who was well down the road to alcoholism himself. At a whim during one of his visits, London harnessed a team to the buggy and whisked Rogers off to visit friends, leaving Charmian and Rogers's daughter Nora at the ranch. When they didn't return that evening, or the next day, or the next, young Nora witnessed the terrible effect that London's binges had on Charmian. "Her laugh fluttered higher and higher and broke like a light globe. Neither of us slept except in catnaps, starting at the sound of a sleepy bird, the wind in the redwoods, the footfall of imagination. . . . Charmian was sharp and bitter. Nothing was ever said between us about drink. A man's family did not discuss this, nor admit it." What disturbed Nora most was that Charmian had apparently given in to these absences. "By nature," she wrote, "Charmian London wasn't a quitter. Even people who didn't like her admitted she had more guts than any other female they'd ever known." At one point George Sterling arrived at the ranch and joined in the vigil.

On such aggrieved nights Charmian could retire to her sleeping porch, fated to her insomnia, but at the back of her desk, taped to the windowsill, she kept a pin-up photograph of her Mate-Man, a stunning full-length frontal nude from his younger days, deep-chested and beautiful and virile, his arms lowered and outstretched as though he was about to scoop her off her feet. On such sleepless and deeply humiliating nights as these she could at least gaze at the picture and conjure earlier days, and repeat to herself that he always, at last, came home.

And so he did. London and Rogers appeared again after five days, riding small burros, reeking of alcohol and body odor, singing and joking. "I am a little confused," said Rogers. "Why am I riding this burro?"

"You are confused," said London, "because at this moment you are not sure whether you are a man dreaming you are a burro or a burro dreaming you are a man. We all have these moments." Unsteadily they made their way onto the terrace.

"You might have waited for me," said Sterling coldly. Charmian busied herself about the house but eventually had to comment, "You have had a long visit this time with your friend John Barleycorn." London began to wax eloquent, refusing to acknowledge the nightmare he had put her through. Charmian gained control of the situation, reminding him that dinner was long since ready, and he had guests who were starving. At that London did apologize, but stumbled and fell as he led the company in to dinner. Charmian endured the return without further criticism or hint of her pain.[9] Nora also read *John Barleycorn*, and she considered it "still the best book ever written on alcohol, I jumped nearly out of my skin for I had heard so much of it as he walked up and down the terrace at Glen Ellen with the sailor's gait and answered violently" any barbs that Charmian ventured.[10]

Not all visitors to the ranch were subjected to such drama. Frederick Irons Bamford was one of his oldest and most useful friends, and although he and Bamford had corresponded warmly, London had actually seen Bamford's wife, Georgia, only once, at her wedding, since their days at Oakland High School, when the vehemence of their political differences had precluded anything like friendship. Her record of their few days' visit to the ranch afforded another unvarnished look at the failing Jack London. He and Charmian were now so traveled that they lived among mementoes. The central room of the cottage was, she noted, "divided by hangings of South Sea Island tappa cloths. The front, or living room part, contained the grand piano, a couch, several chairs, and two beautiful Korean chests." On the oblong dining table in the rear portion of the room, Nakata had created a centerpiece of fresh pomegranate cuttings around a bowl of goldfish the same color as the buds.

Her view of London as distant and occasionally curt, even with Charmian, showed that he had not mellowed since a similar demeanor had been recorded by Joseph Noel before the sailing of the *Snark*. There were a couple of times when Georgia caught London looking at her, and she thought he might engage her in a private conversation, but he did not. "I was reminded of the old days," she wrote, "when he would not speak to me because of my capitalistic associations, as he thought."

She was aware not to expect the Londons to appear before noon, as they did their work in the mornings, but in the afternoons they went swimming in their new lake, and visited Aunt Netta at Wake Robin Lodge, where Georgia was shown the great shire stallion, Neuadd Hillside, who had become London's pride and joy, and was an engine of ranch work. She and Charmian rode to the ruins of Wolf House, Charmian indicating where the principal rooms had been and how she had planned to decorate them. Georgia was struck by the irony that London the implacable socialist had created such an opulent retreat only to see it come to ashes. At dinner with other guests, including a Silesian who had accompanied them up from the station, she found London more his old self, passionate in discourse and game for argument. "I could vividly see the Jack of the olden days exactly as he leaned, sprawled and slouched over his desk at High School. . . . He spoke with a violent jerk to his voice, much as he had when giving a talk on the beauties of Socialism—anything to hammer his idea 'home.' He waved his arms and ran his fingers through his hair so that it became as disheveled as it used to be. The only difference from long ago seemed to be that now he was sure of himself."[11]

Still, Georgia sensed a sadness behind his showy bluster, a discontent at growing older, a sense of losing the inspiration and sense of discovery that was part of the package of youth. She sensed London becoming jaded. In early October he and Charmian boarded the graceful old *Roamer* to poke about the inland delta. He still worked, and kept George Brett supplied with books that sold well and were lucratively serialized. Like a dying star bursting into a supernova, London abandoned the short story for a rapid series of novels: *The Mutiny of the Elsinore* came out in September 1914, *The Scarlet Plague* and *The Star Rover* in 1915, and *The Little Lady of the Big House* and a collection of previous stories, *The Turtles of Tasman*, in 1916.

They sailed the *Roamer* all the way up to Stockton, where they moored her and traveled with a tour to Truckee, in the Sierras near Lake Tahoe, to attend the Winter Garden Festival and frolic in knee-deep snow. By the end of January they were back at the ranch, but the cold and damp had excited an onset of rheumatism that caused him much pain. London had long told friends that one of the advantages of carrying his office "under his hat" was the ability to work anywhere. He loved the ranch but was not daily needed there, for Eliza ran the place beautifully. February would be a good time to leave for Hawaii and see if he could recover some vitality there. He and Charmian were in San Francisco to see the opening of the great Panama-Pacific Exhibition and then left the next day on the S.S. *Matsonia* for five months in the islands.

The many photographs of them on this stay in Hawaii portray a laughing and contented couple, locking elbows back to back in their bathing suits and hoisting each other in the air. Others show him lounging and writing, barefoot and wrapped in a Japanese robe. He could no longer surf, but the successful Outrigger Club now stood where they had once spent happy weeks in a tent cabin, and there were endless parties either for them or with them. There was no cure, of course, for failing kidneys, especially since he bullishly ate and drank as he pleased, but the curative trip had its effect; he felt better, and when they returned to the ranch in late July, he was ready to tackle the mountain of correspondence that had accumulated in his absence.

Much of his daily correspondence was from writers—beginners seeking advice, journeymen needing encouragement, even established professionals looking for a moment of commiseration. London answered them all doggedly, helpful or encouraging by turns, even when he did not feel like it. The leader owed no less to his pack.

J. Torrey Connor, who headed the fiction section of the California Writers Club, wrote to ask how London had become such a success. His answer was as revealing as it was flip: "(1) Vast good luck (2) Good health (3) Good brain (4) Good mental and muscular coordination (5) Poverty . . . (8) Because I got started twenty years before the fellows who are trying to start to-day." He also paid a tribute a final time to the influence of reading Ouida's *Signa* when he was eight years old.[12]

Of his many correspondents, one particularly distressing case was the hard-headed Mary Austin, who had taken up residence in New York only to discover that the romance of the desert Southwest carried less clout than it once did. She determined to become more of a generalist, and Harper had let her a contract for a life of Jesus of Nazareth, whose full-bloodedness and passion, she was convinced, had been drained and sooted by centuries of cant and candle smoke. The result was *The Man Jesus,* a prescient book that anticipated the "historical Jesus" movement by more than half a century, but for which she took a critical beating.

Austin wrote London a bitter complaint about the experience; it was a subject upon which London, whose attraction to the teachings of Jesus offset his alienation from accreted religious doctrine, was in sympathy with her treatment. "I have read and enjoyed every bit of your 'Jesus Christ' book as published serially in the *North American Review,*" he answered her, but he was baffled that she was so offended that most readers did not understand it. "Long ere this," he added, "I know that you have learned that the majority of people who inhabit the planet Earth are bone-heads." He offered the example of his own *Sea-Wolf* and *Martin Eden,* both of which were attacks upon Nietzsche's *Übermensch* idea, but "nobody discovered that." He suggested that instead of complaining, she should draw contentment from her frequent characterization as the greatest American stylist, conferred on her by H. G. Wells and others. "The world feeds you," he concluded, "the world feeds me, but the world knows damn little of either of us. Affectionately yours, Jack London."

The world, however, was not feeding Mary Austin as generously as it once had. Though she needed new work badly, she continued to alienate publishers and her career took a nosedive. Under assumed names she was reduced to factory work, making mannequin wigs and artificial flowers; she even sold pencils and undertook a relationship with a Chicago concrete laborer. Her fate was a cautionary tale of artistic ego, and ample vindication for London's lifetime of cautious management of his career, his cultivation of publishers and ultimate return to the safe harbor of Macmillan.[13]

The previous winter and spring in Hawaii had proved to be so restorative that the Londons returned, boarding the S.S. *Great Northern* on December 16 and heading out into the Pacific once more. They attended a New Year's Eve reception in the Iolani Palace, where they were presented to the former queen, Liliuokalani, who was now quite elderly, and who had accepted her overthrow but was still bitter about it. There was a lesson in her politely frosty conversation with them: like London, she had once cared for a cause—her nation and people—more deeply than for her own welfare, but she had made poor judgments in pursuit of her goals. Like London, she encountered opposition to her ideas that proved irresistible, and now she had come to some wisdom, too late to matter to anyone but herself.

London's differences with American socialists that began over his reportage of the Mexican civil war widened in their differing views of the Great War that was raging in Europe. He had expended much of the fire of his youth in the cause of social justice, but now socialist rhetoric took an increasingly anarchistic tone, where he saw in the conflict the chance for democratic ideals to triumph over the hidebound medieval anachronisms of central European autocracy. He also saw how the few gains made for common people during the Progressive Era had doused the fire of what American socialism had been in pressing for meaningful reforms. He also had been reading Carl Jung and realized some of the missteps he had taken in his own lifetime of advocacy. As all these factors worked within him, he sat down and wrote an important letter:

> Honolulu, March 17, 1916
>
> Dear Comrades:
>
> I am resigning from the Socialist party, because of its lack of fire and fight, and its loss of emphasis on the class struggle. . . .
>
> My fighting record in the cause is not, even at this late date, already entirely forgotten. Trained in the class struggle, as taught and practiced by the Socialist labor party, my own highest judgment concurring, I believed that the working class, by fighting, by never fusing, by never making terms with the enemy, could emancipate itself. Since the whole trend of Socialism in the United States during recent years has been one of peaceableness and compromise, I find that my mind refuses further sanction of my remaining a party member. Hence . . . my resignation.
>
> If races and classes cannot rise up and by their own strength of brain and brawn, wrest from the world liberty, freedom and independence, they never in time can come to these royal possessions.

The necessary corollary, he concluded, was that the oppressed people who had their freedom handed to them "on silver platters" would not know what to do with it. He resigned for his wife as well and closed the letter, "Yours for the Revolution, Jack London."[14]

When the episode had passed, Charmian asked him, "What will you call yourself henceforth? Revolutionist? Socialist? What?"

He got over the anger of the moment, but it left him saddened. "I am not anything, I fear. I am all these things. Individuals disappoint me more and more, and more and more I turn to the land."[15] Beauty Ranch had proven to be the one entity that had not disappointed his spiritual investment.

While in Hawaii, the Londons reconnected with Louis von Tempsky, the polo-playing manager of the Haleakala Ranch. Nine years had elapsed since the saucy fourteen-year-old Armine and her sister had engaged London in the crimson-splattered raspberry fight high on the slopes of the volcano. Not only had she survived his brutal critique of her juvenile writing efforts, she had determined to attempt a career in literature and now submitted some of her recent work to him. Unfortunately for her, she still thought that her schoolgirl's effort at manuscript preparation was good enough, and again he let her have it:

> I do not go into any question of style, treatment, pitch, taste, handling; I have marked only for one particular thing. . . .
>
> This particular thing is slovenliness. There is no other name for it. . . . The editor does not exist who would read five pages of any manuscript so slovenly typed as these MSS pages of yours have been typed. . . .
>
> Such slovenliness advertises to any editor, with a glance at a couple of pages, that you have no sincere regard for literature, no sincere desire to write literature. . . .
>
> Please believe that I still love you for all of your other good qualities, but that such love for you does not mitigate the harshness of my chastisement of you for . . . submitting such horrible, awful, and monstrous typed manuscript to me!

And further deponent sayeth not.

Affectionately yours,

Jack London

P.S. Just the same, you ought be damned well ashamed of yourself!

Again the young von Tempsky survived the barrage; she was thirty-five when her novel *Hula* was published and turned into a movie starring "It Girl" Clara Bow. She went on to publish several more, and London, who often advised his friends against pursuing literary careers and then admitted his sympathy when the advice was ignored, would have smiled.[16]

Three essays about Hawaii that London wrote for *Cosmopolitan* stemmed from this sojourn, published in the months directly preceding his death, and demonstrated his continued deftness at mixing consumer interest with social commentary, amid his undiminished capacity to tell a story. Hawaii as an independent kingdom had been doomed, he wrote. Either Japan must acquire it, or the United States. The last king, David Kalakaua, recognized this, and chose Japan, offering his daughter and heiress Princess Kaiulani in a royal marriage to the imperial family. Had it not been for the Japanese loathing of diluting their pure race, the tropical paradise might have been theirs. Just as he had in *The People of the Abyss,* London cited census figures to back up his assertions: in 1914, there were well over three times as many Japanese residents in the Hawaiian Islands than any other national group: Chinese, Filipinos, Americans, or even native Hawaiians. Yet while all the other groups were cross-mating with Polynesian abandon, only six Japanese had married outside their own. Instead, wrote London, "the *haoles,* or whites, overthrew the Hawaiian Monarchy, formed the Dole Republic, and shortly thereafter brought their loot in under the sheltering folds of the Stars and Stripes. There is little use to balk at the word 'loot.' The white man is the born looter. And just as the North American Indian was looted of his continent by the white man, just so the Hawaiian was looted by the white men of his islands. Such things be. They are morally indefensible."

London went on to acknowledge the conflicted conscience of the concerned American, admitting on the one hand the moral turpitude of how Hawaii was acquired, while confessing joy and relief in the acquisition. Better our navy in Pearl Harbor than Japan's. (The transfer might have been inevitable, but it was not forgiven. At the New Year's Eve reception where the Londons were presented to former Queen Liliuokalani, she shook hands with them, but according to Charmian, she looked like she would rather have killed them.)[17]

❧ ❧ ❧

The Hawaii articles for *Cosmopolitan* were some of his last quality works. His literary output, still a thousand words per day, every day, was workmanlike, certainly better than what most other publishing writers were doing, but lacked the inspiration of his earlier years. As many literary scholars have noted, his best work was behind him. And that isn't surprising. London became a writer first to support himself, and second to find himself. He accomplished the first goal, ensconced on one of the most beautiful properties in California. At the second goal he succeeded in a personal way, for ever since he had sought and devoured education like a starving man when he came home from tramping at nineteen, he knew what he believed and why, and he could argue brilliantly why others should believe it, too. But he did not succeed in a public way. His desire to kindle revolution, or rather, his desire to see social justice done, even by revolution if it came to that, was disappointed. Like the rest of the ardent socialists of the day, he prophesied as inevitable a revolution that never came.

It is easy for modern eyes to see the early twentieth-century socialists as naive and slightly ridiculous. No nation more than the United States has ever had a stronger vision of its own political and moral righteousness, even when that vision has been misdirected and even manipulated into willfully not recognizing societal evil in its midst. The very idea that Americans indoctrinated with their own patriotism would ever take to the streets to force radical governmental change now seems slightly laughable. It seemed less so then, for socialism itself a century ago was seen as a more idealistic concept—hence its support by respected clerics such as New Haven Pilgrim Church's Dr. Alexander Irvine, who invited London to lecture at Yale in 1906. In books such as

The People of the Abyss and *The War of the Classes*, and in fiery lectures from coast to coast, London argued the best case that he could that the United States, indeed all of the capitalist West, had fallen short not just of their professed ideals, but of fundamental justice to society's most vulnerable people. And the country collectively shrugged. London had already succeeded for himself in the capitalist system, and if the country did not care to supply the full measure of fairness he called for, he could, himself, retire to his ranch to raise pigs and eucalyptus trees.

Some conditions did improve, and the muckrakers had indeed helped to make things better. *The Jungle* of Upton Sinclair, an ardent London admirer, caused passage of the Pure Food and Drug Act. Another law, restricting child labor, was enacted thanks partly to the *Woman's Home Companion* issue of September 1906, which focused national attention on the subject and in which London had written the lead article. However, the reforms—and they were significant—that managed to struggle into existence during the Progressive Era sucked popular support from the remainder of the socialist agenda. Workplace safety and compensation for workplace injury, a livable or at least minimum wage, old-age pensions, recognizing the legitimacy of labor unions—all of which London demanded for the dignity of the workers who generated the nation's wealth, all lay in the future, some far in the future, some still not fully achieved. But to the extent that he wanted to be able to make them happen, he didn't.

London devoted much of his last energy to fiction—*The Acorn Planter* and *Little Lady of the Big House* both came out in 1916. Perhaps because he no longer suffered from the depression that plagued his earlier years—an angst that lent immediacy to the conflicts of his earlier work—the later pieces, including *Valley of the Moon*, which marked his return to Macmillan in 1913 and was particularly idyllic, were written with his mature polish but simply did not grab and throttle a reader. George Sterling noticed the decline, and his commenting on it led to heated arguments. As Joseph Noel logged, "Jack had said that 'The Little Lady of the Big House' was the greatest story ever conceived by man. After one reading George had declared it mediocre. Time has vindicated this judgment. Jack suffers in this novel, and in other late stories of his, the fate of every writer with too well-defined style. He sounds like a burlesque of himself."[18] *John Barleycorn,* which recounted those earlier days and recaptured their vital struggle, was probably his last really important book. *The Star Rover* shows a last burst of imagination, hearkening back to *Before Adam* for its inspiration of recounting lives unknown, but drawing as ever upon both his outer and inner life. Protagonist Darrell Standing is an agronomist (drawing upon London's studies to improve the ranch) who is wrongly convicted (Buffalo penitentiary again) and condemned for murder. He transcends the tortures of his captor the warden (a dash of "A Thousand Deaths") to live via astral projection the adventures of a Roman legionary, an Elizabethan soldier, a French nobleman, and various other lives. The book was a flop and existed rather within the pale of Noel's closing judgment, but also was better than its fate. It displayed a more spiritual aspect than London's previous books, and was better appreciated by following generations.

Back at the ranch by July 1916, he was able to visit Sacramento for the California State Fair on September 3, but it was increasingly obvious to Charmian that her Mate-Man was in a downward glide. To the chronic uremia that must kill him were added kidney stones and their unique brand of agony, and acute rheumatism. It is also possible that he was undergoing a regimen of salvarsen, a difficult and dangerous arsenic-based treatment for venereal disease. Although she had never made an issue of it, she was aware that he had had sexual flings when out "pirooting," but learned to content herself with the security that he would always come home to her.

London's chronic pain had its impact on his still voluminous correspondence, usually impatient and sometimes vituperative. This was shown most vividly in his breaking with Spiro Orfans, a carpenter and socialist from Seattle with whom London had always enjoyed fencing and arguing politics. Charmian had never liked him and considered him something of a non-contributing hanger-on, but London had stoutly defended him as having paid his way with the pleasure of his company. He had been equally loyal to his other acquaintances from former and poorer days, the tramps and socialists who helped mold him into the writer he was. But now London felt that Orfans' mooching had been excessive, and let him know of it in no uncertain terms.[19]

To the tramps and former tramps who wanted less of him, just desired to associate themselves with his name, he could be more generous. "One thing... you can take straight from me," he wrote one named Charles Brown, "because of my own tramping experiences you can scarcely find a tramp today in the United States who has not hoboed with me, slept with me, gone to jail with me, etc. etc. Of course they all claim this whether they really have or not, and who am I to say nay to their stories?" There were a few times he drew a line; once was with Leon R. Livingston, who had tramped across the continent more than fifty times under the road name of "A-No. 1" and became a lecturer on hoboes. He had taken to telling audiences that the great Jack London abandoned the road on his advice, and requested London to send him an autographed photo of himself acknowledging this as fact. "You are making a mistake telling folks this fairy-tale," London answered him. "No, it is impossible for me to do as you ask me to do." London's reasons for resuming sedentary life, to study and write, were well known. "I can go pretty far, but I can't make a direct and palpable liar out of myself." To cushion the blow London invited A-No. 1 to visit the ranch again.[20]

Otherwise there was a sharp and crabby turn in his correspondence in the fall of 1916. "Why did God make you to love a fountain pen when your handwriting is so hard to read," he inquired of Mrs. H. P. Agee of Honolulu. Even Sterling felt his sting after he called off a visit to the ranch when he missed the car that London had sent to pick him up at the Santa Rosa train station. He bluntly accused the Greek of "laziness or uncaringness on your part, implying that you don't care a whoop what unfair stresses and strains you throw on me and my ranch people."[21]

London had not been speaking idly when he told Charmian, in the wake of his resignation from the Socialist Party, that he felt himself drawn increasingly to the land. Back in California, disillusioned and increasingly ill, he devoted himself like Voltaire's Candide to improving the Glen Ellen ranch. At the end of October he answered an inquiry from *Countryside Magazine*'s Geddes Smith, that he was "that sort of farmer, who, after delving in all the books to satisfy his quest for economic wisdom, returns to the soil as the source and foundation of all economics." And being Jack London, he was methodical in his approach. "I am rebuilding worn-out hillside lands that were worked out and destroyed by our wasteful California pioneer farmers. I am not using commercial fertilizer." Rather, he wrote that he was following the Chinese model, rotating nitrogen-gathering cover with manure fertilizer, which had worked for 4,000 years, and he was getting results. Using a nitrogen-enabling soil additive marketed under the name of Westrobac and plowing under the first crop, they were able to harvest from one field planted in a mixture of oats and vetch an impressive two tons per acre, and that was in a dry year.[22]

One inestimable tragedy struck on October 22, when gigantic Neuadd Hillside fell dead in his pasture, and the event signaled a flurry of new difficulties. After nine years of faithful service, Yoshimatsu Nakata left the Londons' employ to pursue an education. He left on affectionate terms, but a new valet, Tokinosuka Sekiné, had to be trained. Edward Payne and his wife, Aunt Netta whom London had once trusted completely, had broken with him to the point of suing him for damages to their property caused by construction of his dam. Two trials over the space of three weeks settled the issue in his favor, but on November 10 he was stricken with food poisoning.

By the third week in November it seemed like everything took an optimistic turn again, and there was reason to look to the future. He was keen on work, and cabled *Collier's* publisher Edgar Sisson an offer to do a "dandy article" on man-eating sharks. There was also a congenial letter from a new literary magazine called the *Seven Arts*, expressing interest in any uncommitted material he lad lying around.[23] His rebound in national notice also included a visit by the Gaumont Newsreel Company, which filmed him on the ranch on November 16. And in ranch affairs, London emerged victorious from the vexatious water rights suit; to shore up good relations he had all the combatants to lunch at the ranch. He gave them a tour of the dam site, and all agreed that the suit had been unnecessary. J. Torrey Connor of the California Writers Club gifted him with a small green Aztec idol for his desk, with which he was delighted. "The god-damned little god has arrived in all his godliness," he wrote her. "I can't thank you enough for parting with your little treasure . . . tell me some more about it—all you know about it, please." His morning reading had come to include an illustrated journal called *Every Week*. "Curses on you," he wagged to the editor. "I wish the man who writes the captions had never been born. I just can't refrain from reading every word he writes." He was planning a trip to New York to look after his affairs, and settle the Millergraph boondoggle with Noel once and for all. Before then, however, he believed he had time to take his daughters for an outing. "Next Sunday," he wrote Joan, "will you and Bess have lunch with me at Saddle Rock, and, if the weather is good, go for a sail with me on Lake Merrit. If the weather is not good, we can go to a matinee of some sort. Let me know at once. I leave Ranch next Friday."[24]

The coming days would be busy. London was heavily occupied with plans for another trip to New York and four days later he rode out to look over another tract of property near the ranch that he wanted to acquire. The next day, November 21, he suffered from vomiting and diarrhea. His dinner did not sit well, and he retired early, forgetting his nightly play with Possum, the fox terrier to which he and Charmian had become so attached. "Thank God," he said to her almost presciently, "you're not afraid of anything." At the cottage on the Frohling property, where they had now lived for five years, they utilized his and her sleeping porches that flanked the entry. When she retired, Charmian glanced over to his room and saw him, green reading visor on his brow, his head on his chest, having dozed off.

Before eight the next morning, Eliza was awaked by a furious pounding at the door of her nearby house; it was Sekiné, distraught that he had not been able to awaken London. He had come to her because he was forbidden to wake Charmian. Eliza found her stepbrother comatose, his face blue, his breathing labored. At the bedside was a syringe, and an empty vial of morphine. Charmian was awakened at once; the phone was out, and the nearest doctor, A. M. Thomson, was sent for. When he arrived he diagnosed an overdose of morphine. London's own physician, William S. Porter, was summoned from Oakland, as well as Thomson's assistant, and Dr. J. W. Shiels from San Francisco.

The physicians gave him 50cc of atropine and got him to his feet, yelling at him, walking him around the room. Charmian shouted that the dam had broken, hoping that would get through to him, but it did not. During the day it appeared a couple of times as though he were surfacing, and Charmian called out to him, "Mate, come back!" They laid him in her sleeping porch, where he was seen a couple of times to pound the mattress lightly with a weak fist. At a quarter of eight that night the struggle ceased.

The question of whether Jack London killed himself has been a live and contentious one almost from the moment he stopped breathing. Charmian was alert to the possibility of her Mate's memory being tainted with the brush of suicide, and even in the shock of the moment remonstrated with the doctors to ascribe his death only to the uremia; her biography of London five years later omits any mention of the morphine. The suicide story certainly had the element of artistic suffering to recommend it; the Carmel bohemians were known for carrying their vials of cyanide in order to choose the time of their exits. When George Sterling learned of the Wolf's death his first reaction was to exclaim that he had killed himself. From whatever impetus, the story was repeated in magazine articles and over the years repeated again in lightly prepared introductions to subsequent editions of novels and story collections.[25] In the first biography of London not connected to the family, Irving Stone's 1938 *Sailor on Horseback*, the event is cleverly phrased that London made a "calculation of the lethal dose of the drug." Common sense weighs against this, however. If London intended to end his life, there would have been no need to figure the weight-to-dosage ratio of morphine; he would simply have taken all he had. In all probability what he was calculating was the maximum dose he could take without harm, but did not reckon on his weakened condition amplifying the medicine's effect.[26]

After his death, Anna Strunsky memorialized him for the socialist journal *The Masses*. Her own literary gift had no trouble summarizing the inspiration he had lent to the movement. Her personal memories, however, were much more affectionate, tender to the point of causing one to wonder whether she did not always regret having not spent her life with him.

> I see him in pictures, steering his bicycle with one hand and with the other clasping a great bunch of yellow roses which he had just gathered out of his own garden, a cap moved back on his thick brown hair, the large blue eyes with their long lashes looking out star-like upon the world—an indescribably virile and beautiful boy, the kindness and wisdom of his expression somehow belying his youth.
>
> I see him lying face down among the poppies and following with his eyes his kites soaring against the high blue of the California skies, past the tops of the giant sequoias and eucalyptus which he so dearly loved. . . .
>
> I see him on a May morning leaning from the balustrade of a veranda sweet with honeysuckle, to watch two humming birds circling around each other in their love ecstasy. He was a captive of beauty—the beauty of bird and Bower, of sea and sky and the icy vastness of the Arctic world. No one could echo more truthfully the "Behold, I have lived" of Richard Hovey. . . .
>
> "Behold, I have lived!"[27]

It is for others to know his life through his attributed credo, written to an Australian activist for women's rights, Vida Goldstein. The original is lost but was recalled by London's great-nephew Milo Shepard:

> *I would rather be ashes than dust!*
> *I would rather that my spark should burn out in a brilliant blaze than it should be stifled by dry-rot.*
> *I would rather be a superb meteor, every atom of me in magnificent glow, than a sleepy and permanent planet.*
> *The function of man is to live, not to exist.*
> *I shall not waste my days trying to prolong them.*
> *I shall use my time.*[28]

EPILOGUE

Charmian Kittredge London had devoted herself to her husband and his career. She had not been blind to his temper or his infidelities, nor was she ever bashful about registering her hurt. She later said that the night he died was the first sound sleep she'd had in weeks. A casket was brought to the ranch; London was laid out in a favorite gray suit and taken to Oakland for a funeral service. She did not go, according that time for his first family and a select few of The Crowd. George Sterling read a poem he composed for the occasion, full of thous and thines and farewells, but he was too broken up to have written anything truly memorable. After the body was cremated, Sterling and some others brought the urn back to Beauty Ranch, where a small crypt had been prepared in a glade where the children of the previous owners were also buried. It was the place he had asked, when the time came, to be interred. A great block of maroon lava, rejected for having been too large to use in building the Wolf House, was positioned over his ashes.

In widowhood, Charmian became the keeper of Jack London's flame, traveling and speaking widely about him and his books. From the same lava quarry that gave rise to Wolf House she built a large, comfortable home on Beauty Ranch, the House of Happy Walls, which she turned into a museum of his papers and artifacts, and she guided the posthumous publication of many remaining manuscripts. She was too vital a human being to grieve for the rest of her life, however. A year and a quarter after his death, she was engaged in an affair with Harry Houdini (sometimes referred to in her diary as "Magic One") and had many other lovers through her long and full life, once juggling over half a dozen suitors at one time.

Even as Charmian burned her lovers' letters before she died, her honesty about London's life and her willingness to cooperate with would-be biographers was equally evasive and inconsistent. She could be sharp in her criticism of books that were prepared without her permission, including Martin Johnson's *Through the South Seas with Jack London*, which she described as "presumptuous." In her own two-volume biography, *The Book of Jack London*, she omitted certain unsavory aspects of his character, although she was candid about others. She encouraged his daughter, Joan, in writing her biography but declined to open her papers, or her memory, to others, and forced at least one unapproved book to be withdrawn from sale. Irving Stone finally obtained her cooperation by persistent and obsequious attention so he could write *Sailor on Horseback*.

By 1940 she was somewhat impaired by a series of small strokes, but she was present in 1943 at the launching of the Liberty Ship S.S. *Jack London*. She was eighty-four when she passed away at home early in 1955; she was cremated, and the great lava stone was moved from atop London's grave to place her ashes next to his.

London's beloved and devoted stepsister Eliza Shepard continued to manage the ranch in an amicable arrangement with Charmian; after her death it passed to descendant Milo Shepard, who oversaw its transition into the Jack London State Park.

Charmian, as executor of his estate, continued to provide for his dependants. Flora Wellman Chaney London, hard to the end, died in January 1922. She was survived by several months by Jennie Prentiss, who because of increasing senility had been placed in a home. Jennie was ninety-one. Charmian was generous in her treatment of London's former wife, Bess, who never ceased blaming her for destroying her marriage. Perhaps the most succinct characterization of Bess Maddern London was that bestowed by her daughter Becky. Once asked what her mother's occupation was, she replied that she was a professional martyr.

Even as she was torn between her feuding parents, Joan London became torn between her mother, who hated Charmian, and Charmian herself, who was blameless in that matter and mentored Joan in her own attempt at a literary career. Even though Joan was painfully aware that her mother had dedicated her life to poisoning her and her sister against their father, Joan's biography, *Jack London and His Times,* is nonetheless flavored with that toxin. Dour and humorless herself, her biography alternates facts of London's life with essays on the development of socialism, a cause to which she was devoted. Becky was too young to share Joan's bitter memories of their father's desertion, and took more after him in hale and adventurous temperament. Their divergent personalities led to rifts between the sisters from time to time. Becky did not visit her father's grave until well into her old age.

Ina Coolbrith, the Oakland librarian who took an interest in London when he was only ten years old, which he never forgot, went on to become the poet laureate of California. She was accorded many honors, including the presidency of the Congress of Authors and Journalists for the Panama-Pacific Exhibition of 1915, and she was twice asked to compose graduation odes for the University of California. She saved some of her best work for her golden years, published posthumously in *Wings of Sunset.* She passed away at eighty-seven in 1928; the legislature adjourned the day of her funeral, and a peak in the Sierra Nevada that overlooks the pass where she first entered the state was named for her.

Anna Strunsky's comradely marriage to William English Walling, a cofounder of the NAACP, fell apart over irreconcilable party differences. As one of a family of Russian Jews driven from home by czarist pogroms, she embraced Bolshevism. He was of a prominent New England family and espoused a milder American socialism, deploring Bolshevism. She was a pacifist during World War I; he endorsed the U.S. role in it. She bore him five children (four lived) before they separated. Walling obtained a Mexican divorce in 1932, which she declined to recognize, and he died four years later. Anna maintained an avid interest in social justice until her death; she was just short of eighty-five when she passed away in 1964.

George Sterling, without his Wolf, went into a long and sad decline. Among the Carmel bohemians it was an article of identity to carry a vial of cyanide, and Carrie Sterling quaffed hers not long after London's death, freeing her widower to relocate to New York, where he was regarded as a once-talented regional has-been. He returned to San Francisco, and by the time the real quality of much of his work was rediscovered, and some honors began to flow his way (H. L. Mencken nominated him as the first American poet laureate) he was too broken down to attend an event held in his honor, and he swallowed his cyanide a few days short of the tenth anniversary of London's death.

Perhaps the strangest tale of the London circle after his death is that of Jack London himself. By the end of his life he had regained much of the popularity he lost during his most intense proselytizing for social justice, but during the national hysteria of the "Red Scare" in the 1920s, regard for him fell again in the glare of shallow patriotism. Under J. Edgar Hoover the FBI compiled a posthumous dossier on his supposed anti-American sympathies, and during the McCarthy era of the 1950s he came into disfavor once more. It was the unsinkable, compelling nature of his stories, however, underpinned still by *The Call of the Wild*, *White Fang*, and *The Sea-Wolf*, that prevented his assignation to literary ignominy. It has been left to our own generation, incensed by financial outrages on the part of corporate tycoons that devastated the middle class and led to the economic collapse of late 2008, to realize that London in his clarion calls for social justice was articulating abiding truths that our country seems doomed to have to learn over and over and over and over.

ACKNOWLEDGMENTS

The idea of publishing a literary biography in today's marketplace is a brave one, so special thanks are owed to my agent, Jim Hornfischer, for his enthusiasm for it, and to the editors at Basic Books, Lara Heimert and Brandon Proia, for their solicitous encouragement during the process. The market being what it is, I was grateful for the positive testimonials of two booksellers, Jo Virgil and Frank Campbell, that they believed people actually would buy a biography of London.

Further, thanks are extended to Dorothy Lazard of the Oakland Public Library, Sandra Johnston of the Alaska State Library, Julia DeVore of the Anchorage Museum at Rasmuson Center, and most particulary to Natalie Russell at the Huntington Library. An extra thanks to Ms. Lael Morgan for lending me her copies of the Londons' photographs taken during the voyage of the *Snark,* and to the Huntington Library for kindly giving permission to reproduce photographs from its London archive.

NOTES

PREFACE

1. The interview with Shepard is archived at the California Digital Library, www.cdlib.org/xtf/view?docld+kt8p30068x&doc.view=content&chunk.id=d0e3759&toc.depth=1&brand=calisphere&anchor.id=0.

CHAPTER 1

1. "A Discarded Wife," *San Francisco Chronicle*, June 4, 1875.

2. Mood, "Astrologer from Down East," 778–782.

3. Quoted in Kingman, *Pictorial Biography*, 22.

4. Mood, "Astrologer from Down East," 792.

5. www.spirithistory.com/96calhis.html, accessed August 16, 2008; Joan London, *Jack London and His Times*, 11.

6. Quoted in Kingman, *Pictorial Biography*, 19.

7. Joan London, *Jack London and His Times*, 13; cf. Stasz, *Jack London's Women*, 7.

8. The details of casualties among the family that owned her was something that Virginia Prentiss would never discuss, saying only that she and her former mistress were the only survivors. Stasz, *Jack London's Women*, 7.

9. London, *John Barleycorn*, Chapter 3. Because of the varying pagination in the many editions of this work, citations from this autobiographical treatment are to chapter.

10. London to Houghton Mifflin Co., January 31, 1900, in Labor, et al., *Letters of Jack London* (hereinafter *Letters*), 1:148.

11. For the obligatory mentions of *Signa* see Kingman, *Pictorial Biography*, 27; Stone, *Sailor on Horseback*, 21; Sinclair, *Jack*, 6; O'Connor, *Jack London*, 33; and Joan London, *Jack London and His Times*, 24. Perhaps the most readable of the widely available biographies, Kershaw, *Jack London: A Life*, oddly omits *Signa* from his childhood reading list at page 16. For varying views of Ramé's life, see Yvonne French, *Ouida: A Study in Ostentation* (New York and London: D. Appleton-Century Co.,

1938), or Eileen Bigland, *Ouida, The Passionate Victorian* (London and New York: Jarrolds, 1950). Ouida's life bore other strange similarities to London's, including her similar output of about forty volumes, and her lifelong love of dogs and horses, for whose welfare she was a passionate advocate. She died in Viareggio in 1908.

12. Ouida, *Signa* (London: Chapman & Hall, 1875), 1–2.

13. Frank Atherton, *Jack London in Boyhood Adventures*, manuscript quoted in Kingman, *Pictorial Biography*, 32.

14. C. K. London, *Book of Jack London*, 1:59.

15. Bamford, *Mystery of Jack London*, 158.

16. "Nobody at home bothered their heads over what I read," London wrote Coolbrith many years later. "I was an eager, thirsty, hungry little kid. . . . You were a goddess to me." London to Coolbrith, December 15, 1906, in *Letters*, 2: 650–651. The *Overland Monthly* later resumed publication, but it lacked the spark of the original, leading San Francisco literary capo Ambrose Bierce, later well acquainted with London, to refer to it as the *Warmed-Overland Monthly*.

17. See London to Marion Humble, December 11, 1914, in *Letters* 3: 1391–1392.

18. Noel, *Footloose in Arcadia*, 20. Noel interviewed Flora in 1905 at the floodtide of London's early fame, but this is a source I have used with caution. His sometimes unsympathetic account of London's life cannot help but have been colored by the fact that London's eventual break with him was acrimonious and even abusive—not unusual, for London. However, Noel was also known to defend London long after he had motive to color his reminiscence in negative ways, as seen in Stasz, *American Dreamers*, 206. Noel's book contains errors, but in general has the accuracy of a skilled journalist writing often without documentary buttressing. Given that *Footloose in Arcadia* is as much about George Sterling and Ambrose Bierce as it is about London, I have used it when it can illuminate and can either be substantiated or is so clearly within London's behavioral parameters that one can presume it is truthful—and bearing in mind that others close to Jack London sometimes went an equal distance to present him in a positive light, as seen in Milo Shepard's comments on Charmian's *Book of Jack London* in "The Jack London Story and the Beauty Ranch," interviews conducted by Caroline C. Crawford, 70, archived at www.archive.org/details/londonbeautyranc00sheprich.

19. Joan London, *Jack London and His Times*, 32–35.

CHAPTER 2

1. Higgins, "Jack London on the Waterfront," archived online at www.jacklondons.net/first_and_Last_chance.html. The sign over Heinold's bar was a reference to the prohibitionist, correctly spelled Carry Nation, famous for breaking up saloons

with a hatchet. In 1998 the owner of the bar maintained that Heinold purchased the dictionary for London when he was ten. San Francisco *Chronicle*, January 9, 1998, at www.sfgate.com/cgi-bin/article.cgi?f=/c/a/1998/01/09/EB29535.DTL.

2. Oysters native to San Francisco Bay were exhausted soon after settlement and were supplanted by oysters from farther north on the Pacific coast; they were the ones replaced by the Atlantic transplants. Booker, "Oyster Growers and Oyster Pirates on San Francisco Bay," 63–88. In fact, the very first game conservation law enacted by California, in 1851, protected the proprietary rights of those who transplanted oysters of other than local species, but it was the railroad that appropriated the law into a scope that none foresaw and created such public discontent. See "Department of Fish and Game Celebrates 130 Years of Serving California," *Outdoor California*, November–December 1999, reproduced at www.dfg.ca.gov/publications/history.html.

3. Higgins, "Jack London on the Waterfront," www.jacklondons.net/first_and_Last_chance.html. London's recollection in *John Barleycorn*, Chapter 7, was that Jennie Prentiss was enthusiastic about lending him the money.

4. One biography that accepts the story is Kershaw, *Jack London: A Life*, 17. However, Kingman, *Pictorial Biography*, 37, points out that Mamie and her sister were chaperoned, which makes this rendition of their first coupling somewhat suspect. One might also note that the expression to "make love" in this era might mean only innocent sweet talk; it did not become the usual euphemism for having sex until some decades later. London did aver to Cloudesley Johns that she was his mistress. London to Johns, March 30, 1899, in *Letters*, 60.

5. C. K. London, *Book of Jack London*, 1: 84–85.

6. Joan London, *Jack London and His Times*, 42–43.

7. London, *John Barleycorn*, Chapters 5, 11.

8. The description of "Old Scratch" Nelson in London's later autobiographical *John Barleycorn* might lead one to think that he had been embellished for fictional use, but a similar description of him in C. K. London, *Book of Jack London*, 89, and his recollection by Johnny Heinold in Higgins, "Jack London on the Waterfront" make it seem a reasonable assumption that his essential character was accurately related.

9. "White and Yellow" was the first story in *Tales of the Fish Patrol*, first published in *The Youth's Companion*, February 16, 1905.

10. London to Corresponding Editor, *Youth's Companion*, March 9, 1903, in *Letters*, 1:348–350. As London inscribed one copy of *Tales of the Fish Patrol*, "Find here, sometimes hinted, sometimes told, and sometimes made different, the days of my boyhood." Joan London, *Jack London and His Times*, 44.

11. In addition to a growing amount of human waste, San Francisco Bay also started receiving the effluent from dairies, slaughterhouses, three oil refineries, and a copper smelter. Booker, "Oyster Growers and Oyster Pirates in San Francisco Bay," 79–81.

CHAPTER 3

1. John Sutherland, "Appendix 1" in London, *The Sea-Wolf*, Oxford University Press ed., 2000.

2. Higgins, "Jack London on the Waterfront," www.jacklondons.net/first_and_Last_chance.html.

3. San Francisco *Chronicle*, August 18, 1906. After the publication of *The Sea-Wolf*, the reporter was seeking to uncover its historical roots. Joan London, *Jack London and His Times*, 49–50, found documentation that the ship was only four years old, but that would not preclude the vessel from masquerading under other names if she was engaging in contraband trade.

4. Eames, "Jack London," quoted in Kershaw, *A Life*, 22–23.

5. Noel, *Footloose in Arcadia*, 223–224. Stasz, *Jack London's Women*, 33, summarily characterized London's estimation of homosexuality as being "repugnant," which leaps rather beyond his views expressed here and elsewhere, or that would be expected by his familiarity with the works of Josiah Flynt and Havelock Ellis. C. K. London, *Book of Jack London*, 1:97–98, wrote that London once defended himself with a dinner fork against the unwanted advances of a Greek sailor. Her comment that, "as for *unnatural* crimes, these were not admissible in his magnificently balanced body and mind," does not showcase her at her most objective. Clearly, based on his remarks to Noel and Monahan, they were at least admissible.

6. London, *John Barleycorn*, Chapter 16.

7. London, "Story of a Typhoon Off the Coast of Japan," *San Francisco Morning Call*, November 12, 1893. In *John Barleycorn*, Chapter 17, London places the hunting off the coast of Siberia, which was not likely as those waters were closed to sealing and patrolled by a Russian cruiser.

8. London, *Cruise of the "Snark,"* Foreword.

9. London, *The Sea-Wolf*, Chapter 17.

10. As with recollections of his oyster piracy, London's fictional accounts of his adventures are sometimes used as source material in biographies on account of their factual basis, but London was given to such embellishment that the actual facts are inseparable from his storytelling. For an adept parsing of this episode, see Watson, "Jack London's Yokohama Swim and His First Tall Tale," extracted from *Studies in American Humor* and accessible at www.compedit.com/watson.htm.

11. London to Mabel Applegarth, November 30, 1898, in *Letters,* 1:25.

12. London, *John Barleycorn,* Chapter 18.

13. London did not record having visited any Asian brothels, but he seems to have mentioned it to his wife Charmian, as in her biography she acknowledges his having been the "squire of more than one Madame Chrysanthéme on her native heath." C. K. London, *Book of Jack London,* 141. See also Joan London, *Jack London and His Times,* 68.

14. London, *John Barleycorn,* Chapter 20.

CHAPTER 4

1. Quoted in Etulain, ed., *Jack London on the Road,* 34. From Davis's going home and London's note in his diary, one might infer that London had pressured Davis to make the venture to begin with.

2. Ibid., 38.

3. Ibid., 56. The ring had been a gift from a dating interest named Lizzie Connelen.

4. Hamaker, "The Commonweal Comes to Kearney, 1894," www.bchs.us/BTales_197905.html.

5. Etulain, ed., *Jack London on the Road,* 47–48.

6. London, *Jack London and His Times,* 75–76.

7. Flora to London, May 22, 1894, in London, *Book of Jack London,* 160–161.

8. Etulain, ed., *Jack London on the Road,* 51.

9. Ibid., 35.

10. Sinclair, *Jack,* 23.

11. London, *The Road,* "Pinched."

12. Ibid. London's outrage on his being railroaded to jail was longstanding and consistent enough that Charmian London, *The Book of Jack London,* 1: 183, continued to plead his case in emotional terms five years after his death.

13. Erie County Penitentiary records, quoted in Kershaw, *Jack London: A Life,* 36.

14. London, *The Road,* "The Pen."

15. See Noel, *Footloose in Arcadia,* 223–224.

16. London to Elwyn Hoffman, June 17, 1900, in *Letters,* 1: 194.

CHAPTER 5

1. C. K. London, *Book of Jack London,* 1: 188.

2. Quoted in Kingman, *Pictorial Biography,* 60.

3. C. K. London, *Book of Jack London,* 1: 191.

4. Joan London, *Jack London and His Times,* 100.

5. Joan London, *Jack London and His Times*, 125–126.

6. San Francisco *Chronicle*, February 16, 1896.

7. Bamford, *The Mystery of Jack London*, 44–45.

8. London to Applegarth, November 14, 1898, *Letters*, 1: 20.

9. London, *John Barleycorn*, Chapter 22.

10. Hopper, "Tribute to London," quoted in Kingman, *Pictorial Biography*, 67.

11. This and following letter quoted in Kingman, *Pictorial Biography*, 18–21. Noel, *Footloose in Arcadia*, 18, also cites Flora's liaison with Lee Smith. Unless he got the information from London, which seems improbable because London was deeply ashamed of his illegitimacy, his source may even have been Flora herself, whom he was known to have interviewed. Stasz, *Jack London's Women*, 14, finds Chaney's account "contaminated by self-defense" but rightly concludes that his paternity was not certain. If Chaney actually believed that he was London's father and was seeking to dodge responsibility, his tendency would have been to communicate less, not at such length.

12. London, *John Barleycorn*, Chapter 23.

13. London to Editor, *Oakland Times*, July 29, 1896, in *Letters*, 4.

14. London to Mabel Applegarth, November 27, 1898, in *Letters*, 22.

15. C. K. London, *Book of Jack London*, 1: 218.

16. Johnston, *American Radical*, 57n43.

CHAPTER 6

1. Mrs. Applegarth to London, July 22, 1897, quoted in C. K. London, *Book of Jack London*, 1: 224–225.

2. C. K. London, *Book of Jack London*, 1: 226.

3. London to Mabel Applegarth, August 8, 1897, in *Letters*, 1: 11.

4. "Like Argus of the Ancient Times," *Hearst Magazine*, March 1917.

5. Fred Thompson diary, quoted in Sinclair, *Jack*, 44.

6. There is a thread of a story that London earned $3,000 by going back and piloting several dozen boats through the narrows. This seems to begin with Stone, *Sailor on Horseback*, 88, but is not credible. See Sinclair, *Jack*, 261n5. The story surfaces in O'Connor, *Jack London*, 88. The germ of the tale may lie in the fact that beginning the next year, the Northwest Mounted Police began requiring that Klondikers hire skilled pilots to get them through the rapids.

7. C. K. London, *Book of Jack London*, 1: 225. See Sinclair, *Jack*, 46, for an assessment of Thompson's assertion. Henderson Creek did later yield millions in gold, but it took heavy machinery to extract it.

8. Quoted in Kingman, *Pictorial Biography*, 77.

9. Quoted in C. K. London, *Book of Jack London*, 1: 235.

10. Jensen, *Jack London at Stewart River*, quoted in Kingman, *Pictorial Biography*, 79.

11. W. B. Hargrave to C. K. London, quoted in *Book of Jack London*, 1:237. By far the best synoptic comparison of characters and events actually experienced by London in the North, and the literary use he made of them, is Walker, *Jack London and the Klondike*, a very useful source.

12. London, Klondike Diary, quoted in C. K. London, *Book of Jack London*, 1: 254.

CHAPTER 7

1. London to Editor of the *Bulletin*, September 17, 1898, quoted in Hendricks and Shepard, *Letters*, 3n; Labor, et. al., eds., *Letters*, 1: 18; and in Kingman, *Pictorial Biography*, 83. One wonders how often and hard this editor chastised himself in later years.

2. "The Mammon Worshippers" finally saw publication in the December 1976 issue of *Saturday Evening Post*—sixty years after London's death.

3. London to Mabel Applegarth, November 27, 1898, in *Letters* 1: 22.

4. London to Mabel Applegarth, November 30, 1898, in *Letters*, 1: 24–25.

5. London, "Introduction," *The Red Hot Dollar*, vi–viii.

6. London to Mabel Applegarth, November 30, 1898, in *Letters*, 1: 24.

7. Atherton manuscript, quoted in Kingman, *Pictorial Biography*, 85.

8. London to Edward Applegarth, September 13, 1898, in *Letters*, 1: 12.

9. London to Mabel Applegarth, December 25, 1898, in *Letters*, 1: 31–32.

10. London to Corresponding Editor, *Youth's Companion*, in *Letters*, 1: 41–42.

11. London to Cloudesley Johns, February 10, 1899, in *Letters*, 1: 45.

12. London to Johns, February 22, 1899, in *Letters*, 1: 46–49.

13. The Fort Tejon Road is now Barrel Springs Road in Palmdale. The railroad needed flatter ground for its booster engines to get up energy to get trains over the San Gabriel Mountains. Harold was populated mostly by Chinese railroad workers; nearby Palmenthal had about sixty families of Swedish immigrants who, previous to starting their journey, had been told that when they began to encounter palm trees they would be near the ocean, and they mistook Joshua trees, giant cacti, for palms and settled in the desert. www.palmdalelibrary.org/history/.

14. Genthe, *As I Remember*, 74.

15. London, "The Impossibility of War," archived online at www.jacklondons net/journalism/impossibility.html.

16. C. K. London, *Book of Jack London*, 319–320.

17. Austin, *Earth Horizon*, 302.

18. C. K. London, *Book of Jack London*, 4–6.

19. Noel, *Footloose in Arcadia*, 150.

20. Not well known today, Peano was born in Parma, studied in Turin, and was working in the Oakland area by the early 1890s. Thirteen years London's senior, he moved to Los Angeles soon after the Londons moved out of Villa Capriccioso. Most at home in the art of architecture, he often worked in hammered or undercut copper, and while most famous for his "Doors of Life," he also designed numerous canal bridges in Venice, California. He died at age eighty-five in 1949. *American Art Annual, 1925*; *Who's Who in American Art 1938–41*.

21. Boylan, *Revolutionary Lives*, 24.

22. London to Johns, February 23, 1902, in *Letters*, 1: 282–283.

23. London to Anna Strunsky, January 5, 1902, in *Letters*, 1: 269–270.

CHAPTER 8

1. George Brett to London, December 27, 1901; London to Brett, January 4, 1902, in *Letters*, 1: 267. The American writer Winston Churchill (born three years before the British statesman of the same name) characterized Brett as having "an undoubted genius for publishing, but he possesses likewise the higher genius for friendship." Quoted in Kershaw, *Jack London: A Life*, 110. Brett had published Churchill's first novel, *Richard Carvel*, in 1899 to great success.

2. Anna (Strunsky) Walling Manuscripts, quoted in Jacqueline Tavernier-Courbin, "Jack London and Anna Strunsky, Lovers at Cross-Purposes," in Hodson and Reesman, eds., *One Hundred Years a Writer*, 29.

3. London to Anna Strunsky, June 7, 1902, in *Letters*, 1: 297, and elsewhere.

4. Stone, *Sailor on Horseback*, 166, and derivative works (e.g., Labor, *Jack London*, 91, and Kershaw, *Jack London: A Life*, 114) give the date as July 21. However, London's first letter to Anna Strunsky written from the train is dated July 18. *Letters*, 1: 301.

5. London to Strunsky, July 18, 1902, in *Letters*, 1: 301; Stone, *Sailor on Horseback*, 166.

6. London to John Spargo, July 28, 1902, in *Letters*, 1: 302. The contemplated article, "How I Became a Socialist," subsequently appeared in March 1903 and was collated into *The War of the Classes* in 1905.

7. London to Strunsky, July 31, 1902, in *Letters*, 1: 303–304, and elsewhere. London sailed on the first *Majestic*, which went into service in 1890 and was retired in 1911; the later, more famous, and even larger *Majestic* was a German vessel (the former *Bismarck*) seized as a war prize during World War I. The captain of London's

ship was Edward J. Smith, who was later given commands of the ever-larger new ships *Baltic, Adriatic, Olympic,* and, to his doom, *Titanic.* Ironically, this first *Majestic* was pulled out of retirement to replace the *Titanic* late in 1912.

8. London to Strunsky, August 16, 1902, in *Letters,* 1: 305.

9. Hamilton, ed., *The Tools of My Trade,* 149.

10. www.hssworld.org/doctorji/abaji narrations/1.htm. Bharatmata is a motherly personification of India, not dissimilar to the role played by Britannia to the English, or Marianne to the French.

11. London, *People of the Abyss,* 63. James Connolly was quite correct in his assessment of the event being promoted as propaganda. After Queen Victoria's nearly forty-year withdrawal from public life, Edward VII was acutely aware of the need to restore the monarchy to public favor. It was he who reinstituted public royal ceremonies now taken for granted, such as the state openings of Parliament, which had fallen into disuse.

12. Marguerite Patton, *The Coronation Cookbook,* quoted at http://news.bbc.uk/1/hi/programmes/ breakfast/1947639.stm. For many of the poor, this was actually their second coronation banquet. At the time the king took ill, the food for the first feast had already been lardered into the palace kitchen. Cartloads of mutton, quail, sturgeon, asparagus, and strawberries were donated to the poor in Whitechapel. Gile St. Aubyn, *Edward VII, Prince & King* (New York: Atheneum, 1979).

13. Auerbach, *Male Call,* 139.

14. London to Cloudesley Johns, August 17, 1902, in *Letters,* 1: 305.

15. Tavernier-Courbin, "Jack London and Anna Strunsky, Lovers at Cross-Purposes," in Hodson and Reesman, eds., *One Hundred Years a Writer,* 30.

16. London to Strunsky, August 21, 1902, and August 25, 1902, in *Letters,* 1: 305–308.

17. Tavernier-Courbin, "Jack London and Anna Strunsky: Lovers at Cross Purposes," in Hodson and Reesman, eds., *One Hundred Years a Writer,* 31.

18. http://users.ox.ac.uk/~peter/workhouse/. Workhouses most commonly occupied not one building but large complexes housing the different wards and functions. Many such structures remain, having been converted to other uses; the Whitechapel Workhouse, however, was demolished in 1965.

19. "The Story of Workhouses," http://users.ox.ac.uk/~peter/workhouse/.

20. London to Strunsky, September 28, 1902, in *Letters,* 1: 312–313.

21. Quoted in Kershaw, *A Life,* 121.

22. London to Brett, November 21, 1902, in *Letters,* 1: 317–323.

23. O'Connor, *Jack London,* 170; Brett to London, December 17, 1902; London to Brett, December 30, 1902, in *Letters,* 1: 331.

24. Johnston, *American Radical,* 76; London, *People of the Abyss,* 288.

25. Boston *Herald,* November 28, 1903; *Cavalier,* No. 11.

26. *London Daily News,* November 28, 1903.

27. Quoted in Kershaw, *A Life,* 120. "If I Were God One Hour" was a poem that was one of London's first published works. It appeared in San Francisco's *Town Topics* on May 11, 1899.

28. London to Ina Coolbrith, December 15, 1906, in *Letters,* 2: 650; Kingman, *Pictorial Biography,* 115. James was not universally well thought of by the native California writers, some of whom thought he was faking his Indian material. Austin, *Earth Horizon,* 296.

29. London to Brett, November 21, 1902, in *Letters,* 1: 318.

CHAPTER 9

1. London, "How I Became a Socialist," *The Comrade,* March 1903. Stasz, *American Dreamers,* 129, and others have noted that London's understanding of Nietzsche was incomplete, as he seemed to equate the *Übermensch* with the "Blond Beast," where in the philosopher's actual scheme the "Blond Beast" was what the Superman could rise above.

2. Bamford, *The Mystery of Jack London,* 129–130. London inscribed the Bamfords' copy of *The Call of the Wild* to them on July 23, 1903; although *The People of the Abyss* preceded it in publication, London gave the couple their copy the following Christmas. Ibid., 174. In fairness, Georgia did possess some grasp of the sentiments of the underclass, citing in her memoir the story of an English judge, when he was unable to understand a defendant who was an old Cockney woman, asking her what class she was from. She retorted that there were only two, "them that 'as, and them that 'asn't." "Perhaps," Bamford allowed, "the old woman was right." Ibid., 92.

3. London to Charmian Kittredge, [early] July 1903, in *Letters,* 1: 370–371. Charmian's own memoir gives a more complete text, adding a paragraph that he chose her because he found in her qualities that he thought he would find only in a man, with woman-love thrown into the bargain. *Book of Jack London,* 2: 83.

4. London to Kittredge, [early] July 1903, in *Letters,* 1: 372.

5. London to George Sterling, July 11, 1903, in *Letters* 1: 374–375.

6. Reproduced in Hamilton, ed., *The Tools of My Trade,* 262.

7. London to Brett, August 10, 1903, in *Letters,* 1: 378.

8. London to Kittredge, January 13, 1904, in Hendricks and Shepard, *Jack London Reports,* 4.

9. London to Kittredge, January 20, 21, and 24, 1904, in Hendrick and Shepard, *Jack London Reports,* 5–6, also in C. K. London, *Book of Jack London,* 1: 404–405.

10. Davis, *Adventures and Letters,* 311; C. K. London, *Book of Jack London,* 402.

11. Dunn, *World Alive,* 115.

12. Ibid.

13. Quoted in Kingman, *Pictorial Biography,* 136.

14. London, *John Barleycorn,* 262–263.

15. London to Brett, April 3, 1904, in *Letters,* 1: 423.

16. C. K. London, *Book of Jack London,* 1: 412–415.

17. London to Kittredge, March 11, 1904, in *Letters,* 1: 419.

18. Dunn, *World Alive,* 119.

19. Hendricks and Shepard, *Jack London Reports,* 76.

20. See, for instance, Sinclair, *Jack,* 106.

21. Hendricks and Shepard, *Jack London Reports,* 105, 103.

22. C. K. London, *Book of Jack London,* 1: 420.

23. Hendricks and Shepard, *Jack London Reports,* 53, 103.

24. Ibid., 123–124.

25. Davis to Mother, June 13, 1904, in *Adventures and Letters,* 305. Six weeks later Davis's disgust with Japanese mendacity was approaching London's own: "The only mistake I made was in not going home the first time they deceived us instead of waiting." Some weeks further on: "So, our half-year of time and money, of dreary waiting, of daily humiliations at the hands of officers . . . was to the end absolutely lost to us." Ibid., 311.

26. Quoted in O'Connor, *Jack London,* 198.

27. Maurice Magnus to London, September 21, 1911; London to Magnus, October 23, 1911, in *Letters,* 2: 1042–1043. Curiously, Magnus framed his question around the character Burning Daylight, but London answered in terms of Wolf Larsen as well. After his death in 1920, Magnus's *Memoir of the French Foreign Legion,* about his service during World War I, was published with a scathingly critical introduction-remembrance by D. H. Lawrence, which elicited disapproval from other writers. Magnus may also have been emboldened to write London on this topic by having read *The Game,* whose praise of male beauty Magnus might well have thought exceeded purely aesthetic appreciation.

CHAPTER 10

1. San Francisco *Chronicle,* June 30, 1904. Given the heat of their on-and-off relationship, Stasz, *Jack London's Women,* 92, found her protestations somewhat wanting.

2. Ibid.

3. Austin, *Earth Horizon,* 301; London to Stoddard, June 21, 1900, in *Letters,* 1: 195.

4. The biographical entry for Stoddard at www.newadvent.org/cathen/14298b.htm draws on previous Catholic accounts based on his teaching career. His

online biography at Wikipedia, http://en.wikipedia.org/wiki/Charles_Warren_Stoddard reprises the same material, with the addition of his sexuality. For an example of Stoddard's defiant living out of his sexuality heedless of the stigma and consequences, see Tayman, *The Colony*, 126ff.

5. Sterling to Bierce, September 5, 1903, and Bierce to Sterling, September 12, 1903, in Bierce, *A Much Misunderstood Man*, 110–111.

6. Bierce to Sterling, June 13, 1903, in Bierce, *A Much Misunderstood Man*, 104.

7. Atherton, "Jack London in Boyhood Adventures," quoted in Kingman, *Pictorial Biography*, 124. Absinthe is a liqueur derived in part from wormwood, an aromatic shrub.

8. Bierce to Partington, July 31, 1892, in Bierce, *A Much Misunderstood Man*, 23–24. Bierce issued the same ultimatum to Sterling: "I hope you will not set your feet in the dirty paths—leading nowhither—of social and political 'reform.' . . . If you do I shall have to part company with you." Ibid., 81.

9. Austin, *Earth Horizon*, 304; Genthe, *As I Remember*, 74.

10. Ambrose Bierce to George Sterling, 13 June 1903, in Bierce, *A Much Misunderstood Man*, 104.

11. Noel, *Footloose in Arcadia*, 200.

12. See for a notable exception Kershaw, *Jack London: A Life*, which is noncommittal on the point but allows it as a possibility.

13. Austin, *Earth Horizon*, 298.

14. London to Sterling, June 1, 1905, in *Letters*, 1: 487–488. Writers who did attempt to gradate masculine affection into terms more subtle than the existing brutal stereotypes were almost universally muzzled. The British novelist E. M. Forster wrote his bravely themed *Maurice* not long after this period, and it could not be published for decades. See also Stasz, *American Dreamers*, 97, who correctly asserts the impropriety of "presentism," in this instance the tendency to impose modern psychosexual mores on a time more than a century ago, when same-sex relationships were often the most important bonds one had, even extending, as she points out, to jealousy of a friend's heterosexual relationships.

15. Hedrick, *Solitary Comrade*, 185–186.

16. Charmian Kittredge London Diary, July 15, 1905, Utah State University, Logan, quoted in Kershaw, *Jack London*, 147, and by many others.

17. Bierce, *A Much Misunderstood Man*, 165.

18. See London, "Brain Beaten by Brute Force," San Francisco *Examiner*, September 10, 1905.

19. London to Johns, December 8 and 14, 1904, in *Letters,* 1: 456–457.

20. London to Bamford, May 8, 1905, in *Letters* 2: 480; commentary in Bamford, *Mystery of Jack London,* 185–186.

21. London to Brett, December 5 and 22, 1904, in *Letters,* 1: 454–455, 458.

22. C. K. London, *Book of Jack London,* 2: 49–52.

23. London to Bamford, August 8, 1905, in Bamford, *Mystery of Jack London,* 194; there are minor differences between this and the version in *Letters* 1: 510.

24. London to Brett, June 7, 1905, in *Letters,* 1: 489. At about the same time, London also tried to lean on Brett to publish a novel written by Ninetta Eames, but at this Brett bridled and refused.

25. "All Gold Canyon" opened a theme London followed through on in such works as *Burning Daylight* in 1910 and *The Valley of the Moon* in 1913.

26. C. K. London, *Book of Jack London,* 2: 33–34.

CHAPTER 11

1. London had never been blind to the value of publicity, having never regretted selling *The Call of the Wild* for a lump sum in exchange for Brett's pledge of promotion. "Fame depends more on the amount of printer's ink you spill in the headlines," he told Joseph Noel, "than on what you put into your story." Noel, *Footloose in Arcadia,* 149.

2. London to Carrie Sterling, 15 & 29 September 1905, in *Letters,* 1:520–30.

3. C. K. London, *Book of Jack London,* 2: 59.

4. Quoted in Kingman, *Pictorial Biography,* 150–151, and others.

5. Hendricks and Shepard, *Jack London Reports,* 253–258.

6. Hartford *Leader,* January 27, 1906.

7. Maule and Cain, *The Man from Main Street,* 89.

8. Williams, *Catholicism and the Modern Mind,* 243–244.

9. Fink, *I-Mary,* 116–117. If Austin was aware of the snub, she chose not to recall it in her memoirs. "One dined so very well at Coppa's: such platefuls of fresh shrimps; such sand dabs and crisp salads; such almond tartlets and Dago red." Austin, *Earth Horizon,* 297. Coppa's was the choice of the bohemians in good part because of the proprietor's generosity with credit extended to artists down on their luck. Failing a change of fortune and repayment, wall space was provided for painters to work off their debt. The famous frieze of black cats was created, over time, in just such a way by Martínez, an artist friendly with both Sterling and London. Genthe, *As I Remember,* 55, 64.

10. Austin, *Earth Horizon,* 300. On the night London and Austin fought over her powers, it was Arnold Genthe who suggested it was time for all to be going, and he

offered to see her home. The forest was black and there were no paths, but Austin refused the loan of a lantern. "Don't you know I can see in the dark?" Her belief was unshaken, deep in the woods, by walking straight into a pine tree. Genthe, *As I Remember*, 75.

11. Austin, *Earth Horizon*, 300, 304. This is an opinion seconded by Stasz, *American Dreamers*, 98. Regarding London's drinking, his more strident defenders insist, for instance, that "there is no reliable record that anyone ever saw Jack drunk after . . . he was sixteen years old." Kingman, *Pictorial Biography*, 190. That just is not true.

12. Austin, *Earth Horizon*, 302. The great tenor Enrico Caruso was also staying in the Palace Hotel that night. Less psychic than Mary Austin, he fled the building in his nightshirt during the quake and swore he would never return to San Francisco.

13. This and previous quotes from C. K. London, *Book of Jack London*, 2: 124–125. The contractor, an Italian, later returned while the Londons were hosting Ed Winship, a Korean war correspondent with London, and his wife, Ida. Fearful of his own temper, London avoided him and had Charmian send him away.

14. London to Coolbrith, December 15, 1906, University of California at Berkeley, in *Letters* 2: 650–651. Oddly, although they lived no great distance from each other and had many friends in common, London had not seen Coolbrith since those library days.

15. London, "What Life Means to Me," reprinted in London, *Revolution and Other Essays*.

16. Honolulu *Advertiser*, June 8, 1907.

17. Shields, *Artists at Continent's End*, 192.

18. Genthe, *As I Remember*, 75. The attribution to Browning was Genthe's, but a computer search of the works of both Brownings yields no such verse.

19. Sterling, "The Abalone Song," quoted at www.ab2000.org.za.absong.html; www.abcamp.com/AbaloneSong.html, and others. Lesser member of The Crowd Opal Heron was said to have contributed the first verse. Genthe, *As I Remember*, 76; Shields, *Artists at Continent's End*, 192, quoting Benediktsson, *George Sterling*, 37.

20. Austin, *Earth Horizon*, 303.

CHAPTER 12

1. London to Stoddard, June 21, 1900, in *Letters*, 1: 195. Stoddard had been only twenty-one when he visited Tahiti for the first time, and later lived two stints in Hawaii. His letters to a friend from that first trip were published as *Idyls*, praised by William Dean Howells as "the lightest, sweetest, wildest, freshest things that were ever written about the life of that summer ocean."

2. Noel, *Footloose in Arcadia,* 191–193. For thoughts on Noel's reliability and his motives in writing about London, see Chapter 1, note 18.

3. O'Connor, *Jack London,* 248.

4. Jack London Scrapbook 47–2, photo 05821, Huntington Library, copy lent by Lael Morgan.

5. C. K. London, *Book of Jack London,* 2: 144

6. London to Johnson, November 12, 1906, in *Letters,* 2: 629; Johnson, *Through the South Seas with Jack London,* 3, 7.

7. London to Bailey Millard, August 13, 1906, and London to Cosgrave, August 21, 1906, both in *Letters,* 2: 600–601.

8. London to Editor, *Cosmopolitan,* and London to Vance, both November 18, 1906, in *Letters* 2: 634–36.

9. Johnson, *Through the South Seas with Jack London,* 53; C. K. London, *Log of the Snark,* 17.

10. London to Brett, May 28, 1907, in *Letters,* 2: 685–687.

11. London to Roscoe Eames, July 11, 1907, London to Ninetta Eames, May 28 and July 25, 1907, in *Letters,* 2: 687, 694–695, 700, 701n5. In one of the coats of whitewash in her biography, Charmian denied any trouble with Roscoe. *Book of Jack London,* 2: 144.

12. Quoted in Tayman, *The Colony,* 198.

13. Johnson, *Through the South Seas with Jack London,* 123.

14. Quoted in Tayman, *The Colony,* 203. In the larger context of Hawaiian history, Queen Liliuokalani might have said the exact same things about Thurston.

15. Stasz, *Jack London's Women,* 123.

16. Johnston, *American Radical,* 129.

17. Johnston, *American Radical,* 129.

18. London to George Sterling, October 31, 1908, in *Letters,* 2: 770–771. Charmian also used the letter as evidence to refute later charges from critics that the novel *Adventure* exaggerated the dangers in that part of the world. *Book of Jack London,* 2: 172–173.

19. London to Bessie, October 27, 1908, in *Letters* 2: 762–768.

20. Hendricks and Shepard, *Jack London Reports,* 259–262.

21. "A Brief Explanation," in Bamford, *Mystery of Jack London,* 222–223.

22. London to Eliza Shepard, February 24, 1909, in *Letters* 2: 792.

23. See Osa Johnson, *I Married Adventure* (Philadelphia and New York: J. P. Lippincott Co., 1940). Martin Johnson was killed in a commercial airplane crash in California in 1937; their travels and films are memorialized in the Martin and Osa Johnson Safari Museum in Chanute.

24. The *Tymeric* went on to tumultuous adventures of her own, grounded and nearly wrecked when a typhoon hit Hong Kong in 1937, and ultimately torpedoed and sunk in the North Atlantic in November 1940.

CHAPTER 13

1. London to Strunsky, January 21, 1900, in *Letters,* 1: 145. London of course did later develop a formidable facility at quarreling.

2. C. K. London, *Book of Jack London,* 2: 184.

3. Goldman, *Living My Life,* 467–469.

4. Stasz, *Jack London's Women,* 142–143.

5. C. K. London, *Book of Jack London,* 2:184. Parsons was a woman of mixed race whose husband was hanged, probably unjustly, for his part in the Chicago Haymarket riot.

6. London to Brett, May 5, 1910, in *Letters,* 2: 888–889. The serialization in the *Herald* ran for more than two months that summer.

7. Quoted in Kershaw, *A Life,* 228.

8. London to Fuller & Johnson Manufacturing Co., March 28, 1910; London to Brett, April 1, 1910, in *Letters,* 2: 881–882.

9. Charmian to Fannie, July 1, 1910, quoted in Kershaw, *A Life,* 230.

10. Hendricks and Shepard, *Jack London Reports,* 293–301.

11. London to Samuels, open letter, July 29, 1910, in *Letters,* 2: 916–918; San Francisco *Call,* August 2, 1910.

12. London to Charmian, July 29, 1910, in *Letters,* 2: 915–916.

13. London to Henry W. Lanier, January 18, 1912, in *Letters,* 2:1063–1064.

14. London to Eliza Shepard, February 12, 1912, in *Letters,* 2: 1067–1068.

15. Stasz, *Jack London's Women,* 110.

16. C. K. London, *Book of Jack London,* 2: 230–232.

17. London to Charmian, August 13, 1912, in *Letters,* 2: 1078–1079.

18. Conrad to London, date illegible, archived online at www.huntington.org/LibraryDir/friends.htm/.

19. Palmer, *Nineteenth Century American Fiction on Screen,* 211.

20. London to Joan, October 11, 1913, Hendricks and Shepard, *Letters from Jack London,* 405–408, *Letters,* 1257–1260; Joan to London, October 28, 1913, in ibid., 1260n.

21. St. Johns, *Final Verdict,* 356–357. Stasz, *Jack London's Women,* 150, citing the same passage, depicts the scene entirely differently: "at the end of the ride, when Jack cruelly announced that he no longer wanted to be Adela's godfather, she realized

that instead of listening to her child's wisdom, he treated her as he would have Joan." This is a very surprising discrepancy from the cited text. Although Earl Rogers's final years were lost to alcoholism until his premature death at fifty-two, his record in murder trials was 74 wins against 3 losses. He was said to have been the model for Erle Stanley Gardner's Perry Mason character. See also Richard F. Snow, "Counsel for the Indefensible," *American Heritage*, February–March 1987.

CHAPTER 14

1. Higgins, "Jack London on the Waterfront," archived online at www.jacklondons .net/first_and_Last_chance.html.

2. London to Fred Barry, June 26, 1913, quoted in Kingman, *Pictorial Biography*, 242.

3. London to Michael McKenna, April 3, 1915, in *Letters*, 3: 1440.

4. Quoted in O'Connor, *Jack London*, 356.

5. London to Editor, *Army and Navy Register*, April 27, 1914, in *Letters*, 3: 1332.

6. Davis, *Adventures and Letters*, 355.

7. Hendricks and Shepard, *Jack London Reports*, 174–175.

8. Davis, *Adventures and Letters*, 355–356.

9. St. Johns, *Final Verdict*, 358–363.

10. Ibid., 361.

11. Bamford, *Mystery of Jack London*, 138–143.

12. London to Connor, November 3, 1915, in *Letters*, 3: 1512–1513.

13. Austin to London, October 26, 1915, and London to Austin, November 5, 1915 in *Letters*, 3: 1513–1514; Fink, *I-Mary*, 172–173. Austin survived the crisis to triumph in her later years. London's irritation at the critical misunderstanding of *Martin Eden* had nettled him since the book first appeared. He inscribed a copy for his friend Fred Bamford, "And not one blessed reviewer has discovered that this book is an attack on individualism, that Martin Eden died because he was so utter an individualist that he was unaware of the needs of others, and that, therefore, when his illusions vanished, there was nothing for him for which to live." G L. Bamford, *Mystery of Jack London*, 176–177. The misunderstanding continues to the present day with such mentions as "Jack London, whose fictional heroes were muscular autobiographical projections magnified by a Nietzschean lens." John Seelye, *War Games: Richard Harding Davis & The New Imperialism* (Amherst: University of Massachusetts Press, 2003).

14. London to Members of the Glen Ellen Socialist Labor Party, March 7, 1916, in *Letters*, 3: 1537–1538.

15. C. K. London, *Book of Jack London*, 2: 337.

16. London to Armine, June 30, 1916, quoted in Walker, ed., *No Mentor But Myself*, 161–162; *Letters*, 3: 1558–1559.

17. Quoted in Hendricks and Shepard, *Jack London Reports*, 380–383.

18. Noel, *Footloose in Arcadia*, 266.

19. London to Charmian, November 19, 1912; London to Spiro Orfans, September 29 and October 19, 1916, in *Letters*, 2: 1100–1101, 3: 1579, 1593.

20. London to Charles Brown, Jr., 28 July 1914, in *Letters*, 3:1357; London to A-No. 1, 28 October 1911, in *Letters*, 2:1047. After meeting on the road, Livingston over the years sent London hundreds of picture postcards from the places visited. See London to Robert E. McNamara, 25 August 1915, in *Letters*, 3:1492–93.

21. London to Mrs. H. P. Agee, October 24, 1916, in *Letters* 3: 1596–1597; London to Sterling, October 28, 1916, in *Letters* 3: 1600.

22. London to Smith, October 31, 1916, and London to Western Soil Bacteria Company, November 18, 1916, both in *Letters* 3: 1600–1601, 1603.

23. London to Sisson, October 13, 1916 in *Letters* 3: 1589; London to Waldo Frank, November 5, 1916, in *Letters* 3: 1601–1602.

24. London to Connor, November 20, 1916; London to Editor, *Every Week*, November 21, 1916; London to Joan, November 21, 1916; all in *Letters* 3: 1603–1604.

25. See, e.g., "Publisher's Preface," *The Sea-Wolf* (Norwalk, CT: Easton Press, 1979), p. iii; Jack Lindsay, "Introduction," *The People of the Abyss* (Westport, CT: Lawrence Hill & Co., 1977), p. 5, etc.

26. Stone, *Sailor on Horseback*, 331. Stone later gained wide fame for his fictionalized portrayals of famous lives, an art form that freed him from following strict factuality when telling a good story. The London effort was his first book. While written as straight biography, it omits source notes and depicts Stone at the beginning of that long career in fiction. Subsequent careful scholars criticized the book for its frequent factual lapses. Stone's characterization of "calculating the fatal dose" certainly adds an element deserving of inclusion in one of London's own short stories but falls far short of establishing suicide.

27. Walling, "Memoirs of Jack London," quoted in Kingman, *Pictorial Biography*, 276.

28. Jack London's "Credo," with Commentary by Clarice Stasz. http://london.sonoma.edu/credo.html, quoting Irving Shepard, *Jack London's Tales of Adventure*, vii.

BOOKS BY JACK LONDON

The Son of the Wolf (Houghton, Mifflin Co., 1900). Stories included: "The White Silence," "The Son of the Wolf," "The Men of Forty Mile," "In a Far Country," "To the Man on the Trail," "The Priestly Prerogative," "The Wisdom of the Trail," "The Wife of a King," "An Odyssey of the North."

The God of His Fathers (McClure, Phillips & Co., 1901). Stories included: "The God of His Fathers," "The Great Interrogation," "Which Makes Men Remember," "Siwash," "The Man with the Gash," "Jan the Unrepentant," "Grit of Women," "Where the Trail Forks," "A Daughter of the Aurora," "At the Rainbow's End," "The Scorn of Women."

Children of the Frost (Macmillan, 1902). Stories included: "In the Forests of the North," "The Law of Life," "Nam-Bok the Unveracious," "The Master of Mystery," "The Sunlanders," "The Sickness of Lone Chief," "Keesh, the Son of Keesh," "The Death of Ligoun," "Li Wan the Fair," "The League of Old Men."

A Daughter of the Snows (J. B. Lippincott, 1902).

The Cruise of the Dazzler (Century Co., 1902).

The Kempton-Wace Letters (with Anna Strunsky, Macmillan, 1903).

The People of the Abyss (Macmillan, 1903).

The Call of the Wild (Macmillan, 1903).

The Faith of Men (Macmillan, 1904). Stories included: "A Relic of the Pliocene," "A Hyperborean Brew," "The Faith of Men," "Too Much Gold," "The One Thousand Dozen," "The Marriage of Lit-Lit," "Bâtard," "The Story of Jees-Uck."

The Sea-Wolf (Macmillan, 1904).

The War of the Classes (Macmillan, 1905). Essays included: "The Class Struggle," "The Tramp," "The Scab," "The Question of the Maximum," "A Review (Contradictory Teachers)," "Wanted: A New Law of Development," "How I Became a Socialist."

The Game (Macmillan, 1905).

Tales of the Fish Patrol (Macmillan, 1905). Stories included: "White and Yellow," "The King of the Crooks," "A Raid on Oyster Pirates," "The Siege of the 'Lancashire Queen,'" "Charley's Coup," "Demetrios Contos," "Yellow Handkerchief."

Moon-Face and Other Stories (Macmillan, 1906). Stories included: "Moon-Face: A Story of Mortal Antipathy," "The Leopard Man's Story," "Local Color," "Amateur

Night," "The Minions of Midas," "The Shadow and the Flash," "All Gold Canyon," "Planchette."

White Fang (Macmillan, 1906).

Scorn of Women (Macmillan, 1906).

Before Adam (Macmillan, 1907).

Love of Life and Other Stories (Macmillan, 1907). Stories included: "Love of Life," "A Day's Lodging," "The White Man's Way," "The Story of Keesh," "The Unexpected," "Brown Wolf," "The Sun Dog Trail," "Negore the Coward."

The Road (Macmillan, 1907). Essays included: "Confession," "Holding Her Down," "Pictures," "Pinched," "The Pen," "Hoboes That Pass in the Night," "Road Kids and Gay Cats," "Two Thousand Stiffs," "Bulls."

The Iron Heel (Macmillan, 1908).

Martin Eden (Macmillan, 1909).

Lost Face (Macmillan, 1910). Stories included: "Lost Face," "Trust," "To Build a Fire," "That Spot," "Flush of Gold," "The Passing of Marcus O'Brien," "The Wit of Porportuk."

Revolution (Macmillan, 1910). Essays included: "Revolution," "The Somnambulists," "The Dignity of Dollars," "Goliah," "The Golden Poppy," "The Shrinkage of the Planet," "The House Beautiful," "The Gold Hunters of the North," "Foma Gordyéeff," "These Bones Shall Rise Again," "The Other Animals," "The Yellow Peril," "What Life Means to Me."

Burning Daylight (Macmillan, 1910).

Theft (Macmillan, 1910).

When God Laughs (Macmillan, 1911). Stories included: "When God Laughs," "The Apostate," "A Wicked Woman," "Just Meat," "Created He Them," "The Chinago," "Make Westing," "Semper Idem," "A Nose for the King," "The 'Francis Spaight,'" "A Curious Fragment," "A Piece of Steak."

Adventure (Macmillan, 1911).

The Cruise of the "Snark" (Macmillan, 1911).

South Sea Tales (Macmillan 1911). Stories included: "The House of Mapuhi," "The Whale Tooth," "Mauki," "Yah! Yah! Yah!" "The Heathen," "The Terrible Solomons," "The Inevitable White Man," "The Seed of McCoy."

A Son of the Sun (Doubleday, Page & Co., 1912). Stories included: "A Son of the Sun," "The Proud Goat of Aloysius Pankburn," "The Devils of Fuatino," "The Jokers of New Gibbon," "A Little Account with Swithin Hall," "A Gobotu Night," "The Feathers of the Sun," "The Pearls of Parlay."

The House of Pride (Macmillan, 1912). Stories included: "The House of Pride," "Koolay the Leper," "Good-by Jack!" "Aloha Oe," "Chum Ah Chun," "The Sheriff of Kona."

Smoke Bellew Tales (Century Co., 1912). Stories included: "The Taste of the Meat," "The Meat," "The Stampede to Squaw Creek," "Shorty Dreams," "The Man on the Other Bank," "The Race for Number Three," "The Little Man," "The Hanging of Cultus George," "The Mistage of Creation," "A Flutter in Eggs," "The Town-site of Tra-lee," "Wonder of Woman."

The Night Born (Century Co., 1913). Stories included: "The Night Born," "The Madness of John Harned," "When the World Was Young," "The Benefit of the Doubt," "Winged Blackmail," "Bunches of Knuckles," "War," "Under the Deck Awnings," "To Kill a Man," "The Mexican."

The Abysmal Brute (Century Co., 1913).

John Barleycorn (Century Co., 1913).

The Valley of the Moon (Macmillan, 1913).

The Strength of the Strong (Macmillan, 1914). Stories included: "The Strength of the Strong," "South of the Slot," "The Unparalleled Invasion," "The Enemy of All the World," "The Dream of Debs," "The Sea Farmer," "Samuel."

The Mutiny of the Elsinore (Macmillan, 1914).

The Scarlet Plague (Macmillan, 1915).

The Star Rover (Macmillan, 1915).

The Acorn Planter (Macmillan, 1916)

The Little Lady of the Big House (Macmillan, 1916).

The Turtles of Tasman (Macmillan, 1916). Stories included: By the Turtles of Tasman, The Eternity of Forms, Told in the Drooling Ward, The Hobo and the Fairy, The Prodigal Father, The First Poet, Finis, The End of the Story

POSTHUMOUS PUBLICATIONS

The Human Drift (Macmillan, 1917). Articles included: "The Human Drift," "Nothing that Ever Came to Anything," "That Dead Men Rise Up Never," "Small-Boat Sailing," "Four Horses and a Sailor," "A Classic of the Sea," "A Wicked Woman," "The Birth Mark."

Jerry of the Islands (Macmillan, 1917).

Michael, Brother of Jerry (Macmillan, 1917).

The Red One (Macmillan, 1918). Stories included: "The Red One," "The Hussy," "Like Argus of the Ancient Times," "The Princess."

On the Makaloa Mat (Macmillan, 1919). Stories included: "On the Makaloa Mat," "The Bones of Kahekili," "When Alice Told Her Soul," "Shin-Bones," "The Water Baby," "The Tears of Ah Kim," "The Kanaka Surf."

Hearts of Three (Macmillan, 1920).

BIBLIOGRAPHY AND FURTHER READING

PRIMARY SOURCES: PUBLISHED LETTERS & DOCUMENTS

Bierce, Ambrose (S. T. Joshi and David E. Schultz, eds). *A Much Misunderstood Man: Selected Letters of Ambrose Bierce.* Columbus: Ohio State University Press, 2003.

Hendricks, King, and Irving Shepard, eds. *Jack London Reports: War Correspondence, Sports Articles, and Miscellaneous Articles.* Garden City, NY: Doubleday & Co., 1970.

———. *Letters from Jack London.* New York: Odyssey Press, 1965.

Labor, Earle, et. al., eds. *The Letters of Jack London.* Stanford, CA: Stanford University Press, 1988 (3 vols.).

PRIMARY SOURCES: DIARIES, MEMOIRS, INTERVIEWS

Austin, Mary. *Earth Horizon: An Autobiography.* Boston: Houghton Mifflin, 1932.

———. "George Sterling at Carmel." *American Mercury,* May 1927.

———. "Three at Carmel." *Saturday Review of Literature,* September 29, 1928.

Bamford, Georgia Loring. *The Mystery of Jack London.* Oakland, CA: Piedmont Press, 1931.

Chaney, W. H. *Primer of Astrology and Urania.* St. Louis: priv. pr., 1890.

Davis, Charles Belmont, ed. *Adventures and Letters of Richard Harding Davis.* New York: Charles Scribner's Sons, 1917.

Dunn, Robert. *World Alive: A Personal Story.* New York: Crown Publishers Inc., 1956.

Ford, Alexander Hume. "Jack London in Hawaii, Rambling Reminiscences of the Editor." *Mid-Pacific Magazine,* February 1917.

Genthe, Arnold. *As I Remember.* New York: Reynal & Hitchcock, 1936.

Goldman, Emma. *Living My Life.* New York: Alfred A. Knopf, 1931.

Hamilton, Fannie K. "Jack London: An Interview." *The Reader,* August 1903.

Heinold, Johnny. "Heinold's First Encounter with Jack London, As Told By Himself." San Francisco *Chronicle,* November 24, 1916.

Higgins, John C. "Jack London on the Waterfront." *Westways,* January 1934.

Johnson, Martin. *Through the South Seas with Jack London.* New York: Dodd, Mead & Co., 1913.

Larkin, Edgar Lucien. "Recollections of the Late Jack London." *Overland Monthly,* May 1917.

London, Charmian. *The Book of Jack London.* New York: Century Co., 1921 (2 vols.).

———. *The Log of the Snark.* New York: Macmillan, 1915.

———. *Our Hawaii.* New York: Macmillan, 1917.

London, Joan. *Jack London and His Times.* Garden City, NY: Doubleday & Co., 1929 (repr. Seattle and London: University of Washington Press, 1974).

Noel, Joseph. *Footloose in Arcadia.* New York: Carrick & Evans, 1940.

North, Dick. "Diary of Jack London's Trip to the Klondike." *Yukon News Magazine,* November–December 1966.

Stevens, Louis. "Jack London As I Knew Him." *Book News,* March 1948.

Walling, Anna Strunsky. "Memories of Jack London." *Greenwich Village Lantern,* December 1940.

Williams, Michael. *Catholicism and the Modern Mind.* New York: L. MacVeigh, 1928.

SECONDARY SOURCES: BIBLIOGRAPHIES

Blanck, Jacob. *Bibliography of American Literature,* vol. 5. New Haven, CT: Yale University Press, 1969.

Gaer, Joseph. *Jack London: Bibliography and Biographical Information.* New York: B. Franklin, 1971.

Hamilton, David Mike. ed. *"The Tools of My Trade": The Annotated Books in Jack London's Library.* Seattle: University of Washington Press, 1986.

Sherman, Joan Rita. *Jack London: A Reference Guide.* Boston: G. K. Hall, 1977.

Walker, Dale L., and James E. Sisson III. *The Fiction of Jack London: A Chronological Bibliography.* El Paso: Texas Western Press, 1972.

Woodbridge, Hensley C., John London, and George H. Tweney. *Jack London: A Bibliography.* Georgetown, CA: Talisman Press, 1966.

SECONDARY SOURCES: BIOGRAPHIES

Barltrop, Robert. *Jack London, the Man, the Writer, the Rebel.* London: Pluto Press, 1976.

Benediktsson, Thomas E. *George Sterling.* Boston: Twayne, 1980.

Calder-Marshall, Arthur. *Lone Wolf: The Story of Jack London.* New York: Duell, Sloane & Pearce, 1962.

Day, A. Grove. *Jack London in the South Seas.* New York: Four Winds Press, 1971.

Fenady, Andrew J. *The Summer of Jack London.* New York: Berkley Publishing Group, 1997 (repr).

Fink, Augusta. *I-Mary: A Biography of Mary Austin.* Tucson: University of Arizona Press, 1983.

Foner, Philip S. *Jack London / American Rebel.* New York: Citadel, 1947.

Franchere, Ruth. *Jack London: The Pursuit of a Dream.* New York: Thomas Y. Crowell Co., 1962 (repr.).

Garst, Doris Shannon. *Jack London: Magnet for Adventure.* New York: J. Messner, 1944.

Johnston, Carolyn. *Jack London: An American Radical?* Westport, CT: Greenwood, 1984.

Kershaw, Alex. *Jack London: A Life.* New York: St. Martin's Press, 1999.

Kingman, Russ. *A Pictorial Biography of Jack London.* New York: Crown Publishers, 1979.

Labor, Earle. *Jack London.* New York: Twayne Publishers, 1974.

Lane, Frederick A. *The Greatest Adventure: A Story of Jack London.* New York: Aladdin Books American Heritage Series, 1954.

Lane, Rose Wilder. *He Was a Man.* New York: Harper, 1925.

Maule, Harry E., and Melville H. Cain. *The Main from Main Street.* New York: Random House, 1953.

Mood, Fulmer. "An Astrologer from Down East." *New England Quarterly,* October 1932.

O'Connor, Richard. *Jack London: A Biography.* Boston: Little, Brown & Co., 1964.

Payne, Edward B. *The Soul of Jack London.* Kingsport, TN: Southern Publishers, 1933.

Rather, Lois. *Jack London, 1905.* Oakland, CA: Rather Press, 1974.

Sinclair, Andrew. *Jack: A Biography of Jack London.* New York: Harper & Row, 1977.

Stasz, Clarice. *American Dreamers: Charmian and Jack London.* New York: St. Martin's Press, 1988.

———. *Jack London's Women.* Amherst: University of Massachusetts Press, 2001.

Stone, Irving. *Irving Stone's Jack London.* Garden City, NY: Doubleday & Co., 1977.

———. *Sailor on Horseback: The Biography of Jack London.* Boston: Houghton Mifflin, 1938.

St. Johns, Adela Rogers. *Final Verdict.* Garden City, NY: Doubleday & Co., 1962.

Walcutt, Charles Child. *Jack London.* Minneapolis: University of Minnesota Press, 1966.

Walker, Franklin. *Jack London and the Klondike.* San Marino, CA: Huntington Library, 1972.

SECONDARY SOURCES: CRITICISM

Auerbach, Jonathan. *Male Call: Becoming Jack London.* Durham, NC, and London: Duke University Press, 1996.

Bashford, Herbert. "The Literary Development of the Pacific Coast." *Atlantic Monthly,* July 1903.

Baskett, Sam S. "A Brace for London Criticism: An Essay Review." *Modern Fiction Studies*, Spring 1976.

Doctorow, E. L. *Jack London, Hemingway, and the Constitution*. New York: Random House, 1993.

Foner, Philip S. *The Social Writings of Jack London*. New York: Citadel, 1987.

Geismar, Maxwell. *Rebels and Ancestors: The American Novel, 1890–1915*. New York: Hill and Wang, 1963.

Hawthorne, Julian. "Jack London in Literature." Los Angeles *Examiner*, January 12, 1905.

Hedrick, Joan D. *Solitary Comrade: Jack London and His Work*. Chapel Hill: University of North Carolina Press, 1982.

Hendricks, King. *Jack London: Master Craftsman of the Short Story*. Logan: Utah State University Faculty Association, 1966.

Hodson, Sara S., and Jeanne Campbell Reesman. eds. *Jack London: One Hundred Years a Writer*. San Marino, CA: Huntington Library, 2002.

James, George Wharton. "The Influence of California Upon Literature." *National Magazine*, April 1912.

Labor, Earle. "Jack London, 1876–1976." *Modern Fiction Studies*, Spring 1976.

Lynn, Kenneth S. *The Dream of Success, A Study of the Modern American Imagination*. Boston: Little, Brown & Co., 1955.

McClintock, James I. "Jack London's Use of Carl Jung's Psychology of the Unconscious." *American Literature*, November 1970.

Reesman, Jeanne Campbell. *Jack London's Racial Lives: A Critical Biography*. Athens: University of Georgia Press, 2009.

Walker, Dale. "Jack London (1876–1916)." *American Literary Realism*, Fall 1967.

Walker, Franklin. "Jack London's Use of Sinclair Lewis Plots, Together with a Printing of Three of the Plots." *Huntington Library Quarterly*, November 1953.

Watson, Charles N. "Jack London's Yokohama Swim and His First Tall Tale." *Studies in American Humor*, October 1976.

———. *The Novels of Jack London*. Madison: University of Wisconsin Press, 1983.

SECONDARY SOURCES: MISCELLANEOUS: BOOKS

Boylan, James R. *Revolutionary Lives: Anna Strunsky and William English Walling*. Amherst: University of Massachusetts Press, 1998.

Etulain, Richard W. ed. *Jack London on the Road*. Logan: Utah State University Press, 1979.

James, George Wharton. *California Scrapbook*. Los Angeles: N. A. Kovach, 1945.

Markham, Edwin. *California the Wonderful*. New York: Hearst's International Library, 1914.

Martin, Stoddard. *California Writers: Jack London, John Steinbeck, The Tough Guys.* New York: St. Martin's Press, 1983.

McClintock, James I. *White Logic.* Cedar Springs, MI: Wolf House Books, 1975.

McDevitt, William. *Jack London as Poet and Platform Man.* San Francisco: Recorder-Sunset Press, 1947.

———. *Jack London's First.* San Francisco: Recorder-Sunset Press, 1947.

Mighels, Ella Sterling. *Literary California.* San Francisco: John W. Newbegin, 1918.

Murphy, Celeste G. *The People of the Pueblo.* Sonoma, CA: W. L. and C. G. Murphy, 1937.

Palmer, R. Barton. *Nineteenth Century American Fiction on Screen.* Cambridge and New York: Cambridge University Press, 2007.

Shepard, Irving, ed. *Jack London's Tales of Adventure.* New York: Doubleday & Co., 1956.

Shields, Scott A. *Artists at Continent's End: The Monterey Peninsula Art Colony, 1875–1907.* Berkeley: University of California Press, 2006.

Tayman, John. *The Colony: The Harrowing True Story of the Exiles of Molokai.* New York: Scribner, 2006.

Von Tempski, Armine. *Born in Paradise.* New York: Duell, Sloan and Pearce, 1940.

Walker, Dale. *The Alien Worlds of Jack London.* Grand Rapids, MI: Wolf House Books, 1973.

Walker, Dale L. ed. *No Mentor But Myself: A Collection of Articles, Essays, Reviews and Letters on Writing and Writers.* Port Washington, NY: Kennikat Press, 1979.

Walker, Franklin. *The Seacoast on Bohemia.* San Francisco: Book Club of California, 1966.

Ware, Wallace L. *The Unforgettables.* San Francisco: Hesperian Press, 1964.

SECONDARY SOURCES: MISCELLANEOUS: ARTICLES & PAMPHLETS

Baggs, Mae Lucy. "The Real Jack London in Hawaii." *Overland Monthly,* May 1917.

Baskett, Sam S. "Jack London on the Oakland Waterfront." *American Literature,* November 1955.

Bland, Henry Meade. "Hail and Farewell to Jack London." *California Writers Club Bulletin,* December 1916.

———. "Jack London." *Overland Monthly,* May 1904.

———. "Jack London, Traveler, Novelist and Social Reformer." *The Craftsman,* February 1906.

———. "John Barleycorn at the Plow." *Sunset,* August 1914.

———. "Making of Jack London." *Wilshire's Magazine,* December 1905.

Booker, Matthew Morse. "Oyster Growers and Oyster Pirates on San Francisco Bay." *Pacific Historical Review*, February 2006.

Briggs, J. E. "Tramping with Kelly Through Iowa: A Jack London Diary." *Palimpsest*, May 1926.

Buchanan, Agnes Foster. "The Story of a Famous Fraternity of Writers and Artists." *Pacific Monthly*, January 1907.

Bykov, Vil. "Jack London in the U.S.S.R." *American Book Collector*, November 1966.

Connell, S. "Jack London Wooed Fame Through the *Overland Monthly*." *Overland Monthly*, October 1920.

Darling, Ernest W. "Jack London's Visit to Papeete, Tahiti." *International Socialist Review*, September 1908.

Debs, Eugene V. "Eugene V. Debs on the Death of Jack London." *National Rip-Saw*, February 1917.

Dickson, D. H. "A Note on Jack London and David Starr Jordan." *Indiana Magazine of History*, December 1942.

Dunn, R. L. "Jack London Knows Not Fear." San Francisco *Examiner*, June 26, 1904.

Eames, Ninetta. "Jack London." *Overland Monthly*, May 1900.

Emerson, Edwin Jr. "When West Meets East." *Sunset*, October 1905.

Fiske, Minnie Maddern. "Mrs. Fiske Endorses Jack London Club." *Our Animals*, July 1918.

Francoeur, Jeanne. "Jack London Is Dead? There Is No Death for Such as He!" *Everywoman*, December 1916.

Friedland, L. S. "Jack London as Titan." *Dial*, January 25, 1917.

Goodhue, E. S. "Jack London and Martin Eden." *Mid-Pacific Magazine*, October 1913.

Haldeman-Julius, E. "Jack London." *Western Comrade*, June 1913.

Hamaker, Gene E. "The Commonweal Comes to Kearney, 1894." *Buffalo Tales*, May 1979.

Hopper, James. "Tribute to London Is Paid by James Hopper, California, 1898." *Alumni Fortnightly*, December 1916.

James, George Wharton. "Jack London: Cub of the Slums, Hero of Adventure, Literary Master and Social Philosopher." *National Magazine*, December 1912.

———. "A Study of Jack London in His Prime." *Overland Monthly*, May 1917.

Kendall, Carleton W. "Jack London." *The Occident*, January 1917.

Kingman, Russ. "Author Jack London Bought Glen Ellen Ranch with $7000 Advance Royalties on 'The Sea-Wolf.'" *Sonoma Index-Tribune*, September 26, 1974.

———. "Author Jack London Was Also a Farmer." *Sonoma Index-Tribune*, September 22, 1977.

———. "How Jack London Planned and Made the Cruise on the 'Snark.'" *Sonoma Index-Tribune*, September 21, 1978.

———. "Jack London Had Vision of a Better Era for All." *Sonoma Index-Tribune*, January 15, 1976.

———. "London's Yukon Cabin Now at Jack London Square in Oakland, California." *Jack London Newsletter*, September–December 1970.

———. "Moving On in the '70s." *The Wolf '78*, January 1978.

———. "The Search: The Mystery of Jack London's *Snark*." *Bay and Delta Yachtsman*, October 1972.

———. "Somewhere the *Snark* Lives." *Pacific Islands Monthly*, January 1971.

———. "Topping the Centennial." *The Wolf '77*, January 1977.

Lachtman, Howard. "Jack and George. Notes on a Literary Friendship." *Pacific Historian*, Summer 1978.

McNamara, Sue. "Jack London at Home." *Writer's Magazine*, August 1913.

Millard, Bailey. "Hard Work Made Jack London Succeed." San Francisco *Examiner*, November 26, 1916.

———. "Jack London, Farmer." *The Bookman*, October 1916.

Murphy, Celeste G. "Library Collected by Jack London Reveals Thirst for Knowledge." *Overland Monthly*, May 1932.

Shivers, Alfred. "Jack London: Not a Suicide." *Dalhousie Review*, Spring 1969.

Sinclair, Upton. "About Jack London." *New Masses*, November–December, 1917.

———. "A Sad Loss to American Literature." *California Writers Club Quarterly*, December 1916.

Stellman, Louis J. "Jack London, the Man." *Overland Monthly*, October 1917.

Sterling, George. "Farewell, Farewell." *California Writers Club Quarterly Bulletin*, December 1916.

Strunsky, Anna. "He Was Youth Incarnate." *San Francisco Labor Unity*, November 27, 1924.

———. "The Meaning of Jack London." *New York Call*, November 28, 1920.

Thomson, Allan. "Doctors Deny Jack London Killed Self." *San Francisco Call*, February 15, 1929.

Tunney, Gene. "Gene Tunney Tells of His Quitting Because of Jack London's *The Game*." *The Ring Magazine*, November 1921.

Walker, Dale. "Jack London: A Writer's Writer." *Art Form*, no. 25 (n.d.).

Walker, Franklin. "Frank Norris and Jack London." *Mills College Magazine*, Spring 1966.

SECONDARY SOURCES: MISCELLANEOUS: ARTICLES WITHOUT BYLINES

"About Jack London." *The Masses*, November–December 1917.

"Adventurous Jack London." *Human Life*, September 1907.

"Chaney Discards Flora." San Francisco *Chronicle*, June 4, 1875.
"The Death of Jack London." *Santa Rosa Republican*, November 23, 1916.
"Fear Jack London Is Lost in Pacific." *New York Times*, January 10, 1908.
"'Get a Gun,' says London, Writer Talks About War." *San Francisco Bulletin*, August 31, 1915.
"Jack London." *Overland Monthly*, May 1900.
"Jack London and Firefighters Save Glen Ellen." *Santa Rosa Press Democrat*, September 23, 1913.
"Jack London at Harvard." *The Arena*, February 1906.
"Jack London at Yale." *Yale Alumni Weekly*, January 31, 1906.
"Jack London Involved in Tenderloin Brawl." *Oakland Times*, June 22, 1910.
"Jack London the Socialist . . . A Character Study . . . His Literary Methods and Aims." *New York Times*, January 28, 1906.
"Jack London's Literary Habits." *Writer's Weekly*, July 1915.
"Jack London's New Haven Speech." *The Arena*, April 1906.
"Kipling Lauds Jack London." *Sonoma Index-Tribune*, September 23, 1905.
"Last Rites for Jack London." *San Francisco Bulletin*, November 24, 1916.
"Little Vessel to Be Ready for Sea." San Francisco *Examiner*, January 14, 1907.
"London on Socialism." *The Advance*, February 8, 1906.
"The Mysterious Disease That Killed Jack London." San Francisco *Examiner*, December 24, 1916.
"Nation Mourns London's Death." *Berkeley Daily Gazette*, November 24, 1916.
"Notes on Upton Sinclair and Jack London." *Courier—Once a Week*, May 20, 1906.
"Oakland's First and Last Chance." *Air California Magazine* 2, no. 10 (n.d.).
"The Valley of the Moon Remembers Jack London." *California Highway Patrolman*, January 1961.
"W. H. Chaney: A Reappraisal." *American Book Collector*, November 1966.

INDEX